Secret of
THE PAST
WHISPERS THROUGH TIME

Book 1 of 3

Sam Caffrey

ISBN Ebook -   9781967840984
ISBN Paperback - 9781967840991
ISBN Hardback - 9781969324000

Published by **Parker Publishers**

First Edition: 2024

Nobody is anybody, but everybody is somebody they want to imagine being.

Table of Contents

Prologue

Paul gives Stephanie a quick peck on the lips as he heads to work. Then, back in mommy mode, she calls to Matthew and Sarah. "Get a move on or you'll be late for school." Rachel moves around the kitchen in her little toy car, getting in everyone's way, smiling up at whoever will look at her. Stephanie rubs Rachel's head every time she passes by.

Making a mental list for the day ahead, Stephanie notes: shopping, dry cleaning, and remembering a costume for Sarah's concert. Finally, they're all loaded up in the people carrier and heading to school. As usual, they arrive just as the bell rings. Matthew and Sarah get out, and Stephanie calls after them, "Love you. Have a good day."

"Oh, Mum," Matthew says back in embarrassment.

As the door closes in the car, her mobile rings. Poking through her bag, she roots it out, not recognizing the number. "Hello," she answers in her normal friendly voice.

"Mrs. Bridges?"

"Yes," she responds, wondering who it is.

"This is Elizabeth from Dr. Finch's office. Can you come in to see Dr. Finch today at noon?"

"What's wrong?"

"Dr. Finch asked me to arrange this following yesterday's tests."

"Is there a problem? Did something show up?"

"I'm sorry, Mrs. Bridges. I have just been asked to arrange this. Also, can you bring somebody with you, please?"

"Okay," she says, hanging up. Panicking, she calls Paul. "Paul, the hospital called. I need to go in today at 12, and you need to come."

There is a momentary silence. "What happened?"

"She wouldn't tell me. Paul, this can't be good. The scan and tests were only yesterday. Please tell me you can come?"

"Of course. I will collect you at 11. Call the childminder to take Rachel."

"Okay. I am so worried. What did they find?"

"Try not to worry. We will face whatever it is. It might just mean a follow-up scan, or yesterday's weren't clear," he says, though the lack of conviction in his voice is obvious.

With that, they hang up and rearrange their days. Calling the childminder, Stephanie can barely hold it together. "Margaret, I got called away and may be late back," she says, asking if she can hold onto Rachel. Thankfully, she can. Starting to cry as soon as she hangs up the phone, Stephanie composes herself long enough to drop off Rachel. Margaret, seeing her puffy eyes, thinks better of asking questions and simply says, "I am free all day, so leave her as late as you want."

With a quiet "Thank you," Stephanie turns to leave.

Across town, Maria is working on a report at the kitchen table, barely able to concentrate from the smile on her face. Mark brings her a coffee.

"Mark, should I be drinking coffee in my condition?" she says with excitement.

"It's coffee, not vodka. And you are pregnant, not dying," he jokes.

Getting ready for the first scan today, Maria can hardly hold back her excitement. "I wonder if it's a boy or a girl, or if we will even ask?"

Mark just smiles back. "As long as it's healthy, who cares? Now finish up there so we are in good time."

The sliding doors of Manchester Hospital open. Rushing through the rain, two couples enter the doors at the same time. The contrasting looks on their faces tell their own story: Maria babbling away with a smile and excitement, and Stephanie ashen-faced with dropped shoulders and head, walking in silence with Paul holding her hand in support, serious and worried. They make their way to the reception desks.

Side by side, the two reception counters are manned. Almost in unison, both announce themselves.

"Maternity Unit."

"And Oncology, please."

Two conversations take place at the same time as the receptionists echo each other. "Name, please, and do you have an appointment?"

A smiling and excited Maria Holmes gives her name, while next to her, Stephanie Bridges, in a low voice, almost whispers her name with nerves. Without even lifting their heads, the two receptionists echo the tired scripted questions. "Is this your first visit?"

And as if mirror images of each other, both ladies answer, "Yes."

As Maria is given directions to go through the double doors and take the lift to the third floor, she beckons Mark to follow her with eager anticipation, heading off before the receptionist can even finish.

In stark contrast, Stephanie Bridges is directed to the same set of lifts and the first floor. Paul holds her hand as they walk slowly towards the lift, trying to delay the inevitability of what may come next.

One hour later, as the lift doors open on the 1st floor, Paul and Stephanie step in and are surrounded by the laughter and excitement of Maria and Mark.

"What will we call the baby? Do you want a boy or a girl?" Maria talks a mile a minute, while Mark looks on with a huge smile on his face.

Unable to say anything, a slow stream of tears trickles down Stephanie's cheek. Paul wraps an arm around her, trying to reassure her that everything will be okay. "The doctor did say that they are having great success with the new treatments. We will get through this."

Exiting the lift, both ladies head for quiet corners of the coffee shop, and Paul and Mark stand side by side, ordering coffees. The contrasting faces of excitement and anguish hover over them. Paul orders Stephanie's favorite flat white with two sugars, her treat when she wants a coffee. He gets his own Americano, not that he cares.

Mark just orders two Americanos, as they are the fastest and he wants to get back to Maria.

Both women place their handfuls of pamphlets on the table. Maria looks at the titles: "Your First Pregnancy" and "What to Expect." Stephanie, on the other hand, has pamphlets titled "Cancer Treatments" and "What to Expect."

Heading back, Mark takes a seat. "Well. WOW, how did that happen?" Maria just laughs, poking Mark in the shoulder.

"Who knows? It could have been anywhere from the kitchen table to the shower. Or maybe that day on holiday when the beach was empty... well, it was quick, but only took a minute. Who cares, Mark, I am so excited."

Mark blushes. "Mmm, yes," he responds, almost as if embarrassed.

"Okay, Mark, I have about two months before this bikini body starts inflating like a balloon. Let's book a holiday. Somewhere hot, with beaches... who knows, maybe we'll find a few quiet spots again. I am about to get bigger everywhere," she jokes. "Let's enjoy me before I do."

Mark laughs. "Maria, you certainly brought 2003 in with a bang, and now out with one, too. And a bit bigger in some places is no harm." He laughs.

"Cheeky bastard. Come on, let's go to the travel agents next. Let's book a getaway and celebrate. I have loads of holidays to take, so why not use them? Let's have fun before you have to share me."

With that, Maria pulls out her notebook from her handbag and starts writing.

"What are you doing?" Mark asks quizzically.

"Making a list of things to do. We will have to go house hunting; we can't bring up kids in the apartment."

"Kids?" Mark looks surprised.

"Of course, two or maybe even three. But definitely two. You know I always wanted children."

Mark shrugs as if he has no say in this.

The list goes on: Book a holiday. HOT. When to tell Jack and HR? Baby furniture. Pre-natal classes.

Then horror crosses her face. "Maria, what is wrong?" Mark wonders.

"My clothes, nothing will fit soon. God, no, maternity clothes. Can't I just skip that part?" she says, starting to laugh. With laughter, Stephanie looks over, mustering a smile behind the red eyes at Maria's enthusiasm. The ladies share a glance.

"Maria, you and your lists. You will nearly try and arrange the birth for a weekend, so I don't miss work."

Laughing, the notebook is put away, and they stand to leave, packing up their work and the baby's first photo. Maria catches the eye of Stephanie as she does, seeing her tears now flowing. Maria just nods a serious nod, realizing that not everyone here has good news today. As they move out of earshot, "Mark, aren't they the couple that came in at the same time as us?"

Looking back, Mark just sees the seriousness of the conversation at the nearby table. Stephanie and Paul slowly thumb through the paperwork they were given.

"Paul, what will we tell the children? My chemo starts in two days. It is all so rushed. What about work?" Stephanie is in tears and panicking. "What if I don't survive this?"

Paul just grasps her hand. "You will be fine; we will get through this. The doctors said there is a good chance." The untouched coffee sits in front of them. They finally pack up the folder of paperwork spread on the table and walk out, even more beaten up than when they walked in.

Heading for the doors and out into the now dry but cloud-covered day, Maria and Mark head out in their two-door Ford Escort. Another thing to add to the list: they need a family car.

Paul sits in the family people carrier as they talk about what to say to the children. "Matthew and Sarah will understand something, but Rachel... my babies," Stephanie cries.

Seven months later, as if by design, Paul walks out the same sliding doors, pushing Stephanie in a wheelchair. Scarf around her head and looking white as a sheet, weight having fallen off her, the bones evident in her face where a healthy glow sat only months earlier.

Mark, by contrast, rushes enthusiastically and climbs into the new family estate he is driving, clasping Maria's list. All he can think is, "Superstition, where does she get it? Can't buy anything for the baby before he is born." Now he is stuck going to Mothercare with a list so detailed it nearly has serial numbers. Tired from being up all night, he knows he must fill that list, knowing how often she was in the shop checking the stock in the last two weeks.

Two hours later, a delivery van is arranged for what felt like the shop stockroom being ordered. Mark returns to Maria and baby Liam. Her mother by her side, Maria smiles the tired but glowing smile of a new mother at Mark as he walks in.

"Well, did you get everything?" she questions.

"Yes, dear. The shop assistant was amused at your list, and when the manager came to help her fill it, he did ask if you wanted a job, as you know more about what they have than most of his staff."

"Smart ass," Maria jokes.

"I will leave you two alone. I will get something to eat. Do you want anything from the canteen?" her mother smiles.

Maria gets out of bed and brings Liam in her arms back to his cot; she catches Mark looking her up and down. "Don't you worry, I will be back in the black bikini before you can arrange for his baby brother or sister. I booked classes."

Mark laughs. "I know, and it was probably the white one coming off that day that's responsible for this fella," he says as he walks over and hugs Maria.

By the time 2006 comes, Maria is supported in the front door. Mark calls for help, supporting Maria with one arm and pushing a stroller with Liam in it with the other. "Help, please, she is in labor. She is early."

Within a few hours, Maria is in the labor ward with Natalie in her arms. As Mark arrives with Liam, Maria sits up.

"I am never doing that again…." Mark just jokes, "No list for this one then."

Maria throws him a glance. "No, and I am never wearing a bikini again. It is responsible for these two; you just can't help yourself, can you," she says, trying to make a tired joke. With that, her phone rings. Looking at the screen, she answers, "Joan, not a good time."

"Okay, Jack is wondering where you are; you are late for the meeting." Maria explains, "Natalie just could not wait. A month early." She then proceeds to tell Joan where to find the files and to have Jack call her.

A day later, Mark pushes Maria to the door in a wheelchair, as hospital policy dictates. As they leave, she sees a half-familiar face but just can't place it.

Paul walks out at the same time, Sarah and Rachel wrapped around him crying and Matthew a few steps behind with his head down in silence. They walk solemnly to their car.

Maria is trying to place him when she hears her phone ring. Looking at it, Jack's name appears. "Jack," she answers in a frustrated tone.

"Congratulations, Maria. I heard it's a girl, from Joan. Hate to disturb you, but do you have any idea when you expect to have the McLaughlin job done? I was asked by Malcolm."

About to give a smart answer, she says, "It is nearly there, just final balancing, really. The team can sort it. I will see how much maternity leave I need."

Mark asks what that is about as she hangs up. "Work. I said I better take it. I am after a promotion."

Heading home to the new house they finally got last year, Maria shifts into mommy mode. Mark says he has taken a few days off but needs to go back to work on Monday. Enjoying a few quiet days, Maria turns her phone off and focuses on the children. Mark is as attentive as he can be, in between phone calls from work, waiting on her and the children's every need.

Paul is busy arranging the funeral and trying to care for the children, who are struggling with this. Having no family himself, he is alone with his only real support from work colleagues. Stephanie had always been the center of his universe.

.

Chapter 1

I lay on the carefully selected soft sheets, with dawn-break sunlight streaming through the slit in the curtains, wondering where the past twenty years had flown to. A tear in my eye as I remember a life that seemed lost. I thought about when I used to be full of life, zeal and passion, and every day used to be an adventure. I turn my head and look at Mark, asleep soundly, a line of drool white on his chin. His simplest touch would send me into a frenzy, short-circuiting my neural networks.

Closing my eyes and flashing back to my younger years, which don't seem that far back, that I can remember. I would have woken as I am now, except I would have been wrapped naked around Mark. Remembering the days I saw I had ten minutes before getting up and used the time to take advantage of naked man next to me.

That was my twenties, a time of unending possibilities- so how did I end up in this one possibility that I'd never imagined for myself? Back then, I was unstoppable; there was no glass ceiling for me and no internet to tell me my faults. I was invincible. And then I fell in love.

I wonder now when my life started feeling so stagnant, was it after our first child? Second? Was it when Mark started coming home late and then quietly turned over and slept without even checking if I was asleep? Was it after I confronted Mark about our dwindling sex life and told him I was desperate for his touch, and he laughed and ignored me?

Sex was just something we occasionally had because it was available, and we're together, I guess. For old times' sake? What once was my every desire was now barely a passing fancy. I snort a short, sarcastic laugh and turn to look at him again. Has he gone off sex, or is it just me? If only he showed half the interest in me that he did when we were young; I hardly turn him on when we're together; how could I make him want me? The marital ennui has had me suspecting and questioning which part of my body is the culprit. After three kids and so many years together, could it be entirely possible I've forgotten to enjoy sex? Am I too greedy to want more? Can safety and adventure ever exist together?

Mark moves in his sleep, and I know that when he wakes in a few moments, it will not be me he would desire as he did a few years ago, but a warm cup of dark, bitter coffee and a cool shower.

Once, a long time ago, my shadow would make him want me; his gaze would set me alight. It was almost pathetic what had happened to us. Our lives had become as unnoticeable to each other as the expensive wallpaper in the bedroom.

In the distance, across the walls, I hear the kids banging on bathroom doors and shoving their books in their bags as the day begins. I look at my watch on the bedside locker: 7.05 AM. I had a few minutes...

I slide my hand under the quilt, beneath the PJ bottoms and the comfortable cotton underwear. My movements are thorough, precise and quiet; Mark wouldn't know anything. My other hand glides across my neck, pausing on that sweet spot where it once tickled me, then continues down, teasing my nipples, giving them the attention they crave. I rub my breasts together and moan; it's more habitual and hopeful than what I'm feeling, but I continue. My hands move in a circular motion between my legs, my eyes closing, imagining it was a man's touch and not my own desperate fingertips.

I rub gently and then vigorously, but there's no pleasure, no evidence of it either. I sigh, frustrated, and mumble, "Even I can't do it". When had I changed from wearing nothing or some silky sexy night wear to pjs and sensible underwear. I don't even recognise myself.

Even more sensory underwhelmed, I shrug off the sheets and get off the bed, shedding off my T-shirt and PJs on the way to the bathroom. I will Mark to be awake and show a sliver of interest in my body, and I turn around, and indeed he is watching me. A faint beacon of hope survives in my heart. Maybe he'll come over, slap my ass, take me into the shower, and we'll finally have a good time?

But he just mumbles, "You go ahead, give me a few more minutes in bed." The days of getting up together and enjoying 10 minutes over a coffee before the kids' surface are gone. The valuable 10 minutes of peace from frantic children.

The faint beacon is extinguished.

I shake my head, now irrationally angry, and wait for the water to warm up. I look at myself; I look a bit tired, and my eyebags aren't doing me any favors, but all this comes with being forty-two. I'm not plastic, of course, I have changed, but I don't think I look any worse for wear. I'm still five-foot-seven, size 12, and have short blond hair that looks unkempt, maybe because it is. Either way, I do try to take care of myself… and don't look bad, I think. I could stand to lose a few pounds; I twirl in front of the mirror and look at myself from all angles. I could tone up a bit; I am always shaved where it counts, not that Mark notices anymore. Yet I hope.

I stand beneath the comforting stream of warmth under the shower, losing myself in its enveloping embrace. It seeps into my pores, the nooks and crevices… eventually, my frustrations blow out of me in a humid sigh. I enjoy this shower, maybe a bit too much. It's all I get before the mayhem of the day starts.

"Maria? Maria! What's keeping you?" I hear Mark knocking at the door. After so many years of marriage, I know my husband was standing with a worried 'v' between his eyebrows, an unintentional frown marring his features on the other side of the door. Why so nostalgic today. remembering hearing his younger self shouting *"Maria? Maria! Space for one more?"*

So, the mayhem starts.

I get out of the shower and wrap a towel around myself.

"All yours," I murmur before pulling on my clothes. Today's suit was already picked out, a white blouse, grey slacks and a strict jacket to go with it. Some sensible, moderately high-heeled shoes and my purse.

I steal a glance at myself as I pass by the mirror; could I look any more like the boring accountant that I was? The old enthusiastic smile full of energy replaced with a tired wrinkling look. I shake my head to rid myself of the pricking thought and quickly go down the stairs and into the lounge and kitchen, where the kids are already up and about. Liam was going through another phase where he would dress up in only baggy clothes, and since he was fourteen and the rest of us were not, we couldn't understand him. I lightly shuffle his hair and smile when he frowns at me.

Natalie is twelve and does not touch anything that's orange. Except for an orange because she likes sour food. And our surprise child, Rebecca, only four, sits on the floor in the middle of the school rush. I pick her up and sit her down on the couch just as I hear the doorbell ring.

One look at the clock, and I know it's our nanny, Ursula, who comes right on time to get the kids ready and shipped off for school. We say hello, and I pick up my coffee and sip it quietly as Ursula picks up a bunch of things at once, kids included, and rushes them about the house, collecting their homework, toys and whatnot on the way. That reminds me, I need to talk to the kids about picking up their own slack more; it was ridiculous how much mess there was in the mornings these days.

Mark and I headed out of the house at the same time, leaving the carnage behind, barely exchanging a smile, much less a word. Our cars are in the driveway. Sensible people carrier, my VW Golf and Mark's SUV. Cars, a house, a mortgage and kids. Suburban bliss, right? Until it is not. Sitting, I sigh, was I happier when we had little, enjoyed what we had, got buy and savored the moments of simple pleasures and lived in the moments.

I started to wish him good luck, but he had already sat in the car and is backing out. I start mine, and we go our separate ways. Mark is like how Mark gets when there's a new project on his hands. His enthusiasm for work has not changed, older yes, but with the same vigor for work, just not for me. He is a dedicated architect, and he sees buildings coming to life in material as miracles. His design just got into the construction stage, and nothing can tear him away from the site these days. The only silver lining? It's the city centre of Manchester, so at least he's close to home. I could see the building from my office window now that the construction had started, but a strange bitterness creeps over me whenever I see it; I have no genuine interest in it.

***

Thirty minutes and a swearing match later, I'm at the office. The traffic was actually light today, and that brightened my mood a bit.

I press the button and wait for the elevator to ride up to my floor. DAF Accountants... I have worked here for the past fifteen years, finally becoming Senior Accountant in the Forensic Department. Although there was none in the department better than me at bringing mismanaged companies to heel or sorting the books and doing corporate due diligence, sales and purchases, acquisitions and mergers, I still haven't made partner.

Or, the company hadn't made me a partner, a promotion that was promised to me five years ago. I was on the partner track for several years now, but in the end, it was the boys' club. My performance was extraordinary, my reputation was cold and fierce, and although it didn't endear me to the people that I worked with, they respected me. And yet I didn't sit at the big people's table. It made me grind my teeth with frustration and anger, two emotions that were primarily all I could feel these days. There is always an excuse to keep women behind in the corporate world. My old enthusiasm to impress to advance and looking at my superior with envy and admiration, replaced with a tired resentment of my superiors and a drive to have my ability and work recognized.

The big boys do have a nickname for me, though, and people around the office act like that's some consolation. Ice Maiden. They couldn't even think of something original. *I was never really that cold, was I?* That was like giving a name to my job description; I was hired to assess the companies and staff, make use of anything worthwhile and throw the rest away. Now what can I say, I'm very good at my job.

I have just finished working on a major project, and I hand in my final report for the Monday staff meeting. Usually, projects are discussed, and status updates and new projects and resources are allocated in these meetings. I sit on my swivel chair in the office, with nothing to do until the meeting, enjoying this welcome reprieve.

At around 2P.M, the meeting starts. The agenda is run through by my boss, and the only new project that comes up is appraising a chain of outdoor shops and assets of the deceased owner. The owner built it up from nothing and managed it all himself; now, the shops are all over the country, more densely located up North and in Scotland, and the HQ is situated in London.

The profile sounded quite impressive, and I wanted this project just because it would give me an opportunity to be away from home for a while. It was going to be just another mid-level company with no apparent successor, to be torn apart and sold for parts. Turns out most of the teams were busy, and some were about to wrap up their work, so the file automatically got pushed towards me.

I swirl the file on the table before picking it up; I can't ever appear too desperate for anything, even the break that I crave. I was told the meeting with the Solicitor was arranged for 4 PM, and they will fill in any blanks that appeared in the file.

I go back to my office and open the file; a miserable groan escapes my throat. The file was a collection of blanks at this point; the information was so scarce I had to search for it. I should be happy I got the client's name; I suppose. I knew what

6

was coming: a train wreck company with clueless employees who would drown me in paperwork as soon as I set foot across the threshold and then be expected to fix everything.

That was all part of the job, but I hated to be underprepared.

All I could tell from the file was that the company belonged to Ralph Michael, 68, now deceased. He was single, with no children or any appointed successor, and although his home was in Fort William, Scotland, he spent most of his time at the London HQ. No net worth. The entirety of his business boasted of shops stocking high-end and boutique outdoor sporting goods, "Outdoor Pursuits", and a rental portfolio.

His will was secured with Bond & Partners in Manchester, with in-house legal counsel all up over it. My eyes scan the assigned Solicitor's name: Senior Associate Paul Bridges. It didn't ring a bell. It would just be another boring suit, thinking he knew much more than I did.

I scan the rest of the entirely useless document I was handed. No value estimates of either the outlets, rental properties, offices or retail stores in London. The owner's London apartment was leased by the company, and the only other home was in Fort William, so… effectively no factual information about anything. A good internet scouring could have told me more, but I was short on time. I'd just hoped the London office kept good books.

***

At four sharp in the afternoon, Paul Bridges arrived at my office.

He looked like he was in his late forties and dressed like any other solicitor from his company. B&P has had a long-standing work relationship with DAF, so I knew a few people from his firm. I was sure he knew a few from mine. Dark suit, white shirt, plain tie. *Hmm, he likes to play safe*, I think. I have a niggling feeling I have seen him before. But cant place him.

He introduced himself and sat across from me, plucking a similar file as the one on my table out of his messenger bag.

But there it was, the only difference between his papers and mine, the will.

He handed me a copy of the will. It was succinct and straightforward. A senior partner at his company was appointed the Executor and Trustee of the will and estate. The first task was to assess and value the assets. The last task was to distribute it as per the associated trust deed. The instructions were clear: the contents of the deed would not be disclosed until the first task was completed, and all associate work was done.

The Solicitor was tasked to appropriately manage the upper echelons of the company and facilitate all that was needed to keep it running alongside the accountants assigned. Paul revealed that he had not come across the deed and was not expecting to until the work was done, as stated in the will. The request wasn't too out of the ordinary because fights do break out among family members and claimants once the new owner is revealed, and the company is soon run aground amid court trials and hearings.

I bring out my papers, and we join our heads to discuss strategy.

***

After an hour, we looked over the mess of papers and agreed that the only move forward now was to visit the HQ and stay in London for a few days to figure out the game plan. We could get the paperwork needed boxed from the HQ and see what we could salvage to make sense of the assets and valuation.

Paul has Nicola Mason's contact details, the head of Legal, who had her fingers in all pies, namely Finance and Operations.

"Hi, Miss Mason, I'm Senior Associate Paul Bridges from Bonds & Partners, with Senior Accountant Maria Holmes from DAF Accountants speaking to you in regard to the will and estate left behind by Ralph Michael...."

After a few minutes' call, we decided to spend Thursday and Friday in London and schedule a 9 A.M meeting with Nicola and the other essential personnel at the HQ office.

I watch his face, a slightly concerned look. crosses it. "Is everything ok?" I ask.

"It is fine, I am usually not away much, I need to organise sitters and make sure home is ok."

So, he has kids, no partner? I ask myself. Snapping back to the present.

Paul gets up and blows a tired sigh, looking around my office awkwardly. He then raises his brows and nods at me, collecting his papers. Neither of us suggested travelling for the London meeting together; I wasn't a small-talk person, and neither was Paul, it seemed. We were pretty formal, but I was like that with all my colleagues, and I wondered how long I would have to work with Paul before the Senior Partner came into the picture. I hoped we would tolerate each other just fine because I was really looking forward to my 'break' in the city.

***

Evenings at home are nice and great for optics. The whole family is together, the nanny in the kitchen wrapping up while the children fuss and talk about their day. Everything I dreamed of for my family future, a nice home, good jobs and financial security, but not what I expected. Their dad is enthralled by unintelligible diagrams on his phone, and the kids couldn't be less interested in what I had to say. I just put it out there.

"So, I have a new project. It will have me travelling between London and Scotland for a few months, at the least," I swallow my food and continue when there is no response, "It's pretty exciting; I haven't travelled in ages," I look around for a response.

Liam shrugs, and Natalie rolls her eyes. Rebecca is blank because she wasn't listening to me in the first place. Mark grunts, and I turn to him expectantly. Looking for a sign of the old Mark, asking me about my job, looking for all the details and seeing if I am looking forward to it and the people I am working with. But the old life I remember seems further away with his response.

"Just make sure you agree the time with Ursula, see if she's available," was all he said.

I nod and raise my brows, utterly disappointed in his lack of interest in my job or anything else happening in my life.

Ursula was, thankfully, available to stay over on Thursday and Friday, so that won't be an issue. But I wondered if Mark would even notice my absence if Ursula was there taking care of the kids, keeping them clean and quiet and fed?

Chapter 2

Thursday morning saw both Paul and I arriving together at the London Office in the financial district. Our destination was the 2nd floor of an older building. Paul held the lift open for me, and together we ascended, the 'Outdoor Pursuits' in bold lettering on the brass plaque our only view. There are a few small businesses on the ground floor, including a bakery and a boutique coffee shop. I speculate the returns on the coffee shop investment because all you could see in the district were suits addicted to coffee. Next door a travel agent and I see a sex shop the next unit down. A little smirk crosses my face. *That looks out of place, but maybe interesting.* There was a time I would have ducked in, taken a look if anything fun. Now, I could not see the reason to even look.

I am dressed to impress, business suit showing all the right curves. High heels showing I am not to be messed with and makeup just touched up before leaving the train.

We meet Nicola, who has worked for Ralph for the last twenty years and manages Legal. Her associate, Helen, who started with her almost 20 years ago greets us with enthusiasm. Nicola is in her mid-fifties, keeps to herself and seems much older because of her dour personality. Her husband managed the London store.

Helen also served as Ralph's PA and dealt with his schedule, diaries, meetings and paperwork. She also took care of all the communications around the late owner and travelled with him sometimes. Although Helen was also around Nicola's age, the two couldn't be more dissimilar in personality.

Helen was chatty, openly curious and obviously very devoted to Ralph. Nicola's laser eyes were boring into me.

Next, we sat down in the scantily furnished meeting rooms, and Nicola began briefing us.

She explains the inner workings of the company, how there were six stores, all independent of the others, managed by its respective managers from staffing to finances. The HQ served as the hub and supplied the shops.

The HQ also housed the Accounts department that dealt with all financial matters: Ordering, reordering, filing returns, creditors, and debtors. There were external auditors, but they were otherwise self-sufficient. We were walking around the department as Nicola talked, and I could see from the hustle and bustle that the morale had not been affected much. There were a few jitters and skittish glances, but that was normal. The boss who kept all the strings in his hand had died, and they had no idea what would happen next. I thought they were pretty calm about it all.

Next, we walked through the stock department, which handled all ordering and product issues. Each order in the shops was sent through here, where it was processed as a group buy and sold to the shop. This way, the outlets did their own accounts and managed local auditors, sending monthly reports back to the head office. Otherwise, Ralph visited the shops a few times in the year, but unless they were losing money, he left them to their own devices.

He, of course, tackled all major issues himself, "but there were not many", Helen insisted.

There were also several rental properties involved, including the ground floor of the building they were in right now, rented to small businesses.

From the way Helen and Nicola talked about Ralph, it seemed he was a hands-on, micromanaging kind of person with thoughts as old as the world. Since he built the company up from nothing, he was the sole commander, and he commanded alone. Now, it seemed the crew was hapless and wondered about the destination of their rudderless ship. There was electricity in the air, with all the gossip about who would take over and what they would do.

Once again, we wandered to the same meeting room as before, and the four of us pulled out a chair and took a seat.

By this time my heels were having an undesirable effect. Glad to sit down as they were cutting into me. Maybe means business to look at, but at a price. Not sure who I was trying to impress here. Paul seemed to be oblivious to me, *I remember when I would turn heads looking like this. Am I getting old and losing it.*

Nicola and Helen too preoccupied with the future of the business to see beyond my job. Pulled out of my thoughts by Paul.

"And what about his personal finances? Any vacation houses, memberships?" Paul asked, bringing out his shiny black pen and a small notebook.

"No, no, I wouldn't know about any of that. Ralph was sweet, but he was a private person," Nicola looked at Helen for agreement. Helen nodded with certainty.

"That's right. We were thick as thieves when it came to business, although his words were the last decision," Helen chuckled, "But I suspect we had never talked about anything other than that, nothing personal. Finances, operations, accounts, orders, creditors… that was all there was with him. It is his life's work, you see," Helen ends forlornly, looking around at the bare walls of the meeting room.

"Although…," Nicola started but paused, and I nodded, encouraging her to continue, "I mean, he was a human, too, right? He didn't exist in a bubble. I know he had personal interests, I'm just not aware what they were," She finished, looking around as if she's spoken too much.

So, no real information about any other assets, but we did find out that he lived a pretty simple life. There was the twelve-year-old jeep, the one that crashed, in Scotland, and his home here was the apartment leased by the company. And that was it, seemingly so.

"We'll leave you both to it, then?" Nicola asked, already scurrying away from the room. Helen followed suit.

"So, I think, let's work with Helen and Nicola, and see how it works here, get the full picture? No sudden changes, and all of that." Paul asked me, although he didn't need to. Paul's firm was the acting executor, and as such, their representative was responsible for all decisions going forward.

I assume he is just courteous, "Sure, that would keep the staff in the loop and maintain the status quo while I work on getting a full personal and commercial financial profile," I agree, packing up my things.

We left the room together, advancing towards the elevator, when Paul stopped in his steps and distractedly asked me to come with him. He went to the reception and beckoned Helen.

"Hey, so we're just leaving, but before that, can you take me to Ralph's office and show me his private safe?" Paul asked.

Helen squinted at us, "Yeah, darling, what safe?" She frowned. Nicola came to the reception as well, looking at Paul questioningly.

"I have never seen a safe, either" she revealed.

"I have the instruction letter here outlining the description of the contents, but it doesn't mention the location of the safe, so I assumed it's in his office. No?" He looked at the women blankly.

"Alright, never mind. I'm sure it will turn up somewhere," he smiled charmingly, and we proceeded to the elevators again.

"You're welcome to come take a look at his office, though," Nicola offered.

Ralph's office was vast but old-fashioned and unexpectedly cosy. There was a window in the corner where the large, rather imposing walnut desk sat, with a glass top beneath which were tucked bits and pieces of paper. The window was shut, but the warmth streamed in through the glass and brought in some hints of nature inside the room. A wide sofa lay across the desk, facing it from a distance, a throw draped over one of its arms.

On the far-right wall was a fireplace that may perhaps still be functional, and beside it lined bookshelves lined with thick, building records. Dates and numbers were strewn across their spines; the shelves were almost bending under the weight of the files. The chair was the swiveling type, with broad leather arms, a backrest, and a small cushion in the set.

The antique clock on the wall ticked loudly as the four people looked on at the papers scattered across Ralph's desk; no doubt he had been looking at them before taking that ill-fated drive to Scotland. Paul cleared his throat, and at that moment, the haunted spell broke; Helen quickly came to the desk and started filing away the papers in their appropriate places.

Paul looked around the office, searching for the safe, I believe, but my eyes were set on Helen.

"Hey, so, will you see that Ralph's recent diaries and the last half's finances are gathered and exported to the meeting room? We'll set up a temporary working space there and see what works from thereon," I am warm but firm. I couldn't work if there was no work for me on time.

"Of course, I will, darling. You see, the staff are very shaken right now, Ralph passed away so suddenly... They'll be glad someone is here, taking charge," She smiled at me warmly, her eyes shining.

I nod sincerely and turn around, raising my brows at Paul.

"I think I'm done, here," I look at him.

"Yeah," he clapped his hands, "Let's call it a day. Nicola, can you please get us both the company key cards by tomorrow? We'll be back in the morning," he looked at me in confirmation; I nodded, "We'll just be here quietly, maybe consult any of you two if there's an issue," he clarified and then smiled his charming smile. The first time he did it was annoying, but I noticed it was his habit. It certainly puts everyone at ease. Exactly contrasting the reaction, I inspired.

The ladies walked us to the elevators, and I got in and pressed the button. Paul stood beside me- close, I noticed- and I took a step back. Leaning against the back wall, trying to take weight off my heels. Helen waved us goodbye, and I smiled tightly before the elevator doors shut and we descended.

Out on the concrete pavement, Paul gestured at me to hold up before I got in my taxi.

"Maria, should we discuss how to best move forward over dinner this evening? I'll come to your hotel," Paul said- asked- willing me to say yes. *Maybe he was not as oblivious to me as I thought.*

We did need to talk about strategy and paperwork, so I said yes. This way, I could stay in and wrap up the business meeting. Two birds, one stone. He opened my taxi door and waited until I had driven away before getting into his own taxi.

***

Finally, out of my heels and suit. A chance to relax. There was a time dressing to kill empowered me and seeing the effect it had. Now it is hard work, and I can't wait to get into my flats and comfort clothing.

Before the meeting drew near, I took a warm, sudsy bath with the relaxing bath oils surrounded by candles in the egg bathtub. I was almost nodding off when I decided to rinse and get ready. I decided to go with a no-makeup look, with some mascara, gloss and concealer. Thankfully, I had brought a black dress that I could dress up or down with accessories, and I climbed into it quickly. I looked at myself for the final time in the mirror, grabbed my purse and phone and exited the room. More sensible shoes, deciding not to kill myself in heels again.

When I entered the dining room, Paul was already seated. He hadn't glanced at me yet, so I had an unhinged, unguarded view of him in his casual, open-necked shirt and jacket and beige jeans. *Business casual suited him*, I found myself thinking. I plucked my drop earrings out of my bag- earrings never do any harm. Running a hand through my hair, I walk towards the table where he sits.

He got off his chair when I came and pulled my chair out for me. I was surprised at his thoughtfulness but took it in my stride. We ordered drinks, and when the menus arrived, we ordered quietly. I steal a look at him over my menu as he reads off his order and thought, 'This is going to be a long dinner.'

Once he was done, I began, "Nicola will-"

"Maria," Paul interrupted me, "I'm sorry to cut in, but should we just chat and have a nice dinner? Let's not talk shop and enjoy our time travelling. I was thinking we will be working

16

closely for the next couple of months, it might be nice getting to know each other," Paul was as sincere as they came.

I smiled and raised my brows, but he was in earnest. I wonder how quickly he would run from the nicety of 'getting to know each other'.

I shrugged, "Sure, let's get to know each other," but didn't say anything else, waiting for him to begin.

In reality, his confession of setting up this dinner to get to know a colleague had taken me by surprise. He was like a different person, a whole 180° from the stuffy box suit I was getting used to.

He wasted no time. He jumped right into it, asking about my family and kids, my husband and his profession. It was like I was meeting an old friend for dinner. After half an hour passed in conversation centered around me, I was more comfortable than I had felt at home for some time.

I felt like I was years younger, forgetting I was married and enjoying the company of intelligent man. I felt more relaxed and alive than I had in a long time.

I told him about Liam's teenage angst and Natalie's aversion to orange food. My comments and stories of my kids made him laugh. There was multiple 'awh's' when Rebecca's turn came and I recounted her recent shenanigans.

It was evolving into a lovely evening of chatting and laughing. It was like an instant click. There was no awkwardness, no strangeness.

He told me about his family, his three adult kids. Matthew, twenty-two, was in university finishing a general business degree. Sarah was twenty, whom he secretly wanted to follow in his footsteps, but she was enjoying her Arts degree in college. And, finally, Rachel, who was sixteen and just in the middle of her teenage drama phase.

He was forlorn when talking about his wife, who had passed away over ten years back suffering from ovarian cancer. So, he had been forced to take a step back from his career and focus on his kids to make it a smooth transition for them.

"It was bumpy, of course; the kids were so young. But I had to be their dad, mom, taxi and laundry. Such is life," he sighs, and I find myself listening to him intently. *Well, that answered the partner question I had about Paul.* Then he talks of his pain; the way he talks about his wife proves he still misses her. Her death was obviously very hard on the family, but they had persevered.

They had their own Ursula as well, a woman named Julie, who had been like a mother to his kids. As they had grown, she had become more of a housekeeper than a childminder.

"Although, she does like to be strict with them, every now and then. Just so they know who cared for them while everything was a mess," Paul laughs gently.

I smiled at him, pleasantly entertained.

Now that the kids didn't need to be watched, Julie could fill in his spot as well, and he could afford much more freedom than he could a few years back. That meant taking a project that would have him travelling and staying away. Although, he said, this was the first job he suspected would have him travelling all the time. But even though Paul was hesitant, his boss had specifically asked- and ordered, more like- him to take on this case.

We were laughing when our food arrived and spoke all the while we ate. Parent to parent, then man to woman, we had lots to talk about. He gave me tips on dealing with children going through puberty and loneliness, and I reminded him how cute the children used to be.

I was enjoying not being a wife or mother and looked at as an interesting woman. Like Monday morning in bed, I was remembering back to my younger days where I felt my blood coursing through my veins like a life force. Then brought back to reality by the next question.

He asked about Mark, who had somehow escaped my mind during all this conversation.

I told him how we met just out of college and quickly got married. That we had been together for twenty years, and he is a passionate architect, always swamped with work. I felt bitterness seeping into my voice as I talked about him and quickly changed the subject to our 'Julie' Ursula, the second mother to my kids, who actually makes it possible for me to travel for work.

I didn't know if I was overstepping, but I felt like asking, so I did, "Did you ever think about remarrying?" I think *looking at him as a man, not a lawyer.*

"No… it didn't even cross my mind. The first few years were tough. The kids, myself… and after that, bar a few disastrous dates arranged by my colleagues, it's always been rushing home from work for the kids. It worked for me, it's not confusing for them, and I've been happy because they are. But now, they're growing up, and don't need me as much. So, I'm forced to get a life," He laughs, obviously referencing his children's thoughts at the end.

The evening passed in nostalgia for our younger days, recalling our loved ones and talking about our children fondly. It was heartwarming when he talked of his wife, and deep inside me, I wanted Mark to get some lessons from him. But maybe it was the wine talking. I wanted to feel loved and wanted and desired like I once did. Feel the effect of the desire that now only lives in my memory. The tingling feeling I wanted once more.

***

This evening was different, was it just me or the air felt different, lighter, easier to breathe in, pleasant even?

Was it my company, or was it the fact that my husband was no longer sleeping beside me, frustrating me with his very existence?

Tonight was lovely, surprisingly. Paul seemed like a genuine man, very family-oriented, soft-spoken and attentive. He enjoyed his job, but it wasn't his whole life. He loved his kids, but he gave them room to grow and flourish; his life seemed in order.

I had an inkling he was in his late forties. He was an attentive listener, and the eye contact during the dinner had been a bit unnerving for me, weirdly, because I wasn't used to being listened to in an informal setting. The realisation shocked and saddened me. Paul wasn't a very exciting or an interesting man, objectively, but still the conversation flowed easily, punctuated by comfortable silences and meaningful glances. Each glance made me feel looked at, seen for me, not my job or a mother.

My only purpose for taking this job and coming here was to get away from home, to let my mind breathe, and to organise my thoughts and feelings that agonised me so. But, after tonight, it seemed this trip wasn't going to be all too bad. With Paul, there was ease in conversation, vastly different from the varying degrees of arrogant Solicitors I usually had the ill luck of meeting. With him, I didn't think about proving myself, putting my foot in the boys' club the whole night. I wasn't an inflexible bean counter, the Ice Maiden that was a frigid bitch.

The events of this evening's relaxed, laid-back and played in my mind until I drifted asleep, cosy inside the cool, crispy sheets of the hotel room against my skin. Choosing to sleep in t-shirt and panties like I did when younger, shedding the sensible pjs reminding me of my age.

***

The following morning, we take a taxi together to the office. I am dressed in a black suit, white crisp shirt, my golden rimmed sunglasses and a pair of pearl drop earrings to match. Low heels for comfort, no need for the weapons I wore yesterday. Paul looks dashing in a black suit, white shirt sans tie; his shirt open at the neck, giving me a tantalising peak to his chest. The missing tie portrays a more relaxed personality.

I clear my throat as Paul guides the driver towards the financial district.

It's almost nine when we arrived, and exchanging not more than a glance, we enter the building. When the lift halts, we are surprised to be welcomed with an unexpected sight: everyone is dressed in casual wear, jeans and loose button downs, trainers and t-shirts. It looks like a Sunday afternoon down at the high street.

Puzzled, we shared a look, Paul's brows furrowed, and I shrug.

We head to the reception to meet with Helen, and she guides us to the conference room which was supposed to be our temporary office for the next few months. Helen unlocks the door and throws it wide open, chuckling nervously, "So, this is it. This room doesn't get used often, so you'd be undisturbed here, at the very least," she smiles at us.

I could see why it was unused: it was just a room, with barely any heating, decrepit and empty. There was a wide wooden table in the centre around which a few rickety chairs stood forlornly.

"Uh-huh," Paul exhales, looking around the room. "It will have to work, I believe."

"It's what it is," I shrug, putting my bag on the table and unloading all the documents and files I have brought. Now that we have a set-up, I won't have to drag all these papers back and forth. That alone is a cause for relief.

"Make yourself at home, any questions and I'm right here, okay, darling?" Helen smiles sweetly at Paul. I snicker, and Paul spots me.

He shakes his head, but turns back to Helen, "Hey, so, I was wondering if I've missed out on something? Yesterday everyone was dressed formally, and today it's very casual out there," he gestured toward the lobby.

"Oh, yes. We usually do dress-down Fridays, and when they asked me if the policies are the same, I didn't want to change anything," she came close to him, and lowered her voice conspiratorially, "you know, honey, they're pretty shaken out there. They've no idea where the ship is heading or who the captain is. I hope this is, okay?" She looks at the both of us in turns.

"Of course, that's understandable. Business as usual. Thank you, Helen" Paul smiles, and asks her to arrange a meeting with the four of us; Nicola, Helen, Paul and I, at eleven. She replies affirmative, and leaves, closing the door behind her.

As soon as she leaves, Paul turns to me meaningfully. I know what's going on in his mind; the situation that could overshadow all our work here.

He looks like he knows we're on the same wavelength.

"So, looks like there's more than just Accounts and Legal here, huh? Staff are obviously worried, and we need them to keep the ship afloat and on course. I think we need to learn a lot about the present before implementing change in the future," Paul exhales, looking at me keenly.

"You're right, we need to settle this quickly and quietly. Let's divide and conquer. Split Helen and Nicola between us and find out the inner workings. At the very least I need to know if the company is even solvent," I agree, my mind already miles ahead.

"Alright, I'll take Nicola and get working on the legal and administration issues. Let's regroup first thing on Monday and see what we can tackle," he pulls out a chair, and takes a seat.

I mirror the same, "I think we should call a general meeting after picking Helen and Nicola's brains. 11.30, full staff. Introduce ourselves, set the record straight. The bottom line will be: it's business as usual and we're here to resolve any issues, make sure the company is secure and the staff are on top of their assigned work. You know, reassurances, morale boost yada yada yada," I speedrun through strategies.

Usually when I come into the company, I am assigned a management team to work with. They're not great most of the time, but it's at least dedicated manpower.

"I figure this whole business was a one-man band. There's no dedicated management, no executives. That means Ralph oversaw and micromanaged everything. All of it went through him, which is great news because we'll get all the info in one place, but also bad news because there's no one else to tell us how he worked, what he was thinking, which direction he was going in," I think out loud.

Paul nodded, quietly listening. I could tell he was formulating a plan of his own.

"Alright, then I'll get a status report on all upcoming and present projects from Helen, and let's see how we can manage that later. You alright to come back next week, all week?" I ask him, unaware that I was hoping he would answer yes.

22

"Yeah, of course. That will tell us how long we are needed in-house. Nicola will run point on briefing you about the status of legalities, and Helen can enlighten me on whatever you two are handling," Paul answered, not realising the smile his former sentence had put on my face.

"Yeah, yeah, sounds good," was all I could murmur, trying to expel this illogical excitement I felt.

We continued going back and forth on strategies, comms and reliable options going forward.

***

At eleven sharp, the four of us met in the chilly, echoing conference room. Once we sat down to talk, Helen and Nicola were pleased to learn we were making some headway and had already settled on an approach to work ahead. We explained how the work would be divided, and that I would be receiving Helen's help while Paul would work with Nicola. The ladies had also brought with themselves boxes and boxes of paperwork that Paul and I needed to go through, bylaws, account sheets. I groan; they really are going to drown me in paperwork, and here I was, angling for a break in London.

The meeting with the ladies wrapped up within half an hour, and I requested Nicola to call a general meeting pronto. At almost half past eleven, Paul and I stand at the front of the cubicles, flanked by Helen and Nicola. I feel a little silly standing on boxes of printing paper beside my assigned Solicitor, but I have done this so many times that I barely cringe. I felt far from the imposing businesswoman who walked in wearing killer heels yesterday. Now I balance on boxes of papers being looked at more like the enemy.

The room was buzzing with anticipation as the employees gathered for the meeting. The nervousness was palpable, and I had already heard whispers of a 'kill list'. When everyone has assembled and the speculative murmurs die down, Paul clears his throat and cues for me to begin. Not sure how I was here and not Paul, after all his company were on lead here. Was he throwing me to the wolves.

"Welcome and good morning, everyone. I am Maria Holmes, Senior Accountant from DAF, and with me is Paul Bridges, Senior Solicitor. We know that change can be unsettling, and the staff here is worried, but we are here to address not only your concerns, but any questions anyone has about moving forward. We believe that we have a tremendous opportunity here to build up on the work that you have already done, and with all of you right by us, we will weather this storm in no time. Mr. Bridges here represents the executors of the estate and thus is in-charge of running the company in the interim, until the successor is found.

"First things first, be assured its business as usual. Helen and Nicola here will see the day-to-day as they have been doing, but any resource allotment, project updates, logistics and deliveries will go through either Mr. Bridges or myself," I finish, and Paul starts right on cue.

"Although I'm the interim in-charge of the company, there's going to be no changes around here. Now, I request each department to prepare a short summary, just a bullet point report on the current projects, resources allocated, team working on it and other specifics. Add in any decisions that need to be made, or any issues you have come across," Paul finished, looking around the room for any apparent feedback.

"Anything related to financials, shops, ordering, invoices, and trading, you're welcome to come directly to meet with me. There will be no radical changes. We are a team, all of us," I make it a point to make eye contact with a few of the front-row employees.

"It was good to see everyone here, invested in the company and doing their very best in these unprecedented times, but rest assured that you have a listening ear in Mr. Bridges and me. Within a few weeks we will get to know more about the company, its culture," I look pointedly at my suit and their casuals, "-its people, and the possibilities that lie ahead," I finished amid a halfhearted applause, and got off the boxes of paper.

Once the general meeting was adjourned, we used Ralph's office to call each of the six shop managers to update them on the newest changes, the chain of command and reassuring them that their interests were protected and prioritised. The managers seemed nervous at first, but subjected to Paul's convincing cajoling and reassurances, they warmed quickly and happily agreed to our few requests.

The rest of the day passed quickly with staff being summoned to piece together vital information and to get a gist of the company morale. Helen and Nicola were on their feet, right beside us, filling in the gaps, proving more useful than I had anticipated. One other thing that I wasn't prepared for was their genuine devotion to the company, even in Ralph's absence.

That evening, Paul and I travelled back to Manchester; separately, after making extensive plans for the coming week. Spending the journey thinking of life, the awakening that seemed to be happening as I remember the young, vibrant adventurous woman I was, compared to the middle-aged accountant existing in life and not living. Determined to regain myself and live in the moment again. Just not sure how. There was a moment of emptiness when I saw his taxi depart, but I shook it off and was thrilled I'll be home soon.

Chapter 3

A new week, same old busy Monday. There was too much on the to-do list, so I came to the office earlier than Paul. I had already sorted the files I had to go through today, when my phone chirped.

A text message from Paul, it read: Coffee in the cafe?

I do need an espresso shot, so I retrieve my reusable cup from my bag and go down the lift, and into the quaint coffee shop on the ground floor of the building. I see Paul engrossed in his phone screen, sitting by the window seat. He looks up as soon as I enter the shop and smiles warmly. I frown slightly and hand over my cup for a refill. Inside the cafe, I am greeted by the warm aroma of freshly brewed coffee, and a pleasant, soft tune fills my ears. Even though the shop is situated in the most boring financial district of town, it was quite cosy, with plush chairs and comfortable couches. I wonder if people here had the time to enjoy these simple luxuries. I remind myself I don't give myself time to enjoy simple luxuries.

I also spy mouth-watering pastries, and warm baked snacks behind the glass showcase. I note down the options for any future fuel-ups. The ambience of the shop is overall chic, modern, but still intimate and comfortable. Not at all professional, and leaning more towards a luxury feel.

On second thoughts, I don't want to have coffee together here with Paul, so I pick up my warm cup, and gesture at him to follow me. He is taken aback, but quickly grabs his charger, phone and bag to follow me outside. Once out in the sun, Paul turns to me in exasperation.

"Nothing worse than the British rails this morning," he shook his head, sipping on his coffee.

"I did not see you on the train, took the 5.55," I look up at his melted caramel eyes glowing in the sun.

"Nope, I got the 6.15. It was bursting at the seams. But, amazing what an extra fifteen minutes in bed can do for you," Paul smiled remorselessly.

We take the lift to our floor, where we set up temporarily, and head to the conference room. The heating has been fixed, and finally, I don't risk blue toes from working here. We quickly come to order and start reviewing the strategies we discussed on Friday.

The next few days are a blur of entropy, reviews, papers, and way too much reading. I am determined to go through the boxes of files and reports I asked for, and Paul does the same. Neither of us exchange pleasantries; it would only get in our way. Just a nod of the head would acknowledge the other's presence, and a wave goodbye was it.

On Wednesday afternoon, we decided to discuss our findings and join heads on issues company-wide. There was progress, and I was pretty satisfied with how things were going on both our ends. We had already started seeing managers, employees and staff regarding their concerns and they were trusting us to make secure, valid decisions for the company.

It was around five-thirty today when I finally finished the tasks, I had set for myself. I was just packing up when Paul peeked into the room.

"Would you like to join me for dinner? Get out of the hotel for once? Room service is making me pull my hair out," he confessed pleasantly.

I agreed wholeheartedly. Although I was staying in a five-star hotel, and the food was decadent, I could do with stuffing myself with pasta or a burger today. We settle to meet at my hotel's reception at seven.

Over the last few days, Paul and I hadn't talked much, barely made small talk. No small talk was good, because I hated to comment on the weather, or the number of people around us, but now I wonder if it could have given him cause to be more comfortable around me. It was just Nicola and Helen liaising between us. Work, work, meet this employee, and work.

Just like that day, I dressed up in black, brushed through my hair so it fell in a pattern around my ears. I decided to get my nude stilettos out and got a matching small nude bag. I kept my makeup minimal; I was tired, and Paul was super casual the last time and I didn't want to overdo it. No jewelry.

He was leaning against the reception counter, pleasantly talking to the receptionist when I came down. He looked at me thoroughly before joining me where I stood and smiled.

"Any cuisine preference? Where would you like to go?"

"Easy, anywhere that's not my hotel dining area," I snort. I feel like I am going on a night out, not a business dinner. The feeling brings a smile to my face. I feel like a world away from reality.

He exhales a small laugh and then takes my elbow. We walk down to Leicester Square and roam until we get even more tired and find a cosy Italian place that smells heavenly. We're greeted by warm lighting that accentuates the romantic setting of the place. There are wooden tables and chairs, and soft Italian music plays in the background. We have barely made it to an open table for two when I'm enveloped in a mouth-watering aroma of fresh herbs, garlic, and tomato sauce.

The smell is rich, inviting, and comforting, with hints of oregano, basil, and rosemary filling the air. I can almost taste the fragrant marinara sauce simmering on the stove, and the freshly baked bread in the oven. My stomach growled with anticipation as my eye caught the extensive collection of wine on the dainty, swirly menu and I ordered a bottle to start the night.

We get to talk about the company, the people there, and it slowly evolves into a similar conversation as the last time we got together. The relaxed feeling overcomes me once more. I can feel the effect through my body, the relaxed feeling of warm blood flowing and a smile on my lips that isn't forced or tired.   He listens intently and offers words of encouragement and support at my narration of life's ups and downs. He talks about his last few days with Stephanie- his wife who passed away trying to battle invasive cancer- and the unexpected turn his life had taken after her death. I feel his pain, his loss of direction. He talks as if this was the first time he has acknowledged his feelings, giving them tangibility by speaking to them out loud. Maybe he was. I feel this inexplicable sense of connection and closeness, somehow knowing that this person comes very nearly to caring about me and my well-being. Not a feeling I can remember since I remember when, I like it.

I sip on my wine until we finish the first bottle, and I order a second. When the food arrives on our table, I smack my lips, ready to devour it. The aroma from my plate of Linguine Alla Vongole wafts to my nose, immediately bringing water to my mouth. I take a bite, and there's a burst of flavor in my mouth: a decadent balance of savory and tangy. I've never had fresher clams, steamed in white wine and garlic sauce until they pop open, thrown over the light and delicate al dente pasta that looks too good to be true.

In the end, I couldn't eat a lot, feeling full from almost two bottles of exquisite wine. I feel myself floating in the air, feeling a bit tipsy but the conversation flows effortlessly, as Paul and I laugh, reminisce and share our hopes and dreams for the future.

The evening slips away as the wine disappears from our glasses- mainly mine. And when I'm laughing a little too loud and losing my balance, Paul takes me by the elbow and hails a taxi. I talk gibberish all the way back to the hotel, quieting down when I notice- out of the blue- that I couldn't remember the last time Mark and I had had a fun evening, a delicious dinner and good company, coming home excited and pulling each other's clothes off as we laughed. Now I imagined that feeling once more. Wanting to feel that wanted. Wanted someone to do that to me again. Remember that was part of my identity that was not overshadowed by the ice maiden.

I'm jerked out of my reverie when Paul opens the taxi door and helps me out and walks me to the reception. I'm hell-bent on making a spectacle of myself but he quickly swerves and glides me away from the reception and into the lift.

"Trust you can find your way from here?" He asks, smiling widely.

I am not tipsy. I am full-blown wine drunk, giggling and laughing, losing balance all around me. I look up at him coyly, standing flush to him, and I see his smile waning and something else clouding his eyes. Or maybe it was just my dirty mind; with newfound horror I pull myself away, and back away into the lift, waving him goodbye. He stands there firmly with his hands in his jeans pocket, watching the doors shut.

I exhale loudly as the lift descends and hit my head. Seriously, I have lost it. I wanted him and did not care why. I walk tiredly to my room, and run a bath, dropping oils liberally into the tub. I strip down and look in the mirror before stepping into the warm, silky water. I run a hand over my neckline, decolletage and down the chest, feeling my nipples advertise my mood. *His loss*, I think, *and my worse luck*. Groaning at my line of thoughts, I shut my eyes, wishing all the embarrassing things in my life evaporated without trace.

***

The following morning, I douse myself in a quick shower and brush my teeth violently. I can still smell wine on my breath, or maybe it's just my overactive mind. The smell, and the puzzling headache reminds me of last night. Oh God, I didn't, did I? No, no, no, I groan.

I threw myself at him, and he didn't even try? Ugh, I could die of embarrassment right now. I hold my head between my hands for a while, and when the fog from my mind lifts, I rationalise.

Isn't his control a testament to his character, that he's a gentleman and wouldn't take advantage of a drunk, stupid woman? And I am grateful one of us held on to their good sense, because after a mistake like that how would we ever work together in a professional setting again?

Shaking my head in regret and frustration, I head into work.

When I get to the conference room, Paul is already there, typing quickly on his laptop. He's dressed in a deep blue suit, no tie, and a light pink shirt open at the collar.

He looks up as I put my bag over the table, and smiles. Then he shuts his laptop, and gets up, smiling at me.

"Do you fancy going to the coffee shop? The only thing worse than the British rails is this pathetic coffee," he looks disgustingly at the Styrofoam cup sitting half-empty on the table.

I nod, trying to appear more composed than I felt.

The coffee shop downstairs is busy, but we spot a few empty chairs by the windows. Paul orders two coffees, mine with a double shot of espresso, and I decide I should stop ignoring the elephant in the room, and just own up to the absurdity of last night.

"Hey, so, listen," I start, "About last night, I shouldn't have drunk so much-"

Paul cuts me off, "Hey, don't worry, there's nothing to it. Both of us had a bit to drink, and had a lovely night out, just two colleagues who had a good time, and then went back to their hotels," he says firmly.

"I'm embarrassed, and sorry if I made you uncomfortable. I don't usually drink a lot when I'm out," I confess, feeling miserable, because he seemed too on top of the situation while I felt like a child.

"Not a thought more about it," Paul declares, "And anyway, it's on my expense sheet. And someone like you would know if it's not on the balance sheet, it didn't happen and does not exist," he smiles mischievously.

I smile warmly and purse my lips.

"Fair enough, I'll quit while I'm ahead," I roll my eyes at him.

And just like that, he put me at ease. No awkwardness, no regrets. Just plain old adults with a sense of humor about their situation. I have a newfound respect for him, at his cool-headed control when it came to handling uncomfortable situations. Hm, he isn't all too bad.

Paul looks at his wristwatch after a few minutes, and I urge him to go, "You go ahead, I have to check in at the office with updates," I smile openly at him.

He nods, and leaves. I look after him for a few seconds, and then pull my phone out to call my boss, Jack, to update him on the current situation. I had made quite some headway with the trove of papers I was given to go over, and I wanted to share some fine details to keep him in the loop.

"Hi, Jack, so I figured I should call with an update before I head in to work today, are you available for a chat?" I'm already pulling out my to-do list and diary where I keep track of all the work.

"Hey, Maria, wait. So, I was talking to Leonard- that's Paul's boss- and we thought we should get a joint update on progress at both your ends, so can you make it for a call at two in the afternoon?"

"Yeah. Yeah, that works," I replied, and cut the call, shoving my stuff back into my messenger bag and hurrying upstairs to let Paul know of the scheduled meeting.

As soon as Paul sees me, he tells me there will be a conference meeting in the afternoon, and that both his and my boss will be in attendance. I purse my lips to keep my smile from showing, and we get to work.

2PM comes around and we gather in Ralph's office to receive the call.

Paul goes first, talking about employees, the current projects the company is overseeing, the managers and their duties, and everything in between.

Next, I summarise, "This is a strange, but very simple set-up. I have looked at the Balance and Trading sheets for the last half of the six shops, and all appear very cash rich on paper. The books seem legit, but I've still asked for the last half's bank statements to make sure nothing is cooked, but otherwise it all looks solid. I can see no liquidity issues."

Paul nods as I finish, and then begins again, "Legally, all is very quiet. The company has been standing still, with no progress or regress for a few years, really. No litigation that's being dealt with outside of the insurance company, and those are small issues too. Nicola deals with supplies, supply contracts, and pricing issues with managers. Overseeing tenants, negotiating lease, it's all Nicola. She's more like a COO than a Legal Head. When Ralph was here, she would oversee the monthly profit and loss reports from the shops and report directly to him.

"The accounting department here is also functional, already dealing with supply chains and keeping the profitability of the main company in check-"

Leonard, Paul's boss and also his friend in some capacity, interjects, "So, what do you both think is next? Do you need more time in London, or is everything good there?" he asks in a heavily Scottish accent.

Paul and I share a glance; we knew this was coming, and we had prepared in advance for it.

"From the company health perspective, there is a definitive lack of management here. With the upper echelon of the company out, the employees are scrambling for a chain of command. Helen and Nicola take care of the day-to-day, but with Ralph here they never made any significant decisions. They can handle almost anything, but there's a vacuum here. We need to sort that out in the interim as the executors until the successor.

"Next, we've got Ralph's personal affairs to wrap up. Even Nicola, his long-term PA has no idea what he got up to, and where. So, the next thing we need to figure out is his financial and estate profile. That might be difficult," he looks at me, and I nod, agreeing, "because from what I've got here, he was a loner, and there's effectively no one to clue me in. I would probably need access to his home office, and his personal papers. Apart from that, the safe that was mentioned in the will has still not been recovered," Paul finishes, giving everyone much to think about.

"What do you guys need, should I send up some assistance?" Jack asks, looking at me.

Paul and I share another glance.

"We definitely need assistance here, because there's too much paperwork to go through, and that's not even considering what we find in Scotland. Plus, some management skeleton here, but I don't think it's a good idea to introduce too much change, and too many people all at once. The last thing we want here is frenzy, and reliable people throwing in the towel," I voice my thoughts.

"Alright, tell me what arrangements need to be made there?" Leonard asks, and I see him pick up a pen to note things down.

"I need assistance with accounting expertise, someone who knows their way around financial holdings and makes sure nothing escapes us. If Jack can spare Maria for a while, until we get through the meat here, I think that will be a valuable help. Since we were the first to get on the scene, I think Helen and Nicola are comfortable with us. But that's for you to decide," Paul puts the ball in Leonard's court.

This part of the meeting we had not prepared for. I did not know what Paul was going to ask for, all I know is I did not want this to end. This job was like a step back in years for me. Reigniting feelings I have been longing to open once again.

Leonard and Jack briefly discuss, and then Jack turns to me.

"Maria, can you afford the time to take this job? I can send up a junior to help out if you want, and I will reassign your smaller tasks, so you don't have to worry about deadlines here. What do you say?"

I take a meaningful pause. *I know what I want and that is to be here.* I can't be to egger.

"I think I agree with Paul here. Employees look up to Helen and Nicola, and we have a rapport with them. Plus, this needs solid Accountancy, and although someone new may get on the job, the morale is delicate. People swooping in and out so quickly may give off a wrong impression. I'm happy to stick with the project for now, and we can revisit the discussion of staying in London until we have all the holdings assessed," I say, mentally calculating how many hours I'd be out, and would need Ursula to cover for the kids.

Jack claps his hands, "Alright, Maria, work with Paul on this and see what needs to be done to find any personal affairs and finances, then put together a profitability report on the company finances, all the shops, and see what the assets end up looking like. Good work, you two," he gives us reassuring support, and the call ends.

I gather all my papers, and before leaving I lean against the door and look at Paul, who is following right behind me.

"Thank you," I say with furrowed brows. I had no idea he would ask for me, even though I was sure he didn't need to; on a big project for DAF, Jack would always need me. But Paul's preference had taken me by a welcome shock.

"Huh?" he raises his brows.

"Asking for me on this job. I was itching for a challenge. This will be different from staring at big numbers all day," I smile, putting him at ease because he looked uncertain, like he should have asked me before recommending me for the task.

"Well, we're away from home, let's indulge in a bit of adventure. And hey, you are actually good company, for an accountant. Last night flew by; it's amazing what a few glasses of wine can do for the mood," he joked coyly.

I blush but then decide to partake, "Oh, I don't remember much. I hope."

He laughs, and we walk to the conference room, where he stands with his hands on his waist, calculating something.

"So, what's next? Should we get out of here and check Ralph's apartment? Maybe he has an office there, to get a feel for the information before delving in. There's also the matter of the treasure hunt."

"Treasure hunt?" I laugh, he is ridiculous sometimes. This behaviour makes me smile and I like feeling playful at work. So long since I had fun in a job.

"Well, the mysterious safe that no one has seen or heard of. I admit, I am curious about it."

Chapter 4

It's around four when we get to Ralph's apartment. It was right around the corner from the office building, and Helen had afforded us an emergency set of keys to get into the place. Her eyes were shining when she handed me the keys, and I asked if she would like to accompany us, but she firmly declined, saying it would be too upsetting seeing so much of Ralph so soon.

I respected her decision, even if her coming along would have made things easier. On our walk to the apartment, I wonder how it felt, to lose such a strong presence of someone who had been with her for upwards of twenty years, in a jiffy. Whatever others said about the Ice Maiden, I could even understand what it meant to work in intimate settings with the same person for two decades. And to lose them to an accident must be so cruel.

Paul nudged me out of my thoughts when we arrived at the entrance of the apartment building. It was a four-story structure, with a vacant shop space on the ground floor, and three apartments stacked above it. As we entered the building, I could see the flight of stairs, and the lifts seemed to have seen better days. The lift had a musty smell, and it creaked and groaned when we called it down. The state was so brittle that I looked at Paul pointedly, and we silently made our way to the rickety stairs.

The third floor was Ralph's. Upon arriving on the floor, Paul clicked in the keys to the lock and threw open the doors. It was a spacious place, with high ceilings, and large windows that welcomed plenty of natural light. The walls are painted a neutral shade, although it was chipping in places now, and there was little in the way of decoration. Once, I mused, this place must have been a home; from the empty vases on every horizontal surface, expensive wallpaper in the bedroom, and hand painted cabinets in the kitchen, I could tell this place had been loved, maybe before Ralph had moved in.

Now, it was just a bachelor pad, with a simple, functional layout and a few pieces of basic furniture. Despite the lack of adornments, the apartment was tidy, and well-maintained. The floors had but just a light layer of dust, and the bathroom and kitchen fixtures were in good condition. There were wall mounted, stainless steel grab bars installed in the bathroom, kitchen and against the stairs.

Across the wall where sunlight streamed in hung a few paintings. I was appreciating the art when I saw a few hooks, from where other canvases may have hung. I walk around the lounge, running my hand over the dusty furniture.

"The sideboard, tables… These vases… all old but look very expensive. So does the art; I wonder if he was a collector?"

A large hook in the centre of the far wall catches my eye. I wonder what had made home on the now-empty stretch of wall and had left behind a blank space that felt incomplete. The large square where the frame must have once hung is slightly lighter than its surroundings, bearing witness to its absence.

"It must have been heavy," I murmur.

The wall itself is unremarkable, with a smooth surface and a neutral colour that blends into the background. There are no visible marks or scratches, indicating that the painting was removed with care. The stark, empty space seems to draw attention to itself, as if it is waiting for something new to take the place of what was lost.

Despite the emptiness, the wall still seems to hold the memory of the painting that once adorned it. I imagine the colours and shapes of the artwork, and how it might have brought life and energy to the room. Without the painting, the wall feels incomplete, like a puzzle missing a piece.

Paul is sitting behind the desk, much like the one in Ralph's office, and watches me looking at the art. I seldom get time to appreciate life's finer offerings, but I know when I see a beloved piece. The desk where Paul sits is not the tidiest; it was in a state of disarray, with papers strewn haphazardly across its surface and spilling onto the floor. The clutter gave the impression of a busy mind, but also suggested a lack of organisation.

There were loose sheets of paper with scribbled notes, receipts, and business cards mixed in with the pages of reports and printouts. It was clear that Ralph had been working on multiple projects simultaneously and had not given a thought to cleaning up. But then he did not have to, he did not share this space with anyone. I wonder how this served as a productive workspace. Paul turns on the computer standing on the desk.

"I need access to this, maybe Nicola has his passwords," he muttered.

"Anything interesting?" I ask, looking at the chaos of papers.

Paul shakes his head, "The usual. Bank statements, bills, regular paperwork... nothing inspiring."

"No surprise there," I say, and walk to the desk, "Nicola said he was reclusive, retired pretty early, and wouldn't leave his room unless it was for work, even when they were travelling. No friends, no personal life. Not a lot to tell. Except she may be nursing a soft corner for him," I chuckle.

Paul was going through the drawers now, one at a time. There was more of the same, stapler, more papers, more files-

"Hello, lookie here," came Paul's excited voice. I looked up from the papers that had caught my eye and saw him looking into the drawer.

"Maybe the old man was not as dull and reclusive as everyone thought," he smiles widely, finally looking up at me.

I frown, intrigued, "What is it?"

Paul holds up a tied-up piece of rope.

38

I look at him quizzically, "A… rope? What's that, sports gear?"

"Nope," he laughs, "Looks like a set of rope cuffs. See, it's already tied to measure," he fingers the dangling wrist cuffs.

A laugh bubbles inside me, "Sounds like experience talking," I tease him, walking back to the empty wall with the hook, and held my arms up. I don't even know how a rope cuff works, or why I did that, but it was funny, imagining the old man with an adult toy.

"Maybe that's what this hook is for, I did wonder if it seemed too sturdy for hanging up just art," I snicker.

We laugh, staring at each other. The air seemed to get heavier, it was getting harder to breathe. I could feel my hands awkwardly hanging over me, but I couldn't move them.

"Maybe it's you who's experienced," Paul shakes his head. "Do you think it will fit?" He playfully teases me back.

"Maybe they would," I whisper, my breath catching in my throat.

He comes to stand near me, my breath heavy, my hands in the air, frozen in the moment.

What have I said, what will he do? My mind races.

Before he brings his hands up, a familiar ringing wrenches us out of the moment. It is his phone, ringing incessantly.

I drop my hands like lead, and flush, wondering what this moment was and what I was thinking being like this.

Paul talks on the call for a few minutes, giving me time to gather my wits. He drops the cuffs when the call ends.

"Let's get back to work," he murmurs, nodding.

There's nothing more to get back to with no passwords to access the computer, and no more toys to tease each other with.

"See you in the morning," I murmur and leave, finally breathing in lungsful of air when I exit the apartment.

The next morning, I pay extra attention to my mascara and eyebrows. I fussed at them until they were in perfect shape, just how I liked it. I smiled; and moved on to my hair, but after watching many hair tutorials on my phone, I decided to give up, and just brushed it straight. DIY hair on the run? Sure. That left me no time to get coffee, but I didn't let it dampen my mood.

Today was different; there was something in the air.

I felt lightheaded, caught myself breathing heavily, thinking back to the moment I had shared with Paul at Ralph's apartment. I wondered if Paul felt even slightly as harebrained as I felt. The unknown added an intensity to the moment, like it existed in just a moment, to savor something.

As I ascended to the second level in the building, I felt a sense of nervousness and anxiety gnawing at my stomach. I tried to shake it off, but it had been long- way too long- since I had felt anything close to this. It seemed my mind would not be satisfied until I was thoroughly embarrassed.

When I reach the conference room that was now our designated office, I see Paul already sat in his chair, two cups of steaming coffee right in front of him. I smile a little, and then walk in, heading straight to my usual chair. He pushes the brown cup toward me silently, and I accept it with a smile.

The day passes in a blur, and there is no mention of what happened, but there is something electric in the air. I know because it's not just me who's been stealing glances at him. Although he has been unaware of it, I've caught him watching me, wondering if what we had felt was mutual. I couldn't help myself; my mind kept drifting back to that moment, to the pure wall and the rope cuffs, and my body started heating up. Under the part that was guilty, there was a hidden part in my heart that yearned to experience that rush of giddiness and excitement again.

The part that hopes Paul feels the same.

Back at the office, after looking through our progress and the documentation we had acquired, it was decided we need not come down to London until next Thursday. Paul and I shared our phone contacts and emails with Nicola and Helen in case they needed to get in touch, and then we were on our way. More than half the work week back at home. That would give me quite a bit of time to think, without being distracted by Paul's presence. Surely my thoughts were misdirected, and I was only missing Mark, right?

After the tedious and frustrating trip back, all I got to see was Ursula leaving after putting everyone to bed and finishing the last of the cleaning around the house. I thank her profusely- God knows I'd be stranded without her- and wished her goodbye. Ursula usually takes the weekends off, but it was Rebecca's birthday tomorrow, and she confirmed she would be available.

When I went to bed that night, Mark was asleep, snoring as he did, and didn't even move as I shuffled in right beside him. I was flush with him, owing to my excitement of seeing my husband after the recent confusion and excitement at work, but he was like a rock. So, I sighed, and turned to my side of the bed, asleep within minutes.

When the light filters in through my favourite off-white, breezy curtains on Saturday morning, I smile. Living in a hotel is good, but you miss your home, your creature comforts. I yawn widely and turn in the bed to look over at Mark. He's stirring, but not quite ready to wake up yet.

"Hey. You miss me all week?" I asked playfully, rubbing his bicep.

Mark is half-asleep when he replies, "Yeah, yeah, the kids were hectic," he mumbles, and squints at me questioningly; I have moved on to rubbing his chest sensually.

I look down at him, feeling horny and playful, and run my hand over his chest and down into his shorts.

Beginning to stroke him, I whisper, "Looks like I was missed by more than the kids," I smile, teasing him.

Mark is groggy, but I have his attention now. He rolls onto his back, "Ah yes, morning glory," He shrugs, "All yours if you want it," he finally picks up on my mood. Took him long enough.

I proceed to pull Mark's shorts down and release him, as he lays there watching me.

Sliding my own panties down, I climb over him.

Directing Mark inside me, I proceed to ride him, slowly, sensually at first, and then passionately.

But under me, Mark's like a dead fish. No impressions of enjoyment, pleasure or even engagement...

Looking down at him, questions assault my mind, 'Is he going to do anything other than just lay there? Where's the passion, where's the love? Where's the togetherness?'

He finishes quickly, and then incoherently mumbling something about the day ahead as he walks into the bathroom for a shower. I lay in the empty bed, thinking of the least fulfilling experience I had just had. I turn on my belly, and groan loudly into the pillow. Damn, I'll need a long shower after this.

I idle on the bed, scrolling through my work emails until Mark pops out of the shower, and heads downstairs to make his birthday special breakfast for the kids.

When I get into the bathroom, I am spilling from frustration, uncoiling within me like a nest of venomous snakes. I want to scream out loud, scratch my nails on the door, but I do neither. Instead, I lock the door, something I don't usually do. Then I start the steaming hot shower, stepping into it daintily, testing the water temperature, to make sure I don't scald myself.

I stand in the hot steam, willing myself to lose the tension in my hips, my shoulders, my jaw. I rub my hands over myself, seeking, always looking, but never finding. I lean against the wall, the water still rolling off me, and close my eyes, my head falling back. My mind subconsciously strays back to last Thursday, at Ralph's apartment. Paul's suggestively raised brow, his smirk, his hot breath over me. My hands raised over my head, watching him coolly saunter over.

My mind lets go of self-respect and logic, and using my free hand, I pleasure myself, in concentric circles, seeking, and finding. Imagining Paul's fingers where mine were, imagining his moans right along mine, until I crescendo and everything falls around me. Every last shred of reason.

42

I slide down the wall, as my knees turn to jelly with the orgasm, breathing hard. I needed that. It had been a long time, and I deserved that, I remind myself, banishing all traces of guilt and shame.

***

The day starts with Mark and I preparing for Rebecca's birthday party. On the little one's request, it was at the play centre and since they could also sort out the party favours, I was only too happy to fulfil her wishes.

The moms and kids are happy and bring many gifts for Rebecca. The attention makes her happy, and even though some little fights break out amongst the children, the moms huddle in the corner, enjoying their free time as we look after our little guests.

Mark and I fuss over Rebecca, making sure she feels special, but the pair of us do not talk. Mark doesn't ask if the new project that I was excited about is going alright, or if I'm tired from all the commutes. He doesn't ask when I got in last night, or how London was. It's frustrating me, making me irrationally angry. Maybe I want to enjoy some attention from my husband once in a while, maybe I'm content because I am dodging a bullet.

Because every time I think of London, I smile. It's unusual, and if I keep it up, even someone like Mark would notice. The events that happened in London also made me blush, as I stopped to remember them, getting lost in taught and being brought back to reality by the housekeeping staff at the play centre. I quickly rushed back to my hosting duties.

When the play centre finished, and the kids and their moms had all gone home, Mark and I filled up the car with Rebecca's presents, and drove back home. On the way, my mind wanders to the shower this morning, to Paul, and I ask myself what I was doing, and if I was even sure about anything. But underneath all the doubt there is a thrilling excitement. It scares me and makes me giddy.

I think I want to find out what results from this bubbly excitement.

On this crisp Monday morning, I am at my office, sitting across the pile of files I've brought with me from London. The work emails regarding strategy, findings and investigations have already begun, and Paul and I are deep in the thread, doing the due back and forth before settling on ideas to move forward.

There's still no acknowledgement of what happened last week, maybe it was just a moment between colleagues, and I am married, and Paul isn't interested. And maybe that is good, because all these reasons are valid and rational.

There's a knock on my door, and I'm cruelly jerked from my thoughts to the present. It's my assistant, Joan. She's been with me for several years now, and I heavily rely on her expertise and experience to go through my day-to-day.

She informs me that all the paperwork has been digitized, and up to date on the office systems so it can be remotely accessed whenever I wish to. It's standard practice, and I thank her. But she's still standing across from me. I look at her questioningly.

"You seem to be getting on very well with your solicitor this time, this Paul." She says as a question. That makes me pause in my tracks, but I carry on as if this was nothing. Joan is close to her fifties, very discerning, has an unmatched styling sense, and even manages to get her hair and nails done weekly. I look at her as a woman now, and although I know she's in great shape, and looks very good for her age. Very professional, but has a reputation for never missing out on any gossip. She certainly knows what goes about in the office, even in mine.

I feel flushed, but I know I can't show it, "Careful, or they'd think the Ice Maiden is melting," I laugh and shake my head, trying to be nonchalant, and getting back to the file in front of me.

"Don't worry, your secret is safe with me. But it's nice to see your emails are getting friendlier and more casual, you know? Or maybe nothing's melting and that's just how Mr. Bridges is with his colleagues," she fishes, determined to see my reaction. She might know everything, or she may know nothing, in any case I need to be careful.

"Oh, by the way, would you terribly mind if I came an hour early and left earlier on the days you're working in London? It'd give me a chance for weekly grocery shopping before going home. Any other days you're here, I will work in the usual hours," she asks, and I nod.

"Alright, sure. Get HR on it and I'll sign off. It's quiet here anyway when I'm in London," I am all business again, desperate to get her off her investigation track.

When Joan leaves, I go to my sent mail and look through the thread. Yep, I do seem very friendly and unprofessional. Huh. I didn't realize I was getting so carried away, and now there was a digital trail to prove it. I change the tone of my emails to Paul now, back to being true to my reputation. I was the Ice Maiden after all.

For the next two days I'm working from the DAF office, I make sure my tone remains polite, but professional and boring. No opportunity for jokes, or innuendos. Just plain old colleagues.

***

On Thursday and Friday, I am in London, and Paul is too, but you wouldn't know because we barely cross paths. The agenda for these two days is working our way through the stack of papers and documents we found in Ralph's office and cabinets.

Paul brings me coffee just the way I like it from the fancy coffee shop on the ground floor both days, and I nod in thanks. Back to work; no wandering eyes, no desperate sighs. I can see him hesitating as he retreats, wondering what happened to the easy banter and the humor between us. I'm sure by now he has assumed that I am married, and don't go around having 'moments', and he has moved on.

Maybe he has heard the Ice Maiden rumors by now.

The weekend doesn't feel like a weekend, but a sick day. Everything feels slow and liquid, and I am just not in a good mood. Mark catches on.

"Hey, you ok? Did something happen?"

"Just tired. Travel, you know?" I reply, surprised he had noticed that I was off. Or did I really not look good? Ugh.

Regardless, I know what's going on with me. The sudden lack of excitement I was enjoying, and getting used to, has left me dispirited. I am now left to my own rational devices, and I do find myself wondering what could have been. I feel silly for getting so invested into crumbs of attention, and I should feel embarrassed because it was not even real. It would be Thursday until I'd next meet with Paul, and until then... cold mails. I'd snap out of it by the time Thursday comes, so I let myself have this pity party.

***

I have just reached my office at DAF, when Paul calls me. I'm a little hesitant to pick up, and debate if I should let it go to voicemail, but shake myself out of this childishness. I am a grown woman- I hope.

"Uh, hey, hi. Hope you had a good weekend, not working... because it was the weekend," Paul stutters and I raise my brows; is he having a seizure?

"So, anyway, Scottish banks have shown up in the paperwork, and there's some other information, are you available to talk right now?"

I give him the go ahead and listen intently to the bits of information Paul has uncovered.

We talk for a few minutes, and then it gets quiet. I am about to say goodbye and hang up when he surprises me.

"Hey, would you mind if I ask you something?"

I frown, "Alright?"

"Uh, have I done something? I thought we were getting along fine, but... well. Perhaps I owe you an apology, I know I overstepped with the joke at Ralph's office, it'd make anyone uncomfortable, I understand. Look, I'm sorry, and really hope

46

we can continue to work together. It's just, I am not particularly used to enjoying someone's company and that might be why I got carried away. Anyway, it was just a joke, and you're married so, I get the hint, I did not mean to offend or disrespect you, either," Paul rambles on in one breath.

This makes me feel guilty. I owe him an explanation. Such a waste of that good apology, though.

"Hey, no, wait, okay. So, yeah, the joke was a bit over the line, sure, but it was the two of us there and it was equally enjoyed. In all fairness, I probably called for the comment. Anyway, that's not it.

"So, my assistant at DAF, Joan, pointed out that my emails were unusually friendly. And that is very unlike me. They call me the Ice Maiden here, and well, you can see how her comment would go down for my reputation. Could do without office gossip and HR visits, you know? I panicked and got cold on us, sorry, I should have told you." Apologies do not come easy to me, but I'm glad I did what I needed to. My heart's beating like crazy, I'm sure he can hear it through the phone.

"Oh, was that it?" He sounds surprised, like he had never thought there would be any other explanation for my behavior other than the reason that he messed up.

"Yep, and I want to continue working with you, too, and really enjoy your humor. It's nice that you're not the regular type of solicitor I am partnered with usually. Let's just watch what we say in the mail, alright?" I'm so glad I'm handling this maturely, because inside I'm a blubbering mess with a heart that is banging like a drum.

"Right-o!" Paul says, and I hear a relieved sigh and chuckle.

"I should have said it first, though. Thanks for being the first to communicate, I really appreciate it. And thank you for the coffee!" I am like a kid full of nerves. I purse my lips, lest I utter something silly again.

"Hah, no it's alright. I was just afraid I had offended you, because I liked the way we were getting on," Paul is relieved now, and am I imagining it, or is he murmuring in the phone now?

47

"Yeah, I did enjoy your weird humor in my emails. Huh," I confess, and soon we say our goodbyes.

I feel oddly relieved now, and the beacon of exhilaration is alight once again.

***

I had just gotten back from my lunch break and was about to snack on my after-meal dessert muffin when my phone pinged. I tap the screen twice to look at it and see it's a random Snapchat invite. I roll my eyes and am about to click delete when my eyes catch whom it's from: Paul! I accept it quickly, and then look at the bright notification on my screen.

I see his little emoji peeking out from the typing bar while I type.

"Hey, surprised to see this invite. You're on Snapchat?"

Three dots appear beside his cute little emoji. And then a text.

"I know, I know."

And then another ping.

"But I labored over it... and I thought we won't miss the banter and the 'odd humor' if, maybe, we could chat here, occasionally. If you want, of course,"

My breath catches.

"That would be nice. No nosey secretaries, plus some of the stuff we're finding needs to be put somewhere other than my weekly report," I type back, adding a winking emoji. I chuckle lightly, feeling elated at our secret little conversation channel.

"Lol, no you can't.

Anyway, say hi here anytime!"

And then his emoji disappears. I figure that's how I know he's online, and reading my texts? Well, maybe it was time to be naughty, just to try it out for fun.... I smile teasingly as I type.

Be careful what you wish for...

***

That night, with the kids and my husband already in bed, I decided to put my feet up and check out the new messaging app.

48

It is just a bit after ten, and my house already seems half-asleep. I tuck myself inside the throw and tap twice on the screen to wake my phone. With a large glass of my favorite red wine, and with Dutch courage in my hand, I send Paul a message. Hopefully he'd reply when he gets up for work tomorrow.

"I wondered if this works… Can't really ask my kids for an in-depth tutorial, now, can I?"

I throw the phone beside me on the sofa, and sip leisurely on the wine.

A surprising ping, and my phone screen lit up. I scramble for it.

It's from Paul.

"Well, of course it does. I suppose you can't."

"What are you up to?"

Something in my throat bubbles. I type quickly.

"Just finished work, putting my feet up. Been a long day, all finally quiet."

He sees my message instantly, and my heart rate picks up again. I tap at my screen again.

"Mind wandered to lunchtime, and this curious app. You did say anytime, I am not overstepping here, right?"

"Not all. If anything, you made my night. Kids are not very present or pleasant company at night. Rachel had a long day and was upset because of something. And Sarah is staying over at her boyfriend's tonight."

I am about to type a question, but it's forgotten when I read his next text.

"Is everything okay, did something happen?"

My heart flutters in my chest. It has been so long since someone was genuinely interested in my day. And asked me about it. Like it mattered to them.

I don't remember how to answer this question.

"Well, you know. Accountants… all the numbers, can hardly keep up. That doesn't make sense. Just one of those days, I guess."

I ramble. On text. Ugh.

But he is as polite as ever.

"I know the feeling. It's like a hamster wheel sometimes, I imagine. Thank God for imagination and escapism, right?"

"Walter Mitty I am not, but it's good to just let the mind go where it wants at times…"

The ellipses at the end make me curious. I wonder what he imagines.

"You can sing that song."

"So… where does this imagination of yours go? Anywhere that might cheer up a boring accountant?"

"Nah, that would be too telling. It goes many places."

Oh, he's teasing me.

"Been anywhere nice recently?"

I know what I'm doing, and maybe it's because I'm behind a screen, or maybe because I'm on my second glass of wine, but I need my hit of that exhilaration that Paul brings with him. I wait for his reply with bated breath.

"Lol, not for the faint-hearted. And certainly, way too adventurous for boring accountants. You know the legals, always living in the grey."

I chuckle.

"Well, we have our moments, too. What we can't live, we can dream of."

I have a wide smile on my face. It's silly. I can see why the younger generation might be so attached to their screens.

"Any nice dreams lately?"

I know I shouldn't do this. I shouldn't, right? Still, my fingers move of their own accord.

"Just one…"

And just then- right in front of my silly, smiling face- Liam is standing before me, holding a consent form from school he forgot to get me to sign. I slam my phone, screen down, on the sofa beside me. He looks puzzled that I was startled and his brows furrow, but he says nothing. He hands me the form for his school outing and tells me I must sign it so he can go. I gulp, and nod, partially trying to calm down the alarm bells ringing in my head. I read the form, only half taking it in, sign it and hand it back. I walk him to his bedroom door and tell him get into bed. I shut the door behind him, and lean against it, breathing hard. Thinking, thankfully it was not Mark who came in to see that stupid grin on my face.

Snapping out of my shock I remember my last message to Paul and run to my phone in anticipation.

It was sent thirteen minutes ago. I wonder if he was still up. It was close to eleven now.

His message read: "Sounds intriguing… do tell."

I shake my head, part desire, part guilt.

"Sorry, maybe I am getting carried away here. Probably the wine."

Paul sees the message immediately, but takes a few minutes to type back a message.

"It's alright, this is a safe space. What happens here stays here." He types back with a wink emoji. Another ping.

"Don't worry if you're not comfortable, I was just teasing you. A play on words here and there, an occupational hazard, I believe."

He's still typing. A ping.

"But you did say hello, and there was something on your mind. Wanna share?"

I take another sip from my almost-empty glass.

"To be honest, I didn't think much beyond saying hello. I didn't even think you would answer."

It's not that I don't want to share, I do. But I wonder if we need to come back from that kind of familiarity, could we find a way?

"I'm here now." He answers simply, and something inside me breaks free. How easily he is there for me, how effortless his support is. I stare at his text for a few moments, forgetting to reply, forgetting what's happening around me.

"How about you just say it, and if it gets awkward or funny, we can just say goodnight and end the conversation. Just like that, no unease."

He insists, but he didn't need to. My mind was already made up. I was ready.

"Sorry," I start typing.

51

"*It's just-*" I stop and erase the words, starting anew.

"*Life has been weird lately. I just feel stuck in a rat race, exhausted between work and kids, with no room for fun. It's been like this for many years, and I guess it just started hitting me how boring I've become.*" I send the text, and he sees it immediately, but I continue typing.

"*Okay, this is embarrassing, but the closest thing I've gotten too fun or excitement is when I got carried away in Ralph's office. I know why I did what I did, going against the wall and teasing you, because, for the first time in a long while, I felt something. I felt my heart pumping, and I wanted to feel it more.*" I hit send and re-read my text. I'm overcome with embarrassment.

"*Ridiculous, I know. It was just a joke. But it made me feel alive.*"

His reply was almost immediate, and my heart was in my throat as I ran my eyes over it.

"*Come on; there's no need to be like that. There were two of us in that room, and for a second, I forgot that I was also at work. To be honest, my mind has gone back to that moment many, many times since. How's that for embarrassing?*"

This was it. The forbidden line I was afraid to cross. How little I care for it now.

"*I know all about where imagination can take you, the places you should never be. I've been there, but where have you been?*"

"*I can tell you've had your fill of wine. Lol, you're brave when you've had a few.*"

His reply is a bummer because I'm excited, and maybe it's the wine, maybe I really have lost my inhibitions, but I want to see where his mind has been.

"*Tell me where you've been, and I'll tell you if I've been there.*" I hit send, knowing full well Paul would not be able to deflect now.

I see him typing, and then not, and then typing again. I do not have the patience anymore.

"*Go on, then. Never known a lawyer lost for words.*" I goad him on.

"*It is very intimate, very personal. And I really don't want to sour our working relationship. We get on, and we've got so many months of work ahead of us….*"

After a minute, this is what he's come up with? Wow, he's really cautious.

"That intimate, huh? Sounds similar to the situation I've got going on here."

"I'd make you a deal. If it sounds too personal or I don't like it, I'll just say stop, and we can return to the regular stuff, alright?"

"Because of the daydreams I've had? No lightweight legal eagle can compare." I add a wink emoji to drive my point home.

A huge smile transforms my face, and I sit back on the sofa, putting my feet up, comfy as a kitten in a basket. A ping announces Paul's message.

"You remember when my phone rang?"

"Very clearly." I reply.

"Well, I should've left it on silent. I've been cursing at it for ringing at the wrong time for ages."

"When you were against the wall with your hands up ... I saw a playful side to you I had not seen before. My mind just went into overdrive... the phone ringing actually saved me because I didn't know where I was going, just somewhere it shouldn't be.

I've thought of you many times since, you are looking at me teasingly in your fitted dress, the killer heels. So professional and proper."

My throat bubbles up with excitement; my heart pounds like a drum.

"Lightweight! Tell me everything you imagined," I nudged him.

"I imagined that the phone didn't ring. And I look at you, leave the cuffs and walk over as I take my tie off. Slowly, as you breathe quickly, I wrap my tie around your hands, latching them to the hook. Your mouth falls open, and I see your tongue running over your teeth, then moistening your lips. Your chest falls and rises; you breathe harder, my hands still on your wrists at the hook."

He stops suddenly, and I'm left wanting, waiting. Maybe he thinks he's overstepping, but I need him to resume. There's a dull ache deep in my belly, and I need to nurse it to satisfy it.

"That's me right now. Breathing hard, wetting my lips..." I type back.

"I imagined we are close, very close. We share an inseparable closeness, our bodies fitting together like perfectly crafted puzzles. Your hand wraps

around my waist, fingers lightly grazing my side, pulling me in. I give into your pull and wrap my arm around your lower back, our bodies melding into one. Our breaths intertwine, and I feel your gasps on my cheek as I nuzzle your ears. Anticipation cackles in the air with each passing moment, intensifying the electric touch between us. Our lips are just a breath away."

"The world ceases to exist for me. Everything falls away, and there's just you and me as our eyes close and our lips meet."

"We kiss through longing and connection. Slowly, lingering, and you lean in, hungrily, sensually."

"Passionately."

"It's tender, and it's everything I hoped it would be."

"When we break away, we're gasping, our mouths red and still hungry, but I'm lost in you, in how you feel in my arms."

"I reach to untie you, getting even closer, closer than I need to, pinning you lightly against the wall. Your gasp is audible as you feel my evident desire against your thigh. You teasingly brush your leg against it, and I know you like it."

"I untie your hands and bring them down with mine."

And he stops typing. Whew. I really got into it, much more than I'd like to admit. My heart is still racing, and I feel excitement pooling in my stomach. I gulp, re-reading his previous messages.

"Wow, so our imagination was in sync."

"I thought it was just me reacting this way... Lucky I was wearing a fool-proof dress." I roll my eyes, recalling how I'd strained getting myself into it.

"I know, lol. I thought the same, then. I still remember your every curve and rise in that dress. But that's as far as I'd get with you in that dress."

"Sure, you remember it," I teased him.

"I do. The high neckline, dark navy, down to the knees. No opening on the front, and a gold zip down to your hips in the back. Deliciously fitted."

My toes curl, and I simper. I bask in his desire and test the power it gives me.

"You were paying attention. I'm impressed."

54

"In my imagination, I was disappointed by it. It gave me the confidence to be cheeky, but it made some things very difficult."

"Maybe next time you will make things easier." There it was, the promise of things yet to come, the sweet symphony of longing and desire. A loud acknowledgment of our undeniable chemistry.

"Maybe I will." I smile and yawn loudly.

"Goodnight, Paul."

"Goodnight, Maria. Thanks for saying hi."

I chuck my phone on the seat beside me and curl inward, replaying everything that had just happened. My mind rolls back to the recent events: me texting Paul, knowing I shouldn't, knowing what would follow, and actively engaging in it. I was exhilarated at the idea, and my cheeks felt warmer, my eyes brighter. I feel alive. Oh, how long have I longed for these feelings to return. I bask in the happiness of realizing there's nothing wrong with me; it's not me who has changed. I've still got it.

I shake off my girlish rapture and get up to go to bed. Mark is asleep when I enter, and I quickly shuck off my trousers, get into the threadbare comfy t-shirt that I usually sleep in, and get into bed. It was late, much past my usual bedtime, but my mind kept recalling what Paul had said to me. That feeling of being wanted, to be desired, kept bubbling up inside me, threatening to drown my sanity.

When sleep finally takes me under, I dream I'm with Paul again, and this time we don't stop at a heated kiss.

***

When I woke up the next morning, I felt like I'd slept better than I had in ages. I was refreshed, and when I passed by the mirror, I was surprised to see I had a smile, a softness in my eyes, and a halo of glow around me. I nuzzle my hair, remembering last night.

While the water warms up, I sit on the edge of the bathtub, running a finger over my nose, my cheeks, and my lips. Imagining his touch, his fingertips. There was a shyness in me now, some part of me that wanted to be coy, to be sought out and craved.

The steam billows around me from the shower and mists on the mirror, fogging it up. I step inside, breathing deeply. Standing under the water stream, I lean against the wall, close my eyes, and slowly run my hands over my naked body. Today when I find my nipples, they are hard, my skin tingles at the sensation of my touch, and as my hand runs down and over my stomach, between my thighs, I am plenty aroused. My imagination brings me back to Paul and pretends it's his hands running over my warm skin.

Suddenly, the bathroom door opens, and with it, my eyes. I quickly lather myself to mask my embarrassment, glad the bathroom was steamed from the hot water.

As I ran around getting my earrings, putting my files in my bag, Mark and I discuss our schedule for the coming week so I could book Ursula.

"Just the usual, Maria. This project is big, and I'll have to work late one evening, anyway. We're falling behind, and they keep scheduling meetings every week. Ask Ursula to stay until nine on Thursday, yeah? If I'm back earlier, she can leave."

I nod, and that's the end of our conversation.

Chapter 5

A day at DAF has never been as restless as today. I feel electric, frizzy with energy. My frustration and irritation are palpable, and I catch Joan giving me a sideways glance multiple times. But I can't help it.

Today I'm finishing with the handover of some of my accounts to my colleagues, to allow time for Outdoor Pursuits. Analyzing spreadsheets, verifying numbers, running due diligence has always been satisfying for me. It's a comfortable pattern that I enjoy. Not today, though.

It might be in no small part due to the fact that my email inbox is empty- well, at least from someone who matters. I quickly refresh my inbox again, and a pang resonates within my chest. I check my Snapchat, and it snatches the very floor from beneath me; the chat is empty, Paul has deleted all that we said to each other last night. Erased clean, like it didn't happen.

Is that what he really wanted? Had he decided after all that I wasn't to be bothered with? Had I come across as too needy last night? My mind reels, reality and self-doubt spiraling into one. I wonder how he'd deleted the messages from *my* phone. Still lost in poisonous thoughts, I limply collapse on my chair, slamming the phone on the table. No cute good morning texts, and last night erased without so much as a word. It was clear what Paul wanted. I have been too hasty.

I hold my head in my hands, cursing the moment that started all this. A wave of sadness envelopes me, drowning me in the depths of regret and embarrassment. I cringe, and sigh, helpless in the wake of my messiness.

And yet, there's not a little part of me that yearns to read Paul and my conversation from last night. I ache to relive those moments, his dreams that sounded so true, so smitten. I wanted to be lost in my daydreams, lost in the sensation that his imagined touch and whispered secrets bring me.

All of a sudden, I remember Paul's paining absence, and snort sarcastically. Here I was acting like a teenager, all hot and bothered at the bare minimum, while he got to erase all that seemed so eventful to me. What had that quiet, settled man done to me? How was I such a mess, reduced to craving his touch as he disdained me.

I shake my head free from the shackles of my overactive thoughts, realizing how uncharacteristic I was being. This was not the kind of stimulation I was craving when I manifested excitement in my life.

***

It felt like a Boston doughnut nut and a double shot espresso kind of a day. The weather was beautiful outside, in stark contrast to the storm raging inside me. I look at the shining sun and the clear blue sky and sigh, trying to internalize the sunshine into my dark mood.

I dust off the crumbs, still thinking about the disappeared messages from my phone- *what if Mark had seen and deleted them?* - when my phone rang. I receive the call without looking at the display name, still lost to my rumination.

"I hope that double shot of espresso won't drive you off the rails," an amused, familiar voice.

"How did you know..." I looked around, partially hoping to see Paul. Some part of me was appalled that I'd forgotten my line of thoughts so quickly. My nerves, fear and guilt simply evaporate.

"Creature of habit, I guess. I have been getting you your coffee for the last few weeks, you know," he sounds out of breath, like he was walking someplace quickly.

"Alright, so you're not a stalker. Yet," I reply, but I'm still confused by his hot and cold behavior. He sounds... normal.

"So, what are you up to?" He asks politely. My patience was wearing thin since morning, and now it threatens to rip.

"Hey, so, I noticed our conversation from last night's been deleted. Was that you?" I burst, spilling my nerves and fear out.

"Wanted to get another look at my dreams, huh?" There's a smile in his voice, and something more. I bite my lip and wait for him to continue.

"Well, that's the point of Snapchat, I guess. The messages are deleted once they're seen. You've got to rely on your own imagination. Be on your toes, Holmes," he laughs, clearly enjoying my social media lack of expertise. A knot in my chest finally loosens, and I smile in relief.

"Oh. Oh, I see. That… makes sense, somehow. Now I feel foolish," I murmur, "It would have been nice to visit you in your dream. My imagination is good, but I liked your input," I know what I'm doing, and I like it. My turn to enjoy.

"Ah, I see. Good to know," he whispers tightly.

I like how his voice catches, but there are other things to discuss. If I have an insecurity it needs to be communicated to him.

"Today was… sad, I think. My imagination was going everywhere, from what happened last night to this morning… I was so paranoid and shaken when I saw the messages were 'deleted'," I roll my eyes, "I wondered if I regretted it, if you wanted to stop, were you hoping it all went away? It was just weird, sorry for the rambling," I finish, feeling quite vulnerable.

There were a few seconds of silence, and I wait with bated breath to see how he would respond to my moment of vulnerability.

"I'm sorry," he says finally, his words etched with genuine regret, "I should have said hi this morning. I guess I thought I was busy, and I knew you would be too, and I didn't want to be a distraction," his words are like a calming salve over my frayed nerves.

"Although, I did want to ask, and this might be a heavy question, so you can answer later, too," There's an uncertainty in his voice that makes me curious.

"Sure, go ahead," I nod, even though he can't see me.

"Can I ask... Do you regret opening Pandora's box from last night? There is still time to resist it, we haven't played any of our cards yet, we're not at a point of no return. And I only say this because you're in a different position than me in this situation... and I don't want you to do anything you'd regret..." he tapers off, holding his breath for a word of my assurance.

He has been graceful to give me time to think about this, giving me a way out too, and he deserves an honest answer.

I take my time to get my thoughts in order. Time has passed for harebrained decisions, and things are getting too real, too fast. I am at my office now, and I lock the door behind me, a sign for Joan to not disturb me. Sighing, I sit in my chair, tapping at my desk.

"I have been asking myself this, too. And avoiding a direct answer. Honestly, I do feel guilty, but not regret. I know that I do not want to stop. Paul, life for me has been so colorless, so stale lately, and for a long while. I feel like I have taken on so much responsibility that no one thinks about me needing anything anymore. Not even myself," I say in a rush, things that I have been overjoyed to feel.

"Last week at Ralph's apartment, I wondered what if your phone had not rung. What limits would I have crossed? The after events in my mind have been mind-blowing, to say the least. I feel alive, and warm, and like a woman again. Not a caricature of ice that I've been reduced to. I don't want that narrative anymore," I say the last part firmly, "So let's just enjoy this for what it is and thank or curse Ralph and his colorful proclivities. Although I do think we'd have gotten here without his help sooner or later," I giggle, and I hear Paul snort.

It's a beautiful sound; casual intimacy that has us giggling and snorting in the middle of a workday. I've never had this, and I didn't know it would feel so free and fun to me.

I continue, "You're a nice guy, and you sort of crept up on me when I was least expecting it. When we went out for dinner that first night in London, and I made a spectacle of myself and yet you didn't try to get it on with me, I wondered if I wasn't attractive to you, but later I surmised you're not that type. It made me trust you." I finish, finally letting it all out. For the first time in my life, I feel like I can hand over all my uncomfortable, messy feelings to someone and they will take care of it, not throw it back in my face.

Paul laughs quietly, "The next time I creep up on you, you will *know*," he teases me, and I chuckle.

"Aren't you glad to hide behind your phone right now? You wouldn't be so cheeky otherwise," I tease him in return.

"Cheeky is acceptable, isn't it?"

"Cheeky is acceptable. Although I'm still the Ice Maiden at work," I roll my eyes at the weird nickname. A maiden, I was surely not.

***

Wednesday afternoon finds Joan preparing for my departure to London. She makes a hotel reservation, a taxi booking, and packs up my files that I retrieved. Business as usual. To outsiders, anyway.

When Thursday morning comes, I take some time loitering on the station, leaving my usual 5.55 for Paul's 6.15 train. I'm bubbly and giggly on the inside as I wait for his train on the platform, excited to be together. But Paul is nowhere. Not in his usual first-class carriage, not in the others. My excitement recedes quickly, and I take a seat, deflated. Why are my plans ruined before the wheels are even in motion?

I shake my head, and my phone starts vibrating. It's Paul.

"Hey, did you miss your train? I wanted to get you breakfast, maybe edge in a chat before we hit the office, but you're not in the 5.55?" His voice was muffled.

"You know what they say about great minds," I snorted, "I took your 6.15 thinking the same. I think we should start sharing ideas like we do dreams," I am smiling with all my teeth and more.

"Before I'm thrown off the train for public indecency, how about we plan dinner tonight? Maybe we can talk, set some ground rules?" Paul is so clear about what he wants, it's kind of attractive.

"Lawyers and their rules. But yes, let's have a nice dinner, and see where the conversation flows. At the very least we'll have good company." I answer, trying to be more spontaneous, trying to be the adventurous person I used to be.

***

Two coffees sit before me, piping hot, ready for a productive Thursday.

Paul enters with Nicola and Helen, and swiftly grabs a coffee without a second thought. I look around to see if either Helen or Nicola pick up on this show of familiarity, but they are deep in conversation with each other. I sigh in relief. London isn't aware of my reputation, so do I really need to be careful? Dangerous thoughts, dangerous questions...

We immediately get to work; Paul lays out a general plan we will be following for the next few weeks. We flesh out a few more issues that the outlets had highlighted, and Paul meticulously addresses each one. As a colleague, I'm often glad how Paul does his fair share of work, going above and beyond to fulfill the duties this temporary role demands of him.

Looking at him I think to myself, He sure looks handsome right now. I stare at him while he talks, his fitted black slacks that he fills out so well, the baby-pink office shirt that stretches across his wide chest, dipping from his shoulder over his rolling back- I startle to a stop. My imagination is in overdrive these days- I need to let off steam. That idea makes me hot and bothered, so I direct my attention back to Paul, who's now talking delicately about something we had already discussed earlier.

"Unfortunately, this may feel somewhat invasive, but we will need access to Ralph's personal belongings, property and office. Since there is no one available to provide us with an outline of what's where, I'm afraid we will have to take this liberty," Paul looks at me, and I nod.

Helen and Nicola take it gracefully, and simply offer their help for whatever's needed going forward. Next, Paul emphasizes his role as a temporary decision-maker for the company until we're done with our tasks and someone else steps in. Helen breathes a sigh of relief that the company wouldn't go through any major changes; I suspect she wouldn't have liked it otherwise.

"Everything's looking great as it is, so just let the staff do their thing, and I'll stay out of it unless something major comes up. Although, I do need to address something serious," he finishes in an ominous tone.

My head snaps up. This is news to me; we discussed everything ahead already, so why did this not come up? A shadow of concern passes over Nicola's face.

He continues, "The coffee here is dreadful," he smiles charmingly, his neatly lined white teeth doing their thing, "I insist we get a coffee machine ASAP. Ask everyone what flavors they like and see what pods are the most popular."

Helen chuckles and Nicola swats the air with her hand, mimicking Paul's smile. I snort.

He looks at me and does his charming smile again, where his eyes scrunch and his dimples deepen. He's breathtaking.

"And that concludes today's executive decisions!" He laughs, and the two ladies join in.

"You'll be quite popular; no one could get Ralph to get a coffee maker. He was a strict tea drinker, God rest his soul," Helen recalls pleasantly.

"Alright, then, just as before, both of us will stay in London for two days a week, but give us a call if something comes up," Paul finishes, and I note the satisfaction on our new colleagues' faces.

I had to confess: Paul was good at this.

Once we're alone in the conference room, I turn to him with a smirk, "You're buying off people with coffee?"

He shrugs, and dusts pretend dust off his shoulders.

Financial statements, contracts, boring documents. Boring day. Although a thorough investigation of Ralph's office reveals his personal banking statements and rental property documents to be missing. I keep a log of everything we've found yet, and a log of what we actually need. The latter list seems painfully short for now.

As we're leaving, Paul stops me and pulls me to a corner.

"So, dinner at seven? Meet me in the reception area. And..." he trails off, lost in my eyes.

"And anything in particular sir would like me to wear? " I laugh as I spur him.

"Well, if you are asking, those dangling earrings you wore when we first went out for dinner? I really liked those," he speaks shyly, and I spontaneously giggle, surprised how shy he could be after all we've talked about. The compliment is a request, and it holds a certain charm, the uncertainty of his words tying my stomach in knots.

I nod, not trusting myself to speak.

***

I look at myself in the mirror; at the way this bottle green dress hugs at my curves, kissing my waist before stretching over my hips. The square front has a low dip, and I hum with approval at how well it fits me. My carefully lined eyes travel to my ears, where the dangling mother-of-pearl earrings sway, a loud yes to Paul's quiet request. Then to my face, and I pay careful attention to my lipstick. Still very unsure what Paul likes.

The clock catches my eye in the mirror, it's almost seven already! I quickly step into my heels and pick up my bag.

When I get to the reception, Paul is there, waiting for me. His back is turned to me, and just a look at those wide shoulders drive me crazy. I pace towards him, and he turns around just as I go in for a hug, which turns into a sweet soft kiss.

He smiles, surprised, and I fix my lipstick, "I couldn't spend an evening longer not knowing how you taste," I say with heat, and I see him respond to it, his pupils dilating.

It's past seven, and we're hungry.

***

Paul opens my door, and we sit in. My breath catches when his fingers curl around mine, forming a vise. He gives the driver the address. I see him checking the location on his phone, as we get close, he directs the taxi to pull over and we get out. I look at him quizzically, and answering my unspoken question, "I just wanted a short walk with you, some contact before a dinner table divided us." and it's a five-minute walk through the winding streets. When we get there, Paul makes a gesture, as if presenting the place to me, and I am pleasantly surprised.

We're standing across from a cozy place, with warm lighting, and a homey vibe. It is a ground floor high, wooden structure, with the menu and the specials of the place in chalk on a large blackboard. Only a narrow door with a hand-painted 'Welcome' sign, and three windows offer a glance inside. It's not crowded, but there are still a fair share of people on the counter, nursing their drinks, and the back space is secluded, with only a few couples. It's perfect. Exactly the scene where I can talk openly about things and have a lovely evening with Paul.

Our table is adorned with a candle, which is so delightful, I'm already smiling ear to ear. Two stems of fresh roses also soak up water from a small fishbowl, adding a touch of muted elegance. We sit across from each other, our faces radiant with anticipation.

I sip my wine, and he mimics me, with a hint of playful twinkle in his eyes.

"Anything exciting happening in the evenings these days?" I start with a thinly veiled cheshire cat smile on my face. He knows what I mean, and his eyes dart around, checking to see if we're being overheard. A nervousness in him.

He clears his throat and raises his brows, "Well, actually, Matthew and I might be going hiking soon. It's been a long time since we went, and we enjoy it. It's an adventure," he says, nodding, enjoying his teasing.

"Ooh, an adventure. Maybe you can give me some tips for our future adventures," I say innocently, cutting my steak into square pieces.

His eyes widen as he gets my meaning, and I enjoy his unguarded surprise, and following desire. I enjoy this game of cat and mouse, but soon we delve into lighthearted topics, our laughter and chuckles filling the air.

The conversation weaves seamlessly between work, shared interests and more playful teasing, each bringing me closer to an intimacy that I had forgotten existed. Time tempts to slip away unnoticed, losing me, but I have something on my mind that I need to get out of the way before... we become something more.

I clear my throat to get his attention, and he picks up on my mood quickly. It brings me joy to see he's attuned to me in such small ways that matter, that I crave.

"So, you know I'm married. You know about my kids, and you're no stranger to responsibilities that come with it. Life isn't terribly exciting, but that's life, I suppose. What I'm trying to say is, whatever happens between us, I will not abandon my family, nor do I want to lose them. This... whatever this is, is just something for myself, an adventure for me, but it comes with boundaries," I lay all my cards on the table.

In a way, a part of me is giving him a way out, gauging his interest and passion for me. That part of me is relieved when he nods somberly, and continues, "No, I understand that. I know, in comparison, I'm freer, but that does not mean I'll be willing to break up a family. This is important, and I'm glad you broached this topic. Your family will be your priority whatever we may become, and that's alright. I am honestly enjoying my time with you so much, just seeing you and having dinner with you, that anything more takes me a bit to process. You make me feel like I'm young again, and hopeful," He smiles genuinely, taking my hand in his, tracing concentric circles on the back of my hand with his thumb. It's embarrassing that such a simple gesture is making me tingly all over.

I put my head back into the conversation.

"That makes me glad, then, that you understand," I say firmly, even though I do not need to drive the point home. His answer was so wholesome that all parts of my personality are fulfilled. For now.

"Your double life… a woman of mystery. I like it," he says, leaning back in his seat and stretching his hands behind his head. Veins pop in his forearm, and I stare, and I know I'm staring but I do not stop.

He continues, seemingly unaware that my brain has completely melted, and I've been driven insane, "With that out of the way, are you keen on seeing where this adventure takes us?"

"Yes," I blurt, then steady myself, "Please."

"So, there's another thing to get out of the way…" Paul starts, and his cheeks flush a bright red. The tops of his ears follow. My brows weave together in curiosity, and I urge him to continue.

"Uh, so. Okay, this is embarrassing. But here it goes: It's been more than ten years since I've been intimate, like this, with anyone. With my wife, we were young, and adventurous, but nothing too crazy with the kids around. All this to say, I might be out of practice," he's fidgeting with a napkin, and I take his hand in mine, putting his insecurities to rest as he did mine.

He continues, "Not imposing anything on you, maybe we won't ever get that far."

Oh, we sure will, I think, and wink at him.

"I appreciate the honesty, but just relax. Whatever happens will happen. Let's just have a good time, alright? At least we don't need to endure this attraction silently," I groan, and laugh, and Paul joins in.

A few minutes later the waiter approaches us unbidden and starts clearing off our table. Not subtle, their attempts to evict us. I look at my watch and am surprised to see it's eleven thirty.

Where did all the time go? Paul picks up on it too, and after settling the bill, he stretches, after sitting here for so long. "Come, now, I better get you to your hotel soon."

The lobby is quiet when we enter my hotel, and Paul walks me to the elevator. He presses the button, leaning close to me, lightly brushing into me, and I take a whiff of his cologne. My stomach clenches. With the privacy from prying eyes provided by a nearby pillar, before he fully pulls away, he pecks me on my lip, lingering. I moan and look to take him into a kiss, my wine fueled desire taking over.

Sensing my obvious desire, he kisses me softly, but it deepens as I pull him in. I want him.

We break contact, and I see him looking around, probably making sure we are not seen, panting I take a breath, and I'm about to invite him upstairs, to hold him by the hand and take him into my bed when he clears his throat, and caresses my cheek, lips, "Goodnight, I'll text you when I'm back in my room."

And he turns around and leaves, adjusting himself as he does.

I am left breathless, panting, and hungering for his touch, watching his back as he leaves. I'm frustrated, but I know he's being sensible. Maybe. *Ugh,* I groan with frustration, and climb into the elevator, taking my heels off as they pinch my feet.

***

Once I've taken off my makeup, letting my hair down and get into a t-shirt, my phone pings. Climbing into the bed and tapping at the screen to awaken it. It's Paul on Snapchat.

"Hope you found the way to your room." It reads, and I roll my eyes. Maybe a bit pissed about being left hanging.

"Well, with no help from you"

"I didn't take you for the teasing type... you kiss me like that and disappear?"

I type back.

"Ah, if only you had said..."

"You know exactly what I want, you in my bed."

"You do owe me something first."

68

"And what's that?"

"A dream for a dream."

"Oh, which one should I tell… there's been so many," It's my turn to tease him, or torture for how he has left me here.

"Whichever comes to mind first." He quickly types back.

"It could get spicy; I've had a few drinks… and I don't exactly need to boost my libido."

"Oh… I picked the perfect time, then," he types back, and I sense his urgency in the text, his desperation. It fuels me. I can play this game too.

Payback time for leaving me hanging starts now.

"Had to get ready for bed alone when I got to my room," I say breathily, *"My black panties and a T-shirt. Tonight, I hoped I'd be sleeping in your arms, naked… my skin hot against yours… but I'll have to make this work. I imagine you here with me, between my bare legs as I sit up and open your shirt… button by button, discovering each inch of your skin with my fingers. I take it off, and I cannot resist anymore. I run my hands over your stomach, your chest… down the happy trail.*

"Your hands run down my sides, splayed, hungry. I feel your nerves, your shyness as my arms reach up and around your neck, bringing you close… even closer."

I imagine his breathing getting faster behind the phone screen. I smile coyly, hyper aware of everything I was doing to him.

"And then I kiss you, soft, lingering, as I dive into your mouth, and you open to me. This is my adventure, and I discover you with fervor. Savouring every second that we are together. And then I go down, lower, from your lower back into your pants, you gasp, and I pause.

" 'You okay, darling?' I ask, and I feel your arms tighten around me, your control wearing thin. 'Take off my shirt.' I direct, and you follow. I want to feel you against my skin, your touch over my trembling body, the nervousness in your fingers as you lift my shirt. All the while, I'm struggling with your belt, finally getting to your pants button."

I pause, imagining how he would look, what I'd do to him if he were here, would I even have time to think, or would I just lunge at him? I wonder for the umpteenth time why he didn't come up with me.

Paul sends another message, and the world ceases to exist for me, I'm just a puddle of heightened sensation, *"A moan escapes me as I feel you against my bare skin. Your body on my body, over my hips, on my stomach. You can see through my pants how hard I am, and your gaze splits back to mine. I see fire in your eyes, and it burns through me as I pull your shirt off of you. 'You're amazing,' I whisper, and see blood rise to your chest, over your neck and to your face."*

"You okay, darling?"

I groan at his text, resisting the quickening ache between my legs.

I type back, *"For the love of God, I'm panting here…"*

Paul returns, *"Take off your shirt… I want to imagine it coming off as I'm saying it."*

I cannot hold back… I start taking off my shirt and then groan, typing him a text.

"You take it off."

"Imagine it is me," comes his text, and as I'm typing a reply, my phone starts ringing. It shocks me, grounding me to reality. Unknown number. It's so late, who could it be?

I reluctantly answer. A familiar voice. A welcome voice, "Maybe you prefer listening to me describe what I am doing over reading and typing."

I moan when I hear his voice. He sounds wild.

"Please," I don't know what I'm begging for, "I am putting the phone on speaker, so I have two free hands, and then I am all yours," I whisper.

"I want you to get comfortable, get rid of all the blankets, I just want one white crisp sheet over you, and you stretched out under it. Your hands glide freely against your skin under the sheet, and you imagine it is me. Got it?"

I am reduced to panting and no words form so I moan in affirmation at his seductive voice and his controlling tone. My heart is jumping from my chest. How can listening to him describe something I can't even feel make me so wet and drive me crazy?

Paul resumes, "Close your eyes, lay back and use your hand to do what I'm telling you I'm doing." The sheet brushing off my skin also, as if he is rubbing against me.

I whisper in anticipation, "Okay, I am stretched out here under the sheets in nothing but my panties."

"Now, no need to speak unless you want to. Just follow what I am describing. I will go slow and easy... stop me if you don't like anything."

I nod, knowing full well he can't see me, but I've lost all sense now.

Paul's wild voice whispers in my ear, "I quickly slide off my pants that you have opened, and I lay down next to you, my body stretched against yours, skin on skin, and you feel so warm. My lips softly caress yours as my finger runs gently over your cheek, down your chin and onto your chest. I go in for a deep kiss as my fingers caress and tease your beautiful breasts, one at a time. Softly rubbing each one and rolling your nipples gently between my fingers. My lips suck on your chin and then neck, as I kiss and caress you with my tongue. I continue for a few minutes, as my hands savour the feel of your breasts, your nipples, my foot runs up over your thighs. You feel my erection through my shorts against you, as you tremble against my body."

"Take off your shorts, I want to feel how hard you are against me," I whisper.

I hear some shuffling and then Paul's voice again, "Yesss. I envelope you again, my fingers giving you a featherlight touches, teasing you, barely touching you. Across over your stomach, and you feel my lips as I bow into the nook of your neck, kiss down over your chest, and onto your erect nipples, I take the first one between my lips, slowly rolling it. I spring free and rub against you, flush against your thigh. As I kiss your nipple and move over to the other, my fingers slide down over your panties. Rubbing you over them with the palm of my hands, my fingers finding you sopping wet. I slowly massage in a circular motion over your panties and feel them getting wetter.

71

"I kiss back up your chest, neck and onto your lips, moving so I = am pressed full length against you. My lips on yours, my tongue inside your mouth as I look down into your face, your expressions, so I can see exactly how you're feeling.

"My fingers move down your stomach and slide down inside your panties, slowly teasing my way down... building the anticipation. I see you convulse, shaking and whisper, 'Are you okay, darling?'"

"Don't stop," I gasp.

Paul takes my cue and continues, "My finger pushes down over your wet clit, and finds your soaking lips. I massage them gently to open them and then you feel my fingers glide inside you. I see you react and whisper, 'Just imagine this is me inside you.' I move away from you, kneeling up, all the time my fingers stay inside you, dancing a rhythm that drives you insane. With my free hand I push your panties down and off, and lay beside you, your leg over my leg, you open to me, our naked bodies becoming one. My hard erection teases your thigh and I work you faster with my fingers inside you.

"Now go on, finish yourself for me. Finish yourself without me doing anything, saying anything, do what you like, and imagine it is me. Let me hear you now."

I'm too far gone again, lost, and I keep working myself with one hand, two fingers inside me as my other hand teases my nipples, massages my breast. I don't want to stop, and I'm building... building.

I hear him pant over the phone with my moans, and that's the trigger, his breathing sends me over the edge and I'm falling. It's like skydiving- a rush of adrenaline, a surge of excitement and then exhilaration as you leap from the aircraft and freefall through the sky with wind on your face and your body weightless. I moan through all of it, and it lasts longer than it usually does.

I'm convulsing with pleasure, my hands and legs numb when I whisper through the phone, thoroughly spent, "Oh, my God... what was that? Are you still there, Paul?"

"Yes," comes his restrained voice.

"You have no idea how hard you made me come… twice. How did you do it…" I ask him as much as I'm asking myself. I didn't know I was capable of experiencing such intense pleasure.

"You've no idea how hard you made me come. Now roll over and close your eyes, imagine I'm still there, holding you close as you fall asleep. Let's feel this feeling. Goodnight," he says, and blows a kiss and after a few seconds the line goes out.

I have a smile on my face, and I feel liquid; submerged in jelly without a care. I've never had a sweeter sleep.

I sleep right through my alarm.

When I wake up, my mind is still occupied with what happened last night, the build-up, the tension and the release. I rewind the moments, relive them. I wonder why he didn't just come upstairs with me, why go through the trouble of resorting to the phone? A large part of me also wonders if just his voice drove me over the edge so exquisitely, what his actual presence would do to me. I shudder, and a bolt of pleasure vibrates through me.

In the bathroom, my reflection is smiling like an idiot, and there's a glow on her face. Her smile seems dreamy, the stress around her eyes relaxed. Even the eyebags seem less weighted. Surreal. Amazing.

Today, the water from the showerhead cascades over me, enveloping me in a misty veil. Steam rises as I lose myself into the warm embrace of the shower. The droplets gently caress my skin, and today I don't tease myself with empty promises of a fulfilling touch. I close my eyes and simply enjoy the soothing melody of the water hitting the tiles, my time of relaxation and renewal.

As the water continues its gentle massage over my shoulders, I recall the feeling of going over the edge last night, and moan, manifesting it back.

When I reach the office, I see Paul entering the boutique coffee shop on the ground floor. I sneak up behind him, and as he turns, I startle him, plucking the coffee from his hands.

"The least you could do is buy me breakfast after last night. You disappeared when I awoke," I murmur, grinning.

He shakes his head, and we find a quiet corner to continue our conversation.

"I hope I didn't go overboard last night…"

"My only complaint is that you weren't there to do all of that in person. How did you learn to do that… it was incredible," I say, recalling his voice over the phone. This has quickly become a conversation that would make any HR manager cringe at a pending sexual harassment suit. Not sure who is harassing who.

"And don't say you didn't know you could… I know you wanted to. So, what was it? What spooked you? And don't say inexperience, because if last night was any indication, you aren't lacking in that department." I raise my brows, letting him know I won't back down.

He looks embarrassed, "OK, it might be because I was a little shy, unsure that no sooner you'd have fingers on me, and I would have just cum on the spot and would have spoiled your night and I just wanted more pleasure for you. I wanted to describe and let you hear what I like and how I would love things to go when we do. See what you liked. As you liked the rope cuff idea, I wondered would you be more adventurous and not like the softer and more sensual.

And as far as experience is concerned, trust me, I have had years dreaming of a night with a beautiful woman … so easy to imagine that with you. hearing you react to my imagination. mmmmmm," he moans quietly.

I cannot stop myself from reacting to this man, "I think I like your bedtime stories Paul; you may have to come up with a few more for me now that I know what you are capable of. I loved every second of it, but you can lead up to your cuffs as well. Let's have an adventure!"

"Oh, an adventure?" he asks with a twinkle in his eye.

"An adventure. Plus, you finishing quickly is a compliment, believe it or not. I understand dry spells, so just relax. And just so you know, it's been way too long, so much so that I enjoyed doubly last night," I grin, and his ears heat up when he understands my meaning.

He clears his throat, and then takes my hand. I look around in concern, and then quickly extricate my hand.

"Now, back to work. You're on Ice Maiden's time right now."

Paul clicks his tongue in affirmation, and we get moving according to plan.

Today we are cataloguing all the information we have found for everyone so far, plus arranging all the papers in chronological order since all the bank accounts, property statements and financial information are unstructured and upside-down in this office.

By the time everyone's leaving, and the day has ended, we've done our best with the filing cabinets in Ralph's office.

It takes till the end of the day, but by then, it seems clear that we did our best and obtained as much information as we can.

After an entire day's backbreaking work of endless shuffling through files and flipping through papers, I lean back and observe the scene. Everyone was leaving and we seemed to be contained in a flurry of papers, manila folders and files.

"One thing Ralph was not short of," I comment, "was companies." Paul snorts.

It seems like he decided to set one up for everything he did. It may have made life complicated for him at times, certainly is for us right now, but financially wise if any of his other ventures failed.

In our hours of flipping through the stacks in the filing cabinets, we had come across a few other company names, and we were looking to see whether there are any assets in any of those companies or if he has any interest in them.

Thankfully, this was one of the tasks we could delegate back to the office and sit tight until the reports came.

As the reports started coming in from the office, Paul sent them back to his secretary and asked her to carry out several registry searches, properties, shareholdings and directorships.

We needed to check property searches in the name of the main holding company and each of the companies under which the shops operated.

When Paul's trusty secretary returned the list of companies, Paul picked the ones that Ralph held shares and sent them over to the accountant's team to get a financial profile on them.

As he delegates tasks and types out instructions, he looks up and smiles over at me, "Better make these guys work or they wonder what you are doing down here and get lazy."

"Can't let 'em get lazy," I smile back.

When it gets too late to work anymore, Paul and I grab our coats and head back to the station for the train trip home. The train is packed, and we are thankful of our booked seat. No chance to change and sit together. We say our goodbyes there.

Chapter 6

When I arrive home at around 9 PM, I am greeted by the sight of Mark and our children gathered in the living room, engrossed in a movie adaptation of their childhood book. It's a familiar scene, and as soon as the children spot me the usual conversations ensue. I inquire about their day, their projects, anything fun happening at school.

A fish market ensues; all the children speaking over each other, detailing everything they had kept pent-up inside until now. The little one had a few play dates scheduled; the elder ones had their outings planned. Liam tells me sullenly that he's going to watch a movie with his friends tomorrow and needs me to drop him by the theatre. I raise my brows, and he rolls his eyes and grits out a 'please' and I shake my head and smile.

I notice Natalie about to burst with excitement, and so I mitigate the disaster by asking her what she's been up to.

"There's a disco at the school!" She blurts and then shrieks excitedly.

"Mom, everyone's attending! It's our first school disco, can I pleaseeeee go?" She asks me eagerly, making her charming puppy eyes.

I look at her dad, his attention completely diverted from the movie now that I'm home and ready to look after the kids. Natalie sees me watching Mark.

"I already asked Dad, he told me to ask you," she pouts prettily, and I melt. She's been obviously so excited about this disco, and there's no harm in a fun little event. Her enthusiasm wins.

"You can go, you know about the-" I'm interrupted by her eagerness.

"- the curfew, and no breaking the rules," she rolls her eyes, and repeats what I've been telling her for years; all my children have learnt my dialogue by heart. It's the only thing that keeps them safe and protected when they're out there, away from my eyes.

"Yeeeeeeee!" she shrieks in delight, and I laugh.

"When are we going shopping?" she asks me, now sitting between my knees as I do her braid.

"Shopping? What shopping?" I am lost at this sudden turn of conversation.

"Mom, I need to get something to wear. I have nothing to wear!"

"Oh, right. Of course. We'll go as soon as you're awake, darling," I pacify her, and look back at Mark. he now has his glasses on, and his laptop in his lap, the movie forgotten and lost in his work.

It's been a few minutes since I've been home, but let alone getting up and showing any affection at my return, he doesn't even say hello, asks me about the commute, or my project. Nothing. Radio silence. Utterly disinterested in my life and his children's.

His indifference surprises me: have I been tolerating this attitude from him for so long that I was numb to it until now? No acknowledgement, let alone a gesture of affection.

During the ride back home from London, I had a lot of time to reflect on my actions in the past few days. Feelings of guilt, fear and delight; an impossible mix. The remembrance of Paul's sultry voice in my ear, my reaction to it, and what he generally made me *feel*.

My mind probes the risks involved: my family, my marriage... my self-esteem and desires. I contemplate what would happen if I sent Paul an email right then and there, saying this was a mistake and that I never should have given in to my insane impulses. To tell him to forget about it, and pretend it never happened. I considered if I should end things, despite how alive I felt, how desired, and womanly, and fulfilled, that maybe I should end it all before it spiraled out of my control.

Arriving home to find the children occupied with their usual activities, with young Natalie just beginning her life, the school disco and shopping, brings me back down to reality with a bang. I know I'm risking this, the children's sense of normalcy and family. But looking at Mark sitting on the couch, in the room but barely there mentally, hardly raising his head, or acknowledging my presence with *anything* when I entered the house makes me think.

Do I not deserve attention, or love? Why shouldn't I turn elsewhere for something my husband is least interested in giving to me? Paul… he is a lovely man whose kind, straightforward, compassionate and has shown every sign that he cares for me. And if last night was any indication, there was much more passion and fun to discover, just the way I needed to.

The idea that enveloped my mind in the train, to email him and deny there was anything between us, evaporates from my brain. Just one look at Paul reminds me why I went down this path anyway. Why was there even a need for me to consider it in the first place.

I tell the children to get ready to sleep and go up to my bedroom and start changing out of work clothes. My stomach is rumbling with hunger, but I need to get the children to bed. I unwind their minds, answer all their questions, and one by one, after about half an hour, they are all asleep. I sigh a sense of relief. Finally.

It's 10 PM by the time I collapse on the sofa with a coffee and a plate of cheese toasties.

Suddenly, a thought crosses my mind, quickening my heartbeat, and a vision assaults me: Paul's voice in my ears, breathless, and my lower half bursting with sensation as pleasure runs through my body, reeling against the boundaries of my sanity.

I gasp, and my coffee almost spills over my cup.

There's this excitement and hunger for pleasure within me that is like a voracious beast that consumes everything, but it only fuels its craving for more. Paul ignited a spark inside me, propelling my anticipation and reintroducing a sense of exhilaration. It inspires me to seek out new experience, to create where there is none, pushing the boundaries of what's sane and insane. The beast within me is relentless, it devours each thrill and adventure, leaving me evermore hungry and stimulated.

The intoxicating allure of my time with Paul beckons my senses to indulge. Indulge until there is no sense or logic. Every time I pick up my phone, it tempts me with his seductive promises of joy and contentment. Immersed in pleasurable sensations that engulf my very being. His every word, every whispered breath tantalises me with temporary satisfaction, leaving me yearning, always ephemeral. Always chasing the next thrill, never satisfying, this beast inside me.

But the beast is both a blessing and a curse.

On one hand it motivates me to explore and grow, to recognize where I've stagnated, and makes me discover new paths of enjoyment. On the other hand, it leads me to an unquenchable thirst for Paul, an insatiable appetite that can never be satisfied, leaving me in a perpetual state of longing and craving.

I can't do it anymore.

I pick my phone and thumb a very quick message, my food and drink forgotten.

Me: *Thanks for the most stimulating week at work I've ever had. Just wanted to say I'm back in my home, in reality, thinking that I can't wait to go on adventures with you, exploring and discovering new things. Just wanted to say that I'm... thinking of you and missing you.*

Sent. I throw my phone away, groaning, and stuffing my mouth with my cheese sandwich. I do realise that Mark is around, and I wouldn't want to appear too deeply affected by or engrossed in someone I was texting this late at night. But this is the turning point: the final stage of guilt that I'm rid of. No more guilt, only excitement of what lies ahead and the experiences I'm about to enjoy. I go up to my room after discarding the utensils in the sink and get into bed.

I don't realise when I fall asleep.

When I wake from sleep, the sun is shining outside and filtered rays' stream in from my window over my eyes. I squint and sit halfway-up, yawning. Habitually, my hand finds my phone and I look at the screen to find a notification of texts from Paul.

I quickly rub my eyes and check his messages.

There is dread, excitement and anticipation boiling inside me in the few seconds it took me to open the messaging app.

Paul: *Hello to you too, Maria. Your message came at a great time, I was wondering if you would think differently now that you were home, with your family. To be honest I was anxious since we parted ways at the station, wondering if anything would change once you see how difficult it is in your position. Nevertheless, I'm excited to embark on this adventure with you, and so glad you are too. As the saying goes, it is what it is, and let's make the best of it.*

There was another message, slightly longer.

Paul: *Now that that's out of the way, I wanted you to know how genuinely I loved working with you all week, simply being in your company and hovering around you. Thursday night was perfect, the dinner and what followed afterwards. Though now I do think I should have gone up to your room, but just how you let me tell my dream makes me think it was better that it happened that way. I surely wouldn't have lasted that long then, lol, but we have all the time now. When we're not together we have our phones and our imagination. It makes me so excited, the way you're up for anything…. Last thing, I know you're with your family over the weekend, so I won't disturb you, unless you decide to text me…*

Wow.

I put my phone down, feeling slightly more prepared to face my day now, and head off to my morning shower with a bit more enthusiasm than I usually have, than I've had in quite some time now. I savour the warm shower and quickly head down for breakfast.

I feel especially motivated today, so I cook myself a fancy breakfast, garnish it with fresh herbs, and quietly sit down and enjoy it. A strange reprieve from my breakfasts consisting solely of coffee and an occasional doughnut.

I debate waking up Natalie, to ask her if she wanted to spend time together but I feel unsure... do I really want to go out when I can relax. After a few moments of contemplation, I remember telling her we would go shopping when she woke. I run upstairs and wake her up. I tell her to get ready to leave in half an hour and that I'm taking her shopping for new clothes. The response, as I was expecting, is excited shrieks and rookie dance moves.

On a normal day, shopping is not something that fills me with any great interest or anticipation, but today I too am in the mood to go look in the shops, participate in what Natalie always refers to as "retail therapy". I've been thinking for a few days that it would be nice to have something new to wear next time I see Paul when we go out.

We spend most of the morning shopping for Natalie. I get the odd opportunity to look at clothes for me when Natalie isn't pulling me along to the next shop before I'm done exploring the one we're at- or pulling me away to go with her to let her try clothes on. The price tag on some of these scanty things makes me baulk, but quickly I imagine Paul seeing me in a few pieces. I get why people buy these.

As we walk along the neatly organised line of shops in the mall, I see some spicy clothes on a few mannequins, and stop briefly, inconspicuously, to look in through the windows. Natalie immediately beckons me, and I follow, quietly longing for some alone time.

Finally, Natalie finds her perfect outfit for next weekend, and we head to the food court. It is nice seeing her so excited about her night out. Though a little frustrated I did not get to explore the shops for myself, I can now really appreciate how she is feeling. I'm sure if I were allowed to be I'd be as excited as her thinking about my next dinner out with Paul.

As we walk toward the food court, we pass a boutique lingerie shop, and I pause, taking a thorough look at the artfully dressed mannequins in lingerie and skimpy silks. *Mmm*, I think to myself and remember how I used to enjoy lingering in this shop, deciding which pieces of lingerie to buy, but I can't remember the last time I bought or wore some. It's depressing. Maybe I could change that.

A question creeps into my mind, "Does Paul like lingerie on a woman?" and I quickly shake my head to snap out of it, and move on as Natalie realises, I have fallen behind. I blush at the thought of her catching me staring at the mannequins and half-run to catch up with her.

Once we're done with lunch, and Natalie is satisfied and gushing about her purchase beside me in the passenger seat, I'm making a plan to get some shopping done for myself soon. No chance today and it looks like I need to make an effort. I find myself really looking forward to it, dressing up sexily, anticipating the feeling of being desired again. Imagine it being taken off me.

When we get home, Mark is on the couch, watching the afternoon game. I say a quick hello in his general direction and hear nothing in answer.

Once the kids are upstairs, I say to him, "It's a shame you're busy, I bought some sexy lingerie today. Maybe we can spice things up a little," I wink, but he's not even looking at me.

He just grunts a non-committal "That's nice." I can tell he's not interested, but I'm starting to think that's a good thing. I don't even feel bad about myself at his disinterest in me. It just means I'm right to want more for myself than his disdain.

I head into the kitchen to make dinner, and the kids come down a few minutes later. Natalie is trying on her new clothes, and she looks adorable. I send her in to show her dad, but she comes back a minute later saying he told her to 'go play dress-up elsewhere'. Natalie is close to tears.

Mark watching Manchester United lose again, and he's not in a good mood. I reassure Natalie that she looks great, and I tell her that I got the same reaction from her dad, and it's okay, he'll like her new outfit once the game's over.

After an hour, dinner is ready and served, and the family gathers at the table. There's not much conversation, but I ask the kids about their day. Liam tells me about doing his homework that his 'mental teacher' is making him do, and then going to the park to play football with his friends. Rebecca tells me about playing with her dolls and dressing up like the princess from a new children's movie. She inquires if I could get her a new hairbrush for her doll, and I smooch her, saying yes.

Mark was silent and unresponsive when I asked him about his day. He didn't ask a single question about mine. After dinner, everyone else left the table without offering to help with the cleanup. I asked Mark to help, and he reluctantly did so, grunting and making faces. It makes me frustratingly mad; why do I care about this man's reaction to me?

When we are finished, I turn to him and ask him what was wrong. He looks at me quizzically, "What do you mean?"

"I mean, I can barely get two words out of you these days," I said. "I ask about your project, and your day, and even though I am on a new project keeping me away, taking me out of the city, your only interest seems to be that I have Ursula booked to stay over on the days I am gone." He silently looks at me. Slightly bored. It makes me so mad.

"Well, what's going on? You seem to have no interest in me beyond a childminder and housekeeper." I throw down the gauntlet. *It's been a long time coming, fine, let's hash it out*, I think bitterly.

Mark is lost for words, and then finally says. "I have no idea what you are talking about."

No wonder I was numb. Otherwise, this man would have driven me crazy.

"You have no interest in me anymore. When was the last time we talked? When we shared a laugh or a good moment together? When was the last time we made love?" I ask, feeling anger and resentment rise up inside me.

He jumps in and says, "Last Saturday. Morning, I remember."

I looked at him in utter disbelief, "That was me climbing on you. When I tried to play, I remember exactly what you said,

'Can't beat nature, all yours if you want it'. Wow, what a way to feel wanted. I did try and play and frankly I would have got more interaction from a banana in the bed with me."

Mark looks offended, but I keep going on, relentless, "You know, I am only 42, I still love you and want you. We used to have sex whenever, wherever we could. I don't expect it to be like that now, but it would be nice if we could still do it without you making me feel like it's a favour from you."

Mark begins to speak, but I stop him, "I am not finished. Leave the sex aside, you never ask what I am doing, what is happening at work, what am I up to. You have more interest in making sure Ursula is here than me. Maybe you are screwing her. It would make sense that way, somehow."

Mark grits his teeth, "Can I speak now?"

I raise my brows and say nothing.

"You know how much you mean to me, and of course I want you." he scoffs at the thought of me believing otherwise. "You know how hard I am working lately, and I am very tired. Me sleeping with Ursula? She has been our childminder here forever. How could you even think that? Whenever you're out working, she is here with the kids, for them. I don't know how you could think that" Mark says, his voice irritatingly sounding betrayed.

"Well then, I know who you are not screwing," I cut back in," Me."

I look at him firmly, "I'm going to make this simple for you. Just start treating me a bit better than just your housekeeper and nanny. How we used to be. That is all I want."

"You're accusing me?" he says, finally bursting, "When half the time I need to call Joan to find out if you are working late or not. She knows more about what's going on with you than I do! Certainly, knows more about where you are, and have been."

Liam comes into the kitchen exactly when I'm about to fire back, and Mark moves away, back to the dish he was putting away, and the conversation ends.

"Mom, are you dropping me to the movies? Remember I told you I am going out with my friends tonight?"

I look at Mark, and he takes my glare as a subtle hint, or not so subtle. He tells Liam they will leave in five minutes. Mark probably takes it as an opportunity for escape.

Twenty minutes later Mark returns and there is nothing more to be said. We go about our evening; I have a little work to do, and Mark throws himself in front of the TV again.

I go and collect Liam at 10:30PM and he tells me about his night out, the movie ending and how he had so much fun. I'm glad to hear he enjoys being allowed out a little on his own since he turned fourteen.

Later that night when we head to bed, Mark offers me a back rub like he used to do. He tries; he stretches me out and removes my t-shirt and begins with my shoulders. It is a bit strained and I'm too tense, but he is trying.

He continues and it ends, as it used to, with us ultimately having sex. It was nice, and it makes me remember all the times we did this without scheduling it.

He tried for the first time in a long time, and it felt a little forced, but he is trying.

***

On Sunday morning, I wake up to gentle sunlight streaming in through the curtains. I lay in the bed breathing deeply. After a few minutes, I rise from the bed and make my way downstairs. The children are still asleep, so I take my sweet time making coffee and breakfast. As the enticing aroma of freshly brewed coffee swirls in the air, I pour the hot beverage into separate mugs, and throw a few flaky pastries on a plate. Balancing it all on a tray, I carry it back upstairs to our bedroom, a smile playing on my lips. I'm eager to start this day on a good note.

I nudge Mark awake and gesture toward the prepared tray I've brought him. While he gets up and rubs his eyes, shooing the sleep from his eyes, I sit at the foot of the bed in anticipation. He takes a sip from his mug. A bite of pastry from his plate. A few crumbs fell over his chest and on the plate. And silence.

I don't lose the spirit and start the conversation, "So, what are the plans today?" I ask with a big smile, hoping I get anything other than the usual response.

"Eh, you know. Liam wanted to go to the park for a football match a bit later in the morning. And there's a football match on in the afternoon," he finishes, looking into his coffee mug.

Not a courteous question about my plans. Or how my week was, or how I expect the coming week to be.

"Do you want to go for a walk or a coffee in town once you get back from the park?" There's still an ember of hope inside me. And he quenches it quickly.

"Oh, the match kicks off at one, so…" He shrugs, pretending our conversation last night didn't happen. As always. Placate me and then pretend it didn't happen.

There's no companionship in this marriage. I have been a fool all this time. I should go out alone, I think, and do what I wasn't able to do the other day out shopping with Natalie.

I leave my cup on the tray balanced over his legs and go get ready. He watches me get dressed without asking anything.

"Watch the kids, will you? I'm going out when you get back, and since time together isn't an option, I'll go alone," I stay there for a moment, giving him an opportunity to change his mind, to offer me anything, to fight for me as I'm fighting myself for him. He doesn't.

I busy myself as my son and husband leave for their outing.

What more must I do in this marriage alone? I think to myself. Here I am, irrevocably drawn to Paul, and still doing my best to stay with Mark. Doing everything to get Mark to show me he cares, a hint of evidence that he's interested in me. All I get is radio silence.

Ursula is off today so I do my laundry and the kids'. Wrap up a few chores around the house, and iron my work clothes for the week. Then I make myself a smoothie and put on some TV. An hour later I get dressed and grab my purse from the bedroom. When I get back to the lounge, Liam and Mark have just arrived home and are in high spirits.

I smile and ask about details as Liam regales me with the events of the match. I am genuinely glad he had a good time with his father, and once depleted, he takes his stuff upstairs to his bedroom. Mark has already sprawled over the sofa, changed the channel and made himself comfortable.

I pick my handbag off the sofa and turn toward the door.

"I'm off," I say irately, and slip on my shoes.

"Is lunch ready?" Mark asks, unbothered, his eyes already glued to the telly.

"I don't know, is it? I huff, planning to fully go off at him if he keeps up this attitude.

"I'm going out for shopping and lunch. Take care of yourself and your kids for once," And before he further spoils my already rotten mood, I take off, without staying to listen to his absolute nonsense. *That will show him,* I huff, and simultaneously wonder where he would get the takeout for the kids.

Frustrated and irate, I turn to lunch for a therapeutic release. The Trafford Center is bustling with activity, and it calms me. Determined to turn this day around, I decide that a satisfying lunch is just what the doctor ordered. I spot a cosy Italian restaurant and I turn to seek solace there; in a secluded corner where I can immerse myself in a tranquil time and watch the world go by. Finally settling into a spot that promises both peace and a perfect view, I eagerly await the food I've ordered. The Italian menu reminded me of my dinner with Paul, and that has already uplifted my spirits…

Knowing myself, I order just a glass of wine, ensuring that I stay fully sober. I know it will be just hours before I find myself behind the wheel again and I was not a fan of being wrapped around a streetlight. Today, I am resolved to stay out for the entire afternoon, savouring every moment, even if it means replacing my wine with endless cups of coffee. Maybe I could try a Frappe, or other creamy drinks my colleagues loved so much.

After a few minutes, the server brings out the pasta I ordered, and I enthusiastically dig in. A few bites in, I check my phone for the latest news: some high-profile politician's scandal, the ever-changing landscape of sports and economics. Just the usual. Flicking back to my homescreen, I see a red badge over the Snapchat app, and I frown. That usually means a message, and I didn't see a notification on my phone lock screen yet. Strange.

I click on the app icon, and find that it is in fact a message, from Paul and received last night. The furrow between my brows deepens: how did I miss his message *last night?*

I open the chat.

Paul: *Hi Maria, just a quick hello. Hope your weekend is going well and you're doing something nice for yourself after a long week. I know I should not bother you at home, so no need to reply, just sitting here thinking of you and thought I should let you know. X*

The message warms my cheeks: at least there's one man thinking of me. He wonders about my weekend and cares about my life. It brings a smile on my face and cheers me up instantly. I close the app and finish my food, enjoying my wine and looking out.

After a while, I bring my phone out and open the messaging app again. Quickly, I thumb out, *"Hi Paul, nice of you to ask about my weekend. Yes, it is fine, and I am finally getting a little me time and out shopping. Just not sure what I'm shopping for yet."*

I stare at it, overthinking my punctuation for a few seconds and then hit send.

I get a fancy coffee and head to the shops, with a renewed sense of enthusiasm and anticipation. The ugly morning mood has been broken and I'm all smiles again. I browse the boutiques and spot a lovely dress, black, elegant and feminine, with a halter top and low back… I wonder if it is too much. I try it on and feel gorgeous in it. I have this inexplicable need to show it off to Paul. I feel sexy with the low exposed back. *What the hell*, I think, and pay for it at the counter.

Moving on, I head to the next shop, and spot a nice pants suit, professional but more designer and fitted than I usually wear. Since I'm going all out, I buy it and two more white shirts to match. A bit more open neck than usual. I just imagine myself in it next Thursday in London, and I'm sold. I pick up a few more casual clothes and head back to the car.

I pass by the sexy lingerie shop again and stop briefly. Rather than looking in through the window like a creep, I head straight inside. All around me, there are so many options. All so sensual. I pick up a gorgeous black lace set that feels feather soft on my skin. I find that there is a promotion, and I could get another second on half the price. Works for me! I find another set in grey, and get it packed, thinking this is Mark's final chance.

Chapter 7

With Monday morning comes the usual flurry of activity and frenzied commotion.

The racing, the banging, the running. Mark in my way, lost ties, undone homework, and angsty teenagers, while Ursula flips pancakes in the kitchen.

Sleep had evaded me last night, and I twisted and turned in the bed, my mind abuzz with the drama and events that had unfolded over the weekend. My mood was like a pendulum, swinging between anger and sadness while I lay under the cool sheets. Sadness for what our marriage had become, and anger at how Mark thought he could pacify me for five minutes and then go about being the same, while also ignoring me. If he believed that a mere five minutes of attention after my endless efforts and complaints is enough to appease me, he was sorely mistaken. I was deluded; he will never change. And I'm finally sick and tired of him. *That's it, I'll be doing it for him no longer*, I decided at 4 AM.

I grab a toast from the plate Ursula has placed on the kitchen counter and take a sip of the coffee. I sigh; it's cooled, and now I'll have to stop on the way to pick a hot one.

***

The traffic on the way gives me road rage, but that's usual. I head into work with a steaming cup of coffee, its aroma waking me right up easing the stress lines around my eyes and on my forehead. I already feel better after the terrible night. Unlocking my office door, I fire off a message to Paul.

Maria: *Good morning! Want the good news first or bad news?*

I take a look at the files on my desk today, flipping through the first one. It was going to be a long and tiring day. I should settle in, and so I did. Removing my heels and replacing them with low comfortable shoes, I sip at my coffee.

My phone screen lights up, announcing a notification. It's Paul.

Paul: *Hey, you okay? Is it the messages, did anyone see them? Tell me both.*

I chuckle at his obvious distress. Poor him.

Maria: *Good news is I can't wait to see you on Thursday. Even got something special planned. The bad news is… well, you've awakened something in me that won't be easily satisfied. You're in so much trouble. I think I might break you, darling.*

There was a sharp knock on my door, and a few moments later Joan entered, giving me a radiant smile. She was dropping off a couple more files on Ralph's case.

"I've got a long list of companies from Paul Bridges' office. Should I prepare a financial analysis for all of them?" She asked, bringing out her little diary she noted all the day's tasks in.

"Thanks, Joan. Yes, let's get a comprehensive financial assessment for each one. Can you get Melanie on this too? I need to know Ralph's interests in these companies, their valuations, and unless it's evident, their business activities based on the latest filings. Oh, also, has Mark been trying to reach me here? He mentioned something." I throw in the last question nonchalantly, waving my hand in the air.

Joan appeared slightly thrown by the sudden turn in conversation, "Not really, Maria. A very few times, he's inquired about your availability when you're usually tied up in meetings, but he said it wasn't anything important and he'll try your mobile later."

I nod and give her a smile as she leaves.

***

I look at the stack of files in front of me with determination. I'm on a mission today. There's a lot of cases to be sorted through and moved forward, and as much as I enjoy my time

92

in London and Paul, I cannot get behind my responsibilities at DAF.

I look through my agendas, perusing each file, my mind falling into the routine like a well-oiled machine, swiftly processing the details and connecting the dots. My fingers dance across the pages, highlighting key points and making notes in the margins. I ask for some more files, and Melanie and I review them meticulously. A few projects were stuck since I took the job in London, and it irked me.

I touch base and get updates on the progress of our current projects, and also the gigs we were pitching for. There are many challenges, but I probe for information, and navigate through the complexities of each project, ensuring that everything is aligned and moving forward.

After delegating some tasks, I tighten a few lazy bones and assess the statuses of the rest of the projects, methodically working through each file. When I resurface from work, it's past noon. I stretch, and my shoulder bones crunch satisfyingly.

I figure I could use a coffee break and retrieve my phone on the trip to the canteen.

Joan is walking hurriedly toward me, looking visibly stressed.

I raise my brows in anticipation as she stops before me.

"Hey, you're on a roll today and your mission is great, but the Ralph Michaels job is huge, and there's too many companies in the list to get data on. Can you tell me which projects are a priority so I can get started on the value-added tasks first?"

She's right, but I really need a break right now to gather my thoughts. My mind's bursting with information on all the work that's still pending.

"Joan, give me a few minutes for coffee and I'll be right back and clarify this for you, alright? Thanks!" And I quickly march off to the canteen, being pulled into its direction by the overwhelming scent of freshly roasting coffee beans.

While I wait for my order, I check my phone and see there's a message notification from Paul. A large smile graces my face, and I half-forget my exhaustion. I click on the notification quickly.

Paul: *That doesn't sound like bad news ... interesting, and fun, I'd say. It has been years since I was found in that kind of trouble. Let's make Thursday night memorable. You have something special to wear, right? How about I make a restaurant reservation? Both will get dressed up and we'll call it a date?*

My stomach flutters from his words.

Me: *Now you're talking! You've already guessed that I'll dress up... hm, we're on the same wavelength again.*

Paul: *Ah-hah! It was just a guess. Looks like I better dust off my tux. Don't wanna look like the beauty and the beast. Leave it to me!*

Paul: *By the way, how are things on that front? Any sign of the Ice Queen thawing?*

I laugh. Ice Queen in his words sounded much better than Ice Maiden.

Me: *Oh, yes, she's sizzling.*

Me: *Decided to work hard and late today. I don't want to give Jack any reason to question how much time I'm spending on Ralph's accounts or if I'm neglecting other responsibilities. Frankly, a junior could handle what I'm doing down there, so I need to be doing the part up here. I don't want anyone scrutinising it. Jack is lazy; once the work is done, he couldn't care less. Plus playing catch up while I'm in London is such a waste... while I could be having so much fun...*

Paul: *Ah, a woman on a mission. All for fun. Do you want me to leave you alone until Thursday?*

Me: *Hmm, do you really think you can get away that easily? No chance. I've developed a taste for you and become used to seeing your messages on my phone. Don't stop. I might not reply immediately while I work, but will get to you as soon as I'm free.*

Paul: *You really are a woman on a mission.*

I chuckle and collect my coffee, now feeling especially rejuvenated.

The day continued, and I immersed myself back in my work. For the office, the Ice Maiden was back and in full force. Barking orders, ringing telephones. There was no break for anyone today.

As the day drew to a close, I received a lengthy email from Paul's office. It was addressed to me, Jack, and Leonard, Paul's boss. I click on the notification and read through the text.

Subject: Update and Further Recommendations for Ralph Michael Estate, London

Good afternoon everyone,

We are a couple of weeks into the Ralph Michael Estate Project, and it hasn't been without its challenges. Ralph has proved to be a shrewd businessman, albeit somewhat reclusive. His sports shops operate as independent companies, resembling sole traders. They all report back to the London headquarters, where the parent company handles sales and centralises orders to maximise manufacturer discounts. It's a clever execution of a good idea.

Each shop appears to be profitable, although the manager's salary for the Fort William branch seems higher than the others. Nevertheless, it is still turning a profit. Maria Holmes has done an excellent job analysing the shop accounts and has built a good rapport with the London staff, who are cooperative and trust her. All the necessary paperwork for the shops and the main business is safely stored at the head office.

Although, the London branch's staffing situation requires delicate handling. The core staff members have been with the company for many years, some for over two decades. They seem to hold a strong loyalty to Mr. Michaels, although interestingly, they don't seem to know much about him outside of the office. The shops and distribution company are running smoothly, so my recommendation is to refrain from making any significant changes at this point. I'd suggest we reassure the staff that no immediate changes are planned after our initial analysis and acknowledge their invaluable contributions to the company.

Late Mr. Michaels personally oversaw all financial matters, conducting his own analysis and supervision. This fact provided relief and lightened our workload as everything was in one place in one system. For now, I suggest leaving that role with Maria Holmes, if possible. While others may be qualified, introducing changes in this area could disrupt the stability we currently have. The last thing we want is bitterness and competition between the high-level employees of the company.

Apart from that, we still need to do a deep dive into the rental accounts and property portfolios and pay visits to the shops, just routine due diligence. Unfortunately, the main office lacks substantial records of rentals, leases and personal accounts, so that's a dead-end. We have initiated a search with financial institutions to identify any funds, and our accountants are analysing company registries for further leads.

Here are my recommendations:

The accountants should complete company searches to uncover any other ventures Mr. Michaels may have been involved in.

Legal should take charge of the bank search process.

Maria Holmes should assume a role within the main company and attend weekly, dedicating 1-2 days based on current patterns. This will ensure that the staff knows there is a boss overseeing operations, rather than an unfamiliar face from a large company of solicitors or accountants.

We should search Mr. Michaels' apartment thoroughly and bring back all papers and computer equipment to the main office for analysis. As for how to deal with his personal effects, clothing etc., all suggestions are welcome.

It would be prudent to have the art and antiques in the apartment appraised, as well as the apartment itself. Although dated, it is a spacious two-bedroom apartment in the financial district and likely holds considerable value.

We should attempt to locate Mr. Michaels' personal safe, which may be found during a search of his home.

I will remain in London to assist Maria Holmes and take on the responsibility of searching for additional assets, business interests, and rental properties. This will allow Maria to focus more on the core business.

We must visit each of the six shops, starting with London and Manchester since I assume they're the easiest to handle.

The remaining four shops in Fort William, Edinburgh, Glasgow, and Perth should be visited by Maria Holmes and me. This will provide an opportunity for the managers to meet us, their new reporting superiors, and allow us to reassure them.

We should also visit Mr. Michaels' Fort William residence to assess its contents and records, both from an asset and documentation perspective.

The last items will take a few days away. I'm estimating 2 days for each destination, except Glasgow, we'll fit it in the schedule, so no overnight stays are needed.

I propose that we send each shop a comprehensive list in advance, including stock take and values, staff details, and up-to-date bank statements. This way, they will also be well-prepared for our visits and assessments.

I apologise if this workload puts Ms. Holmes under more pressure, but these are necessary steps to ensure a smooth transition. Please let me know your thoughts on these recommendations.

Furthermore, I think it's also in our favour to determine at this point whether the business and properties are to be sold eventually or kept intact. Considering the associated costs, we must exercise caution and avoid any extravagance, especially with regards to the ultimate beneficiaries. I suggest discussing this matter further in the coming weeks and making appropriate recommendations.

I await your feedback and instructions on the aforementioned points.
Yours faithfully,
Paul Bridges
Senior Associate

Whoa, he really does nothing half-heartedly, huh. As soon as I'm done reading the email, my office phone rings.

I answer distractedly, "Holmes."

"Oh, hi, Holmes on a mission. Did you get my email?"

"I did. Just finished reading through it."

"I was asked for an update on our current work there. I hope I didn't put too much work on you? I don't want our time in London to be an obligation, I just thought it all made sense and it was better coming from me as a recommendation to Jack and everyone. If you prefer less time away, I'm sure I can justify it in the next update, not a big deal at all," he says in a rush, making me think he's nervous and it is a big deal after all. The thought makes me giggle quietly.

He continues, "Now the main reason for my call was to hear your voice and say hello. Are you done for the day? How was your day?"

I chuckle, endeared by him, "Thank you, Paul. Your email was perfect, exactly what they must have been expecting from us by now. You were very formal, and of course it's all justified. And yes! I want to spend more time in London with you there. Unless you become a bore, I don't see why you should change your recommendation."

He exhales in relief on the other side of the line, "Great, great. And this won't be too much work for you?"

"Thankfully nothing big is on my desk right now. Let's see what Jack says," I reply.

"And how was your day?"

"What do you want to know?"

"Anything, as long as it's you are talking," he replies unexpectedly. It makes me chuckle.

"A charmer! Your coffee-machine buying tactics won't work on me. But my day was dull, just chock-full of work. Productive, though. Nothing too exciting. What are the work plans for London this week?"

"I was thinking let's start by heading to Ralph's apartment first," Paul suggests, his voice filled with a sense of purpose. "We can box up all his belongings and bring them back to the conference room in the office. We need to search for the safe and see what other paper trails we can uncover. It might not be the cleanest or most glamorous task, but it's necessary."

I consider his proposal for a moment before responding, "That sounds like a solid plan. However, I do have a meeting at 4 in the afternoon nearby."

Paul's concern is evident in his voice as he asks, "Will you be back in time for our dinner date?"

A mischievous grin spreads across my face as I reply, "Paul, do you think I would miss our dinner date for anything? No way! We'll meet at our usual time, 7pm. And I'm excited to see where you've chosen for us to dine."

Amidst the excitement, I feel the need to clarify something, before we miss each other in pursuit of the other again. "Oh, by the way, just to avoid any confusion, I'll be taking the 5:55 train to London on Thursday morning, returning at 6pm on Friday. I've got seat 34A in first class each way. We've been on the same wavelength too much, let's not miss each other now."

There's a moment of silence on the other end of the line, and then Paul's voice, filled with warmth, responds, "Thank you for letting me know. I appreciate your attention to detail. And prepare for what I've planned for dinner, should be fun."

"I'll be observing with a shrewd eye," I laugh, and roll my eyes.

"Yes boss, no pressure, of course."

***

Over the course of Tuesday and Wednesday, Paul and I engage in a playful back-and-forth of text messages, alternating between teasing and flirting. Despite the lighthearted banter, I can't help but feel a nervous excitement building up within me. The prospect of our dinner on Thursday evokes a strange mix of anticipation and nostalgia, as if I've been transported back to my teenage years experiencing the thrill of a first date.

Throughout our exchanges, Paul displays a delightful blend of attentiveness and playfulness, making me feel special and cared for. His thoughtful gestures and affectionate words put me at ease, easing the butterflies fluttering in my stomach. It's refreshing to be on the receiving end of such genuine warmth and attention.

As I read his messages, a smile tugs at the corners of my lips, and I find myself eagerly looking forward to our upcoming evening together. There's an undeniable chemistry between us, and I can't help but wonder what surprises and delightful moments await us during our date.

Chapter 8

Thursday morning arrived with a sense of anticipation as I stepped onto the train. The familiar, boring carriage was exciting today, and as soon as I made my way to seat 34A, I spotted the back of a man's head peeking over the seat in front of me. My heart skipped a beat, elated at the sight of Paul, and a thought crossed my mind. With a mischievous grin, I tiptoe to the seat, unable to resist the temptation to playfully tease him.

"Hey, there, you come here often?" I quip, walking toward him, my voice filled with playfulness and mock suave.

The head turned, and to my horror, revealed a completely different man, a stranger rather pleasantly surprised at my confident greeting.

"Not often enough, I think," he replies, smiling openly.

Ugh, I groan internally, *not a screw-up early in the morning.* Embarrassment washes over me like a wave onto the shore.

"Uh, sorry," I mutter, and quickly take my seat, stow my luggage and bring out my laptop to hide my reddening face. *Way to extricate myself from the awkward consequences of my own actions.*

Undeterred by my apology, the stranger smiles, and tries to strike up a conversation. He appears friendly, and we engage in some harmless small talk. After a few minutes, I open my laptop, and feign busyness, in hopes he would get the hint.

Spoiler alert: he didn't.

"So, how often do you travel on this train? Are you gonna stay over in London?"

It's curious how he's so resolute about continuing the conversation when I'm so obviously not into it. Plus, I don't want to answer the questions. I'm still thinking of a way to maneuver the conversation in a different direction, away from personal information, when a voice cuts through the tension.

"Excuse me, I think you're in my seat," the familiar voice calls, and I look up in relief to see Paul, standing over the man. "Here, 34B," he shows his ticket.

"Oh, I'm 34A," I say, looking at the man in front of me meaningfully.

He checks his ticket. "Oh, silly me, I'm 24B," he mutters, then looks at Paul, "Would you mind swapping seats? Saves me the trouble of packing up and moving."

I look at Paul.

Paul replies lightheartedly, "Ah, I'm a creature of habit. 34B has been my lucky seat, I suppose I want to have an especially good day today." I giggle inside at Paul's playful charm.

I quickly stand, hinting at him to get up and leave, and he finally takes the hint, sighing.

As the stranger leaves, he mutters something unintelligible to Paul, the latter chuckles but doesn't let on what the man said.

Taking his seat beside me, he flashes me a mischievous grin, "You always manage to find yourself in interesting situations, eh? Replacing me first thing in the morning…" he shakes his head in mock heartbreak.

I punch his bicep and regale him with the embarrassment session I had to endure, and Paul laughs.

"Wish I could've seen that. Even better, watching you try and get out of it. Anyway, I'm on my lucky seat, let's make today special," he nuzzles my nose lightly.

With a playful wink, I replace my laptop back into its bag, and we chat about the weekend, some light-hearted banter, if there's been anything interesting.

The ride was smooth, and we ordered some breakfast. I indulged in pancakes with my coffee, and Paul fed me the little strawberry with cream. I nibbled on it, cherishing the soft moment of this casual intimacy. As soon as we arrived in London, we hailed a taxi and made our way to the office together. We didn't stop to drop our bags at our respective hotels; there was no time.

Nicola checks us out from toe to head and then gives a playful smirk, "Ah, smart! Celebrating casual Friday already?"

Helen joins her, and they share a curious glance, and I see her winking at Paul. He brushes his lapel self-importantly.

I hide my chuckle.

Paul explains, "We're going to be out of the office today, going and sorting out Ralph's apartment. Move all paperwork back to the office here. Hauling work, not a suit morning. We'll be back soon after lunch though, but if anything important comes up, we're just 'round the corner."

Helen and Nicola nod, and Helen clicks her tongue, "I don't think there's anything immediate here. You both can go work peacefully."

Paul goes to his table and collects a few documents, surrenders them at the reception and we head out, Ralph's apartment keys jangling in Paul's palm.

Before we leave, however, I request the reception to drop a stack of cardboard boxes at the apartment, and once full, pick them up by one. We are assured a van would come collect all Ralph's packed up belongings, mostly office files, by the time we're done.

As we step into the apartment, an eerie feeling comes over me. Paul and I exchange a glance, saying what was unspoken with our eyes.

Someone has been here.

The air feels damp and heavy as we step further into the room, our senses on high alert. Maybe the intruder was still inside the building? And then, to my surprise, a noise echoed from one of the rooms, breaking the silence and unsettling my nerves.

And then footsteps. Coming towards us. We watch in absolute surprise as a figure- a woman- emerges from Ralph's bedroom, and shrieks, startled, when she sees us standing there. In a moment of desperation, she aims a surface cleaner towards us, her fingers poised over the trigger of the plastic spray bottle. Paul and I look at each other, and he runs his tongue over his bottom lip, his hands in front of him as if in surrender.

With a mix of curiosity and mild bewilderment, I mustered the courage to ask, "Who are you?" The words slip out of me tinged with astonishment.

The woman, clearly taken aback by our presence, stammers, "I'm Rachel. I come here every Thursday to clean. I've been working here for the past five years. Who are you?" The question comes with suspicion.

I exhale in relief, and so does Paul. False alarm, I guess. I feel Paul's reassuring, steady hand on my back. The cleaning lady is too suspicious to notice.

We introduce ourselves, showing her our keys as evidence. Paul suggests that she contact Ralph's office to verify our authority. The office summarizes the purpose of our visit to Rachel and instructs that she cooperate. Once Rachel is satisfied, she quickly opens up and starts talking. Beginning with a complaint of how messy we left Ralph's apartment the last time we were here.

When the call ends, Paul begins, "Ms. Holmes and I are responsible for all Ralph's affairs henceforth. May I ask what are the terms of your employment? Since we'll be looking after the contract you had with Ralph now."

Rachel's mood becomes somber as she processes the news about Ralph, and answers haltingly, "I just come and clean every Thursday morning. I take the laundry and bring it with me on my next visit, change the sheets, cook and freeze some food."

"Right, okay. So, I'd like you to continue what you do. Except there's no need for laundry, sheets and food now. I'll sort out the contract soon, and you'll be updated when it's done." Paul debriefs her.

Rachel appears relieved, and quite open. Paul senses the opportunity to get a few questions in.

"Also, have you noticed any paperwork or odd objects stored in the apartment somewhere? Maybe there's a drawer somewhere?" Paul leads.

Rachel ponders for a moment, "Not that I've seen, and you best believe I clean every corner. No drawers with papers, except in the office. Sometimes there is scattered paperwork around the desk, I believe Ralph brought the work home with him. But drawers in the house are for personal stuff," Rachel reports succinctly.

Curiosity piqued, Paul inquires further, "Have you ever come across a safe in the apartment?"

Rachel shakes her head, "No, but there's a locked chest in his bedroom that I've never seen inside. I've seen no safe. Also, it's almost ten, and I'll be done and out of your hair soon. I come at eight and leave by ten. Shall I take any laundry today?"

"Yes, please do that. For next week, though, could you pack all the clothes, linens, shoes and accessories to donate? Pillows, quilts, blankets and sheet and towels everything can go," Paul asks her in a friendly yet authoritative way.

"Yes, sir. Some of the stuff is in very good condition," she observes, thinking.

I can sense her direction of thoughts, "If you need anything from the packed stuff, you can have it. The rest we will have picked up," I look at Paul as I say this, and he nods. Rachel seems pretty happy with the arrangement, and cheerfully continues about her business.

I take a seat at the table and go through my emails. There are a few updates from the projects that were stuck, and I fire off new instructions. People at DAF shouldn't think I've fallen off the face of the earth while I'm in London.

Once she leaves, and we bid her goodbye, I turn to Paul with a whistle.

"Whoa, for a second, I thought there was a woman involved. Would have made things interesting. Nope, it's just his cleaning lady. As it stands, she knows very little about him, much like all the others in Ralph's life. Isn't it strange, though, how little everyone knows about him, no matter how long they have been with him?"

Paul's eyebrows are furrowed, and he's pondering something as he nods.

"Very curious, yes."

As the sun reaches its zenith and the day gets sweatier, we get busy packing up files, documents, and personal correspondence. Every envelope of bank statements, To-do lists, and sticky notes are carefully sorted into neatly labelled cardboard boxes.

"I think we're done with everything here," I exhale, giving a once over to the ransacked room, and pull the drawers of the sturdy oaken table for a last check.

A smile alights my face as I dangle the notorious rope cuffs in front of Paul.

"How shall these be filed?" I look at him coyly.

He winks and smiles, "'Needs Further Investigation' box, I think."

"Oh, speaking of further investigation. Let's check out the locked chest Rachel was talking about."

Paul looks at the time: we still have about half an hour until the van comes back to pick up the boxes.

"Well?" I wiggle my brows. "We might find more *interesting* stuff inside."

"You're in a mood today, aren't you. Well, lead on to the bedroom, who am I to hinder your investigations?" He smirks, and exhales dramatically, "The things I gotta do at work."

He follows me to the scantily furnished bedroom, and we come to stand against the padlocked wooden chest nestled in the corner of the bedroom. Over it lay an old, dainty crocheted cover. I kneel beside the mysterious chest with anticipation and curiosity. I look at Paul and I know we're both wondering what secrets lie within. There were intricate carvings around the latch, secured by a heavy lock. We hadn't found any keys in the drawers or cabinets, so we searched the room. We look in the vanity and the bedside tables, but our search yields no key. We had to look for other avenues to unlock it.

"Are you hiding any impressive lock-picking skills?" Paul asks me.

"Nope, not this time," I shake my head, and from the corner of my eye I catch a loose nail that attached the clasp to the wood of the chest.

"Actually, hold the lid open for me," I murmur, and go in search of a knife. I find a blunt but sturdy one in the kitchen and quickly return to the bedroom. Paul is holding the weighty lid open as far as it would allow. It would do.

I slide the knife between the latch and the wood, and push, turning it hard at an angle. After two tries, the latch gives, and the lid springs open.

"See? I get what I want by hook or by crook," I smirk, and throw open the chest to look inside.

Disappointment and confusion dance over my brows and in the lines on Paul's forehead as we realise the contents of the chest. Why was I expecting something completely different, something more like the cuffs...

But all we found was old tickets, movie stubs, faded receipts, brochures, event posters...

This was sentimental, I realise. Finally, something of substance regarding Ralph. He was an astute businessman, a micromanager, but also a nostalgic man.

Numbers and words jump at me from the collection of Ralph's keepsakes. Dated from 1980s until late 2000s, up until eleven years ago. The last hotel receipts are dated approximately eleven years ago, after which we find no more newer bits of paper.

"Oh, well. I have to say this turned out very differently than what I'd imagined it would be. Expected a treasure trove of toys or something alike," Paul mutters, sifting through the contents of the chest, "Let's keep these together in a box, maybe mark it as 'Personal'. And leave it for now. Obviously, this meant a lot to Ralph, maybe the beneficiary can sort it out on their own," Paul exhales.

We go through the bedroom again, under the mattress, behind the vanity, just to make sure we haven't missed anything. I hear a ping on my phone, and see that it's Joan, updating me on the status of various issues I was currently addressing. While I read it, Paul writes a note addressed to Rachel to take all the boxes, including cutlery and linen to donations and charity, leaving behind the personal box.

Some food was starting to rot in the unplugged refrigerator, and he includes a deep clean of the refrigerator and kitchen cabinets into the note.

"I guess now we're done here. Time for-" Paul is interrupted mid-sentence by the chime of the doorbell. It is two men from the van, and they haul the Paperwork boxes out, with instructions to safely place them inside the conference room that served as our joint office.

"Hi, I'll head out, check into the hotel. I'll drop my bags before coming back to the office," I pick up my bag as Paul was helping out the workers with the boxes.

"Alright, see you at the office after lunch."

"Otherwise, hotel reception at 7," I instruct, careful not to say too much while the company workers were around. I didn't think there was anything wrong with two colleagues joining each other for dinner, but it didn't hurt to keep the details to a minimum. Things escalated very quickly in that context; I'd come to realise.

***

The afternoon evaporates like a thought in the early morning, leaving behind nothing but a faint sense of lost time.

When I get to the office, Nicola is ready to regale me with the usual events around the company. I surmised that everything was running smoothly, and I just had to sign off on little matters, easily sorted. She is very succinct, which I appreciate, and reassures me that every project is being taken care of, and the company's working like a well-oiled machine. She also gives me an update on company structure and responsibilities, as I am only getting familiar with personnel. In the end, I'm pretty satisfied with how things were going, and thanked Nicola for all her efforts.

"Oh, also, there's a trade expo around this time every year in Holland that Ralph religiously attended. It's the only one he went overseas for; God rest his soul. Let me know what you want to do about the bookings, flights and hotel rooms, there's still a bit of time until we need to decide," says Nicola, cutting off a task off her to-do list in her little brown notebook.

"Alright, thanks for letting me know. I'll take this up with Mr. Bridges. Meanwhile, email me a recommendation, someone who knows the inside out of trade, knows what stocks and equipment we have, and what needs to be purchased," I say, and Nicola nods "The usual buyer also goes to this and the other events.", she says as she leaves.

Even though the day is about to end, I haven't spotted Paul since I came from my hotel. I debated sending him a text, but then see another long email from Joan, detailing privileged information and reports on Ralph's companies of interest. Somehow, even though the initial number was very high, more companies have sprouted up, and I groan, knowing this increases my work.

I reply to a few points in Joan's email and get cracking on the company searches. Afterwards, the correspondence is quick, and I quickly allot more work to my team at DAF. There's too much to do, and there's too little time for new companies to be appearing at this point.

At 3:45, I pack my things, and leave the office, done for the day.

I spot Paul in the corridor the same moment he spots me. We smile at each other, and I wink, and reaching up to him I whisper, "I'm heading to my four o'clock. We'll see how lucky you can get tonight," And I leave Paul behind, smiling but slightly confused if he should know what my four o'clock was.

Exactly at 4, I'm stepping inside the hair salon close to my hotel. I saw it on one of my walks last week, and decided, what the hell. I deserve to feel pretty and pampered, too. Once I'd picked my dress and lingerie, and dinner was decided with Paul, I rang up the salon and booked some services. I didn't want to overdo it, so I decided to just get my hair done, a body wax and a little skincare treatment. I was itching for a manicure and pedicure, but there was no time. I was too bubbly and excited for the date tonight.

Partially because I was doing this after so long, I couldn't even remember the last time I got my hair and nails done for a night out, an event or a date. But that was the past. I moaned in relaxation as the salon technician lathered my face in a cool gel, and I reclined, my brain finally going silent.

***

Finally, at 6:30, my hair is done, my skin is glowing, and my body feels velveteen. I moan from the feeling of being pampered, and even without makeup I know I look gorgeous right now. I pay in cash at the reception, and quickly hurry back to my room, mindful not to encounter Paul and spoil the surprise I had prepared. There is mischief in the air, sexy playfulness that I thrive on.

As soon as my room door shuts behind me, I rush to bring my dress out from the wardrobe. It appeared flawless, not a single wrinkle in sight. I smile widely, appreciating Its halter top design that gracefully highlighted the shoulders and exposed just the right amount of skin, leaving a tantalising hint of allure. The plunging neckline dipped seductively, drawing attention to the décolletage with an air of subtle confidence.

Crafted from luxurious fabric, the dress flowed effortlessly, cascading in gentle waves that danced with every movement. It fell below the knee, embracing my curves and accentuating a flattering silhouette. The low back, a captivating feature, added a touch of sensuality, leaving an indelible impression as it revealed just enough skin to tease the imagination.

There's very little time, so I hurry on tiptoe and retrieve my lingerie and stockings, a garter to go with it, and lay it all out on the bed. I shed my work clothes and slip into the lace bra set I got on my shopping spree last week. The cups of my bra embrace my body with gentle elasticity, offering support with decadent luxury. The delicate fabric is adorned with intricate patterns and delicate floral motifs, adding a femininity and grace that I sorely missed.

As the lace brushes against my skin, it feels like a gentle caress, invoking a tantalising sensation. The fabric moulds to my body, accentuating my curves and contours in a way that is both flattering and enticing, something I was excited to find I had retained over all these years. The softness of the lace against the skin makes me aware of what I'm wearing, making me feel mischievous and sexy.

This was as much for myself as it was for Paul, and I delight in knowing how he will find me.

I reach for my dress and realise with panic that my bra straps would be visible since the dress plunged low in the back, compromising the flawless look I desired. This was a dilemma... *what to do?* Did I have anything else that could work? I knew there was nothing. And then a rebellious idea crossed my mind- *What if? Could I?* I shut my mind to the loud ringing bells of caution and take off my bra.

I slip into the dress, and even without the constraints of underwear, my dress is snug enough to provide some support at the top. I palm my breasts, shrugging, and decide this look was better. I needed to dare to embrace my body, my sexy side again. I look in the mirror, and see a confident, elegant woman that had a sparkle in her eyes. Not to toot my own horn, but I looked positively ravishing. Some eyeshadow, lipstick and blush, along with my heels and a dainty necklace complete the ensemble. I look at the clock: six fifty-five. Paul must be waiting downstairs already. The thought clenched my heart, and I giggled in excitement.

I get my blood-red wrap, for the chilly evening and grab my bag, almost running to the door. Before shutting it behind me I look back to see if everything is in place perfectly. We were going to come back here, and I didn't want a thing out of place. On second thoughts, I spray a little bit of my perfume onto the pillows and bedsheets and smile a Cheshire cat smile.

My plan tonight was flawless.

***

Stepping out of the elevator into the reception area, my eyes sweep the surroundings. Paul is already there, his gaze fixed on me as he approaches. He comes toward me with a purpose, and I almost whimper seeing him dressed up. I would confess I wanted to take him upstairs right now, everything be damned. And then, with a gentle touch, his hands rest on my waist, pulling me closer as his lips meet mine in a tender kiss. As he pulls away, he lingers for a moment, his voice a soft whisper.

"You look absolutely stunning this evening. You surely delivered the surprise you promised. Breathtaking," he murmurs in an exhale, nuzzling my ear.

A smile plays on my lips, and he takes my hand in his. "The restaurant is just a short car ride away," he says.

"Thank goodness for that," I sigh, "These heels may be beautiful, but they're not made to walk in," I laugh, and he joins in. We head towards the front door, where the concierge awaits, ready to open it for us.

Paul lets me exit first, his fingers grazing gently across the exposed skin of my back, sending a delightful shiver down my spine. My skin tingles where his fingers were a moment before, and electricity courses down my back. He acts impervious to what his touch has done to me.

The concierge follows closely behind, leading us towards a parked BMW by the curb. I glance at Paul, my curiosity piqued.

"I had planned to book a hotel car to drop us off and pick us up," he remarks. "They recommended this car, much more elegant than a taxi. Especially considering how breathtaking you look tonight; I must tip whoever suggested this to me."

The car door is held open for me, and I gracefully step inside. The chauffeur starts the car and Paul takes his place on the other side, a warm smile gracing his lips. In this moment, everything feels surreal. I feel transformed, as if stepping into a new version of myself, and I am thoroughly enjoying every minute of it. This seems like an altered reality, a parallel universe where I'm actually living my life free of monotonicity and boredom. Cinderella before midnight.

As we make our way to the restaurant, small talk fills the air, both of us mindful of the stranger driving the car. "I can guess what your 4 PM appointment was for now. Your hair looks exquisite, it really suits you," Paul comments, twisting a piece of my hair over his finger. "And you were right, I stand corrected."

A playful glimmer lights up my eyes. "Of course, I'm always right, remember? But tell me, what was I right about this time?" I inquire with a teasing smile.

He gazes at me, his expression filled with genuine admiration. "I thought my surprise would have been... well, more surprising. But I am in awe, feeling completely out of my league in your presence tonight," he confesses, his voice tinged with a mixture of excitement and vulnerability. "You're so beautiful, and I can't believe that... you're here."

I glow in the praise he showers over me, always so genuine and heartfelt. The validation fulfills something inside me, a balm over an ache that had begun to harden my heart and numb my feelings. I feel like I'm melting now, mushy on the inside in the best way possible. Words spill from my mouth, unfiltered and true.

"And you look absolutely dashing yourself. New suit, crisp shirt, and tie. That's all you, has always been. But what you see in me right now is simply the side of me that you're awakening. So, trust me when I say, you are not out of your league. You're responsible for this transformation, so you can only blame yourself." I actually feel this to be the truth.

At this, he takes my hand and kisses it softly, barely touching his to mine, knowing full well how he was teasing me.

As we arrive at the restaurant, Paul swiftly steps out of the car and circles around to open my door. It's a small gesture, but it speaks volumes. A gentleman, making an effort to make this evening special. It's been a long time since I've experienced such thoughtfulness.

Just from the entrance anyone could tell the restaurant was upmarket.

The table we're brought to exudes an air of sophistication, adorned with fresh flowers arranged in an elegant centerpiece, pristine white linen, perfectly pressed and draped over the surfaces. Each table setting is meticulously arranged, gleaming silverware meticulously aligned, and crystal glassware sparkling in the ambient light.

As we take our seats, I sink into the comfortable plush chairs.

The soft glow of candlelight dances across the table, adding a touch of romance to the ambiance. The silver service style further adds to the refined atmosphere. The waitstaff, dressed in impeccably tailored uniforms, have an air of professionalism and grace, serving meals in polished silver trays. Their movements are measured and deliberate, displaying a mastery of etiquette and a deep understanding of fine dining service.

Once we're seated, we peruse the menu, though dinner is the furthest thing from my mind. My thoughts are consumed by the evening ahead and the anticipation that hangs in the air. I wish Paul could read my mind and tell me all the things going on in his, what we'd do tonight, why he has that look of mischief in his eyes. I can scarcely sit still, or form thoughts from the anticipation of what comes when the evening slows, and comes to an end.

Our small talk mingles with the clinking of silverware and the gentle murmur of other diners.

We order our starters and mains, and Paul hands me the wine list.

"Are you trying to get me drunk again?" I playfully remark.

He chuckles and responds, "Do you think it would work?"

"Well, if you are trying, I certainly expect more than just a phone call to end the night this time," I tease, a mischievous twinkle in my eye. He shakes his head, his ears reddening.

I select a bottle of wine from the list. "Let's make it just one bottle tonight, so we can savour every moment. I want a clear-ish head this evening. It's been far too long since I've had a night out like this."

As the food begins to arrive, we continue our conversation, comfortably chatting about everything and anything. Paul asks about my dress and shopping trip, and I share the story of the lingerie from Victoria's Secret and the strap situation, playfully revealing, "You can see which way I went in the end."

"Oh, the hardship," he responds with a grin. "I'm sure we'll manage." but I see him looking at my décolletage, his eyes hungry. A surge of power runs through me.

The evening drifts along as we enjoy our meal and each other's company. The dessert trolley arrives, followed by coffee.

"Let me know when you're ready to head back. I'll need to call for the car a few minutes ahead," Paul is smiling, and I see where his mind is at.

"Why not call it now? We can always grab a drink in the hotel bar, or not..." I suggest, my eagerness palpable.

The car arrives, and once again, Paul graciously opens the door for me. We make our way back to the hotel, and as we enter, he asks, "Would you like a glass of wine?"

"Yes, but I want you more. So, let's skip the bar," I reply with a playful tone, holding him by his lapel, urging him to walk with me.

"Alright, give me a minute," he says, and unsticks himself from me and heads towards the bar. I watch as he retrieves a bottle of wine and two glasses before walking back to me.

"Now who said you can't have both?" he says, his eyes sparkling with anticipation and affection.

***

As we enter my room, Paul sets the wine on the dresser loudly, and I gracefully slip off my wrap before we are entwined in an embrace. Paul pulls me in, one arm around my exposed back and the other tenderly caressing the side of my face as he leans in for a kiss. It starts off gentle, but soon grows deeper and more passionate.

Feeling his hand on my back, holding me firmly and protectively, sends shivers down my spine. He confesses, "I wanted to do that since the moment I saw you step off the lift."

114

His fingers find their way into my hair, and he looks at me lovingly as he softly kisses my neck.

He teases me playfully, "Seems like a shame to ruin all the effort you went through with your hair today." He says, running his fingers languidly through my hair.

I smirk, "The only shame will be if my hair doesn't have the just-fucked look soon," I blurt out, surprising even myself with my boldness. But I mean every word.

I boldly push his jacket off his shoulders and tug at his tie, needing to feel his skin against mine. Paul takes control and spins me around, his arms wrapping around my waist, pulling me close as his lips find my neck from behind. My head tilts back, giving him full access to my erogenous zones.

His other hand is now between us, working on unbuttoning his shirt while he continues to shower me with kisses. My heart skips a beat as he discards his shirt, his bare chest now pressing against my back. I can't resist reaching around to undo his belt, hurrying to undress him.

I'm working on his belt, but he pulls me even closer, and his hand glides up my back, reaching to release the strap of my dress. With a gentle tug, my dress falls off my shoulders, hanging loosely at my waist, held up only by his arm wrapped around me. His other hand slips under my arm, crossing over my chest, and I gasp softly as his warm palm cups my breast, sending shivers down my spine. My nipples harden into pointy hills, inviting his touch.

I gasp and arch my back and hear his whispered question, "You okay?"

My breath hitches- his question barely registering- and I nod through my desire. "Don't stop, please. I want you," I gasp, my words filled with raw need.

He releases his grip on my waist and turns me; my dress falls to the floor, and I kick it away. My body tingles with anticipation as he takes me in, his eyes locking onto mine, and we both know there's no turning back now.

I finally have the chance to look at him again. I tug for the last time and pull his belt open, overwhelmed by the urgency to have him closer. As I release his pants, he takes my mouth and kisses me passionately. Gently, he leans me back onto the bed, his eyes filled with longing.

Standing before me, he pushes his pants down, revealing his desire straining against the fabric of his shorts. I can't help but feel a surge of excitement as I watch him undress, his every move sending ripples of anticipation through me. I lick my bottom lip, impatient.

With a tender touch, he takes off my heels, caressing my legs as he goes. Moving back over me, he captures my lips in another kiss, this one hot and passionate.

"I want to taste and savour every inch of you," he murmurs, his mouth wet on my skin, and his whispered words send shivers down my spine.

His lips journey across my neck, trailing down to my chest. With each soft kiss, my body tingles with delight, and as he takes my nipples between his lips, it's a blissful yet agonising sensation that leaves me wanting more.

His lips continue their journey, moving down my body, and his hand follows, gently tracing over my stomach. My heart races with anticipation, and I can't help but moan softly as I feel his touch. With every movement, he's building up an exquisite tension, and I can barely contain my desire for him.

His hands gently trace over my panties, feeling the undeniable evidence of my arousal. I squirm with anticipation as he kisses me over the delicate lace, following the tantalising path of the panty line. His wet mouth lodges over the dampening fabric, and I moan. The sensation is electrifying, and I can feel my heart racing.

With a seductive smile, he takes hold of the sides of my panties, and I lift my hips to help him slide them off. He continues to shower me with kisses, driving me wild with desire. As the last barrier is removed, he buries his face between my legs, tasting me with an intoxicating fervour. I gasp and moan, my body quivering with pleasure as he explores every inch of my essence.

"I want you inside me," I whisper, my voice heavy with need.

With an effort at patience, he sheds his shorts, revealing his throbbing erection. I reach out, unable to resist, and wrap my hand around his length.

"I've been dreaming of this moment all week," I moan and grin like a Cheshire cat, and his reaction is immediate. I feel a surge of satisfaction knowing that I have been on his mind just as much.

He positions himself on top of me, and I eagerly part my legs, inviting him to enter. My fingers knot in his hair, guiding him towards me, and the moment our bodies join, it's like a symphony of pleasure.

"Oh, my God," a moan escapes my throat.

He starts to move, and a wave of pleasure washes over me, and I can't help but surrender to loud moaning. Pleasure builds in my stomach, arcing through my back, down to my legs.

"I don't know if I can last long," He grits out, his strokes slow and long.

"We have plenty of time and a long night ahead," I grin, encouraging him to let go and enjoy the moment. In the same moment, like a surprise, I'm at the edge of the precipice, and in surprise I fall, loud and appreciative of the man above me.

For the first time in what feels like forever, I feel cherished and adored. He moves slowly and tenderly, his focus solely on pleasuring me. It's a new experience, and I find myself lost in the sensations he evokes.

His body tenses, and I know he's close to climaxing. I wrap my arms around him, holding him close as he releases inside me. I shower him with affectionate kisses.

As we lay together, our bodies entwined, he pulls me in close, and I rest my head against his chest. "This is an amazing night," I murmur, my heart filled with contentment. We're sprawled over each other, relishing the afterglow of our passion.

After a little while, I feel him harden against me, and a knowing smile creeps across my lips. He's ready for another round, and I'm more than willing to oblige. With a playful glint in my eye, I look up at him, knowing that the night has only just begun, and there's plenty more pleasure to explore together.

***

For the next two hours, our time is consumed by passionate kisses, tender caresses, and discovering and exploring each other's bodies. He counts moles on my body, and I run my hands across the planes of chest hair, nuzzling, enjoying and embracing the deep connection that has come to grow between us. Every touch ignites a spark, and every kiss deepens our desire.

When we eventually make love again, the intensity of it is unrivaled, as I submit to the pleasure and sensory tingles that overwhelm me. The room echoes with the cries of my pleasure.

In contrast to before, this time there is no rush to reach the finish line. Our lovemaking is a symphony of passion and desire, orchestrated with a profound connection. We move in perfect synchronicity, one body, one life. Paul is an attentive and passionate lover, engaging my senses and igniting a fire within me that makes me lose my mind. We get into a delightful rhythm, surrendering ourselves to the waves of pleasure, both physically and emotionally, as we explore new depths of intimacy together.

Once the tide breaks, and I slowly come to my senses again, I find myself consumed by bliss and satisfaction. Our bodies intertwined, we lay spent and breathless, savoring the aftermath of our intense lovemaking. The room is filled with a sense of contentment, a deep and profound connection that transcends the physical.

"Stay," I murmur sleepily, as the sun starts to break through the night.

I longed to wake up by his side, to bask in the warmth of his presence as a new day arrived.

"Alright, let me put in an order for breakfast," he whispers, and I nod, nuzzling into the crook of his neck.

118

In a couple of hours, Paul wakes me, and we take a bath together. Both of us relaxing in white robes, quietly playing with each other's bodies when there's a knock on the door. Paul gets the door, and the sound of wheels rolling lets me know our breakfast trolley has arrived. The enticing aroma of coffee wafts in the room as we indulge in breakfast in bed, savoring each bite and relishing in the casual intimacy of our togetherness.

Paul licks a chunk of jam off my lips, and I kiss him deeply.

"Such a shame we have to go to work," I lament, and sigh, "At least it's not me who has to do the walk of shame to their hotel," I tease him playfully.

He smiles mysteriously and shakes his head.

"What's so funny?" I ask him.

"The walk won't be that bad. I am only 4 doors down the corridor." He flicks my ear.

"What?" I am so confused right now.

With a mischievous grin, he reveals his secret. "I actually changed my hotel booking on Monday to stay here. I was hoping that our night together would unfold as beautifully as it did. It's much more convenient being in the same hotel." He kisses me, proving his point.

I chuckle, appreciating his foresight. "Smart man," I moan, kissing him again.

We get done with the breakfast, and Paul suggests we meet half an hour later at reception. Once he leaves for his room, I lay out my ironed outfit for work, a casual ensemble and quickly get into it. When I went down, once ready, Paul was already leaning against the counter, waiting for me.

"Taxi will be here in five minutes. Let's commute together to the office."

"No posh car today," I joke, "You're slipping now that you've had your wicked way with me." I laugh.

"Ah, take a look in the mirror and you will know why." he says, and I know he's talking about my just-fucked hairstyle I am wearing to the office today.

And my mind goes back to last night, his fingers in my hair, his lips on my skin...

I gasp, and find him staring at me, no doubt knowing what I'd just thought of.

In that moment, I realised that Paul is unlike any solicitor I've encountered before. He possesses a delightful sense of humor, a cheeky playfulness that sets him apart. Yet, he remains a true gentleman, displaying genuine care and consideration without a trace of arrogance.

***

As we make our way to the office, a noticeable shift occurs in our demeanor as we both adopt our professional facades. Stepping inside the conference room, we drop our bags with a sense of relief, grateful for the casual Friday attire that allows for a more relaxed atmosphere.

Paul heads towards the conference room to begin tackling the boxes, while I settle into Ralph's office, ready to dive into the tasks at hand. We work diligently, fully immersed in our respective assignments. Paul suggests we meet at lunchtime to share our progress and findings. I notice him feeling a bit curt, withdrawn, and an eerie feeling takes over me. I try to disregard it and focus on the work at hand.

Over lunch, I sense a hint of nervous restlessness from Paul. Curiosity gets the best of me, and I ask him directly, "Are you okay? What's wrong?"

He shakes his head, "Last night was truly amazing. The entire evening and waking up next to you... I didn't think I'd experience that again, waking up next to a beautiful woman and wanting to stay there. But this morning, I couldn't help but wonder... after such an incredible night, do you still want me? Do you have any regrets?" There was open vulnerability and sincerity in his eyes, although his words catch me off guard momentarily, I quickly gather my thoughts and respond with unwavering honesty.

"You made me feel like a woman in ways I haven't felt in a long time. The excitement and anticipation I feel when I think of you, your texts, and our time together, combined with the incredible night we shared, only solidifies what I know in my heart. Yes, I want you and all this wherever it goes. From laughs about rope cuffs, to sharing a coffee and a kiss. So, darling, rest assured that you're not going anywhere. You're stuck with me."

Even I surprised myself with the depth of my emotions and the sincerity of my declaration.

Paul's response is filled with a mixture of relief and excitement. "Okay," he replies, his smile growing wider. "Let's do this. Let's see where this adventure and Ralph's mysteries take us."

Suddenly, a thought crosses my mind and I grow serious, "I do have one major issue, though," Paul immediately sombers and I continue, "As an accountant, it will pain me to pay for two separate rooms when we both know you'll be in mine every night." I confess with a playful grin.

Paul chuckles, understanding the predicament. "We can't exactly reveal the true nature of our relationship to Jack and Leonard. They'll think the Ice Queen is melting, and my colleagues will likely be shocked at this side of me. But don't worry, I have a plan."

Intrigued, I raise an eyebrow, "What do you mean? What are you planning?" I inquire, a curious smile forming on my lips. Paul simply smiles back and winks, leaving me filled with curiosity for the surprises he has in store.

Next, we discuss announcing me as the head of overseeing day-to-day business. Helen and Nicola are already debriefed, but a professional announcement would be sent out to let all the other employees know.

Suddenly, I remember Nicola's update.

"Also, there's some trade expo in Holland that Ralph attended regularly. It's coming up and Nicola wants to know who will be sent this time, now that circumstances have changed. There is a usual buyer for the shops who goes, but Ralph for some reason always went to this one. There's still some time, but it's crucial things like this are sorted out beforehand," I recount to him, and he nods, thinking. "Let the buyer take care of it as usual, but let's talk to her and see if there was a reason, she knew Ralph went there."

At 2:30, we have a meeting scheduled with Nicola and Helen. Paul reiterates that all inquiries and instructions should now be directed to me on a day-by-day basis.

"I'm available, right here for any necessary assistance, but having a designated point of contact will streamline communication and ensure efficiency."

"Understood," He smiles warmly.

"Oh, and also, since we have you both here, perhaps you can assist us further. You've done a fantastic job with all the company paperwork and business analysis, and we are incredibly grateful for your support. However, when it comes to Ralph's non-company assets, it becomes more challenging. Can you provide any insights into how he managed those?" It was a clever technique, because honestly, we were at a loss how to go about it, so why not ask the people who might have an inkling?

Nicola sighs, "To be honest, Ralph was incredibly private, and I never came across any non-work-related paperwork. He was a creature of habit, arriving at the office before 8 am and leaving around 7 pm. The only thing I found intriguing was his consistent two-hour lunch break from twelve to two in the afternoon. He would leave the office at twelve and return at two. For someone who worked so diligently, and was so anal about punctuality, it seemed unusual to me, but he was never accountable to us, and it was not our place to question him. He was an excellent boss, fair and kind, but he kept his personal affairs private."

Helen nods her agreement, "I also noticed his lengthy lunch break, and I knew better than to inquire about it. I never knew where he went during that time. I apologise for not being able to provide more assistance."

"Oh, it's alright, we'll work something out," Paul smiles charmingly.

I take my head in my hands. Uncovering information about Ralph's non-company assets will prove to be the most challenging task. However, we remain determined to explore all avenues and seek further clues that may shed light on the personal aspect of his life.

Once Nicola and Helen departed, I shared something else with Paul that I'd noticed in the expense and salary sheets, "You know, it's quite intriguing. I couldn't help but notice that Ralph never actually took a salary from the company. His withdrawals were minimal and seemed to be solely for business purposes. It makes me wonder, what was he relying on for his personal finances?"

There is no answer to mine or Paul's questions yet, so we get back to work, trying to unearth any clues.

As the workday came to an end, we made our way to the train together, and enjoyed a pleasant dinner during the journey home. When the train got near to our station, a tinge of disappointment crept over me as I realised that I wouldn't be seeing Paul for a whole week.

And then, unbidden came a rush of memories from the previous night, washing over me, and I couldn't help but feel a renewed sense of excitement for next week.

As we prepared to part ways upon reaching our destination, Paul gently placed his hand on the small of my back. "Have a wonderful weekend, and I'll be sure to text you. But please don't feel obligated to reply. I understand that you could be tied up."

"I wish. Maybe another time?", I say innocently, and his eyes twinkle with amusement.

"Ah, the box of further exploration," he chuckles.

"I may be just a boring accountant, but who knows where this adventure might lead if you tempt me." We shared a laugh, bidding each other farewell before going our separate ways.

Chapter 9

The weekend passed in the same monotonous fashion as many others before it. Somehow, weekends didn't feel like breaks anymore, it was just added stress. It was the two long, silent days punctuated with piles of laundry, the kids' and Mark's demands that I needed a break from now. The only meaningful conversations I had all weekend was the kids occasionally extorting me for money, or whatever they had seen on the internet and wanted now.

Mark spent the weekend hiding out, watching the game and the various commentaries on it afterwards. It didn't prick me how he did not afford me a moment of his time, a single glance to notice my hair. The freshly done look was in its last days and the blow-dry had fallen flat but by then the rich colour of the dye had deepened and developed beautifully.

I had put my new dress in the back of the wardrobe where I knew Mark would never find or see it, so I wouldn't have to answer any questions. The lingerie, on the other hand... well if he sees it, or asks me about it, it would be easy to say that I bought it and wore it for him, and he ignored me. *Good to see you noticed it in the drawer and not on your wife.* I was trying not to be bitter about him, about how pathetic he is, but my anger did boil over sometimes.

Now that I had finally felt desired after ages and remembered what fun felt like, I was getting more and more annoyed thinking about how he neglected me. I also found myself feeling less guilty, because I deserved this.

Seeing the dress and lingerie also got me thinking more and more about Paul, about what had happened when I was wearing the dress and lingerie. It led to us exchanging some playful pictures and reliving some of the heavenly Thursday night over text messages.

I got into work early on Monday, thankful for the chance to be back out of the house and saw an email from Paul. I was just in cc'd into an email addressed to his boss and Jack. I checked and saw that it was sent late on Friday night. I clicked on the notification and started reading.

Subject: Update on Ralph Michael's Estate

"The last two days in London were enlightening both as to what we found and what we did not.

We met with Rachel, Ralph's cleaner, on Thursday morning. She was very cooperative, but we seem to have made no progress on finding the location of Ralph's safe. Upon us asking Rachel if she was aware of a safe's location, she came up blank and did not even know of a safe's existence in Ralph's home or office. We have at present asked her to dispose of all clothing and linens and the contents of the kitchen cabinets. We have also cleared all paperwork from the apartment after going through it. Our hope is that the apartment will be effectively cleared out very soon except for the furniture and the art pieces.

There is little by way of personal papers still turning up. The company paperwork is in good condition, and I think the accountants have a good handle on that. We advised key staff that the reporting structure is now to Maria Holmes, and they seemed very content with the arrangement. We assured them I was there also for assistance, should the need come up.

I asked Helen and Nicola about his assets and paperwork that are not related to his businesses. Neither knew anything, according to them, he happened to be a very private man and an even more reserved employer. The only comment of note was that he worked from 8 AM to 7 PM but took a 2-hour lunch every day without exception, from 12 PM to 2 PM. However, it appears nobody knew where he went. This may be nothing of significance, but he was obviously going somewhere, so I will be keeping this lead active.

As executors of the estate, I am concerned about costs since we will ultimately be accountable to someone. We are incurring high hotel bills which, although necessary, is a worry considering the gravity of the situation and how much longer it might take us here to wrap this up.

Therefore, based on these concerns and from some financial calculations I have performed, I would like to make the following proposal. DAF would need to check and confirm if I am correct here and if it is acceptable to them and feasible for the company.

The apartment is an asset of the company, and currently has ten years left in the lease. I am not sure why such a long lease was agreed to, or whether the idea was to keep it or for it to be sold eventually. Either way, we don't have a function for the apartment currently and as an asset, it should be put into use. However, the apartment needs a freshening-up to maximize its value.

I would suggest, as the apartment is now empty, that we get it cleaned up, repainted and renovated to an agreeable condition, for whatever we decide to do with it. If the beds or at least mattresses are then replaced, new linens and towels are added, this could be used as a London base when we are working down in London.

There is already a cleaner at the apartment who comes in once a week and takes care of the household and does all the cleaning and upkeep. Using the place as a London base would cut down hotel bills as well since the cost of repainting and basic beds and linen would be small in comparison to City Centre hotel costs for a couple nights a week for the foreseeable future, that we are currently incurring. Irrespective of who is sent down, it would allow a place to work away from the offices, without prying eyes.

It is a two-bedroom apartment, with a kitchen, bathroom and Wi-Fi. Personally, I don't mind moving out of hotels and into the apartment when I'm staying down in London because of all the tourists in the City Centre and because I tend to dine out anyway. But the accountants may prefer hotels and are entitled to the same, as they wish. This is merely meant as just a suggestion and purely depends on whether everyone agrees with my idea. This is in keeping with Mr. Michaels' ethos, since he was not a fan of extravagance. Also, I believe that having a dedicated London base might prove to be more productive than working out of hotel rooms. The company can be billed for everything as it is a company asset, and they get all the bills as is for its upkeep and maintenance.

Please have Maria Holmes or whoever you find appropriately advise you in conjunction with the accountants if my tax logic is correct.

It might be a good time to get into contact with the shops as well and to arrange to visit each property in the next few weeks. We can run everything here and coordinate by group email here, or I am happy to just coordinate diaries with Ms. Holmes and we will work it out between us and report back. Either way, my observations and comments are meant as recommendations.

Regards,

Paul Bridges.

I gasp and then smile. Oh, I like how his mind is working here… and sent Friday evening too! So cheeky of him not to tell me.

I wonder if I should reply to the email, giving my approval, in a professional capacity, of course. But I decide to wait to hear from Jack first and feign ignorance. I opened Snapchat instead and send Paul a message.

Maria: *Setting up a love nest in London, are we? And asking our bosses for their approval no less… Oh, you're not just a pretty face. I'm curious to know what else you have planned for the apartment.*

Paul: *Heaven forbids… surely as an accountant, you can see the merit in this? Think of all the huge costs we'll be saving. Shocked that you would suggest ulterior motives from me. After all, it's a two-bedroom apartment and if we happen to overlap there, then…*

Maria: *And here I was thinking you were just looking to have me all to yourself. A girl cannot but wish. Oh, to feel wanted. Although, I was thinking two rooms might be wasted on us since you're not going to be getting out of mine.*

Paul: *Well, let's see what your reply to my email is or what Jack says. I won't care one way or the other and I'll just say fine to whatever you say.*

Maria: *Well, I did spot Ralph's four-poster bed, which is sort of unusual for a man on his own. But I can certainly think of a few ways I could put it to use? You could help me with it too… So, my vote is to change the mattress and keep the bed.*

Paul: *Oh, you're getting brave here… and what else?*

Maria: *Easy, see if we can find a use for his cuffs or hook you found or whatever happens to turn up when we're there… Oh, I am brave… and aching to be with you, to be honest. The idea of the apartment has gotten my mind in overdrive already.*

Paul: *Well, I've done my part ... it's all up to you now. See if you can get the sign off on it and let me know what would be the reaction at home? With the apartment and maybe us staying the odd night in London?*

Maria: *Feck home... Mark doesn't care enough to ask, and I can simply say I am using the company apartment in London. I am there too often, and hotels can't be justified when the apartment is sitting empty and furnished. I'll tell them there will only be some boring lawyer here and there sometimes, but it probably wouldn't even overlap with my schedule.*

Paul: *Even just to be able to leave clothes behind when we're coming or going and if there is anything we want for us ... it's all just there.*

Maria: *Okay, got to go. Jacks just summoned me to the Monday morning scheduling meeting...*

I arrived at the scheduling meeting, and we went through the work at hand. The meeting was mainly me catching everyone up on the progress we had made on Michael's estate, followed by an overview of where we were still struggling, and a discussion on how the company was doing overall. I also outlined the smaller projects I was working on and gave an update on all ends. There was nothing much too exciting from any other department, and the meeting was thankfully over in half an hour.

I was poring over some notes I had made during the meeting and when it ended, I gathered my papers and turned to leave as Jack called me back. "Morning, Maria. Good work in London. Really glad to hear of the progress."

"Morning, Jack. Thanks! Anything I can do for you today?" I ask, feeling a conversation coming up.

"Can we have a chat about Michael's estate and companies?" he asked. "Looks like it'll be a lot of work, and you'll be having to spend a lot of time in London for the next few months."

I nodded. "Yes," I said. "But at least the companies can afford us."

"Yeah, so about that, the lawyers were on this morning and I don't know if you saw the email this morning from Paul Bridges?" said Jack.

"I saw it but didn't get a chance to read it yet. Haven't been able to make time this morning," I said coolly, indicating the paperwork in my arms.

"Well, they seem a tad worried about the costs here and suggested we bill ourselves directly to the company for all your work. Therefore, reduce the estate bill in the end," Jack said looking up at me expectantly from the conference table.

"Hmm" I nod thoughtfully. "Makes sense, I suppose. That might be a smart idea."

"There is another part, however, I'm not sure how much you will like it though," he goes on. "They are talking about maybe getting the company apartment decorated a little, renovated and redone perhaps. In order to establish that as a work base and no longer put everyone in hotels in London."

I decided to play a little put out and pretend to consider it seriously. "Oh, I don't know … the apartment is very dated and would need everything redone in it. Plus, I must admit I'm getting used to the room service and my laundry done."

"Look, read the email from Paul and see what is suggested," he pushes. "If you agree in principle, let me know. But if you prefer hotels, let me know too, and I'll fight for it. But it would make life easier if we could cut some costs and bill it all to the company. The lawyers brought us into this job, not our clients and I want to appear cooperative."

"Alright, I'll check Mr. Bridges' email and let you know what I think," I say.

Jack smiles at me, "If you have any particular requests for the apartment, you just let me know, all right?"

I let the morning pass by and call Jack at three in the afternoon, "So Jack, I looked at the email… and if it helps you, I think it's a fine idea. But it does need to have new mattresses and all new linen, and the cleaner must keep coming regularly. The apartment needs painting and must be made more comfortable. It's not bad, and truthfully well located, just dated and a tad dilapidated."

"That's great, exactly what I wanted to hear from you," Jack replies happily, happier than even me at this news, I laugh to myself. "Can you send a quick reply to the email and outline that, so it is coming from you. And thank you, Maria… this does help cut costs here."

I write out the email and before I sent it, decide to send Paul a message. I pick up my phone and decide to drop him a call instead.

Paul picks up, "Hello?"

I just come straight with it, "Well, hello, lover. How are you?"

"Mmm. you're on speaker here, I'm in a meeting right now."

Panic hits me like a bucket of ice-cold water and I freeze. After a few moments of silence, Paul chuckles, "I'm only joking. Sorry, darling. How are you doing?"

"You made my heart nearly jump out of my mouth there. Now I'm nearly tempted to not tell you my exciting news. But anyway, Jack asked me about your email this morning after the meeting and said that he's coming under pressure to reduce costs a little. He wants to be seen to keep ye happy, and I pretended I did not see your email yet. He said the apartment use would be helpful if I was happy with it but left it to me. I made him work for it, so he thinks I'm doing him a favour. You know I'm after the new partner position also, so I want to appear co-operative.

Anyway, Jack asked that I reply to your email and include my list of requests."

"Mm, your requests. We know you're not shy about coming forward, so what are you asking for?"

"A giant freezer to store you once I'm through with you," I joke.

He snorts, "Seriously, though, that's great … But what do you want to ask for? We know where your mind goes."

"Why Mr. Bridges, what are you suggesting? Mind you, I'm sure we can have our own fun along the way. This is fun, exciting, even." I said, pleased. "So, anything you think I should include in my wish list that you haven't?"

"I don't think so, just say maybe accommodation may be covered," Paul adds thoughtfully. "But eating out is allowed on expenses, not expected to self-cater and if you need anything for the apartment, you can simply order via the company, within reason."

I smiled into the phone. "I'll add all that and send the email your way soon. So, how is your day going? I've booked my train tickets for this week's trip."

"Oh, I haven't booked mine yet. I was waiting to see your reply to my email. Any chance you could stay from Friday night until the Saturday evening train? I was thinking maybe you could hang on for Saturday and go shopping for the apartment and we'll get everything we needed to get that out of the way? There'll be no time when we're working during the week. We could have a nice day, relaxing Friday night, lazy breakfast, and just wander in the London shops Saturday before coming home."

"Let me see, I'll check with my sitters, but that's a great idea. I'll suggest it in the email too. Otherwise, how are you?" I ask.

"I'm good, I'm really happy now." I could just picture him smiling. "Now, I must head off here. Duty calls."

I make a list of all the things the new apartment would need, and also all the other requests to be made. Then I wrote the email, making sure to ensure it came across as me generously doing Jack and the others a favour by agreeing to the idea. I replied to the email and asked for the extra day in London to buy what was needed, as well as all of Paul's requests.

A while later, an email pinged my computer again. Paul had emailed back:

Re: Update on Ralph Michael's Estate
I'm perfectly happy for Ms. Maria Holmes to sort out whatever she wants and make the necessary arrangements for the apartment. I'm happy to simply go along. All I require is that a fresh mattress be ordered for the second room and fresh linens too. I do not want to use someone else's. On my next trip down to London, I'll make notes of anything else that may be needed in the apartment and let Ms. Holmes know.

Regards,
Paul Bridges

From the email, I saw how Paul was intentionally trying to make our relationship seem as professional as possible by avoiding the possibility of being seen doing this with me.

Chapter 10

A new Thursday saw us both reserve the same seats on the train again. As I boarded, I noticed the same friendly man from last week, and before I could look away, he spotted me and smiled and waved. He started walking toward me, and I cringed, trying to think of a way to dissuade his friendly attempts. The man was perfectly fine, and normally I would encourage some friendly engagement, but these were not normal times. I was with Paul and did not want to think of anyone other than him.

Just as the man approached- ready to strike up a conversation, I'm sure- I felt a gentle touch in my hip. Subtle, but enough to feel saved, and I finally sighed in relief. Not sure if the other man noticed the touch, but I think he did, Tension drained from my body as I looked up sideways to see Paul following my line of sights, a mischievous smile on his face as the approaching man appeared confused.

"Ah, I feel like I'm just in time to grab my lucky seat," he spoke loudly, and I was sure the man could hear him, too, "Hey, you wanna get breakfast two weeks in a row? People might start to talk," he jokes the last part and I laugh.

The man stops dead in his tracks, and takes a seat elsewhere, his eyes on us as we walk together, to our designated seats.

"Come on, now, that's just terrible! You're tormenting that poor man," I say, my mind already picturing our day together.

When we reached the office, Nicola immediately ushered us inside the conference room, and sat us down.

"So, I had a weird call yesterday. It was some man, asking if Paul could call him back. I asked him what it was about, and he just said it's private and not about the company," Nicola talks haltingly, a deep 'v' between her brows. She looks at us questioningly, as if we might recognize this strange man.

If it was not about the company, and this man wanted to talk to Paul, could it be that our secret had leaked? Panic swims in my brain, and my eyes widen as I seek any expression of concern on Paul's face.

"Did he say anything else? What does he want to talk about?" Paul asks calmly, trying very hard not to appear worried.

"No, nothing else. Call him back to talk about Ralph, he said," Nicola shrugs.

A huge sigh of relief escaped me inconspicuously, and I could finally see straight.

Nicola hands a sticky note to Paul; Adam Wright is scrawled over it in a neat script along with the caller's number.

"Alright, I'll get on this," Paul murmurs, and nods at Nicola and me, and the two leave the conference room together. I sip at my coffee, rolling my eyes at panicking uselessly. It was almost hilarious. It also made me realise that all I really care about is the office coming to find out about Paul and me, not my husband. It should've saddened me, but I'm past that stage of mourning my marriage now.

I sip on my coffee and organise my workstation in the fifteen minutes it takes for Paul to wrap up his call with the mysterious Adam Wright. He peeks inside the half-shut door, and then comes inside and walks to me with a spring in his step. I look at him, bemused.

"Can you spare an hour?" He asks me cryptically.

"Sure," I frown, and get my going-out shoes on.

As we venture out of the office, I'm still unaware where we're headed. Paul pauses at the office door, "You say you are open-minded, let's put it to test, shall we?"

I shake my head, nervous where this was going, but excited at the same time. What was he doing in office hours?

He looks at me intently before continuing, "Have you ever paid attention to the businesses on the ground floor?"

I ponder for a moment before responding, "Well, there's the coffee shop that we both know. A travel agent. And what appears to be an adult shop? Fet Boutique. Why in the financial district escapes me. I've only been to the coffee shop, though."

Paul's eyes lit up with a mischievous glimmer. "Well, we're going to remedy that today. On ahead to the adult shop," he announces like we're going on a voyage.

Taken aback, I exclaim, "What! I certainly didn't expect that."

Paul chuckled in response, "And yet you didn't say no. Quite interesting. But before that, about the gentleman who rang. Adam Wright manages the shop in question and asked for time to discuss a few things. When I inquired further, he asked what's going to happen with the shop now that Ralph has passed. So, apparently, Ralphs owns it and has an office there as well. Naturally, I suggested we pay a visit and have a conversation."

I was still processing the new information, but I half-joke, "No shopping, then? That's a bit disappointing. But seriously, though, I never saw that coming. Ralph owns an adult toy shop, huh?" I baulk, still processing the unexpected turn of events.

A short lift ride down, and a few paces, and we arrive at the shop.

Adam Wright, manager of Fetish Boutique greets us at the door, and takes us inside to his room at the back of the shop. I look curiously at the paraphernalia in the shop, wide-eyed and awe-struck. I wonder if I could even guess what half of these things are used for.

The interior was a vibrant mix of colours, textures, and enticing visuals. Vibrators, dildos, and other pleasure-inducing devices were showcased in all shapes and sizes, each with its own description at the bottom. Lingerie, both delicate and alluring, hung from racks, inviting my curiosity and an itch for exploration. I ached to get a feel of the fabric on my fingers, but we were here on another mission. It was obvious I'd never been in a place like this before. *Ralph owned this place?* I look around more: the walls were adorned with provocative artwork and suggestive images, creating an atmosphere of both playfulness and desire.

The layout of the shop was carefully organised, with different sections dedicated to various interests and preferences. There were discreet corners behind silk curtains for more intimate and private discussions, allowing customers to explore their desires with the guidance of knowledgeable staff. The soft murmur of conversations, whispered questions, and giggles filled the air, adding to the lively atmosphere.

In one corner, a display of BDSM accessories caught my attention. Leather restraints, floggers, and bondage gear entice my adventurous soul, just something about it promised a world of heightened sensations and excitement. Nearby, a collection of sensual massage oils, candles, and luxurious body care products made me think of indulging in some intimate moments with Paul. Before I got carried away, I hurriedly follow Mr. Wright and Paul into a room with a plaque on the door that read 'Manager'.

In the back of the shop, Adam Wright, a well-spoken, well-kept man in his fifties explains how he's been managing this store for over two decades. Ralph had entrusted the manager with the running of the store, along with all other duties, essentially ceasing to be involved around ten, eleven years ago, Adam recalled. And since then, Adam had been running it independently; as long as the store remained profitable and self-sustained, Ralph did not interfere.

"He was sort of a friend, Ralph. His office is in the back, accessible through here, or from a side entrance. He visited every day for a couple of hours, and we'd often have tea, while I updated him on the shop's affairs. He had the sole keys to the office, so he could visit whenever," Adam said casually, unaware that Paul's ears had perked up. He'd catch the scent of the same bit that I did.

"You were Ralph's friend? He was a very private man, I don't think any acquaintance has called him a friend yet," Paul said nonchalantly, trying to make Adam talk.

But at Paul's further digging, Adam became guarded.

"Of sorts, yes. Ralph was a private man, yes, but also lonely. We spent so many years together. I'd like to respect his privacy, and not divulge anything privileged unless it's pertinent to your work." Adam said tightly, "He was a good man to me, and I ought to return the favour now that he's no more."

"Alright, let's talk business, then. What are the accounts like? Profits, stock, margins?" I direct my questions at him.

"Profits are good, business is thriving as much as it has. No huge overhead, no rent since Ralph owned the building. We are fully functional and profitable, stocks are good, and everything is smooth. But the question arises, what is going to happen to this shop, and the staff, now that, well, now that circumstances have changed?"

"No need to worry about that, Mr. Wright. Everything's business as usual. Although I should tell you that I am serving as the executor of estate, and Ms. Holmes here will be overseeing all matters regarding company management and operations. If there's anything you need to discuss, please leave a message at the reception. We are here in London Thursday through Friday."

The manager nods, and we talk a little about account sheets and I ask him to get me the previous year's accounts and statements in the coming week. Next, he asks if we'd like to see around, a glint of mischief in his eyes, and we oblige, curious. Careful, not to appear too interested, we glance around. The shop seemed to offer a wide range of items, ranging from scary-looking 'toys' to scanty leather 'clothes'. There was a distinct rubber-like smell in the air, and I could follow it to the various suspended intriguing objects from the ceilings and walls, and mannequins in harnesses. My finger brushed over the price tag of one very complicated looking harness donned by a winking mannequin; and I was properly astonished how much people were spending on their leather- more than what I typically spent on my work clothes.

After a brief exploration of the shop, we conclude our visit by exchanging pleasantries with the manager. Paul expresses our gratitude for Adam's assistance and his decision of reaching out to us. I inform him that I'll return later to gain a better understanding of how things operated within the establishment, and to collect the account sheets he had promised. With a final handshake, we bid farewell and made our way out of the shop.

Paul and I walk to the coffee shop, still disbelieving of where we'd just been. It was hilarious in a way. My work life had never been as interesting as this before.

Paul gets our coffees, and sliding mine towards me, he begins, "Well, I don't think you should be disappointed about not getting to shop there *yet*. It looks like we are now running that too, so we'll be in and out, I believe," He smiles quizzingly, "Honestly, I never saw that coming. What else is out there we are yet to discover about Ralph, I wonder? The plot thickens."

Suddenly I remembered something.

"Hey, you remember that set of keys we found in his office desk drawer upstairs? I never did figure out what they were for, but I left them there. I wonder if they are for the Boutique office, or perhaps the shop?" I gush to him with an excited glint in my eye.

"Yeah? Do you think so? Do you wanna find out?" Paul asks, equally excited.

After several weeks of being stuck between the office, and Ralph's home, we finally had a new place we could redirect our efforts toward.

I rush upstairs, running by a surprised Nicola, but I don't stop to explain. We'll have ample time later. Right now, I needed the keys, and Paul was waiting downstairs.

I retrieve the keys and find Paul in the same spot where I'd left him.

With the keys in hand, we made our way to the side entrance of the building. With a little bit of trial and error, we found the appropriate key, unlocked the door and stepped inside.

The room before us revealed itself as just another office space, furnished with a desk, computer, cabinets, and other essentials. The atmosphere was slightly dim, with dark, wood-paneled walls and no windows. However, the lighting was warm and inviting, casting a cosy glow upon the room. The walls were adorned with tasteful artwork, adding a touch of elegance to the space. In the corner, a large leather armchair stood, accompanied by a floor lamp behind and a footstool in the front. Unlike all other of Ralph's office space, this place felt like a real personal space.

As we explored further, our attention was drawn to the large desk in one corner of the room. In the centre of the table, stood a framed photograph. He gestured at me to come see: an old picture of Ralph with a woman. I could tell from the photograph that the couple were happy and content in each other's company. The woman was undeniably attractive, with a petite frame, and noticeably younger than Ralph. It was an old photograph, evoking a sense of nostalgia. Nearby, on a small table near the armchair, there was another photograph of the same woman by herself. She had a beautiful smile, and it was not difficult to tell that it was for whoever was behind the camera. Paul and I exchanged glances, both wondering who she was. No one around Ralph had ever provided any insight into his personal life, much less a partner. *Where was this woman now?* I wondered.

We continue our exploration, and soon find that the office housed a collection of paperwork related to the properties and private banking that we'd been missing. This was vital data, something that would speed up the process of the appraisal. It was also a treasure trove of information that shed light on Ralph's private affairs. We realised that this was the private office where he spent his dedicated two hours of lunch every day, likely even enjoying it in this woman's company.

Satisfied with our discoveries, but sure there was more to discover, we lock up the office and made our way back to the conference room above. We decided to revisit the new office and delve deeper into its contents when we had more time. I did not take any papers with me yet. With the clock striking noon soon, Paul and I agree to reconvene over lunch to discuss our findings and plan our next steps. The mysteries

139

surrounding Ralph and his hidden life were slowly unravelling, and I couldn't help but feel a mix of excitement which was in good part curiosity.

Paul was working with some people in another department while I was still stuck in the proceedings around company asset appraisal. With new companies popping up like weeds in monsoon, I did not have a minute to lose to get on top of it. A half hour after noon, my phone pings.

The notification is from Paul.

Paul: *Saw a sandwich bar on the corner about a block down, want to meet up there for lunch? Let's go separately, after the mystery call and arriving together today, I don't wanna raise the ladies' curiosity more.*

Me: *Sure, yeah. I will head down now and order ahead for you. See you soon.*

I shut the files in front of me, and stretch my legs, yawning. My phone pings again.

Paul: *Great, I'll be just a few minutes after you.*

***

During our lunchtime discussion, we carefully weigh our options regarding Ralph's personal office and how to handle its contents. It was evident that Ralph had deliberately kept this office hidden from the rest of the staff, which led us to believe that he had his reasons for doing so. Even Nicola and Helen were not aware where he went in his two-hour break, even though it was just downstairs. It seemed Ralph went to a few pains to conceal this part of his life from them. Paul and I concluded that there was no need to involve the office staff in this matter right now, especially since they couldn't offer any additional insights.

Even though the office appeared meticulously organised, almost to the point of an obsessive-compulsive level, it was filled with financial documents, files, and various records that would require thorough sorting and review. My brain was already in overdrive, thinking of all the ways I'd need to index the information. Paul proposed a practical solution — hiring a secretary for a few days who could come in with a scanner solely and independently working in this new office. They would digitise each file, ensuring that they were properly indexed and organised in the same order as found in the office. This would allow us to access the files on the go and on our devices, also enabling our own support staff to analyse the information and follow up on outstanding balances. Simultaneously, the physical office space would remain intact, serving as a potential workspace for us if the need arose.

I suggest that Paul would take the responsibility of speaking with the shop manager.

"Can you make sure Adam understands that it's going to be business as usual? Also, give him your contact number so he knows that's the preferred point of contact. I have a feeling the staff shouldn't know about any of this yet."

"Yeah, I share the same sentiments. Since Ralph kept this separation between the shop and the office, I feel it's only right we do the same. Plus, it's going to be a sight to behold if Adam gets in touch about stocking and storage details of the shop with Helen or Nicola." Paul laughs, and I chuckle.

For sure. It was surprising enough for *me*.

And there was an elephant in the room. The apartment.

Curious about our plan for the place, I ask Paul what he has in mind.

He grinned and replied, "I'm way ahead of you on that one. I contacted Nicola for Rachel's contact number since I found out she's the one responsible for coordinating her cleaning services. I assumed the office had her details, considering they were paying her. And of course, Nicola was on it."

Paul went on to explain that he had spoken to Rachel on Tuesday, requesting that she clean out the apartment as soon as possible. He also inquired if she knew any painters in the area, because we wanted to spruce up the place. It turned out that her husband was a painter, and since Rachel was a long-term employee, she'd have her husband tackle the job next week. They estimated it would take a crew two days to complete two coats of paint.

"I think we should visit the apartment after the work is done to assess its condition and see how else we can liven it up,"

Paul says, and I spot something else in his gaze that vanishes in a split second. He continues, "I need to go in the evening anyway, see how Rachel has done. Need to give the go-ahead on moving the boxes out, preferably to a charity."

"Alright, then, I'll go with you," I say, and curl my pinky around his.

When we arrive at the apartment in the evening, it appears different from before. It felt empty, more than usual, completely devoid of warmth and personality. The paintings and furniture remain, but all personal belongings were packed away and stacked neatly, following Paul's instructions. The main furniture pieces were still usable, although perhaps not to my taste. I hesitated to suggest replacing everything with new furniture just yet, even though the existing one made me feel uncomfortable.

We ventured into the two bedrooms to explore their potential as our living space for the next following weeks. The main bedroom had a commanding presence, dominated by a grand four-poster bed, matching wardrobes, and a chest of drawers, all made of dark timber. An armchair sat in the corner, and a wall-mounted TV completed the setup. The space was sufficient, very big on storage options.

I smile at Paul and playfully remark, "I wonder what your room is like. I should take a look now, since you won't be spending any time there later."

We made our way to the second bedroom, which, in stark contrast, appeared plain and devoid of any personal touches. No painting, not even a vase graced this room. A metal bed frame stood bare, lacking a mattress. A wardrobe and a simple dresser completed the furnishings.

"Perfect for a man. Very functional," I comment. "It seems like a room that was furnished as a bedroom but was never used. Like a guest bedroom, maybe."

"I will make a list of the items we need. Let me know if I'm missing anything. How about you choose the paint colours for the apartment? Uh, about the furnishings. Let's see what Ralph already has, but let's not get too attached to Ralph's previous choices. A few stock pictures for some colour, maybe some artwork could do beautifully," Paul shares his intentions.

I nod, mostly just taking in the space and envisioning how it would seem when Paul and I live here together. The thought stuck in my throat, making it difficult to breathe.

We agreed that leaving one empty hook on the wall would be a prudent decision. After all, we didn't know what had been hanging there, and it might resurface, potentially catching our interest and ultimately the beneficiaries. It seemed a shame to have to replace that hook when there might be a hidden gem waiting to be revealed.

Excited about the prospect of making the apartment more modern and inviting, I took out a notepad and started jotting down the essentials needed to transform the space. As I consider the colour scheme, I share my thoughts with Paul. He simply nods and agrees, giving me free rein to choose whatever colours I felt would create a warm and contemporary ambiance. It was a refreshing level of trust, interest and collaboration between us.

"Now, how about dinner?" Paul asked, breaking my concentration. "Where would you like to go this evening? I presume you booked something nice since it's your turn this week."

I paused for a moment, momentarily taken aback. *Was it my turn? Heck.*

He chuckles, and I realise he's joking.

"Come on, let's head back to the hotel, change, and then we can find a cosy place to dine. Do you have a preference or mood for something special tonight?"

"Not really. Actually, the place where we went the first time, remember? Put our feet up, greasy food and a bottle of wine kinda evening." I say, relishing discussing date plans with a man who actually cares and doesn't make me feel alone when I'm with him.

We make our way back to the hotel, each retreating to our respective rooms to freshen up.

I unzip my bag, and this time, I indulge in the complete set of lingerie that I couldn't wear last time. It felt exquisite against my skin, and the knowledge that I was in such luxurious undergarments underneath the simple flowery dress added a touch of confidence and sensuality to the evening ahead. I couldn't help but smile, appreciating the little moments of delight that life was recently offering me.

As we sat down for dinner, the atmosphere between us was charged with a mix of friendship and flirtation. Engaged in lively conversation, we delved into deeper topics, exploring each other's lives and aspirations more thoroughly than ever. Playfully, I tease Paul by discreetly playing footsy under the table, my eyes sparkling mischievously. Each time the waiter approaches, I intensify my foot's movement, subtly caressing Paul's leg, his inner thigh, going close to the V between his legs, drawing a blush to his cheeks and a stutter to his words.

When the waiter finally leaves, I laugh, unable to endure the absolute delight I feel watching Paul all flustered.

Paul clears his throat and orders another bottle of wine. As he pours, he looks at me closely, "Are you truly okay with all this? Moving into the apartment, everything moving so fast?" he asks, genuine worry etched on his face.

I pause, placing my hand on his to reassure him. "Thank you, Paul, for caring about me, but there's no need to worry. I'm not a delicate flower. I know my own mind, and I'm here because I want to be," I lower my voice, just so he can hear, and resume my foot game under the table "I'm wearing bespoke lingerie right now because I fully expect you to take it off me later," I lick my lip with a playful glint in my eyes.

But he has communicated his concern, and I must put it to rest.

"I chose the apartment because the idea of it, the possibilities it holds, excites me in ways I've never felt before. And even if things don't go as planned, we're both professionals who can work through it," I added, my foot continuing its secret rendezvous beneath the tablecloth, grateful for the oversized fabric that concealed our playful interaction.

Paul's gaze meets mine, and I can sense his concern clouded by desire. The footsie game had heightened the tension between us. "I don't think it will go wrong," he responded, his voice difficult but confident. "We're not working together full-time, so it's okay. Plus, you've brought a newfound energy and passion into my life. The undeniable chemistry between us, and the mystery surrounding Ralph, the thrill of discovering what lies ahead have given me a renewed sense of purpose."

A radiant smile illuminates his face, his words dripping with desire.

I continue my merciless game underneath the table, feeling him getting aroused, seeing his pupils dilate and his mouth open in a gasp, "That day against the wall, it shocked me. I never would have done that back home, let alone with a virtual stranger. But it also filled me with exhilaration, anticipation, and an insatiable desire. Something within me has awakened. And I sense that you, too, are awakening to new possibilities." I laugh and punctuate my pun by massaging his length with my foot, causing Paul to breathlessly shift in his seat.

"I'm willing to try anything once, and if I enjoy it, I'll try it again. There are things I hadn't even imagined in my 20s, but now, with age, experience, confidence, and the comfort I feel with you, I want to explore, to have fun. You are my guilty pleasure, my secret indulgence, reserved just for me," I confess breathily.

Finally realising his endurance, Paul seizes my foot, pulling it against him for a fleeting moment, massaging it, and when it tickles, I feel the tingles somewhere else, too. He doesn't release it, teasing me for all the time I did the same to him. Smiling, he leans in and whispers, "You're driving me crazy with desire." His voice is like a nectar of pheromones; I drink it up, feeding on the way his voice breaks with the struggle to keep himself in check.

The tension between us grows, electrifying the air around our table. With each passing moment, the tendrils of our connection twists around themselves becoming something new, something stronger. The promise of what lays ahead becomes more tantalising than ever.

"Oh, don't you worry about that. I'll handle it later. What I meant to say is, if I want to stop, I'll say so, just like you can. But when it comes to asking me about what we're doing here, all I want to hear are phrases like 'Ever think of trying...' or 'Would you like...' And to be frank with you, I want you to take control, to take me. I enjoy moments when you're soft and sensual, but I also want to see you strong and dominant, tapping into that primal energy. As long as we maintain respect, anything is possible. If you still haven't figured it out, it's much easier now that I've spelled it out."

Paul's mouth almost dropped open, clearly taken aback by my directness. After a moment, he composes himself and replies, "Well, good thing we have that sorted out. And if it helps, that sentiment goes both ways. I feel like I've awakened from a decade-long slumber, with so much catching up to do. I've always been quite adventurous, but somehow forgot about it along the way. In my thirties, I dabbled a bit with what we found in Ralph's desk and beyond, but it's been a while. The only rules I have are the same as you: mutual respect, ensuring enjoyment for both of us. and let's just revel in our double life down here and leave our cares from the outside world behind," he finishes, saying exactly what was on my mind.

I chuckled at his response, feeling a sense of comfort in his openness. "Well, good to know you have some experience," I teased, a mischievous grin forming on my lips. "Lead the way, Mr. Experience. I can't wait to be educated. Or is it 'trained'?" I let out a playful laugh, recalling the quick recognition he had shown when we discovered the rope cuffs. "Ah, now I remember. You seemed quite familiar with those cuffs, earlier. A little experience, I suppose?"

Paul's eyes gleamed with desire as he replied, "Right now, darling, all I want is to enjoy you. No toys, just us. We *will* explore the realm of toys together in due time."

A shiver runs down my spine at his certainty.

As we finish our dinner, I smirk, "Are you able to stand yet?" I whisper with a suggestive glint in my eyes. Paul knows exactly what I mean and replies, "Just about."

We rose from our seats and made our way back to the hotel. It was a short walk, and along the way, Paul wrapped his arm around me, holding me close to him.

We pause for a moment when I catch Paul looking at something in the distance, and he points out a furniture shop, piquing my curiosity. I look at him questioning, and he gently tilts my head up, planting a tender kiss on my lips. "How about tomorrow, before work, you head down here and see if you can order all the furniture we need for the apartment?" he suggested. "Delivery can be arranged for next Thursday morning when Rachel is in. It will give us more time to personalise the space on Saturday."

Entering the hotel, Paul releases his hold on me, careful of the setting around us. Though it didn't really matter, since we were already known as regulars, but we preferred not to attract too much attention or invite unnecessary gossip from our colleagues. We made our way to the room, and as soon as we stepped through the door, it was as if a switch had been flipped.

We embraced each other passionately and his mouth lands viciously on mine, and I bit his lip. Paul wastes no time in undressing me. My shoes, socks and the airy dress quickly find their way to the floor. Meanwhile, I eagerly undid his clothes, deciding to take his shorts off along with his pants, delighting in the sight of him exposed.

To my surprise, he lifts me up and carries me over to the bed. I still have my lingerie on, adding a layer of seductive anticipation to the moment. He gently lays me face down on the bed and whispers, "Relax."

I can hear him retrieving something from his jacket. With him straddling my ass, I feel his warm hands applying oil to my shoulders. He leans in and says, "Tonight, let's start with a massage. I'm in the mood to explore every inch of you." My arms nestled under my head; I gaze up at him with a playful smile. "I'm sure I'll cope," I replied, brimming with excitement. I see the full-length wardrobe mirror out the side of my eye. I have a perfect view of everything Paul is doing to me. This feels surreal. Seeing him and I watch intently for what is to come next.

Paul's hands glide over my body, his touch slow, sensual, and attentive. As he works his way down, he skillfully undoes my lingerie and slides it off. His fingers find nooks and crannies in my body that I didn't know even existed, lighting my body on fire. Time seemed to blur as he lavished me with pleasure. From the raw passion we shared at the door to this tender moment, I marvel at his ability to pace and control himself.

I moan in delight, relaxing, as Paul lifts my hips and delicately slides a pillow beneath me. I could feel his warm breath against my neck as he leans in to kiss me.

With my hips raised by the pillow, he enters me slowly, inch by inch. I savour every sensation, every intimate unison. I surrender myself to him, allowing him to take me completely, and he does so with passion and tenderness. We move together, our bodies intertwined, synchronous as the pleasure builds within us. He drives me off the edge, once, and then again, until I can no longer feel anything around me. Except for the feeling of his naked skin against mine—it is intoxicating. Time seems to fade away as pleasure and its realisation becomes one.

Glancing at the clock, I realised it was already 1 am. *Where had the night gone?* We lay there, basking in the afterglow, and eventually drift off to sleep, with his fingers tracing invisible patterns on my skin. We sleep naked, entangled in each other's arms, enjoying solace and contentment in the warmth of our embrace.

***

The next morning, I am awakened by the sound of the shower running. Paul is awake, and got into the shower so quickly? I stay in bed for a few minutes, recounting the events of last night, but then curiosity gets the better of me, and I decide to test the bathroom door. To my delight, it's unlocked, and I quietly open it, stepping inside a steamed-up bathroom.

Through the mist, I could see his silhouette under the shower. I watch him for a moment, observing him while he is unaware of my presence. And then, without hesitation, I step in behind him, wrapping my arms around his wet body. "Now here is a way to start the day," I whisper, my nakedness pressed against his. I can feel him gasp, but he doesn't say anything, just tilts his face up to the shower, enjoying the warm stream.

My hand moves from his stomach, down the hairy trail, exploring him intimately before fisting his length. I feel his arousal growing under my touch, an immediate response to my caress. I hold onto him, slowly caressing him as he moans, kissing his back, reveling in the sensation of our bodies pressed together. He begins to turn, but I gently halt him. "No," I whisper, my commanding voice filled with a mix of desire and dream. "Just relax and enjoy. I know we've very little time," I kiss his shoulder, "I promised to take care of this later. Let me take care of you now."

I continue to stroke and pleasure him, pressing myself against him, attuned to his quickening breath. My touch intensifies, adapting to his body's response. My hand goes up and down, slick from the lather of the soap. The warm mist clouds around us, enveloping us in an ethereal embrace.

Paul lets go with a moan and a grunt, jerking against me, breathing harshly. He pants and then immediately turns around, kissing me passionately. His tongue delves into my mouth, searching, claiming, his mouth moves over my skin, over my neck, at my ear. He bites me, pecking and nibbling, and I shudder with sensations.

After a few more exhilarating minutes in the shower, we dry off together and exit the bathroom. As I glance around, I notice Paul's bag. He sees me looking and explains, "I lugged it over before stepping into the shower. I knew I would be joining you here soon, and after such a wonderful night, I wanted to be here when you woke up. I didn't want you to wake up alone in the room."

I could get used to his thoughtfulness. I think I already was.

"Come on, let's get dressed and grab some breakfast. You have work to attend to, and I have some shopping to do," I order.

We quickly gather our things and head out of the hotel, ready to start our day. I bid him goodbye at the hotel door, and we parted ways.

Arriving at the furniture shop Paul had pointed out earlier, I was relieved to find that they had a great selection of furniture and even offered high-quality linen and pillows. It made my task much easier, since I could check off most of the items on the list in one go. From stylish furniture pieces to kitchen essentials, I quickly filled the shopping cart, and struck off items from my list. With almost everything done, I make my way to the checkout counter, excited about the transformation of the apartment.

By the time I was done with the shopping, it was already late morning. I reach the office at eleven, my spirits high from the thoughts of sprucing up the living space I was going to be sharing with Paul.

Paul is heading out just as I enter the conference room, so he pulls me inside.

"So, I talked to the office, and they are arranging for an agency secretary to join us next Thursday. They would assist us in scanning and organising the files in the new office, ensuring a smooth transition. They know it's for the downstairs office, so the secretary can directly go work there, Nicola and Helen need not liaise with them in any way," Paul briefs me on the day's events.

I nod, relieved that we would have professional support in managing Ralph's private office.

"Uh, I was just heading down. I'm mostly done here," he says, looking around in the conference room, "But I think I should take a look at everything thoroughly downstairs. I don't want the poor temp shocked by any surprises," he wiggles his eyebrows.

Chapter 11

When I walked into Ralph's office that morning, I was able to appreciate how organised everything was, something I hadn't had a chance to do the first day I'd stepped foot in there. The office was a library of information; everything had been meticulously organised, labelled and filed away in an alphabetical order. It was almost to an extreme degree but at least in this office Ralph appeared to have invested some time and effort into organization. I wondered if Ralph had spent most of his two hours here meticulously organising everything in the office.

One of the office walls was entirely lined with steel-grey file cabinets, with drawers each marked and labelled. One of the tall cabinets was simply marked "Banking" and it held all the statements we needed of his personal and investment accounts. The cabinet held documents of accounts from all over the place, yet everything was perfectly organised in an alphabetical order.

Each account and policy separated into. its own folder, making it easy to find what we were looking for. I suspected that Ralph had recruited professional help, because this just didn't seem like his work. Things like organisation and attention to detail was lost on great men with so many things to run.

I walked through the room, scanning the cabinet labels. I passed the cabinet labelled 'Pension and Life policies', followed by another cabinet marked 'Property' and slid open the first drawer.

Each of his properties appeared to have a folder of its own and surprisingly, the folders contained the deeds for each property as well. This was everything I had been looking for, for so many weeks! I felt like a child on Christmas morning. I rifled through the labels on the folders; a folder for each of the six shops, one for the building that we were in, separate ones for the apartments, and one folder marked 'Home'. Out of curiosity to see what Ralph considered 'home' out of all the properties he owned, I slid out the last folder and slid it open to see that it was the house outside Fort William. There was a folder for the warehouse, another for the distribution centre and a stock warehouse for the shops.

The bottom drawer of this cabinet was marked 'Leases' and contained a folder for a popular coffee franchise and another for the travel agency on the ground floor of the building. I rifled through the files looking for the one particular lease that I had expected to be in there. After almost emptying the bottom drawer out, I wondered why there was no lease for the adult shop. Was it just not in the cabinets here or did he just not lease the adult shop? The lack of it seemed strange to me.

I moved on from that cabinet to the one marked 'Property Accounts' which wonderfully held all the records of billing and costs for each property in the 'Property' cabinet, all except the apartment. That wasn't strange or curious, I figured, because that was because it was managed by the main company directly.

I spend the rest of the day looking through the cabinets and added the documents we had acquired from the apartment and the other office. Someone had improperly tried to file the documents we had obtained so I also reorganised some cabinets that hadn't been refiled correctly. I also made a mental note to mention the lack of the lease for the adult shop and anything else I found out of the ordinary to my team at DAF to investigate.

Meanwhile, Paul had spent the entire day at the apartment and came back to the office only in time to leave for the day. Both of us hadn't talked during the day like we usually did, so seeing him after all day made me smile like a schoolgirl. By the time we got off work, it was a cool, breezy evening outside, so we decided to walk back to the hotel.

As we strolled, the cool breeze became chillier, and Paul and I gushed about how neatly the office was organised, far more so than the main office. It had made my life so very easy.

I could tell Paul was uneasy about something, so I paused, and let the silence encourage him to open up. After a few minutes, he looked up and softly confessed, "I found the safe," with a slight oddness in his manner.

A few beats passed and I waited for him to elaborate. "Well?"

"I sent an email back to my boss and I updated him on our progress, our findings and on the shop and the office. I left out the nature of the shop though. I only said that it looks like he owned a small shop as well, but it was leased out and independently managed. I will talk to him about that in person, as I feel this was a tiny part of what he owned but it could end up being his label," he said in a rush.

"And the safe? What are you holding out on me, Paul?" I asked, puzzled by him glossing over the discovery of the safe.

"Yeah, I found it," he said slowly. "My boss has the combination and the instructions. It's a bit weird. He told me he would come talk to me about it on Monday."

His explanation seemed lackluster, but I figured he would tell me when he knew more and the mystery around the safe would clear up. I let it go and suggested that we head to Leicester Square for the evening. Leicester Square was always lovely this time of the day, and it's always nice to just get out, we rarely had an abundance of time together and going walking about in Manchester wasn't exactly possible. We headed off and ended up wandering around the Leicester Square area and looked at the shows that are playing.

We headed into a small, romantic Italian restaurant called Bella Italia for dinner. We were both not in the mood for anything fancy, just a simple, intimate night out with pizza and wine. When we got back to the hotel after dinner, we enjoyed another gorgeous night together. Paul may have said he was out of practice, but I could see in his manner it had all come back to him.

Tonight, Paul was far less frenzied. He was more sensual and passionate. He took his time getting me going, playing with me for a proper half hour before even taking off his clothes. We made love slowly, passionately, taking our time. He was patient, in control, and when I jumped off the edge, he followed me, down into the abyss of mind-numbing pleasure.

***

Saturday morning rolled around, and Paul and I headed out early, deciding that finding a café around Covent Garden might be nice for a change of scenery and might offer some diverse cuisine from what we've been eating for the past few days; hotel food and coffee. We wandered up to the main area, passing Cotswolds, North Face and other outdoor and sports stores.

"Take notes, that's the opposition," I jokingly said, and Paul laughed.

We window-shopped our way up to the middle of Covent Garden, found a lovely breakfast café and ordered a simple breakfast.

"There's only so much hotel food you can cope with," Paul said, as he scanned the menu. We ordered coffee, some eggs for me and a croissant for Paul. We ate lazily, talking while savouring each bite of the food, spending an hour over breakfast.

When we left, Paul saw a toy shop and ducked in saying, "Give me a few minutes." I followed him inside as he's poking around in bins and racks of children's toys.

"Rachel likes some of this stuff," he said. I watch him looking through the store; it's comforting watching him looking for something nice for his daughter, being a father, a real father. The sight of it makes my heart both ache and sing. This is a side of him I am not used to seeing, or just haven't seen yet. He does not talk too much about his kids, but it warms my heart to see he is thinking about them. While we're

154

there looking for something for Rachel, I take the opportunity to look for something Natalie and Rebecca would like.

As we're both looking around, I realise how much we must look like a couple, poking around the shops on Saturday morning, getting breakfast, and shopping for the kids. We wander through the shops and stalls, and Paul asks me, "Do we need anything else for the apartment, or should we even be bothered with it now?"

"I was thinking we really just need cutlery, some silverware, maybe a toaster and kettle," I list off the things I had not yet crossed off my list, "There's a cooker but I have no intention of ever using it. Oh, and a microwave. That might make things easier."

Paul laughed, "You seem to know exactly what we need, so how about we get you the company credit card and you can just place an order for it online through Amazon? You have the card details I presume. Just order it all and get it delivered to the office here."

"Ah, excellent male logic", I poke fun at him. "Why do something when a woman can do it instead?" I shake my head laughing, knowing I prefer online shopping anyway. "And alright, I'll sort it out over the next few days."

We stroll all the way from Covent Garden up along to Oxford Street, wandering in and out of shops and window shopping. We debate going into the newly built Apple store, and eventually decide to just take a look. People are just beginning to mill in, and Paul and I look over the new phones, and both comment on the new features, and I'm sure both of us are thinking how much our kids would love these. The price on these quickly makes us exit the store, laughing loudly.

As I'm leaving, laughing without a care, I think about all the perfect moments we've had together lately. Waking up together, the showers, the breakfasts, and lunches. The dinners, and the perfect night to end the day.

On the high street, I window-shop at all the clothing stores, my heart wanting to spend all my money on the beautiful pieces. After walking around for half an hour, it suddenly dawns on me, "Paul, you must be bored senseless," I say, embarrassed. "I'm sorry for making you walk around so much!"

Paul smiles at me. "I'm actually really enjoying myself, surprisingly," he said. "It's nice to see you looking at all the things you like, the shoes, the clothes. You look like you're having so much fun, you almost forgot I'm here," He chuckles softly, "I like seeing you just being you; relaxed, normal. It's not often that we get the chance to do this."

I smile back, "In that case, we're going in here," I said, pointing to an upmarket boutique. "I'm going to try on some of those clothes, and you can watch me shop, and I'll let you carry the bags."

Inside, I try on a backless black dress. It's gorgeous and perfect for a night out. When I walk out of the dressing room, Paul just says "Wow, you look stunning, darling."

When I come back out, I leave the dress and head for the rack, looking through more dresses. Nothing else catches my fancy so I head for the door. Paul looks confusedly at me, "You were gorgeous in that, you should buy it!"

I click my tongue, "Maybe another time. It's a common design, and too pricey here."

He catches my hand in both of his. "Come on, let me get you the dress," he says and then lowers his voice to a whisper. "Afterall, I hope I'm going to be the one taking it off of you."

"That sounds perfect but no, really," I protest, uncomfortable that he's insisting on paying. I really wasn't used to this.

Paul looks back at me very seriously and says, "Come outside for a minute."

I frown and we leave the dress shop and sit on a bench outside.

"Maria," he looks me in the eyes. "However, and whichever way we look at this, we are in a relationship. I know it is far easier for me than it is for you; I know you must be careful and I'm sorry if I forget that at times. I have nobody to answer to but myself."

I nod in agreement, and he goes on, "Good, now you agree we are in a relationship. After all, we're setting up our little love nest here, right?" he smiles." I think since that's the case, I can go shopping and get the woman that I care about something nice to wear," he says gently. 'It is not about whose card it is on; it is about doing something nice for someone important to me. Now, we are getting that dress."

I protest again, just a bit less than before, and he sighs, "Alright, what if I do this for you, and you can do something for me later, would you go for that?"

I think for a second, and ultimately shrug at him in half-agreement. *What is he planning on doing to me now?* I think. *And when he is taking it off of me?* I add to my thoughts.

"Good, now let's get that dress, I will tell you what you can do for me later," he says.

I protest that it's unfair, that I want to know but he's adamant and refuses to budge.

"Anyway, bad news," I say, trying to deter him. "I can't bring it home. There's not enough space in the back of my closet to keep hiding dresses to wear out with you."

Laughing, he replies, "Just as well, you have an empty wardrobe in our love nest here now. Come on, let's go."

He buys me the dress; I love it. When we head out and wander on, I grab his arm as we stroll up the street, swaying and talking.

It was a lovely, relaxing morning, and we chatted about everything except work. On Oxford Street, he looked in a few windows. "You see something you like?" he asks as he looks into a shoe store. "Yeah, let's go in and see," I replied.

Inside, I walk over to the men's section and see Paul beckoning me to the women's section. "My condition for letting you do something for me is you let me get the shoes to finish the dress off."

"That is not fair." I protest. I begin to argue, smiling at him.

But he stops me. "Well, you agreed to this, didn't you? Filthy mind of yours thought I was going to do something to you. Tut tut... get that mind out of the gutter," he laughs. "But you can message me what you wanted me to do later instead," he smiles his charming smile at me.

We look at the collection and when I see a pair I like, I pick them up, when I go to turn them over, he stops me.

"No checking prices, you have to get what you like. Let me do something nice please. You have no idea how much I am enjoying this. Been ten years since I went shopping with someone else instead of my kids and for something other than kids' clothes, and then it was just me and the kids, and me telling the girls, you can't go out in that, more like a belt than a skirt!" he laughs.

On my fourth pair of shoes, we finally had a winner. It's a pair of high heels, glamourous and perfect to go with the dress.

After a leisurely day filled with coffee-fueled strolls through shops, we grab a delicious lunch at one o'clock. After lunch, it was almost time for our train at three, Paul called a cab, and we made our way back to the apartment. Upon our arrival, I carefully hung my dress and placed my shoes in the closet, feeling a mix of emotions. This was really happening, I thought.

As we headed down for the three o'clock train, I was thinking of getting back to the kids, to the house. Thankfully, the train was much quieter than usual. First-class was half empty and nobody was around us, so we could talk freely.

Taking the opportunity, I asked him a bit more about his kids. He had spoken about them so lovingly before.

"Matthew and Sarah are great kids, they're twenty-two and twenty now. Sarah's always been mature for her age, twenty going on forty, you know. I suppose she had to grow up fast. We get on well. She tries to be a bit mothering, especially now that she's gotten older. She's great with Rachel, really helps her and Rachel listens to her. She has a boyfriend now, he's alright." Paul said, the last of it indicating he thought nobody is good enough for his little girl.

"She is away a good bit with college in Glasgow, at least that is what I tell myself, that she's not with her boyfriend. We still make time. We have the odd day every few months when we go into the city, just the two of us. We get lunch and go shopping. We have a mutual unspoken understanding now. We have a nice day, she gets to go clothes shopping on my credit card, and I don't argue." He laughs.

"As she's grown up, we chat openly about what is going on in life, more hers, because mine is boring apparently."

I smile, "That's how kids are."

"Don't I know it," he says. "Matthew is just finishing university; he did a business degree and he's looking for work now but lacking some direction. He is laid back, just worries about what food is in the fridge and his next night out," he chuckles.

Then continues. "But they are great when it comes to me. If I need to be away for work, they make sure that is no problem and keep the house running and one of them is always home for Rachel. Rachel rules the roost, she is a bit spoiled, because she was the youngest by a few years. Everyone sort of looked out for her. She still needs me, just calls me the ATM jokingly. God knows she has a temper when you say no to her, but cools off eventually. But she is no longer the baby, has her own friends and life and I just hope she stays on straight and narrow. She's great at school and thankfully uses Sarah as a role model. But the only person she listens to is Julie. She's the housekeeper and nanny. More for Rachel, but I just call her housekeeping, so they don't complain about it. Rachel does not like the idea of having a nanny; she is too old for that now. Julie is fine with that also; she sees the kid's side. She has been brilliant the last ten years. Would have been lost without her."

He showed me a photo of the three of them from his wallet. It is an old photo, Rachel smiles toothily at the camera, and the other two smile, looking almost identical.

We're almost heading into the station and Paul says, "Sorry for prattling on about my kids the entire time."

"No," I say. "I like hearing about them, they sound like amazing kids."

159

"That they are," he says. "I would love to learn more about yours next time, but just what you want to share. If you prefer not to, that is perfectly fine."

I agree and we part ways on the train. *Another week is over*, I think.

Mark is at the station to collect me, so Paul makes sure to give us a wide berth and heads to the restroom. Surprisingly, Mark asks about my few days and what kept me in London. I told him about the project taking a twist, that we'd found the clients private office and all his financials. He was a wealthy recluse who had assets everywhere, but lived a basic, no fuss life.

I decided to tell Mark about the apartment in London, saying we had been told that because the company has an empty two-bedroom apartment around the corner from the office, going forward, whoever was in London for this was going to have to use that. The company could not justify expensive hotels when there was an empty apartment sitting there, I explained. I also mentioned how effectively, I had been seconded two days a week to manage the business until it all wrapped up, so I was going to be working more for the company than the estate.

Mark surprisingly asked another question about the apartment, so I added how I was told to go buy some furniture as I refused to use the bed and linens that were in the apartment. I only agreed to use the apartment if fresh bedding were added.

I made sure to sound practical and like me.

"Looks like I will be there one night a week, maybe two once in a while, until the new owner takes over. Funny we have no idea who that is," I said.

"Can't you find out from the guy from legal who it is? They must have the paperwork," Mark asks.

His attention catches me by surprise. "The guy from legal is now not really involved in the company as much. He's dealing more with all the other estate work" I decided to keep going, though I'm a little panicked. "It turns out the client owned the adult shop on the ground floor, but was just handled by a manager. He had a private office also behind the shop, accessed from around the corner, and all his noncompany details there. He was a strange man by the sounds of it, but nobody in his personal life that we have come across. The legal people are now going to work from the second office when they are down."

I played it all off passively, and never referred to Paul by name, just as the legal guy. But I was surprised, Mark was so interested, which was unlike him. Was he trying? Was I too harsh on him? I was about to feel a little guilty when the other shoe dropped.

Mark says, trying to be casual. "Oh, right. There are a few matches coming up abroad over the next few months. The lads are at me to go."

I was about to make a smarting comment about it but decided not to. After all, I am the one on the offside, I realise. "Mmm." I say." Buttering me up, are you? I suppose there's not a lot I can say as work is taking me away so much and it'll be that way for a good while."

He looks sheepish. "A few of the matches are on Thursday nights when you will be in London."

"Okay," I say. 'Give me the dates and I will change my London days or cancel them if I can't manage those Thursdays, you might as well make a weekend out of one or two if ye want. You are working hard these days."

Mark looked stunned. Honestly, I thought, if I told him I am sleeping with Paul right here, right now, he probably would have said 'fine' because he'd got his real love, football.

Anyway, giving him these breaks, may give me a few options to get time away myself. Who knows when I may want it now?

Any feeling of guilt that had come over me a few moments ago, disappeared fast, Mark had only pretended to be interested in me to get his boys' weekends away.

When we head home to the kids, I get big bear hugs from the girls. They've missed me. "So," I say to the kids, "How about a takeaway and movie night. Whatever you want." I feel guilty for leaving for so long, so I decided to make sure I am entirely there for the kids for the rest of the weekend.

We actually had a nice weekend; there was calm, no parties, or demands. We headed to the park with the kids on Sunday, which made me think of all that I have and also of Paul's wonderful relationship with his kids.

Mark came along with us too, but he spent the time watching the match on his phone and I wished he might as well have just stayed at home.

Chapter 12

I was burrowed into a pile of files at the DAF office this morning, making headway through the projects in the pipeline. Once the due diligence and approval was out of the way, I could assign these tasks to my team, and they'll take care of it. I could see my workload lighten in a few days. As long as my team didn't run into any major issues, which it sometimes did. I could only hope for the best. Even though London wasn't too terribly taxing, and since Paul was there it was actually fun, the commute, back and forth and handling so many different things at once were tiring me out.

I sigh, wondering why Thursday was so far away and why did two days with Paul fly by so quick. I wondered if the exhaustion I felt was not because of the commute after all, but from having to wait to meet Paul, and the pretension that came with the whole affair. That made more sense.

I was reading through the endless pages in front of me, thinking about patience, Paul and pretend games when my phone rings. I look at the screen: it's Paul. I frown; why's he calling at eleven in the morning? Excitement and intrigue floods through me.

I receive his call, "Hey, everything alright?"

"Maria, yes," Paul says breathlessly, "Everything's okay. Something out of the ordinary happened today. This morning my boss handed me a sealed envelope. It was heavy, and the words on the front piqued my curiosity. So much secrecy around this envelope… Why didn't Leonard give this to me when I got this case?"

"Well, what did the front of the envelope say?" I ask through the air of mystery.

"It says, 'To be handed to the solicitor responsible for handling my affairs, and responsible for opening my safe. Instructions are to be followed precisely.' What could be so secretive that it requires such careful handling?" Paul says, and I hear fluttering of papers on the other end of the phone.

"Huh. So, what is it?"

"I've discovered the code to open Ralph's safe and the passwords to access his computers. The instructions are clear: open the safe, retrieve the envelopes, and deliver them to their intended recipients. There are also photo albums, to be left untouched for now, but slated for destruction later as per instructions."

"What's the deal with Ralph?" I wonder aloud, and Paul hums in agreement. Was he just a dramatic man, making a mountain out of a molehill, or was the information he died hiding just so groundbreaking?

The directives only heightened the sense of frustration and anticipation we already felt. Paul didn't share the details of the photo album, but I could tell he wanted to. I wonder what other revelations awaited us behind more sealed envelopes and strictly worded instruction letters.

"I must confess, I have not yet opened the instruction letter or any other little envelopes inside, but curiosity is getting the better of me. Let's take a look at the safe first thing on Thursday, eh?"

"Yes, of course. I'm curious to know too what went inside the life of this recluse. Anyway, did you make your train reservation for Thursday?"

"Will do that this evening. What about the apartment? Did you manage to get whatever stuff you will need there? Plus, there will be Rachel, and we'll have to see what we need her for from now on."

"Oh, I did. Went on Amazon and ordered some bathroom and bedroom accessories. Kitchen pots and pans, utensils, all that. With any luck the apartment will be usable very soon."

"Thank you for that. So, it all seems on track. It will be lovely to have that space for us, where we can relax together without keeping up appearances. Leave a few things behind, get comfortable," Paul said the last bit in an intimate whisper that tickled me.

Hotel room comfort was transient, but I'd had some extraordinary time in mine. Before the images from those nights play in my mind right on cue, I divert the conversation to the more unpleasant matters at hand.

"Also, on another note. Since it's football season now, Mark wanted me home for some Thursday evenings. I was wondering if we can change around some of our upcoming trips." I hated asking him this, I wanted more time for us, not to cut down the already limited hours we had together.

"Of course, I'll work around anything I can. Maybe this would open doors to us getting a weekend getaway together?" He said like he'd read my mind.

"I'd love that," I whisper, completely forgetting I was still seated in my chair in my office. Paul took me to places I couldn't even imagine existed.

"That would be lovely," he agreed, "My kids are grown up, so they're busy with their lives and won't even miss me. Would probably invite their friends and have a party. Right now, I'm just looking forward to Thursday, our breakfast and chat in the train and sitting across from you, seeing you in person. Anything special you'd like to do on Thursday night darling?"

"Not much. I guess I'm just looking forward to seeing the apartment on Thursday. We'll see what else we need to make it more comfortable. Maybe we can get a quick bite, sort out the apartment, then curl onto the couch with a trashy movie and a bottle of wine with you."

Paul chuckles, and I smile at his charming voice. We talked for a few more minutes, promising to see each other on Thursday in the train.

The rest of the week passes by in a blur of office work, endless files, Joan's keen reminders of the children's teacher-parent meetings, doctor's appointments and more of the same. As usual, Paul and I exchange messages before starting our busy days, finding comfort in the connection we share even when apart.

Working late, I've also picked up the habit of spending the night slumbering on the couch, and neither Mark nor I find each other's absence an inconvenience. When I idle back to our bedroom in the morning, Mark is silent, unperturbed, and gets dressed for his office as usual. I follow suit.

When Thursday morning comes around, my excitement is palpable. Although I do make sure it's contained when I'm with family, I'm not as particular when I'm outside. My heart flutters as I climb onto the station platform anticipating our reunion, knowing Paul will be around soon.

I look forward to our breakfast- not because of the forgettable British Rail food, but the company I usually have during this time. Everything else fades into the background when he's around- much like right now, as I feel myself levitating, watching him seated while I walk to meet him. A sudden, overwhelming desire to kiss him bubbles inside me, but I contain myself until I'm seated, and my breath is restored.

As soon as I sit down, my hand naturally finds his, and I whisper, "I missed you." He kisses me on the cheek lightly, and I crave more, but people have started filing around us, and I'll probably be thrown out of the carriage if I succumb to my feelings right now.

Paul's smile lights up his face as he replies, "Not as much as I missed you, darling. I even did the unimaginable," He chuckles, as my brows furrow, "I went shopping with you in mind."

Curiosity piqued, I urge him to share the surprise he has in store, but he playfully teases me, insisting that I wait until later.

"Delayed gratification," he wiggles his brows.

I laugh, knowing that whatever it is, it will be worth the anticipation.

As we travel, I ask about the police. With a perplexed look on his face "She asked about the estate and did we come across anything unusual. When I asked for more information, she was coy, simply saying just tidying up a few loose ends from the accident."

We arrive in London and hail a taxi, travelling straight to our hotel together. Paul is staying in the same one as mine, and we hurriedly drop our bags, meeting together to hail another taxi. Once we're close to the office, I get off, eager to see the transformation of the apartment and Paul follows.

I turn to him, "You go on ahead and see the safe, I'll be right there once I check the apartment."

Paul holds onto my wrist and pays the taxi, and then turns to me.

"Safe can wait a while, I want to see *our* apartment with you," he says, looking deep into my eyes.

I nod, and we walk together over the next block.

I throw the apartment door open, and in the same breath I'm taken aback by the sight before me. The painters have done a fantastic job, and Rachel has tidied up so wonderfully. The scent of fresh paint lingers in the air, as I walk through the rooms, a smile on my face. The doorbell rings and Paul checks the door: the furniture delivery has just arrived. From within one of the rooms, Rachel's head peeks out, and she smiles, pleased at our pleasant surprise at the transformation she has helped out with.

Paul smoothly takes charge, arranging for the beds and mattresses to be set up while I admire the newfound freshness of the place. It was not half too bad. I hear one of the delivery guys ask Paul where the mattress would go. Paul indicates to him with a gesture, and then slips the young man £20, "Thanks, can you make sure the beds and mattresses are in place. And take away the packaging. Another £30 if you can get rid of the old mattress."

The young man runs a lazy gaze over the crisp notes in Paul's hand and then back at Ralph's flimsy, well-worn mattress. He nods and collects Paul's offering and goes about his business.

Rachel does her own thing independently, busily organising and tidying up the last of the boxes.

I've looked around plenty, and I check my watch habitually. I'm a few minutes late for my meeting with one of the shop managers. That outlet was running steadily low on profits, and I had arranged for a meeting to discuss why that was happening.

"Hey, I think I'll go to the office now, I have a meeting." I say to Paul, giving him an opportunity to explore the safe and discover everything Ralph was keeping secret.

"Alright, let's meet here in the afternoon at one?" Paul asks me and I nod, realising we would need to discuss the contents of the safe away from prying and wandering eyes. This would be the perfect place since the apartment would be deserted.

Before I returned to the office, I turn to Paul, "What was this surprise shopping you mentioned?" I ask him.

He winks, "Keep thinking about it. See you later!" he teases me, and I pout, leaving behind me a laughing Paul.

***

Time becomes liquid, thick and viscous, slowly edging towards the big bold one on my office clock. Paul hasn't rung, and I don't want to disturb him during work, especially now that work needs privacy and sensitive handling. A few minutes past one, and my phone rings. I answer eagerly, knowing it's Paul.

"Are you alone?" he asks mysteriously.

I confirm that I am, and he continues.

"I successfully opened the safe. There are three envelopes inside—one addressed to the beneficiary, another for Adam Wright, and the last for the solicitor, so me."

"What about the photo albums?" I inquire, my curiosity aflame. I wonder what story the pictures told, if there were any

168

of the mysterious woman who's framed photograph sat in Ralph's office in the Boutique.

"The albums," he sighs, "This is like an encyclopaedia, filled with memories, emotions, and hidden truths. The albums seem to hold the key to this mysterious puzzle that surrounds us. There is no definite explanation, no story yet, but I can sense one exists."

"Yeah?" worry at my lip; *what was going on?*

"Yeah. But there are specific instructions not to show them to anyone just yet. Hopefully I will be able to tell you more in time. Maybe if we do the next part quickly, we might get more pieces of the puzzle," Paul exhales.

"Oh, you're in a teasing mood today, aren't you? I may have to torture this out of you later," I joke, and Paul chuckles. He respects the instructions left in his charge, and I respect him for that.

He clears his throat, his business voice back on, "Are you done finalising the valuation on the shops? I have instructions on how to proceed on that front, if you're done."

"I am, yes. The valuations are complete, but we still need stock verification and some minor due diligence. Everything seems in hand. They all seem to be very cash heavy, and no profits have been taken for the last decade, I presume," I rattle off the facts, looking at the little diary I keep in London to take quick notes and make summaries.

"Alright, then. According to the instructions, we don't need to wing it anymore. Ralph wanted every manager to stay on as they have been, unless there are extenuating circumstances. I'll meet with the managers and reassure them that there are certainly no risks to their jobs, provided that the profits stay above the threshold." I hear a soft rustling as I hum my agreement, imagining Paul's keen gaze running through all the tasks he now had to complete.

He continues, "I think I also need to visit the house in Fort William. Assess and evaluate it. It says here there is some contents in the house that need to be destroyed. And a set of keys. I assume I am supposed to go alone, but since there's no clear specification here, you should tag along. You're gonna need to see it anyway."

When Paul finishes, I ask, "When do you think we should visit Fort William? I think we might have to keep a day or two for that separately."

"I was thinking we could schedule that for Monday morning. We can take our time getting there, take in what there's to see and discover. Then meet the manager of the shop in the afternoon. Drive there, enjoy the scenery, stay overnight at a charming country hotel. See if your schedule will allow that."

"Alright, I'll let you know about that. Let's schedule the managers meeting on Friday in the afternoon. I'll get Nicola and Helen on that. This is going to be a huge, formal announcement, right? So, let's do something around it."

"Like a social evening? That could be perfect. We can ask them to come to London with their plus ones. Everyone enjoying themselves at the hotel, with drinks flowing, dinner and ample opportunities for interaction. I think the managers should actually see us to get comfortable with us."

"Right. And what about the London staff?"

"Well, Ralph wanted me to reassure them that the shops were secure and would remain intact for a minimum of ten years. As long as there's consistent profitability, there would be no disruptions to their existing operations. Same goes for London staff. Additionally, they would retain their positions if they wished to continue their roles, ensuring continuity and stability. Let's also book rooms for the London staff at the hotel, establish some good rapport with the people here while we have the opportunity," Paul went on.

With each detail thoughtfully considered, our plan took shape over the several minutes, and we looked forward to the upcoming discoveries that awaited us in Fort William and the events we were hosting in London. We decided we wouldn't come to London until Friday either, so there will be no Thursday night we could spend together. But, if all worked out we will have Monday and Tuesday together. I planned to invite

Mark to the Friday evening event, but I knew he would decline it. Which would be perfect.

"Can you coordinate the plans with Nicola and Helen? I'll see you at the apartment when you're done," Paul exhales, finally running through his list of to-dos.

"Roger that!"

With a sense of urgency, I get to work, eager to quickly sort out my schedule for the coming week. After going through my schedule with Joan, I found my Monday and Tuesday at DAF relatively clear, giving me the flexibility, I needed for an unexpected trip. I swiftly moved my Tuesday meeting to Thursday, ensuring everything would be properly covered while I was away.

Next, I sent an email to Jack, updating him on the evolving puzzle and the new developments. I explained that I had to travel to the Fort William shop and estate on Monday and Tuesday, but I'd be back in the office next Thursday. To pre-empt any worries he might have, I reassured him that I would take care of everything and ensure smooth operations in my absence. Like I was already doing anyway.

Now the last thing. I dial Mark's number and wait for him to pick up.

I told him about the trip to Fort William, and how relieved I was that the other shops were exempted from inspection. The prospect of less time away from home seemed to lift his spirits. Then, I revealed the exciting plans for next Friday night, with a meeting scheduled for the managers in the afternoon, followed by an enjoyable overnight stay for everyone and their partners.

"Can you make it? It's going to be a wonderful night away from home, kids, in a hotel…" I inject expectation in my voice.

Fortunately, Mark was already committed to work on Friday, leaving me feigning disappointment, looking forward to a Saturday in London with Paul.

Done with that, I summon Nicola and Helen to my office. I disclose some of the information Paul had uncovered so far, emphasising that there would be no changes to the current arrangement for the foreseeable future, thanks to the instructions in the will. Although they seemed partly relieved by this assurance, curiosity shone brightly in their eyes as they pondered over the secrecy in the will.

"Also, Paul and I decided we will have a social event for the outlet managers and London staff. All the managers are expected to attend the meeting next Friday at 2 PM, followed by drinks, social and a stay overnight. Please arrange for the meeting as well as the hotel booking for all the managers and their plus ones. The London staff will also be included in the same arrangements. Reserve rooms for yourselves too, and Paul and me," I quickly list off all the tasks,

After they leave, I chuckle to myself, knowing Paul and I will be cozied up in one room. My excitement was palpable.

Nicola and Helen set to work, putting the wheels in motion for the meeting and event.

***

The clock struck two PM when I turned the key in the apartment door, feeling a mix of excitement and anticipation. Whatever awaited me inside, I was determined not to be late for it. The safe and, more importantly, why Paul was teasing me had been at the forefront of my mind all day. As I stepped in, there he was – Paul, already there with coffee and a sandwich, ready to welcome me.

Without even sparing a glance at the room, my eyes locked onto him, and with eagerness, I asked, "Where do we start?"

Before I could comprehend, he rushed towards me, leaned in and kissed me intensely, with a passionate forcefulness that surprised and thrilled me. He pinned me to the wall, his hand confidently exploring my curves, pulling me closer as we shared the fervent kiss. It was unlike anything I had experienced from him before outside our hotel room, but I embraced it fully, reveling in the feeling of being wanted, desired, and cherished. The undeniable evidence of his arousal against me only fueled the intensity of the moment.

As we came up for air, I couldn't help but ask, "Where the hell did that come from? I love it, by the way. Anytime you want to do that again, I'm all for it. But my, you seem like you've had quite the morning."

Looking into my eyes, Paul spoke with a mixture of emotions, "You have no idea. Someday soon, I hope I can tell you everything," his eyes betrayed the intensity he felt, "But for now, let's focus on exploring the apartment."

As we toured the space, I marveled at the transformation that had taken place. The room was no longer the same, as if it had come alive with new energy. Pictures adorned the walls, adding character and charm. The place was impeccably clean, and I noticed fresh cushions on the couch and chairs, a lovely plant in the corner, and artificial flowers on the dining table, adding a touch of warmth and homeliness.

We moved towards the bathroom, where towels hung neatly, and everything sparkled with cleanliness. My eyes widened as I noticed a large shower with glass doors tucked in the corner, inviting relaxation and luxury.

Next, we ventured into the bedrooms, and I gasped with delight. Both rooms were flawlessly arranged, with beds adorned in crisp white linen, folded over, just the way I liked it. A few throw pillows adorned the main bedroom's bed, while bedside lamps illuminated the room from the nightstands. I was puzzled; I hadn't purchased those.

"Wow, you've been busy," I remarked, genuinely curious. "How did you even find the time to shop?"

Paul grinned mischievously, "Well, let's just say I managed to multitask efficiently. Seeing the smile on your face is worth every second of it."

"But I can't take all the credit," Paul confesses with a smile, "I called Rachel and explained that we're eager to get everything set up quickly. I asked her if she could put in some extra hours today to make sure the beds are made up as soon as the delivery arrives. Flowers, pictures, the plants, things that make it seem like a home. Some overtime pay, and here we are!" He looked around proudly.

Overwhelmed with his thoughtfulness, I hug him tightly, "I love this. I love that you put in effort to make it a home for us."

Then, Paul took me to the bedroom and handed me a flat box that lay on the bed, and my curiosity piqued. "Here's a little something for both of us," he said, his eyes twinkling with excitement.

I unwrapped it to reveal an exquisite black silk chemise with delicate white lace trim, designed to just skim my thighs. There was also a matching black silk robe that complemented the set perfectly. Butterflies flutter in my stomach.

"Oh, darling, this is lovely," I gush, genuinely touched by his thoughtfulness. "But why? What inspired this beautiful surprise?"

Paul's voice softened as he sat me down on the edge of the bed and ran his fingers gently through my hair. "I would love intimate moments when we curl up together, especially when we could watch your favourite movies in bed or on the couch. While your dresses are delicious, I thought you might appreciate something more comfortable to wear during those cosy times. Plus, I imagined how sexy you'd look, and it was no debate then," he chuckles.

His words warm my heart, and I remember mentioning how I'd love to have a movie night together. "You're right," I replied with a smile. "We can order a pay-per-view movie from the hotel since we're not completely set up here yet, but we're getting there. It'll be wonderful," I say softly.

Paul beamed with satisfaction.

"Alright, before I get carried away let's have lunch." Paul exhaled, and I laugh at his obvious effort to restrain himself in this moment.

I looked at him leaving, my heart racing from his passionate greeting and the effort he put into making the apartment feel like home, I couldn't help but tease him. "After that greeting you gave me, the effort here, a bed in the next room, and you're talking about food."

With a mischievous glint in his eyes, Paul replied, "Oh Maria, that greeting was me trying to restrain myself. If I start anything now, I won't be able to stop. Can't you see how turned on I am for you right now?"

I could very much see how turned on he was. It made me want to rip his clothes off him with my teeth.

His words sent shivers down my spine, and I felt a rush of desire for him. "Paul, where are those cuffs?" I asked, eager for his touch, for his passion for me. "If that's what you want, get them, pin me to the wall, do as you please," I moan, reaching for his hand.

He shook his head slightly. "They're gone. Ralph's instructions were clear - they had to be disposed of so no one else could use them."

I was still curious about what was in that safe, the mysterious letter, and the intriguing album he had found. Whatever it was, it seemed to have awakened a new side of Paul, and I loved it.

"To think you want me to the point of just wanting to take me like this," I said, almost begging him to take his way with me right now. "I told you I like it a little rough at times, animalistic," I whisper, "Whatever you saw today, and what you want to do with me- now you know that's what I want."

The idea of putting on the lingerie he had gifted me crossed my mind, but Paul read my mind. "No, darling, not tonight," he said, his voice husky with desire. "I'm not in a silk, lace, and delicate mood right now. I don't know if you can tell. I won't be able to control myself."

I couldn't help but feel intoxicated by his presence, his raw masculinity, and this passionate assertiveness. "Sweet divine, you have me all worked up here. All hot and bothered," I croon. "I love this side of you, but I'm telling you now, if you're going to act like this, you better not hold back. Now, what's next?" I demand, wishing him to take charge.

He looked at me with a serious expression, his eyes locked onto mine. Something shifts in his expression, and I smile.

"Take off your panties, now," he commands.

Liquid pleasure courses through me, and my back arches at his words. I gasp, my breath hot.

I am wearing a fitted dress that reached just below my knees, reminiscent of the one I wore on the first day here. It had a zipper at the back, but the neckline was lower this time. I don't hesitate; I lift the dress slightly to access my panties and sensually slid them down and off. Holding them up between two fingers, I teasingly dangled them to the side before dropping them, his eyes following my every move, and the magnetic energy crackles between us. He licks his bottom lip, and that does unimaginable things to my insides.

He walks over to me with an intensity I hadn't seen before, grabbing me and pulling me close. His lips meet mine in a fierce, hungry kiss, sending a surge of electricity through my body. In one swift move, he lifts me up and presses me back against the bed, urging me to lie on my back.

Without a word, he uses one hand to open his pants, exposing his throbbing erection, which is pressed against me as he pushes my dress up. He firmly grasps my hips, pulling me toward him with a sense of urgency. With a deep and powerful thrust, he clashes into me, and I feel every delicious inch of him inside me. One handheld my hip firmly, while the other grabbed my shoulder for leverage.

He moves inside me passionately, his movements hard and relentless, pushing me into the middle of the bed with each forceful thrust. I could feel myself becoming wetter with each movement, and the pleasure was almost overwhelming. I watch him, mesmerised by the sight of him sweating and panting as he pumped into me with an insatiable desire.

Within a few minutes, pleasure builds within me, and I can't hold back. I climax hard, and soon after, I feel his release inside me, both of us panting, lost in the raw, primal intensity of the moment.

After he pulls out, I could feel myself still dripping with desire. "Excuse me, sir," I said with a teasing glint in my eye as I tried to make my way to the bathroom before my dress got any messier. The urgency and passion of the moment were so overwhelming that I didn't care about my dress, but I had to return to work, and it wouldn't do to be in a state.

Upon my return, Paul looked at me with a mix of surprise and remorse. "Oh, sorry, I don't know what came over me. I just wanted you so badly," he confessed, now running his gaze over the crumpled dress.

I couldn't help but smile, feeling incredibly desired, "Paul, that was incredible," I tell him. "You have no idea how that made me feel - so wanted. And knowing how soft and passionate you can be, I know that was pure desire for me. Take it from me, anytime you feel that urge, go with it."

In that raw moment, I had seen a new side of Paul emerge, and I was eager to explore more of it. Our connection felt so secure now, and I knew that our desires for each other were only growing stronger.

As we sat there, the curiosity about Paul's mysterious morning was consuming me. "You have me so curious about your morning," I said, looking into his eyes with a mix of intrigue and playfulness. "Will I ever know what happened to make you like this?"

Paul's expression softened, and he ran his fingers gently through my hair. "Oh, I hope so," he replied, his voice tinged with both excitement and restraint. "But for now, I must respect all the instructions and keep it under wraps. Hopefully soon, I will be able to share with you what I saw and learned. But for now, Maria, you just have to settle for me," he croons and kisses me.

His words spark a mixture of emotions in me. Part of me was intrigued by the mystery, but another part was content just to have him by my side. "Well, I guess I'll have to make do with that," I said, offering him a playful smile. "Now, we better get back to work. Lunchtime is gone, and we've spent too much time lost in each other."

As I searched for my panties and pulled them on, we prepared to head back to work. Paul took care of the uneaten lunch, and we both tried to refocus our minds on the tasks at hand. It was hard work, because my mind would *not* stop replaying those moments.

The rest of the afternoon was a blur as I delved into the financials and dealt with the usual work queries. However, my head was only half there. My thoughts kept drifting back to our lusty lunchtime encounter. Paul's sudden shift in demeanor had surprised me, igniting a fire within me that I couldn't ignore.

I was dubbed the Ice Maiden due to my cold, stoic exterior, but with Paul, something was different. I found myself burning, yearning for his control, his passion, and his dominance. It was as if a hidden part of me had awakened, craving his touch and surrendering to his desires.

***

As the workday came to an end, I couldn't help but wonder about the newfound desires- that I'd long suspected- Paul had unlocked within me. The mystery of his morning piqued my curiosity, but the mystery of my own emotions was equally captivating. What had he done to me, and how did he evoke such intense feelings? I knew one thing for sure - I was eager to explore this new side of our relationship and see where it would lead us next.

As the day drew to a close, my mind was a whirlwind of emotions and desires. I couldn't fully explain what was happening between Paul and me, but I didn't want to overanalyze it either. All I knew was that I wanted him - more of him, and the more I saw him, the stronger that desire grew. Today had revealed a side of Paul that I hadn't seen before either, a man who could take control with such intensity, and it was an incredible turn-on. I found myself yearning for him to lead, to take charge, and the thought of being cuffed to that hook sent a thrilling shiver down my spine. My feelings had evolved from a simple flirtation over four months ago to something profound and passionate, I realise.

From those initial sparks of attraction, we had grown closer, delving into each other's worlds, sharing intimate moments, and confiding in one another. Today, Paul had elevated the intensity, raising the bar in a way that left me hungry for more. I had expressed my feelings to him after the encounter, but I knew I needed to talk to him again tonight, to see where his thoughts and desires aligned with mine.

Heading back to the hotel, I called Paul to check in with him.

He had been going through the property folder, searching for any new leads or clues. He had even examined the bank statements and accounts, hoping to find a trail of money that might shed light on the situation.

"So, here's an intriguing discovery- the lease on Ralphs' apartment. I went through the contract and the company is leasing this space and has ten years left. This explained why we couldn't simply hand it back; the surrender costs were too steep. However- and get this- guess who's the landlord of the space? That's right, Ralph owns not just his apartment, but the entire building. He is the proprietor of the commercial ground floor and all three apartments!" Paul finishes, sounding shaken.

The pieces of the puzzle were starting to come together, but the mystery seemed to deepen further.

"Is there any reason he would lease to himself?" I sputter in shock.

"Uh…" Paul thinks for a few moments while I get into the taxi to take me to the hotel, "I think tax relief on the rent? Could there be any other reason? But since he's the landlord, he has to pay income taxes on the rent. I guess it could be to hide his assets from his employees. Considering how he has built separate companies for everything; it looks like he's just paranoid about losing what he's built. Every major asset he has got is tied to just one company on its own island, so if that island goes down, it goes down alone."

I nod, even though Paul can't see me.

"Another piece of the puzzle fell into place. While I was combing through the bank statements, I found a main account where all the rents from the apartments and shop units under

179

the main office, as well as the rent for the main office itself, were deposited. It seemed that Ralph had been using these rent accounts as his personal funds, covering his living expenses and other costs. Unsurprisingly, he only utilised a fraction of the collected rents. It doesn't show any extravagant personal spending. Any travel expenses were billed to the business. So, the rent account has been steadily accumulating funds over the years, becoming more than healthy in terms of its balance."

"I see. Alright, bring the bank statements with you, and other accounts sheets you have found too. I'll take a quick look and see how it affects the appraisal now."

"Roger that. Have you reached the hotel?"

"Just around the corner. Hey, when you get here, book your room, but bring your bags to mine. I'll get a second keycard."

"Yes, ma'am. How about we get a quick bite and have a relaxing night in? You pick a movie, and I'll get a bottle of wine," Paul clicks his tongue and I hear shuffling papers at the other end and know that Paul is getting ready to leave. I have just a bit of time until he's here.

Tonight, luck was playing fun games. Joan had booked a room for me, but when I got to the reception, I found out that they had overbooked and there were no regular rooms available. Instead, since I was a regular guest, they graciously offered me a mini suite, which I accepted with no qualms. The space was vast, with a working table and a large cosy couch.

Even with all this space, Paul would have to get another separate room, and although it seemed a bit wasteful to book two rooms, we needed to do so to avoid any unnecessary questions from our offices. I'm putting on the final touches on my make-up when Paul enters my suite with his bag in his hand and his jacket slung over his shoulder. Even the sight of him makes me want to jump at him, but I know I need to talk with him about this afternoon before we jump in bed again.

We decide to go to the hotel bars for dinner, and I pick at the simple offering with my fork. Over our meal, we talk about the day, pondering over Paul's discoveries. There is a moment where we both drift away from the conversation, and I know as much as Paul does that, we travelled to our heated moments this afternoon.

After dinner, Paul gets another bottle of wine from the bar, and we return to our room. His clothes hang on the back of the chair from when he changed earlier. Something about the domesticity of that simple thing makes something clench around my heart. I'd love this to be a regular thing with Paul.

We turn on the TV, more as background noise than for entertainment. Paul asks me to pick a movie, and since I'm not too particular, I choose a light comedy that's more like brain popcorn. It will suffice for the conversation we were going to have. Paul excuses himself for a moment, and I nod, calling at his back, "I'll make myself more comfortable."

He turns, and I see a hint of a smile at the corner of his mouth as he leaves.

I know what he's thinking; that I'll change into the chemise he surprised me with. But seeing his clothes strewn over my room, a special thought had crossed my mind.

When he returns to the room, he finds me sitting on the couch, curled up under his white, now wrinkled work shirt from today and my panties. I can see the surprise in his eyes; he was not expecting to see me in his clothes, but I can tell he doesn't dislike it. No, far from it, if the glint in his eyes is any indication. On some level I can tell Paul understands it's a gesture to show how much I cherish his presence.

"Come here, darling," I whisper, jerking him out of his surprised trance. I love the idea of wearing his shirt, feeling his scent all over me. The soft fabric against my skin reminds me of him, and I relish that feeling.

I pat the couch next to me, and he eagerly comes over and sits down. I adjust myself to get comfortable, curling my head into his shoulder with his arm wrapped around me. It's like finding heaven in his embrace, and his hand gently lands on my exposed thigh. I close my eyes and nuzzle him, whispering, "This is exactly what I needed. I've been longing to feel you close to me all day, to feel your touch." He kisses the top of my head.

As we cuddle closer, the movie playing on the screen becomes mere background noise. My focus is entirely on the warmth and comfort of his embrace. My head is quiet, my thoughts peaceful. My fingers trace gentle patterns over his chest through the fabric of his shirt. Leaning in, I whisper to him, "You know, I loved every second of today, especially at lunchtime. But now, I want to hear about it from you. Where did that come from? What did you find in the albums that got your heart racing? I'm curious what you saw that had us ending up like that," I add with a blush and a playful smile.

My heart pounds in my chest as I wait for Paul's response. He looks a little flustered, his mind obviously revisiting the intense moments we shared earlier.

"I can't tell you what was in the albums, not yet" he starts, his voice filled with a mix of longing and frustration. "The instruction is very particular, but I know there's still a chance for me to share it with you someday soon. The truth might be overwhelming, and I'm not even sure if you'd want to know. I don't know the entire thing either. But you need to understand how much I want you, how deeply we've connected over these past months, and how close we've become.

"When I saw the apartment's potential earlier today, I was strangely already excited. The idea of living with you has stoked my desire like nothing else," he continues. "But then I went to Ralph's office, and as I looked through his safe and albums, you were all I could think of. It was a whirlwind of emotions – the thrill of the apartment, the anticipation of being with you, and seeing Ralph's cherished memories all stirred up my feelings for you. I was overcome with desire, wanting to create our own memories, and fulfill my desires for you. And then you walked into the apartment, and it was like a dam broke, and I couldn't hold back any longer. The passion and longing I had for you just exploded, and I had to kiss you like I did. I wanted us to become one in that moment, own each other… but I didn't know how.

"Your words, 'Don't hold back,' reinvigorated me, gave me the freedom to let go," he confesses. "I couldn't stop myself, and I wanted to see how much you were truly mine, how much you'd follow my lead. And when you played along and teased me, it only fueled the fire within me. I may have been in a position of authority, but I can't control my feelings for you. The more time we spend together, the stronger my desire for you becomes. It might be a complicated situation, but I can't help the overwhelming emotions I have for you. With you, everything feels limitless, even though I know we have our limitations. Much more than normal couples have."

My heart flutters as I look up at Paul, and I can see the sincerity in his eyes, all his emotions laid bare. "Oh, Paul, you have no idea how much those words mean to me," I reply, my voice filled with affection. "I am completely yours, and I want to explore every facet of our connection. With you, I feel safe, loved, and desired. I know you would never hurt me, so I want that rawness from you, that hint of danger that quickens your breath." I'm panting from the motion in his words, and the steady throb of feeling in the bottom of my stomach.

Feeling emboldened by his confession, I decide to take the lead. I sit up and move myself to straddle him, feeling his hand on my back through his shirt. I feel his arousal under me, and I move ever so slightly, making him gasp. I run my fingers gently over his face and through his hair, tilting his face up to meet mine. I kiss him softly at first, savouring the taste of his lips, and then passionately, letting the desire between us build. Our movements are slow, deliberate, as we explore each other's mouths.

Smiling warmly, I break the kiss but keep my forehead pressed against his. "Take me to the bed with you, darling," I whisper, my voice tinged with affection and desire. "I know how difficult it was for you to express your feelings, but I want you to know that I feel the same way, if not more." My words are filled with a promise of intimacy and connection, inviting him for a night of passion in my embrace in our bed.

And slowly, throughout the night, I let him know exactly how deep his affections run.

Chapter 13

Next day at the office was a whirlwind of activity. While the agency secretary Paul's company had hired was diligently handling the scanning and paperwork, I was working on sending it to Manchester for sorting and scheduling. Once I was back at DAF, I'd need to go through it manually and then delegate the records to my team. With the upcoming meeting on Friday, the hosting preparations were also underway, and I had to divide my time between the paperwork and the event preparations. Nicola and Helen were also running around, their eyes glued to the to-do-list on their company tablets. The weight of the upcoming meeting was not just weighing on our minds.

This was going to be Paul's first official meeting with the managers of all outlets, and his appearance had to be perfect. We spent a significant portion of our day in the office meticulously planning and strategizing our approach. We had our PR and Marketing Team curating speeches, providing valuable insights and discussing potential questions that might arise in the meeting with us.

After being at it for almost five hours, we rounded back to the same thing again. The one question we had no answer to, nor an idea where to go with it: Who was the new owner of the company and the boss. No matter which direction we tried, Paul or I were nowhere close to being satisfied with what we could tell the managers about this. Uncertainty loomed, especially with the meeting so close and all the top people confirming their attendance, but we had to face the situation head-on.

As the day drew to a close, my heels feel numb but throbbing with pain at the same time. We head for the train station together, taking our usual seats, the conversation from the night before still lingering between us, unsaid. However, words weren't necessary to convey our feelings, and the connection that had blossomed between us.

Once we're settled in our seats, Paul discreetly touches my hand, rubbing his thumb over the ring on my ring finger, the subtle warmth in his touch activating my tired body. The train ride home is pretty quiet, each of us lost in our thoughts, comfortable in the silence finally afforded to us after a busy day. When our stops are announced, I startle awake to a terrible ache in my neck from nodding off in my sleep, my head finally coming to rest on Paul's shoulder. By the grimace on his face, I can tell the discomfort has been mutual.

The train is emptying, but we're firmly sitting on our seats until it clears entirely. We look at each other with longing once it's time to leave. His voice is soft as he whispers, "Text me over the weekend, let me know where you'd like me to pick you up on Monday. I've booked a country house hotel in Fort William for our Monday night."

I couldn't help but smile and wink at him mischievously. "Perhaps we'll uncover some of Ralph's *spicy* mysteries in Fort William," I playfully suggested.

He scoffs and leaves ahead of me.

***

The weekend is uneventful and uninteresting, but Monday morning arrives with a sense of anticipation. I had asked Paul to pick me up outside my home, not wanting to raise any suspicions by meeting elsewhere. With a 5am start, the neighbourhood is still quiet, everyone snugly tucked in their beds as we embark on our long drive ahead. The sat-nav estimates a 6-hour journey to Fort William, but with a few planned stops, and driver switches, we expect to reach our destination around lunchtime.

The wheels hit the road and I can't help but feel a sense of adventure brewing within me. The thought of exploring a new place with Paul by my side was exhilarating. We both are dressed casually, embracing the laid-back vibe of our road trip. The drive took us through the breathtaking landscapes of the Lake District. The rising sun painted the sky with hues of orange and pink, casting a golden glow over the serene lakes. It was a spectacular sight to behold.

Caught up in the beauty of the moment, I am admiring the sunrise when Paul suddenly pulls over to the side of the road. He gestures at me to step out of the car, and without hesitation, I follow his lead. Standing there, with the picturesque landscape unfolding before us, Paul leans on the front of the car and gently pulls me close from behind, enveloping me in his embrace. I sigh loudly, enjoying this moment of intimate togetherness.

We both gaze at the stunning view, and I feel an overwhelming sense of contentment and freedom. Paul's arms wrapped around me made me feel safe and cherished. There was an air of simplicity in that moment, yet it held a profound significance for both of us. "Isn't this fabulous?" he murmurs, the warmth of his breath on my ear sending shivers down my spine. "I love being able to stop like this and just hold you as I want. It's a shame we don't have more time for moments like this."

With the world unfolding in front of us and Paul's tender touch, I couldn't help but agree wholeheartedly. There was something so special about the spontaneity of our journey, the freedom to explore and embrace our surroundings without the need to hide. We stand there, watching the sun paint the sky red, enveloped together for long minutes.

In the end, we both know we're on the clock, losing time we have promised to people. Reluctantly, we tear ourselves away from the mesmerising sunrise- *How long has it been since I have enjoyed the simpler things in life with someone?* - and turn to leave. Paul pulls me into his side unexpectedly, and I gasp, chuckling.

"What are you doing?"

"Immortalising this moment with you," he murmurs cryptically, and my queries are answered when he whips out his phone. Pulling me even closer, with the radiant sunrise as our backdrop, he snaps a selfie of us, both of us smiling and looking genuinely happy. I look at the picture afterward; it's simply gorgeous, and I wish I could keep a copy of it as a memento.

Paul looks at my dipping mood and reads my mind, "This is the first of many of our memories," he says, his voice warm with affection. "I've wanted a picture like this of us for ages, just to have a visual reminder of our memories. It's perfect, a snapshot of this lovely road trip and adventure we're embarking on. Something we'll treasure for a lifetime."

Paul's words touch my heart, and I know this photo was the beginning of many cherished memories to come. I nod and smile weakly.

Once we're back in the car, Paul exhales and grunts, "Now, come on, let's get a coffee at the next service stop and keep going."

With that, we continue our journey through the picturesque Lake District. The scenery was nothing short of breathtaking, with the sun shining brightly, accentuating the vibrant colours and delightful scents of the area. The views out over the glistening lakes were awe-inspiring, and I found myself feeling so at ease and relaxed in Paul's company.

As we drove northward, the landscape changed dramatically. We left the lush and serene lakes behind and entered a much planer terrain. But the beauty of the journey didn't diminish; instead, it transformed into a majestic scene as we approached the mountains. The imposing peaks towered on either side of us, their grandeur almost overwhelming. Water cascaded down from the mountainsides, even in the summertime, adding a touch of wildness to the landscape.

The sight of those majestic mountains left me in awe, and I couldn't help but feel a sense of wonderment after such a long time.

With Paul by my side, the journey took on an almost adventure-esque quality, and I knew that this road trip was more than just a drive to Fort William; it was a journey of togetherness. As we pressed on, I realised that the memories we were creating together would be etched into our hearts forever, and although I really wanted to keep that photo of us, in my heart I would remember that moment with all its magic.

The drive to Fort William was the most fun I'd had on any road trip. We munched on snacks, played country music, sang loudly and off-key until the other grimaced, and laughed out loud on terrible jokes. The air was so fresh, entirely different from London, and it seemed I had changed as well. A comfortable lightness had swept over me, and I was bubbly as champagne.

As the sun peeked over the clouds, the scene became even more devastatingly beautiful, and we couldn't resist stopping at a lay-by to take in the magnificent view of the mountains, basking in the warm embrace of the sun. The landscape before us was both stark and beautiful, with the mountains standing tall and bare in the summer sun. There were sparse bushes, but not much vegetation endured. I couldn't help but be amazed by the stunning scenery, and a sense of wonder washed over me. *How had I never ventured to this breathtaking part of the country before?*

Our journey continued, following the roads that led us toward Glencoe and eventually Fort William. Along the way, we passed a sign for Chalets in the Woods, which piqued my curiosity. We watched hill walkers crossing the roads near the car parks, ready to embark on their countryside hikes and adventures and I felt a twinge of envy. A day spent hiking and wandering amidst this picturesque wilderness with Paul by my side seemed like a dream.

We were turning on a treacherous slope when Paul shared a somber fact with me.

"They say this is around where Ralph had his accident. Somewhere nearby."

The thought of the stark contrast between the sun-kissed mountains we were witnessing and the wintry landscape with snow-capped peaks and icy roads in colder months, a car going out-of-control, Ralph helpless in this remote area, brought a hint of sadness.

As we approached Fort William, Paul decided to stop and check the map and directions to the cottage we were heading to. He parked the car on the side of the road, taking a moment to ensure we were on the right path. With an exhilarating *hurrah*, he announced that the cottage was just a few minutes away, situated after crossing a nearby bridge. Although I had insisted throughout the journey for him to take a break while I drove, he had been adamant to drive. It was gentlemanly of him, but I could imagine he was tired now. His thoughtfulness warmed my heart.

We pulled off the road to the left, and the cottage soon came into view. It was a vision of tranquility, nestled at the foot of the mountains and set back from the road. The white cottage exuded country charm and was well-maintained. I noticed, and so did Paul, how the surrounding woodland secured the privacy of the cottage dwellers in a ring of seclusion, making it an ideal retreat away from the hustle and bustle of the world.

We arrived at the cottage just after noon, and almost collapsed from tiredness. The journey had been picturesque, and wrought with emotional moments, and it had taken too much out of me. I wasn't twenty at all, that was for sure. Still, with each advancing step toward the cottage, I felt increasingly grateful to be sharing this experience with Paul, and I knew that our time in Fort William would be nothing less than a discovery further into our relationship.

Paul takes out a set of keys with a flourish and approaches the door. "Deep breaths," he whispers, "Who knows what surprises Ralph has left for us on the other side."

I know he's just kidding because as we step into the cottage, a musty and damp air greets us, confirming my suspicion that the place had been left untouched for quite some time. The immaculate exterior contrasts sharply with the neglected interior, giving it the appearance of a deserted and unlived space. It was like stepping into a bachelor pad frozen in time. Old paintings adorn the walls, showcasing scenic views, but there are no personal photographs of anyone, except for one moth-eaten, browning picture of an elderly couple, which I presume to be Ralph's parents. Surprisingly, there are no pictures of Ralph, not even from childhood, and that makes me feel the solitude and loneliness that envelops the house.

Paul deposits the keys on the centre, low legged table and we proceed to explore every nook and cranny of the house. Paul meticulously checks all the drawers, cupboards, and single heavy oak wardrobe, while I observe in awe. The house seems to yield little in terms of valuable possessions, mostly just Ralph's clothes and a few personal effects. Paul carefully records anything significant that we found during our search, taking note of each detail. He takes a few pictures, and I see him attaching them in an email.

After spending about two hours thoroughly examining the cottage, and recording our flimsy findings, we get ready to move.

A thought crosses my mind, "Paul, didn't you say there were instructions to dispose of something here?" I inquire, "What did you expect to destroy here? I was hoping to uncover the big secret, but it seems we'll have to wait a bit longer."

Paul nods, lost in thought, "Nothing to destroy here, it appears. The directions led to nothing, so perhaps Ralph had it all managed before his passing. The instructions were written several years ago, so that could very well be the case. It seems this adventure will test your patience for a little while longer." He smiles teasingly, keeping the answers just out of my reach. I'm excited to find out what he's been keeping from me, but my curiosity is tinged with disappointment now. What if it's something banal, how interesting could the old man have been anyway?

Still, I was invested in exploring this intriguing tale.

We set off for Fort William, and despite my love for the road trip, I was tired from all the driving. Nevertheless, we arrived in town after a thankfully short drive, and decided to explore a bit before heading to the shop. The town had a charming, cosy feel to it, with its few markets and restaurants. Some restaurants boasted a waterfront location, and I wondered if this was a fishing town too. The outdoor and adventure stores scattered around the town hinted at its popularity as a climbing destination, which was a given since the town was at the foot of the towering Ben Nevis.

We didn't have to look around much to find a delightful café and quickly got seated for a light lunch there. After all the snacks on the journey here, I wasn't in much mood for food, so I got salad and a toffee sundae in a plastic cup. Sitting by the window, Paul and I observed the laid-back atmosphere and holiday mood of the town. We were dressed super casually- far from the usual formal attire we were accustomed to in the city. It felt like a completely different world from our typical days.

Finally, it was 2:30 PM when we arrived at the shop. Dressed in jeans and casual t-shirts with sunglasses, we blended in with the other customers. The shop was impressive, showcasing high-end outdoor clothing and a specialised climbing section. As we ventured to the back of the shop, our eyes widened at the sight of a climbing wall, complete with a sign warning that it should not be used without supervision. The reception was busy booking climbing sessions.

The shop's interior was ballooning with an adventurous spirit, and I couldn't help but imagine the thrill of scaling those walls. Paul and I exchanged excited glances, both silently contemplating the possibility of engaging in such an exhilarating experience. It was clear that this town was a haven for outdoor enthusiasts, and we wondered how it would be if we could immerse ourselves in this world.

Looking around in wonder and awe, I'm sure we came across to the staff as other wide-eyed customers. Thus, it was no big surprise when a friendly shop assistant approached us, offering her assistance.

"Can I help you with anything?" She smiled her friendly smile at us.

"Sure, is Caroline around?" I ask, without missing a beat.

The assistant is a bit taken aback, but she recovers quickly and points to a woman behind the till. I looked at the counter; Caroline looked like she was in her early 30s, fit and attractive. A perfect brand image. She was dressed in casual outdoor clothing adorned with the shop's logo and has a no-nonsense demeanor. She was helping a customer with their purchase and total when we walked up.

Once Caroline finished with the customer, we introduced ourselves. She appeared a bit serious and nervous at first, but Paul quickly reassured her, "This is just a routine visit, we're merely here to observe and learn about the shop," He starts in a conversational tone and continues, "We were at the house earlier, that was the primary reason for our visit. But we're here to let you know that all shops stay the same, and nothing is to change. Do you mind giving us a tour of the shop now?"

We explore the shop with Caroline as our guide, and soon her passion for the business becomes evident. It's obvious she takes immense pride in her work, and the quality of the gear the shop offers. It's clear that she wasn't just a manager clocking in hours. Paul continues to engage with her, asking about Ralph and his involvement in the shops. In a few moments Caroline visibly relaxes and shares what she knows about Ralph.

"I've known Ralph since I was a child. My mother worked as a manager here, and after she passed away in 2007, Ralph offered me her position. I've been here since then. Which seems like all my adult life." Caroline scoffs.

"Did Ralph come here often?"

"Often, yes. About once a month at least. He was a good man, never interrupting my flow or challenging my decisions. He let me do whatever I liked with the place," She looks around, and I realise the unique character of the shop comes from her personality. She continues, "Although, you see that back climbing wall? I wanted to move it to a bigger place on the side, but Ralph put his foot down. He would often humorously say that this wall stays as is, he can put up a new wall, but no taking this one down. I bothered him a lot to get a clearer explanation but never received one from Ralph. He would simply say, "The wall is responsible for a lot," and I heard him saying the same to my mother, although she was in on the joke," Caroline pouts, perhaps remembering her dead mother.

Caroline could prove an incomparable resource on Ralph's life, and I could tell Paul had picked up on it. We finished our tour around the shop, and Paul conversationally asked her if she could accompany us to the coffee shop on the corner where we could talk more.

"We could get something to drink, and we could talk some more shop and business," Paul asked expectantly.

"Sure, of course. I didn't know what the nature of your visit was, so I got some more help around the store than usual. Some of the staff don't start their shifts until the evening, but I thought I should be available if we needed to do an in-depth review of stocks and books," Caroline answered seriously.

I knew exactly why Paul was inviting her over for coffee, and it was not because of the books or account sheets. It was solely because she was the only person who felt comfortable talking about the enigma that was Ralph and was relaxed about it. We needed to extract as much information from Caroline as we could.

We walk to the coffee shop Paul had mentioned and in a cosy corner, nursing our drinks, Paul encourages Caroline to begin.

"We will talk about the stocks later, first let's talk about Ralph. We need to understand the man to understand the business."

Caroline nods, understanding that any insights into Ralph could prove helpful in our work. She leans back, takes a sip of her coffee, and starts to speak. She reveals that she has known Ralph her whole life since her mother had worked at the shop as a manager.

"Did you know this was his first outlet? The first of the six." she gushes proudly.

"My mother was not just the manager, but also a buyer for the group. That meant attending trade shows and ordering stock for all the shops, introducing new lines, and so forth. In the early years, Ralph used to visit this shop frequently, often staying at the cottage, which was his parents' home, where he had spent his childhood growing up. He had a deep love for the mountains and the landscape here, and led mountain walks for tourists who visited every season."

Caroline described Ralph as a lovely man, always kind and friendly towards her. She fondly remembered her younger days when she used to do her homework in her mother's office, and Ralph never minded her presence.

"It was odd, though, that he had never married or even had a girlfriend, as far as the gossip knows. I found it such a shame, growing up, considering what a good and fair man he was. When his parents passed away, they left him the cottage, and he held onto it dearly, spending time there despite having no other family." Caroline takes a pause and then continues.

"As time went on, Ralph's visits to the shop became less frequent. After my mother passed away, he managed the shop himself for a while before appointing a manager. The manager left not soon after, and that's when Ralph chose me for the job. He continued to keep an eye on the shop's progress in my early days as I settled, but my charge was smooth. His visits became less frequent, I assume he thought he needn't pay much more attention to it since it was going well."

Caroline's voice took on a somber tone as she continued to recount her memories of Ralph. "I sensed a change in him over time, a subtle shift in his demeanour that left him less joyful than I remembered. In my mind, I attributed it to the heavy burden of his expanding business empire, with six shops and distribution operations demanding his attention. Ambitious plans for further growth loomed on the horizon, but somehow, they never came to fruition. It seemed as if Ralph had lost interest in his own dreams. Looking back, I realise it

194

was not the business, Ralph was never too stressed by it, but something else. Like a light had left his eyes, or something.

"Anyway, until the end he was protective of me, always concerned for my well-being. I guess he was attached to me, despite his reserved nature. However, he guarded the inner workings of life with utmost secrecy. Whenever I asked how he was, the response was always the same - 'Fine, busy as ever.' Whatever his struggles or feelings, he kept them to himself." she looked away in the distance, probably imagining all the times he'd said it to her. I wonder if she thought she should have asked him more, while he was still around to answer her.

Caroline couldn't help but notice that Ralph didn't seem to indulge in personal luxuries either, despite his apparent wealth. The profits from his successful shops were left untouched in their accounts, and he drove an old Land Rover that she confirmed had been with him for years. She remembered her mother's insistence that he get a better car for himself, especially for winter travels to the area, but he resisted change. Even when encouraged to buy a new car in 2006, he stuck with the familiar Land Rover, sometimes leaving it in London, but often using it for his visits to the mountains.

The tragic accident had shaken Caroline deeply. Ralph had met with an unfortunate fate, hitting a patch of ice on the road that led to a disastrous crash. The funeral, she recalled, was a small and somewhat lonely affair, attended by a handful of faces she recognized from the London office and a few others she didn't know. Most attendees appeared to be work connections, leaving an impression of a solitary journey to his final resting place alongside his parents.

When Paul inquired about the cottage, Caroline described how a handyman tended to the exterior maintenance, ensuring the grass was kept trim and the facade was painted and clean. No pipes or holes in the old roof leaked under his charge The bills were sent to the shop, and the expenses were taken care of accordingly.

"I've never been inside the cottage, though, so I can't really tell you about it. Maybe Ralph employed a cleaner? But this is a small town, and I would be aware of it if it was true. I don't even know if anyone other than him had the keys to the cottage. Ralph was wildly protective of his space." Caroline finally finished, and Paul appeared to be lost in his thoughts.

We finish our drinks in silence, Paul asking a question here and there, but there's no more to be gleaned from Caroline anymore. Her words lingered in the air, but Paul and I tried to push aside the weight of loneliness and solitude that enveloped Ralph. We thanked her for her insights and assurances, promising to meet her again in London on Friday. As we bid her farewell, Paul's voice was tinged with authority as he advised, "Let's not rush to make any changes in the shop that Ralph wouldn't approve of. Let's wait and see what the new owners have to say, I'm sure they'll appreciate you holding off any changes in his memory."

Caroline nods dutifully and rattles out the directions to the hotel we'd booked for our stay.

We have a bit of time until we would need to get ready for dinner, so Paul suggests we take this opportunity to properly see Ben Nevis. We veer off the main road, greeted by signposts for the famed Ben Nevis Trail. As we arrived at the foot of the Trail, weary walkers were returning from their adventures in the highlands, shedding their day bags and fatigue. All around us people were buzzing with a sense of accomplishment and relaxed friendship with new and old friends from their walk.

Crossing a quaint bridge over a shining river, we took a leisurely stroll along the trail, immersed and inspired by the scenery around us. It was like we'd walked right inside one of those exceptionally beautiful landscape paintings. Although we were not dressed for serious trekking, we embraced the beauty around us, ignoring the weird glances we received from people in professional gear. It was no wonder Ralph had spent a lifetime being in love with this place. I scarcely wanted to leave here to go to my room.

On our way back, as we crossed the bridge once more, Paul stopped and leaned on the railing, gazing at the gently flowing river beneath. I stood beside him, struck by the natural beauty

196

that unfolded before our eyes. "It is beautiful," I murmured, my heart skipping a beat.

Paul's touch warmed me as he wrapped his arms around me from behind, his chin resting gently on my shoulder. His affectionate embrace made my heart flutter, and I felt a surge of emotion as he whispered softly, "Yes, beautiful doesn't even begin to describe what I see." His words carried a double entendre, capturing the essence of both the breathtaking scenery and his feelings for me.

In his embrace, I feel cherished and protected, cocooned from the world as we stood in awe of nature's grandeur. The passing walkers faded into insignificance as we shared this intimate moment together, appreciating the beauty surrounding us. The river's soothing melody played in the background, creating the perfect soundtrack to our serene embrace.

In that instant, time seemed to slow down, and nothing else mattered but the bond we shared.

After a few minutes, Paul held my hand and pulled me to the car.

"Alright, we better find our hotel quickly. I have dinner booked for seven-thirty, but it would be nice to relax before that," Paul said, looking at my tired eyes.

Thankfully, the satnav indicated that we were just a few minutes away from the hotel. I sighed in relief; today had been way over my physical activity limit. As we enter the hotel, I just know Paul has outdone himself this time. The reception area exuded a timeless elegance, adorned with antique furniture and classic décor. A friendly staff member greeted us warmly, and Paul checked us in with a beaming smile.

We were both exhausted from the day's travels, but we smiled at each other as we made our way to our suite. Ascending the grand staircase, we reached the top floor where our room awaited us. Stepping inside, I couldn't help but marvel at the opulence surrounding us. The suite was full of old-world charm, with its ornate wallpaper, rich wooden furnishings, and tall windows draped in elegant curtains.

In the heart of the room, an open gas fire cast a warm glow, even though the season didn't call for it. The ambiance it created was enchanting, and I imagine how delightful it would be to cuddle up by the fire here with Paul during the winter months. To one side of the room, there were two small, cosy couches and a coffee table. It was the perfect nook to sit and enjoy each other's company, to share laughter and intimate conversations as we sipped on fine wine.

Even though I'm tired, and sleep is knocking at my eyes, we explore further, and enter the bathroom, and I am struck by the contrasting modernity of the space. It seemed they had combined two rooms to create this sprawling, lavish suite. The centerpiece was an indulgent jacuzzi bath, beckoning us to immerse ourselves in its soothing waters. The thought of enjoying a luxurious bubble bath together brought a smile to my face. After today, I wanted nothing more than climbing into the tub and letting go of everything.

The room also boasted a large walk-in shower, adorned with sleek tiles and modern fixtures. There were his and hers sinks, each framed by ornate mirrors, adding a touch of sophistication to the space. I playfully remark, "This bathroom is larger than my bedroom. After today I'd feel like I live in a closet abc home."

Both of us chuckle.

Feeling weary yet content, we drop our bags and collapse onto the plush bed. We lay there, relishing the comfort of the mattress and the warmth of each other's presence. Wrapped in each other's arms, we enjoy the simple pleasure of being close, sharing quiet moments of affection. The soft glow from the bedside lamps illuminated the room, casting a warm glow over us as we drifted into a state of pure bliss.

As the minutes passed, the outside world faded away, and soon my surroundings did too. I don't know when I fell asleep, but it was the best sleep I had gotten outside of our hotel in London. After a restful slumber wrapped in the warmth of Paul's embrace, I woke to the aroma of freshly brewed coffee.

It was around 6:30 in the evening, and I couldn't believe how sound I had slept.

As I stretched, arching my back and yawning, Paul gently handed me the coffee I was smelling, and I took a grateful sip, savouring the rich, comforting flavour. Paul reminds me of our dinner reservation at 7:30 in the hotel's dining room and it dawned on me that I must have dozed off without realising it. Despite feeling a bit drowsy, Paul had a thoughtful surprise for me.

"Come, I have drawn you a bubble bath. You loved the jacuzzi so much. Maybe a soak and a glass of wine might help you come back to me," He laughed, seeing me yawn again.

The idea of soaking in warm, fragrant bubbles sounded heavenly, and I eagerly agree.

I playfully ask him to join me. The bath looked spacious enough for both of us, and after the busy day we had, sharing this moment together was perfect.

I head to the bathroom, and upon entering, I am greeted by a delightful sight. Paul did not hold back on the bubble bath; it was nearly overflowing with fluffy bubbles. While Paul fetches me a glass of wine, I quickly undress, letting my clothes fall to the floor without a care, knowing I wouldn't be wearing them again today. As I eased myself into the warm, bubbly water, the jacuzzi jets hummed to life, sending gentle ripples through the surface. I could feel the water's comforting embrace, almost like a soothing massage, as I adjusted my position, letting the jets caress the tight spots on my back and shoulders.

Just as I was getting lost in the bliss of the moment, Paul walks in, holding two glasses of white wine. The sight of him made my heart skip a beat. He smiles warmly, admiring the sight of me, content neck-deep into bubbles. Paul settles behind me on the ledge. He hands me a glass of crisp white wine, and as the soothing liquid caresses my mouth, while his skilled hands begin to massage my shoulders. A contented sigh escapes my lips. "Oh, this is heaven," I moan and sigh, fully enjoying his touch.

His hands moved with precision, tracing delicate patterns over my shoulders and chest. It felt like he knew exactly how to ease any tension, and I couldn't help but appreciate his caring gesture. After a couple of minutes, I reach for his hand, gently guiding him closer. "Come in with me, please," I whisper, yearning for his body against mine.

Paul rises from the edge of the tub, and I watch him undress. Even after all this time, the sight of him still stirs an electrifying response within me. He slides into the bath, sitting opposite me. Our eyes lock, and I playfully tease him with a subtle touch of my feet against his arousal, igniting a spark of desire between us. Without any hesitation, he moves me around in the water and I come to nestle between his legs, leaning back against his chest. He wraps his strong arms and legs around me, cocooning me in his affectionate embrace. I'm overwhelmed, basking in the sheer bliss of our intimacy.

Paul's gentle caresses continue, his fingers brushing over my breasts in the water. Each touch sends a slight electric charge through me, heightening my senses. We linger in the warm bath, losing track of time, cherishing the moment of peaceful togetherness. But as 7 o'clock approaches, reality- and Paul- calls me back.

"Come on, Maria, we have a dinner reservation," Paul gently reminds me.

Reluctantly, I replied, "Must we?" I wanted to stay wrapped in his arms forever. But he chuckles, "Come on, we have plenty of time to relax later."

With a sigh, I move, and we step out of the bath. Paul was right, I do actually feel refreshed. Paul, ever thoughtful, wraps a warm towel around me and begins to help dry my body. It was such a simple gesture, yet it warmed my heart.

"Looks like the cold air is getting to you, too," I joke, teasingly winking at his fading arousal.

"Gee, thanks. Such an ego boost," he teased back, and we both laugh. He grabs a towel and heads to the bedroom, and I follow.

As we prepare for the evening, we slip into a tandem. I take my time savouring the moment, as I observe Paul dressing, unpacking, and slipping into a pair of pants and a shirt. I particularly enjoy his rolling muscles and broad flexing shoulders, his shirt tight over his body. It felt so natural, like we had been doing this routine for years.

The June evening outside was beautiful, with the sun casting its warm glow on everything around us. There's a little breeze and I opt for a short summer dress, buttoned up the front, keeping things simple and comfortable. The bath had slightly messed up my hair, but I did my best to fix it before we headed downstairs.

In the hotel dining room, we enjoy a relaxed dinner, reveling in each other's company and the holiday vibe that fills the air. Everyone around us seemed to be on vacation, creating a lively atmosphere. It was a refreshing change from the usual sedate and business-like atmosphere of London hotel dining rooms.

After dinner, Paul suggests we take a leisurely stroll through the gardens and down to the water's edge, where we could have our green tea to end the dinner. It sounded like a wonderful idea, and as we walk hand in hand, I feel so carefree and at ease. We stand stationary, looking at the water lapping at the edge, Paul's arms around me, enveloping me in a warm embrace.

We discover a secluded bench hidden away among large shrubs, still basking in the evening sun as it begins to set. We settle on the bench, and Paul encourages me to stretch out and relax.

I did as he wanted, lying down with my head in his lap, gazing up at him. He tenderly strokes the side of my face in silence. His other hand rests on my stomach, and his fingers gently caress the fabric of my dress, sending tingles of pleasure through my body. My hand brushes over his, silently conveying my appreciation for his touch, but not enough to interrupt his gentle ministrations.

Our eyes lock, and he flashes me a soft smile as his fingers playfully unfasten just one button on my dress, exposing a hint of my warm skin. The sensation of his touch was electrifying, and I could feel my heart race with excitement. All I could see was the adoring gaze in his eyes, as his fingers continued their soft exploration.

I shifted my position, sitting up and leaning back against Paul, my head resting against the side of his face, and my legs still stretched along the bench. His fingers were making their way out of my dress, but I stop him gently, holding his hand. In a hushed whisper, I urge him, "Don't stop," and unbutton the next button under the one he had already undone, granting him more access.

Though the garden was quiet, we both knew he could easily withdraw his hand if anyone happened to approach. Nuzzling in closer to him, I couldn't suppress the soft whimpers escaping my lips as his touch ignited a fiery desire within me. I gave his hand a slight push, silently urging him to go further. He obliged, sliding his hand into my dress, reaching down until it reached the top of my panties. He stops there, massaging in feather-light touches, teasing me. The anticipation is almost unbearable, and I crave his touch inside the delicate fabric.

His hand continues its exploration, and I close my eyes, savouring the sensations as his fingers caress me through the lace. Slowly, ever so slowly, his fingers move downward. His hand presses flat against me, his palm rubbing gently over my clit as his fingers find their way between my lips, pushing inside me with ease. I am throbbing with desire, my body soaking with longing.

His middle finger delves deeper, gently sliding in and out, the friction hot against my clit, each movement sending waves of pleasure through me. I couldn't help but moan softly, feeling myself drawing closer to the brink, clutching hard at his thigh.

"My god, darling, if you don't stop, you will make me cum," I gasp, the sensations becoming almost overwhelming.

In response, he kisses my ear, whispering, "I better not stop then."

With that encouragement, he adds a second finger, his palm still moving over my clit. His fingers pick up pace, moving in and out with increased urgency, while his palm applies gentle pressure, heightening the pleasure even more. I am on the precipice, my body trembling with anticipation. Then, in a breathy whisper, he coaxes me, "Cum for me... cum, I want to feel your wetness all over me."

His words were all the permission I needed. I surrender to the overwhelming pleasure, my body spasming as I climax, releasing my desire over his fingers and hand. I moan, biting at his bicep, the pleasure running through me like a hurricane.

After Paul slowly withdraws his fingers from me, his fingertips trail up my stomach and out of my dress, and I turn my head to gaze at him. The desire in his eyes is evident as he lifts his hand to his lips and tastes me from his fingers. "You taste divine," he murmurs before kissing me deeply and passionately. My body was still humming from my climax, and I was still swollen and sensitive.

With a smile, Paul takes me off the bench by my hand, and I lean against him as we head back inside. He deftly closes the buttons on my dress and takes my hands in his as we leisurely make our way back to the hotel.

"Come, we can't have you catching a cold," he chuckles.

The warmth of the evening surrounds us as we strolled hand in hand.

Upon reaching the room, Paul looks at me and notices my fatigue. "You look tired," he observes, concern etched on his face. "Come on, let's get you into bed." He helps me out of my dress, gently laying me out on the soft mattress. My bra soon follows, as he moves to my bag to find the black chemise. "Put this on, honey," he says tenderly, helping me slide it over my head.

Paul undresses down to his shorts, and together, we slip under the cool sheet, the night air still warm around us. With Paul's arms wrapped around me, and fully content, I drift off to sleep.

***

I experience a night of deep and uninterrupted rest.

I must have been completely out, as I woke at 8 am to the soft clinking of room service delivering a breakfast trolley that Paul must have ordered. My senses gradually awaken, and I see Paul in his casual shorts and a T-shirt, attending to the arrangements. He pours me a steaming cup of coffee, and I observe him with affection as he moves about the room.

I get up from the bed, still wearing the black chemise he had chosen for me the previous night and join him at the table for breakfast. We sit across from each other, the morning light streaming in through the window, creating a warm atmosphere.

After enjoying that first coffee feeling and breakfast, I decided it was time for a shower. With a playful suggestion, I invite him to join me if he fancied it. Stepping towards the bathroom, I lift the chemise over my head, as I smoothly step out of my panties, all the while feeling his gaze over the naked inches of my body. At the door, I glance back at him, my eyes locking onto the sight of his body, naked and already aroused. A sense of desire and anticipation fills the air. Yesterday I was too out of it to reciprocate, but I had woken up charged.

Without uttering a word, I smile at him and turn, walking into the bathroom. As the sound of running water fills the room, I feel his presence behind me. I wrap my arms around his neck, pulling him close for a tender kiss. "Come inside, darling, I want to get wet," I whisper, pulling him under the stream of the shower, my eyes sparkling with mischief.

With a grin on his face, he wastes no time and jumps in with me. The water flows over us, washing away any lingering fatigue from the night before and renewing our energy for the day ahead. We savour every moment, taking our time to explore each other's bodies, caressing and teasing with gentle touches and passionate kisses. Paul washes himself, and then with tender care, he turns his attention to me, tracing every curve and contour. It felt so natural, so right, to be intimately

204

connected like this. We don't rush, allowing the warmth of the shower and our affectionate touches to envelop us.

The time seemed to slow down as we basked in the pleasure of each other's touch. There was no pressure, no hurry, just two souls entwined in a moment of intimacy. I couldn't have asked for a more perfect start to the day.

***

Eventually, the time came to get ready for the day ahead. We pack our belongings, and check out of the lovely country hotel, and hit the road around 9:30 AM. My mind wanders to Ralph's cottage we had passed earlier. I thought we might stop by, but Paul surprised me when he drove right past it.

Curious, I ask, "Aren't we going back to the cottage?" His eyes shadowed as he replied, "We left early so we could enjoy a nice stop for lunch in the Lake District. Let's take a walk, soak in the sunshine, and make the most of this romantic adventure."

I place my hand on his thigh, giving it a gentle squeeze, "Who said romance is dead? What a lovely idea."

We arrive at a charming lakeside restaurant for lunch, the sun casting its warm rays over the tranquil water, reflecting sparkles on our faces. After savouring a delicious meal, we took a leisurely walk around the lake, hand in hand, reveling in each other's company and the stunning scenery. As we walked, time seemed to stretch, allowing us to fully immerse ourselves in the moment.

We found a soft patch of grass near the water and laid down. The minutes turned into an hour as we lounged lazily on the grass, content in the peacefulness of the moment. "Better get back to reality soon," I say reluctantly, not wanting this perfect day to end. Before we leave, we take one last photo together, stretched out on the grass by the serene lake. Paul was smiling in the picture, and I couldn't help but feel a deep sense of gratitude for these precious memories we were creating together.

***

Once back in Manchester, the familiar chaos of family life greets me right at the door.

The house was filled with the sounds of squabbling children and Mark, who seemed completely oblivious to the pandemonium around him, was engrossed in a phone call. He barely glances at me as I walk in, muttering, "Good, you're home, your problem now. They've been like this for an hour." He disappears in the adjacent room.

I looked at the children, trying to make sense of the situation. They were all arguing over which takeout to order, each one stubbornly insisting on their favourite. It was already 8 pm, and I couldn't believe they hadn't had dinner yet. "You haven't had dinner yet?" I ask incredulously.

In unison, they reply, "No."

Yet again I have to take charge of the situation. I ask each kid what they wanted, quickly deciding on Chinese since it was the fastest option and the older two didn't have any issues with it. I suspected the third wouldn't have any complaints when she'd see her siblings enjoying it. Once the food arrived, calm settled over the house as everyone quietly dug into their meals.

What a rude but necessary awakening to come home to such chaos.

Mark, as usual, showed complete indifference to the family dynamics, leaving everything for me to handle. After the kids were settled in bed, I thought I'd finally have a chance to talk to him. But as we sat down together, it became unsurprisingly clear that it wasn't going to be a genuine discussion. He casually mentions, "I'm heading away with the boys for a weekend in July, golfing. I need a break. I assume you have no problem and can cover the kids." He's still on his phone. I wonder how his project is going, for him to have time to go golfing.

He did not check with me to see if I would be available; rather it was a directive. He spoke about his plans and then got up to leave the table without even inquiring about my trip to Scotland. I couldn't help but feel exhausted by his weaponised incompetence. Feeling disappointed and drained, I simply reply, "Scotland was lovely, thanks for asking, but very tiring."

He stops for a moment, looks at me briefly, and says, "Okay, well at least that's finished," before walking away.

Exhausted and emotionally drained, I decide to retreat to bed early. I had to wake up early for work the next day and had a lot of catching up to do after being away today. As I drifted off to sleep, all I could think was that it was becoming increasingly frustrating, with Mark's disinterest in our lives and his tendency to delegate all responsibilities to me. It was time for a serious conversation, but it seemed like the timing was never right, and I was left feeling alone and unheard.

Chapter 14

I had just arrived at work, to my DAF office, and was barely sipping my coffee when my phone rang. It was the Junior Accountant who I had assigned the task of going through Ralph's office paperwork. She requested that I come down to her office to look at her discovery, so I obliged and made my way there.

With a proud flourish, the Junior accountant greets me, and presents her report "I am finished. I went through all the bank paperwork, statements, and investments." She hands me a meticulously prepared balance sheet, and as I scan through it, I can't help but be impressed by her thoroughness.

She continues, "There does not appear to be any loans or liabilities that I can see. This guy was very wealthy."

Her words pique my interest, and I ask to confirm, "Despite his wealth, it seems he spent very little on himself, no travels, shopping sprees or holidays?"

"None," she confirms, "That's what it looks like. It's quite unusual." Her brows furrow. It *is* quite unusual which is why I must suspect something was going on. Was Ralph saving all his wealth for someone? His successor, perhaps?

As I delved further into the balance sheet, my eyes widened in shock. The magnitude of Ralph's wealth was staggering. Yet, he seemed to live a surprisingly frugal life. It was puzzling, and I wondered what his reasons might have been.

My voice is tinged with disbelief when I inquire again, "Are you sure about these figures?" My eyes rove over the hefty figures underlined on the page.

The Junior accountant nods confidently, assuring me that she has thoroughly examined every detail. She explains that they were still waiting for a property valuation of Ralph's apartment building, which hadn't been accounted for in the balance sheet. I had called an auctioneer ahead and given him the details of the building and gotten a tentative valuation that I'd used for my notes. Soon we will get the estimated value, but for now I have a clear idea of Ralph's finances.

The report she has presented is nothing short of remarkable, revealing the vast wealth of Ralph's estate. This inheritance would make the recipient unimaginably rich, with cash and property assets beyond compare. Since the inheritance was in cash and property, the taxes could be paid without financing or property sale. The more we uncovered this case, the more the mystery around Ralph deepened. His financial choices and lifestyle contradict the typical behaviour I'd come to expect of someone with such wealth. I couldn't help but wonder again about the hidden motivations and secrets behind his seemingly modest existence. Why would a man live without making a family, without having any hobbies or rich personal interests, I wonder.

"Thank you for your work. Let's get you prepared to sit in on the meeting with the solicitors. Make sure you have a comprehensive report outlining this discovery, and send the report beforehand to Paul Bridges and." The Junior assistant's face split into a large smile; the opportunity to be part of this high-level gathering was a well-deserved recognition of her hard work.

As I walk back to my office, I feel the atmosphere in the workplace was charged. Whispers and glances follow me, and I couldn't help but wonder what had sparked such interest. Was my appearance somehow amiss- did I wear my clothes inside out today? Or had someone discovered my secret relationship with Paul? My thoughts were interrupted when Joan, my coworker, approached me with a sheepish expression.

"What is it?" I exhale, taking my seat behind my desk.

"Maria, there's something you need to know," she began hesitantly. "A new Partner is being appointed, and the word is that it's Justin." The world falls around me, and the ground escapes my feet. Joan gives me a pitying look, and something inside me breaks. I experience clarity like I have never before.

In an instant, fury consumes me. I had worked tirelessly, spent so much time and effort training Justin, and watched him move to different departments. I was his supervisor for the first couple of years, and Justin has worked in my team ever since. For the board to go over my head and choose my subordinate whom I'd trained was Illogical and humiliating.

This promotion was supposed to be mine, and now it felt like a betrayal. I seethed with anger, feeling the injustice of being overlooked despite my outstanding performance and contributions. Everyone in the company was aware that I ran the department and managed cases that were important to handle or even cases other department heads had given up on. My mind raced with all the reasons why I deserve this promotion more than anyone else, and it was infuriating to see my hard work disregarded.

Taking a deep breath, I tried to regain composure and perspective. I knew I had earned this promotion, and it was a slap in the face to be passed over for someone else. My personal life was a mess, and now my professional life is facing a similar challenge. I needed to confront the situation head-on and make my voice heard. Enough was enough.

Determined to fight for what was rightfully mine, I steeled myself for the battle ahead. No longer willing to tolerate being overlooked or undervalued, I fix my dress and take a look at myself in the mirror. My eyes were spitting fire, and if Jack knew what was good for the company, he'd tell me that this news was false. It was time I got the recognition I deserved.

I barge into Jack's office, his casual dismissal of my worth and potential stings at me like a thousand bees; and still he's casually sprawled on his swiveling chair when I enter.

"Are you OK?" he asks condescendingly, a faint curtness in his tone.

"Is it true, is Justin making partner?" I demand, my voice ice cold with fury.

Jack seems taken aback at my vocal addressing of the situation, but he confirmed the truth of it. "Well, yes, it was felt that it's maybe not your time yet," he replies, trying to appear composed.

Glaring back at him, I can't hold back any longer. "It will never be my time, will it? I am just a woman, never a part of your old boys' club," I retort bitterly. "I should have made partner years ago if it weren't for this backward system."

Jack makes a feeble attempt to pacify me with empty words, "I am sorry, give it time and you will get there." But the lack of conviction in his voice was apparent. I knew deep down that this glass ceiling was real, and no matter how much time passed, they would always find a reason to deny me what I deserved.

I shake my head, at a loss for words in my anger, and leave Jack's office, my frustration only intensifying. Instead of returning to my desk, I needed to escape the suffocating atmosphere of the workplace. I walk out, needing to find a quiet space to clear my head. Tears threatened to burst first from my tired eyes. I walk bitterly through the commercial streets, and I find myself dialing Paul's number on my phone. In the past, Mark would have been on speed dial in situations like these.

When Paul picked up, his warm voice greeted me tenderly.

 "Hey honey, how are you?"

But as soon as I began to speak, my emotions got the better of me, and tears streamed down my cheeks. This vulnerability was rare for me, but Paul's voice provided a much-needed refuge and outlet for feeling these terrible feelings assaulting me. He hears my sniffling.

"Hey, hey, what's wrong, are you okay?" he asked with genuine concern.

I pour my heart out to Paul, telling him about the recent events that had left me deeply upset, and was now all snowballing to hit me with the biggest slap of despair.

"I don't know what I should do. I genuinely enjoy my work, I really do, and I'm good at it. But the complete lack of acknowledgment used to weigh me down, but now it's straight up humiliating. And things at home aren't good either. Nobody even bothered to ask me how my trip to Scotland was when I got back. I feel like I'm just taken for granted and used."

Paul heard my lamenting quietly, perhaps trying to absorb everything I had shared. Then, with need in his voice he asks, "What can I do to help? Where are you right now?" I hear some shuffling on his side, like he was gathering his things while talking to me.

Amid my tears, I managed to reply, "There's nothing you can do, Paul. I decided to leave the office for a while to gather myself together. It's frustrating because everyone knew that job should have been mine, but once again, I was passed over for it. I came to the park down from my office to clear my mind."

Unexpectedly, Paul says, "Give me 10 minutes, and I'll be there with you."

His response catches me off guard. "Why?" I ask, genuinely taken aback by his offer to meet. I knew he was my rock, but being there for me in my times of need? I was not used to people caring for me this deeply.

Paul replied with a smile in his voice, "Because right now you just need someone to talk to, and I can be there in a few minutes. But if you'd rather not, that's perfectly fine too. Just let me know."

The thought of confiding in Paul was comforting, but there could be prying eyes anywhere here. "I would love to see you," I say, "but I'd prefer somewhere private. There's a hotel just across the square with a bar full of nooks and crannies. We can talk there without the risk of being seen. That would really make my day."

I decide to call Mark; he picks up on the last ring. I tell him about the injustice of it all, and how I feel my hard work never pays off. He tries to console me, "It's a real shame that things didn't work out as you hoped, but maybe it'll lead to even better opportunities. Let's talk later. " His voice irritated me; it was evident that he wasn't overly concerned about the situation.

I had just walked into the bar, still moping in a corner when I saw Paul come in.

His mere presence lifted my spirits, and we talked until lunchtime.

"Do you think it's time for a new job? You're very good at what you do and seeing you breaking down from unappreciation is such a shame," Paul says after I have reiterated the events for him.

His question is certainly food for thought. Despite enjoying my work and having good relationships with my co-workers, the lack of recognition and the recent disappointment has made me question my future at DAF. It's not like I didn't know this would be their ultimate decision, but finally my eyes have opened.

"I don't know, honestly. It's a big decision, plus Ralph's case is almost finished. We have a very clear idea of his assets now. Actually, you'll get the report by tomorrow, but I was properly shocked at the figures," Talking about the report reminds me of the solicitors' meeting next week, and I put my head in my hands, moaning loudly. "To think I would have to sit and smile at the meeting, pretending everything was fine, while they reap the reward of my efforts." I exhale, my spirits in the gutter again.

Paul gently rubs my back, "Yeah, the Monday meeting to finalise the figures of the estate, and then the beneficiaries would be informed about their inheritance. I'm curious who the big man left all his wealth too. It might be Caroline. Or Helen or Nicola. Maybe all three, or maybe a charity. Whoever it is, once that's done, it won't be our problem, anyway," Paul gives me a look of conviction.

I nod, also curious about the benefactor. However, Ralph didn't seem like a man who would donate his wealth to charity after his death, nor someone who would give it to one of his colleagues. Just the fact that this was a secret was enough to tell me Ralph was hiding something from everyone in his life.

213

I manage a small smile, "Well, the only silver lining is that I got you from all this. Without you and everything we have together, I think I'd be at my wit's end by now. I'm close, but still."

Paul takes my hand, "I'm not going anywhere. How could I? You woke me up, and now I'm looking forward to rebuilding my life … with you." I'm a bit surprised at his declaration, but I know he's trying to comfort me. And the idea is indeed comforting.

I lean in and plant a tender kiss on his lips, grateful for his presence in my life. Despite the disappointment and frustration, I knew I could count on him.

I prepare to leave, but Paul still looks concerned.

"I better be getting back now. I'll be okay, don't worry. This isn't the first time it's happened; I'll get over it. Plus, the official partner announcement is still away so I'll live. For now," I smile at him. He takes my hand and kisses it, then watches me leave, my shoulders hunched.

Later that night, when I return home, Mark is on his phone, waiting for me. He sits beside me on the couch and gives me his whole attention in an effort to console me about the job situation.

"It really sucks. It would have meant more work, but you deserve the promotion."

I nod sullenly, spent from today. It had been a terrible day, with people giving me pitying or 'serves-her-right' looks left and right. I loathed gossip, and there was nothing I disliked more than my colleagues whispering it amongst themselves. To be the sole subject of it was even worse.

"Also, I was thinking why don't I accompany you to London for the dinner event on Friday? You're right, it will be a nighttime away from home, and I want to meet the people you have been working with for so long. What do you think?" He smiles like he's making a big concession for me.

I nod, smiling a little and close my eyes, leaning back against the couch thinking if this day could get *any* worse.

214

The only thing I was looking forward to was my Friday night with Paul, and the following Saturday morning. But it was becoming increasingly difficult to hold onto it while I braved through this absolute hell of a day. I grimace, thinking how I would break the news to Paul that Mark had decided to attend the event. The thought of the two of them being in the same place together made the prospect of this whole thing even worse.

Later that night, I am sitting alone in my study wanting to connect with Paul after his show of support today. I sent him a Snapchat, as we often do at night these days.

Maria: *Hey there, thanks for coming over. It meant a lot to me.*

Paul: *How are you doing now? I wondered if you'd be in the mood to talk or not, so I left you be.*

Maria: *I'm always in the mood for you, but thank you. Sorry I was in such bad form today, especially after the lovely time we had on Monday and Tuesday. It was a real sucker punch.*

Paul: *Don't worry about it. I'm here for you, even during tough times, alright? It's not just about the sex, even though we've got that department wholly covered.*

My heart flutters, but I need to tell him about Mark's plans.

Maria: *Received some more bad news :(Mark is trying to be whatever he's trying to be, so he said he's coming to London for the dinner on Friday evening.*

Paul: *Ah, I see. Don't worry, darling. I'll be on my best behaviour, and these things are bound to happen. We would have to meet sooner or later. It might have been a day you could have done without, but at least he's trying to support you. Leave it with me. I'll change my rail ticket to a later train, so we won't meet until the evening.*

Maria: *UGHH! Thank you for being so understanding, really. But honestly, I'm more frustrated that I can only look at you and not touch or engage with you much this weekend. Who knows what will happen after Monday? We might not even have London for much longer.*

Paul: *Don't worry about that now. Let's focus on getting through Friday, and we'll deal with Monday when Monday comes. We'll work something out. Try not to think too far ahead.*

Maria: *I really hope it works out. I can't bear the thought of not having you and waking up next to you, especially on the days I've come to think of as ours.*

And then, suddenly, he shares two pictures that take a second to load. And I'm lost in my feelings when I see he's sent the pictures he took in Scotland this week. We look so happy, it's heartwarming. I cherish this reminder of our beautiful moments we shared.

Paul: *Think nice thoughts and cherish the memories when things get a bit hard.*

We continue to exchange messages, finding comfort in each other despite the challenges ahead. With Paul beside me, I feel a glimmer of hope, even amidst the difficulties that might come our way.

***

Friday comes quickly, and early in the morning I board the train with Mark, feeling a mix of nerves about the upcoming meeting. As fate would have it, the man I had encountered earlier in the year was on the same train again. My heart skips a beat as he glances at me and notices Mark sitting beside me. He raises his brow as he studies the two of us, and I silently hoped he doesn't say anything. Thankfully, he just looks back down at his newspaper without uttering a word.

Mark takes our bags to the hotel while I take a taxi to the office. I meet Paul there, and together, we finalise the last of the details for the afternoon meeting. The clock strikes 1:30 PM when we leave the office, and Nicola and Helen join me as we make our way to the hotel to get ready for the event.

I chose a salmon pink suit for this afternoon and slipped into a pair of nude heels. I style my hair in loose curls, scrunching them in a bun, and Nicola helps me with a little eyeshadow. The ensemble looks pretty sophisticated as I take a look at myself in the mirror. Paul has gone out to get doughnuts at a famous place nearby and since the meeting is scheduled for two PM, we need to leave while he's still out. I hurriedly gather my files and notes, and Nicola, Helen and I jump into a taxi.

Inside the boardroom, all ten of us sit around the table, the six managers, and Helen, Nicola, Paul and I ready to address the matters at hand. Helen briefly makes an introduction for Paul, and I outline the work we have been doing. Afterwards, Paul takes the charge and explains to them that although we haven't yet discovered the owner of the shops, there is an iron-clad clause that prevents them from being sold or undergoing any major changes that could affect the current employees for at least ten years.

"This means that everyone is secure in their position, bar any extenuating circumstances, for the foreseeable future. For this to remain in effect, each shop has to remain profitable. Nicola and Helen would continue to be the primary points of contact, ensuring consistency for the employees." Paul goes on to talk about the company values, his own role from hereon, and the expectations we have from each manager.

The main purpose of the meeting was to bring all the managers together, giving them the opportunity to meet each other since they might not have done so before. It was also an opportunity to address any concerns and provide everyone with the same information to ensure transparency and reassurance.

Once the meeting came to an end, I observed that the managers appear content with what they have heard, and Paul opens the floor to questions.

A voice from the back raises the issue, "Will we be dealing with you going forward, or is there going to be someone else involved?"

I step in to respond, "Mr. Bridges has been handling the estate and legal department, and I've been managing the accounting aspects. As of now, the shops will continue to operate as they have been, and orders will proceed as usual, regardless of who the new owner may be. Hopefully, we'll have more clarity on this in the coming weeks once the succession is uncovered."

Not many other questions were raised, and the meeting concluded around 4 o'clock. As we left, I couldn't help but feel

217

a sense of relief that things had gone relatively smoothly. The uncertainty about the future still lingered, but for now, we had done what we could to provide stability and reassurance to the team.

After wrapping up the meeting, Nicola asks everyone to grab their keycards for their rooms from the hotel reception, which were all booked and ready. The main dining room had been reserved for 7:30, where a social dinner was planned for all employees and their partners. The best part was that the bar tab was covered by the company, ensuring everyone could unwind and enjoy the night.

As the dinner time approaches, I can't help but feel a cloud of anxiety over me. The thought of Mark and Paul being together in the same setting made me uneasy. I knew I would be reduced to wondering if Mark suspected anything between Paul and me the entire evening.

Once at the dinner venue, I welcome whoever I come across, while Mark and I walk through to the bar, hand in hand. We're all dressed in smart casual attire, including Mark and me. The tension inside me is mounting, knowing that this evening could potentially get very awkward at best. Then, as if on cue, Paul makes his entrance, dressed in a sharp suit and tie—a departure from his usual attire at the office or casual outings. He spots us and immediately makes a beeline in our direction.

Greeting me warmly, he turns to Mark, "And I presume this is your better half." They shake hands as I introduce Mark to Paul, feeling my nerves on edge.

Mark is ordering drinks for us and asks Paul what he'd like.

In a serious and somewhat droll tone, Paul declines, "Not tonight, this may be in a social setting, but it is still work-related for me. I don't have fun on the job," he chuckles.

My breath quickens but Mark doesn't notice anything. Instead, he tries again, "What about your partner? Maybe a margarita?"

Paul shakes his head, "I don't have a partner; just three teenagers and myself to look after. I'm widowed," he explains, when Mark looks lost.

Mark purses his lips, "Ah, I'm sorry to hear that."

The conversation dwindles, and I can't help but feel a mixture of emotions—relief that Paul has handled the situation tactfully, but also a twinge of sadness for him. He was surrounded by couples having a fun evening, while he was alone.

Paul graciously thanks us for his water, and excuses himself, stating that he needs to fulfil his host duties and socialise with everyone at the gathering. As he walks away, Mark turns to me, making a face at Paul's back, "There's a solicitor if I ever met one. Can't even relax when he's out. He seems so serious; it must have been dull working around him all this time."

"Boring," I agree with Mark. But inside I couldn't help but smile, fully aware of Paul's intentions. He was trying to deflect attention from any potential personal matters by portraying himself as serious, boring, and overly formal for the night. Seeing through his facade, I decide to step away, telling Mark that I need to call and check on the kids.

Instead, I type out a message to Paul: '*Thank you xxx. Your effort tonight means more to me than you know. I appreciate how you're protecting me in your own way. You've certainly earned some brownie points, and I can't wait to see how you plan to collect them.*

I add a wink emoji for good measure.

Just to be cautious, I quickly sent a text to the kids, asking if everything was alright, in case Mark inquired about them later.

The rest of the night passes uneventfully, with Paul maintaining his serious demeanour. Around 10 PM, he comes to us and bids us goodnight, and I can't help but wish I was joining him. I know this must be hard on him as well, me going to sleep in another bed while we were here.

Mark and I follow suit about thirty minutes later, and I notice that the room is particularly nice and spacious. I suspect that Paul has arranged for an upgrade for us without mentioning it. Mark has already had a few drinks, but he gulps a few more, becoming playful, although I'm far from the mood to humor his advances. Nonetheless, I play along, knowing he'd fall asleep in a few minutes. Afterwards, I sadly recount the rare moments of lightheartedness between us, even if they were somewhat alcohol-induced on this particular night. Eventually, Markl drifts off to sleep, and I lay beside him, deep in thought.

The following morning, after a pleasant breakfast, Mark and I head back home.

Chapter 15

Monday morning, I got onto the elevator at Paul's office with my coffee cup steaming in my hand, and spotted Jack, my infamous boss, and Melanie, the young junior assistant who had prepared the summary of the accounts for Paul. The meeting is scheduled first thing in the morning, and although Jack's face makes me bristle, I persevere. I've been working too long at this. With the documents in hand, we make our way to Paul's office as instructed. We're directed to a spacious boardroom where Paul, and his boss Leonard are already sitting around the table, waiting.

When everyone has taken their seats, Leonard nods, and then starts, "Good morning, everyone." "It seems things are finally coming to an end after a busy six months. Let me thank all of you for your work, starting with Paul and Ms. Holmes."

Paul and I incline our heads and murmur formalities.

Leonard continues, "So, we have a summary here that we're here to discuss. Let's go through it and see what the bottom line is."

All of us look closely at the files lying in front of us on the table.

Melanie, brimming with pride in her work, confidently took the lead at my encouragement, and began presenting. The figures were nothing short of staggering, not just in terms of properties, including shops, offices, distribution warehouses, apartments, and a shop unit, but also in the form of substantial bank accounts and insurance policies. It was evident that Ralph had spent very little over the past decade, instead focusing on accumulating cash.

I observe with satisfaction how everyone's mouths drop at the entire sum of Ralph's fortune, and wonder if they might be envying the secret benefactor.

Once Melanie concluded her presentation, I took over the floor to address the concerns I knew Leonard was mulling over. "The next matter at hand is taxes," I began. "However, providing a precise tax calculation hinges on knowing the specific beneficiaries who will be inheriting what from Ralphs estate. I understand that the beneficiaries are scheduled to join today's meeting to address this." I look at the solicitors pointedly.

Paul's gaze was affixed to the words on the report. A thought crossed my mind: was Paul told who the benefactor was yet? Maybe before the meeting started? Leonard clears his throat.

Not today, Miss Holmes. Although, I'm aware of just one beneficiary."

I frown, vaguely disappointed. But that only one person would inherit everything meant we could proceed with some rough calculations based on that assumption. I go through my notes and quickly provide an estimate, explaining that even after accounting for all the necessary taxes, the beneficiary could expect to retain ownership of all the businesses and continue to receive income from them. In addition, they would have ownership of the properties and likely possess somewhere between 2.75 to 3 million in liquid personal funds. In whatever way the beneficiary was living until now, Ralph's death would change their life.

"However, there are significant funds tied up in companies that can't be withdrawn without incurring additional taxes. Nonetheless, the businesses are performing exceptionally well, with the shops alone generating profits well over a million annually, alongside the income from head office distribution and rentals," I finish.

Paul unexpectedly spoke up, "On the note of the benefactors skipping this meeting, I just want to make sure everyone here understands that the managers and staff are understandably anxious about the uncertainty surrounding the new leadership. They deserve to know the future of the company. When is this mysterious benefactor going to show up anyway? Someone needs to come into the picture. Quickly." He looks pointedly at Leonard.

That satisfied my wonderings; Paul still didn't know who'd be taking over either yet.

In response, his boss gave him an equally pointed look and replied, "Let's give it a few weeks and please ask everyone to be patient. I'll reveal the instructions when the time is right. In the meantime, both of you should continue to run the business as you have been, with the current staff in place."

I couldn't help but feel disappointed that the mystery beneficiary's identity and plans weren't unveiled today. But this meeting was out of the way, I wouldn't have to sit beside Jack anymore, and it was good to see Paul, and I hoped that we might be able to catch a few minutes together later.

There's not much to discuss afterwards, and the meeting concludes. I sit back, reluctant to share a taxi ride back to the office with Jack. Melanie and I go to the restroom for a few moments, and before she leaves, I tell her to let Jack know I will not be traveling with them since I needed to sort out a few matters with Paul before Thursday. I watch Melanie leave and whisper something to Jack, after which they walk towards the exit and out of the office. I believe Jack felt the same way as I did about sharing a car ride, as he didn't put up a fight, rather appeared relieved. When I return to the conference room, I find it empty, but an assistant takes me to Paul's office. It is a modestly sized room with sleek surfaces and steel-grey upholstery that makes everything seem sterile. Very unlike Paul. He has his phone in his hand when I walk in, which he quickly tosses, and comes over to greet me. We take a seat on the sofa, a low coffee table between us.

"Hey, do you have time to go over the list of qualified persons we could send to the trade exhibition thing? It's this Friday, and Nicola will have a stroke if I don't finalize this today."

"Oh, of course. I should've done those ages ago. Let me see," He gestures at the file, "Wait, actually, let's do it over coffee." He looks at his watch. "I have a little bit of time."

I agreed, and as we are about to head out, the same assistant who showed me to Paul's office comes running after us in her heels, threatens to topple over as she stops, rights herself, and says Mr. Bridges is being summoned. She looks agitated. Paul frowns, and shrugs at me. I can't help but notice that he looks a bit concerned, and I wonder what the sudden urgency is all about. They can't spare him for fifteen minutes.

"Leonard asks that Mr. Bridges does not leave the office and reports in ten minutes," she repeats when Paul dawdles.

"Alright," he huffs, and we sit in his office, going over the candidates who are a good choice to represent the company at the trade show. We had to look at many aspects; the representative will also be in charge of placing orders for stocks and seeing them through.

There's a knock at his door, and he looks at me, "I hoped to get you coffee or something, but let's get a raincheck on that?"

"Sure, yeah." I reply, and we exit his office together.

The assistant is there; we say our greetings and I see him head off in a different direction.

***

Later, I found out what the fuss was all about. And oh, boy was it a discovery.

After the shock of the surprise wore off, he told me how Leonard was acting a bit off. He asked Paul to take a seat, and promptly handed him an unmarked envelope, saying, "I don't know what's inside this, but my instructions were to give it to you at this point. Take it home or find a quiet place to read it. I think everything will become clear then."

That's when Paul discovered the mysterious envelope was addressed to him- by Ralph. He said he was unsure then, unable to make out the head or tail of the situation. There was no context or explanation. "I don't know if the contents still

224

hold true- it seems old." Leonard had tried to help. Paul was stewing in curiosity and confusion, but he walked to a cafe and tore the envelope open. The said letter was dated five years ago. He said he went to his office and read the letter.

Afterwards, the shock had been so great that he'd walked numbly until he'd reached the same hotel, we had used to book rooms for our last Friday event. There in a daze, booked a room and he took the room keys while the receptionists mumbled faintly around him, their words seeming distant and incomprehensible amid the turmoil within Paul. He came to collapse on the bed, looking wide-eyed at the ceiling, his mind consumed by the contents of the letter.

A few moments later, he'd gathered strength to call me.

I was puzzled when I received Paul's call.

"I need to see you. Everything's... crazy. Upside down." I frown, unable to make sense of what he's saying. "I need to see you," he repeats, "I don't know who else to talk to about... this. I'm at the hotel where we did the event." He gives me the address, tells me the room number. All methodically, like he was in a trance.

"Hey, don't worry, I'll be there in about forty-five minutes, alright? You hold on." I was worried; never had Paul called me so out of his wits.

"It's not about us, don't worry," he says as an afterthought, and then the call drops. I look at my phone as if asking it for an answer.

When I get to the room, panting and out of breath, I see him holding a few sheets of paper in his hands, looking at it like it's magic.

He looks up at my arrival and I freeze: he's paper white.

"Hey, what's happened? Are you okay?" I immediately go to his side, taking his face in my hands, clasping his fingers to rub some warmth into them. I did not think he was fired, or anything of that sort. No, he was fundamentally shaken. This was no professional setback.

He pushes the sheaf of paper towards me, and it falls limply into my lap. "Just read this."

I hold it up and start reading in the dimly lit room. The letter read:

5th March 2013

Dear Paul

I'm sure this letter is shocking for you., I'm sure. You must be wondering why me and why you. Allow me to make you aware of your birthright, too late, but it is only fair you must know.

I was born in 1950 to a family where I was brought up as an only child. a time when the world was just beginning to recover from the cruel scars of war. I grew up in a loving family, an only child of my parents. However, fate had taken a turn before I was even born, and as I reached my late teens, I came to discover a hidden truth. It was revealed to me that I had a sister, a sibling who had been born to my parents a decade before me. Some pestering and confrontations later, my parents confirmed I was correct in my discovery.

In those difficult times, my parents faced financial hardships, caused by the ravages of war. They were young; merely twenty at the time. Unable to bear the burden of their first child, they made the painful decision to place my sister up for adoption. Life, as it often does, took a different turn for my parents, and when I came into this world a whole decade later, they were in a more stable position to care for a child. And so, they raised me as their only child, near the breathtaking landscapes of Fort William in the beautiful countryside of Scotland.

As I delved deeper into the history of my family, I confronted my parents with questions about my sister. Eventually, they confessed the whole truth, revealing the heart-wrenching reality behind the adoption. It was an unimaginably difficult choice for them, something they had to do to save themselves and the child from utter ruin.

The knowledge of my sister's existence weighed heavily upon my heart. I grappled with a curious guilt, knowing that I had been fortunate enough to grow up in a loving and secure environment while my sister was sent away. She had the claim to a happy childhood, and loving parents as much as I did, and yet she'd been deprived of it while I had obliviously thrived. The need to seek her out, to ensure her well-being, gnawed at my conscience, and when I was able to afford it, I began my quest to track her down.

The journey to find her was arduous and filled with obstacles, as her adoption records were sealed. But I persisted, undeterred by the challenges,

226

driven by the desire to connect with her. I will not bore you with more details of how I came to find out about your mother- But at last I finally discovered her fate. By now, you may have already deduced the truth- as fate would have it, I am your long-lost uncle, a relative you never knew existed, although not by my choice.

Alas, the reunions I yearned for never came to pass. On several occasions, I reached out to my sister, hoping to bridge the gap and form a connection that had been denied to us both. But she chose to keep her distance, having grown up without the warmth of a family, she was afraid of facing the specter of what could have been or should have been. Though I respected her decision, it weighed heavily on my heart, intensifying the guilt I carried with me. Through our seldom encounters I saw some of the bitterness she held within, and my presence seemed to magnify the void she felt in her heart. I understood the depth of her feelings, and as much as I longed for a connection, I knew that forcing myself into her life would only deepen her pain.

With the weight of lost time upon my shoulders and the knowledge that your dear mother has passed away, I feel compelled to confide in you now. In the course of my own journey, I watched from afar, admiring your life, and it brought me great joy to witness your accomplishments and successes. With the same admiration in my heart, I chose your firm to handle my will, ensuring that you, as an unbiased observer, could examine my life without the burden of strained emotional attachments. It was crucial to me that you be given the opportunity to learn about who I was and form your own impressions, without being influenced by my connection to you.

And so, it is now that you hold this letter, a revelation of my past, my financial standing, and my reasons for choosing you to oversee my estate. I trust that my financial makeup has remained strong and robust since I am penning this letter in 2013.

Through all this my objective has been clear— to have you observe the wisdom of conducting my affairs in isolation, and the immense importance of depending upon good people. While I keep each aspect of my businesses separate, I nurture a deep appreciation for the people who contribute their time and dedication to ensure that bottom lines are met. Good managers and loyal team members are the backbone of all my endeavors.

I imagine that by now, you have seen how Nicola and Helen have played pivotal roles at the head office. Their job descriptions are an entirely

227

different thing, but their dedication and trustworthiness have won them my utmost confidence. Over time, I have begun to rely on them, especially during periods when my focus has waned. Their suggestions and proposals don't even warrant a once-over— that is the kind of people I have cultivated around me.

If you so choose to carry on my legacy, I hope you will extend the same trust and respect that I have placed in Nicola and Helen. They may not fully comprehend the depth of my faith in them, but it is my earnest wish that you understand the profound role they have played in my life and business.

Throughout my journey, I have carried a sense of guilt, believing that my prosperity was built upon the sacrifice. It stems from the awareness that my parents helped me establish my first shop in Fort William. But their financial support came at a cost—a cost I feel was paid by my sister, whom they could not care for. It is with this knowledge in mind that I have decided to entrust everything I have to my name to you, my sole family. I feel the foundation of my wealth- material and non-material- is intricately tied to my parents' decision regarding your mother. Thus, I bestow upon you everything I have amassed in my lifetime, subject to certain conditions. I will come to these conditions later.

You may perceive me as a solitary figure, leading a quiet, simple life. Indeed, that is how I find myself now, but my story is far from complete. Much of who I am today has been shaped not only by the decisions of my parents but also by an unexpected chapter unfolding in my life.

You have by now seen the part of my life that I wished for you to see. A hardworking man who has amassed a sizable fortune. But there is another path I took in life that I have protected from even the most zealous diggers. This was a different path from my usual business pursuits, one that would be my first introduction to the complexities of human relationships.

In the earliest days, when the shop in Fort William was a significant part of my life, I worked alongside the staff- among whom was an assistant named Lillian- Lilly. She was ten years my junior, a young woman of twenty-five, recently married and a new mother. From the beginning, we got along remarkably well, despite the obvious professional boundary that separated us. She was dedicated, tired and hardworking, and I admired her steel spirit.

As the years passed, our bond grew stronger, and an emotional intimacy developed between us. Yet, I remained her boss, while she was bound in the shackles of her marriage. Lillian's husband was an abusive and alcoholic man, causing her much pain and sorrow. But she held fast to her duty as his wife, committed to standing by him.

Over time, our relationship would take a different turn, evolving into a deep and intimate connection that neither of us could resist— nor did we want to. But Lillian made it clear that she could never leave her husband, regardless of her feelings for me. Her sense of duty and commitment to her marriage remained unwavering, leaving us in a bittersweet and guilty emotional entanglement.

As the businesses flourished, so did my bond with Lilly, the woman who captured my heart entirely. She became the singular and irreplaceable presence in my life, and I knew deep within me that she was the one, the only woman I could ever love. As my empire expanded, I entrusted her with the management of the Fort William shop, while I ventured to London to develop other branches and establish a distribution hub.

Despite the distance, our bond remained unyielding. I returned to Fort William whenever I could, seeking any excuse to be with Lilly. I appointed her the shop's buyer, a role that necessitated her presence at trade shows, where I was in attendance as well. Even beyond business engagements, we found reasons to spend quality time together: Lilly was a mountain guide, and I often joined her on guided walks, relishing every opportunity to be by her side.

As the years unfurled, our love only deepened, and we came to cherish every moment spent together. Our connection was profound, intimate, and secret, known only to us. Occasionally, we were careful – devising fake guided walks to ensure we could share an entire day together, far away from prying eyes, either in my cottage or at another trusted location.

For two decades, from 1987 to 2007, we lived a lifetime of love and devotion, supporting and cherishing each other in ways only true companions can. Lilly was my world, my confidante, and the center of my universe. I knew that she was all I had and the closest I would ever come to a relationship of this magnitude.

Then, in 2007, tragedy struck, and Lilly was taken from me by a sudden illness. The loss was unbearable, and I found myself shattered, a mere husk of the man I once was. I immersed myself in my work, seeking solace in the routine, while distancing myself from emotional and personal connections. But even in work there was no peace. I was coming to resent everything.

I am sure by now you have observed the finances of the shop in Fort William and met the staff, and the manager- Caroline. You might wonder why the finances of the shop are slightly askew. There is a reason for this. Caroline is Lilly's only daughter, who was only 22 years old when Lilly passed away. At the time, she worked as an assistant in the shop, and I made a promise to Lilly that I would ensure Caroline's well-being and security- not that the sweet girl isn't capable.

I have kept my word by making Caroline the manager and offering her a good salary along with a profit-sharing arrangement- something I introduced just so Caroline would have that advantage. My aim was to fulfill the pledge I made to Lilly, to ensure that her daughter would be cared for and protected.

Caroline is unaware of the true nature of my relationship with Lilly. We took great pains to conceal any hint of deeper connection, masking it as a friendship and a professional partnership. All our trips were justified as work-related endeavors, even though our hearts were entwined. No one had any cause to suspect us.

That brings me to the next part of the story, something very private, and very close to my heart. It's a precious memory that I would not be retelling, but I have some explaining to do regarding some stuff you may have stumbled upon and the peculiar instructions that must have puzzled you to no end- might even have raised an eyebrow or two.

It was around the year 1990; we were working on setting up a new climbing wall in the shop. Lilly and I found ourselves engrossed in the work, ropes, lines, and safety measures were the order of the day. We had the shop to ourselves as we usually did, and amidst the work existed an unspoken joy in our companionship, something that could make any task enjoyable.

I was checking on the safety of the knots and one of the lines, as fate would have it, decided to tangle itself around my arms, leaving me in a somewhat amusing and precarious position. Imagine me, suspended with my arms ensnared in ropes, up on my toes, struggling for freedom. I called for help and in came Lilly. Oh, how comedic and delightful she found my predicament. She stood there laughing for a solid minute, before she came close to untie me. But I was mistaken; she started teasing me, going through my pockets, dropping things on the floor, touching my chest, and my face. Laughing and saying I was at her mercy, and could I guess what she'd do next?

It was just harmless toying; but she got me wondering how liberating it felt to give myself over to her. Moreover, Lilly's playfulness, her newfound initiative to take control, was a revelation. Confidence oozed out of her, and I found myself entranced by this unexpected aspect of her character. I knew she was a strong woman, but she was also abused, and although she could hold her ground, I hadn't seen this side of her before. She was captivating. That day I fell in love with her all over again.

With a few deft maneuvers, Lilly eventually untangled the ropes, and we continued our work, the laughter from that moment echoing in the air. It was a glimpse into a different side of her, one that intrigued me and left me pondering the nature of power dynamics. The joy that can come from relinquishing control, even if just for a moment. I found myself revisiting that evening time and again in the weeks that followed, captivated by the liberty of losing control. Given my penchant for micromanaging, this was a bewildering departure from my usual self. The internal conflict was undeniable; the peace of surrendering clashed with my need to dominate.

One night, as Lilly and I found ourselves sharing a moment, I confided in her about my musings. To my astonishment, she revealed the thought of me at her mercy was occupying her waking and sleeping moments. Being in control over a person especially as assertive as me made her excited beyond words, and that she would love to explore all the places my mind had been.

And so, we embarked on a journey of exploration, a journey that would stretch across the next 17 years of our lives. You might wonder why I'm sharing this intimate chapter with you. There are two reasons, you see.

Firstly, as part of the instructions I left for you, there were certain items scattered across my office, apartments, and even the house in Fort William, all remnants of that private facet of our lives. I have no desire for this part of our story to be exposed to anyone else's gaze. Perhaps the albums stored in my safe added another layer of confusion, prompting questions about who I really was and the character I possessed.

Then there's the matter of the adult store that you must have already uncovered—a curious addition to the equation, sticking out like a sore *thumb in the image I've projected. In our exciting, labyrinthine journey, Lilly and I recognized a glaring gap in the market: a dearth of well-crafted, high-quality products tailored to our particular lifestyle. In collaboration with Adam Wright, who we found on our journey, we successfully established the adult-toy store, a one-stop shop that stocked refined merchandise for those sharing our interests. While I preferred to stay behind the scenes, Adam worked tirelessly to get it off the ground and soaring.*

Secondly, there's a saying that to truly understand a man, you must walk a mile in his shoes. My journey to and through this lifestyle afforded me the latitude to delve into my intimate bond with Lilly, and experience life from a different perspective. Despite the preconceived notions that might surround the lifestyle, the heart of this experience lay in the profound and affectionate relationship forged on the foundation of trust with the woman I held dear. There was nothing tawdry or shallow about it; rather, it was mutual respect and joint exploration on both our parts.

I don't ask you to follow in my footsteps, but if you're inclined to want to know and understand me, perhaps you might consider venturing a bit, peering behind the curtain, so to speak. Should you opt to do so, look through the albums with your significant other. Within those pages I have cataloged all of the places we visited, events we enjoyed, and faces we encountered. These albums are the memories of our shared life, safe from any misconceptions that may color them in the public eye.

These, for me, are the true treasures, my life alongside Lilly, a sentiment so cherished that I've entrusted them to the privacy of the safe alone. Adam and his wife are the only people who know of my relationship with Lilly, and also that she was married.

If you do end up wanting to know more, you'll find a chest in the bedroom in my apartment. There are flyers, tickets, and programs there that catalog our escapades- a diary of our journey. Those bits of paper are like a journal, documenting our secret lives, our explorations, and the myriad adventures we undertook. You won't uncover any explicit accounts of our shared joy, for that remains our intimate keepsakes, but you will receive a lot of information.

Speak with Adam; a letter will be dispatched to him once it's confirmed I'm no longer in the picture. He will tell you more about me, whatever you want to know. He's the one person I trust completely when it comes to the lifestyle. He will offer any help or advice you need.

This will be your adventure, as it was Lilly and mine. All this I share with you just so you know I have lived a fulfilling and happy life, with the person I loved. It does feel good that someone else will know about my true life.

One month from today, I direct you to destroy the albums and everything you find inside the chest so that no trace of any of it remains. If you do have a partner that you trust with this, I allow you to share it with them. Apart from that, no one must know. This I firmly request of you.

If you choose to explore, I wish you to have fun and experience even a percentage of all that I did. The toy shop is now yours, and so when the lights are off, you're free to do whatever you want. It's your adventure. Now, back to the conditions I place upon you should you accept your inheritance:

1. *The shops will not be sold for at least a decade as long as they are profitable.*
2. *I have adored Caroline as if she were my own, and I require her to always be cared for. If any of the shops are ever sold, I bequeath her 20% sale profits or her shop in Fort William. This was my promise to Lilly, and now yours to me.*
3. *All my long-term staff must be reassured of job safety.*
4. *Nicola and Helen are to be given generous packages if the shops are sold.*

All other liquid assets, properties and business is for you to do whatever you wish for. Enjoy your life and make it count.

If you choose to not accept your inheritance, I wish you every happiness in life. There is an alternative trust for my assets and the process to transition there will begin once you decline this gift. You will never be told of this alternative, nor be able to know what happens to it from thereon. Once you say no, there's no going back.

Take your time, and I do hope you accept, since I believe you're entitled to it after your mother. The executor has received instructions to await your decision, so I suggest you weigh your decision accordingly, on your own terms.

Sincerely,
Your Uncle, Ralph Michaels.

The sheaf of pages falls from my hands, landing softly over my shoes. I look at Paul dumbly, and he nods, staring at the ground. My jaw has promptly landed on the floor.

"Are you kidding me? What the hell? Did you have any idea?" I whisper, shocked to the core.

"None at all," Paul exhales, "I was completely in the dark. I know my mother was an only child who was adopted when she was young, but she never wanted to talk about it. So, we never did. I had no idea that Ralph even existed… and now…"

Paul is shaken, and I get it. I'd be completely floored too if a dead uncle appeared out of thin air, offering me incomprehensible wealth. I pat him on the back, and he looks up at me.

"What am I even supposed to do, Maria? About any of this? My mother must have been in so much pain… She didn't want anything to do with him, yet he honored her request. And the Lilly story?"

Over the next few hours, we engage in a deep conversation, pondering over the intricacies of the letter and the doubts that clouded Paul's thoughts. I knew I must be a patient listener, to be by his side since the ultimate decision of accepting or declining Ralph's legacy rested squarely on his shoulders.

A few hours later, he decisively dials Leonard's number. Placing the call on speaker, Paul confronts him bitterly, "You obviously knew I was the beneficiary. Why didn't you tell me, not even a hint?"

Leonard's voice was firm, "How could I? And what would I even say? All I knew was that he was your uncle, and nothing more. You were unaware, and his intention was for you to get to know him without any preconceived notions."

Paul sighs, "What am I even supposed to do?"

Leonard's only answer was, "Take some time off, let this sink in. Your responsibilities can be handled. Give yourself the space you need."

"I'll still go to London this week and tie off the loose ends for a while," Paul says, and the speakerphone conversation concludes. He looks at me, his eyes carrying a plea.

"Please tell me you'll be in London this Thursday. I don't want to face this alone."

With a reassuring nod, I confirm that I'll be there, adding a lighthearted remark, "Guess now fate has been mischievous, maybe I should be calling you 'boss'."

He half-smiles in response and massages his temples.

"Oh no," he groans, "I've suddenly inherited all these staff and responsibilities. But let's stick to Paul for now; we can figure out the 'boss' part in due time. Speaking of things to wrap my head around: Lilly and the cuffs, the albums—everything falls into place now." He sighs.

A smile dances on my lips as I can't help but tease him, "So, does this mean I'll finally get a peek at those albums? The curiosity's been eating at me."

He turns to me, his eyes clearing up, and responds in a playful tone, "Does this mean you're applying for the position of my significant other?" The levity in his words brings me relief. He takes my hands in his, "Thank you, you've been a great help today, being there when I needed it. But on a serious note, I'd appreciate it if you could mull over the situation. I need impartial advice from someone who sees beyond balance sheets."

A hearty laugh racks through him, echoing in the room, startling me, "What's so amusing?"

He chuckles, "Just realized, I asked an accountant for advice without considering the numbers on a balance sheet."

"Well, stranger things have happened," I remark.

Chapter 16

Sitting on the train, I anxiously awaited Paul. His uncharacteristic tardiness was making me restless. I grew more puzzled as the time passed, and the doors were about to close any second now. I had texted him a few minutes ago to ask where he was, but he hadn't replied yet. Just as the train doors were closing, he rushed onto the platform and boarded the train, hurrying over to me at our usual seats.

"Hey, what happened? Are you okay?" I asked, concerned.

"Hello, darling," he said, sighing deeply as he sat beside me. "I'm quite alright. Sorry to worry you, I'm just tired. Past few days have been quite a roller coaster, as you know. I haven't been sleeping well, and constantly thinking about the letter, Ralph, my mom. Just been a wreck. I lay in bed this morning for half an hour thinking about what to do for the day and tomorrow in London." His eyes were bloodshot, and a thick vein drummed on his forehead.

"Hey, hey. It's alright. Just lay back, we'll get breakfast and let's chat," I said, thinking that we both needed some food and coffee before we began the conversation. There was only one topic of conversation in our minds after all. Once our breakfast arrived, and the strong, familiar scent of coffee hit me, Paul turned to me.

"Well, what's been going on with you?" he asked. "I know I've been a bit self-absorbed this week, and you've been my sounding board all this time, even though you've been having a rough time. Talk, I want to be there for you too."

His unexpected concern for me caught me off guard, "Really?" I asked.

"Yes," he said. "Tell me what's going on with you, Maria. You've only been patiently listening to me for the last few days."

"Well, work is okay, at least from a professional perspective," I said. "There are a few new projects in the pipeline, and although I have been getting empathy, the fact of the matter is that I was still passed over for promotions. It all feels superficial. Things are strained between the upper management and me. I kinda lost it yesterday," I shake my head and snort bitterly.

He's still looking at me expectantly, so I continue, "He came down to ask about one of the other projects, one that's not even mine. He asked me to review it and instruct the team handling it about what to do. So, I looked at it and the solution was right there. The team hadn't figured it out, but I turned to him and told him that it is above my pay grade to interfere with another department and team. I said that's partner-level responsibility, and thanks, but I'll just stick to mine. He said I'm experienced and appeared confused! The nerve of him! So, I said 'Maybe ask Justin, since he is obviously more valuable and experienced.' That seemed to get the message across, and he left looking rather displeased."

It was still early morning, and the train was quiet which made my rant sound even louder than I expected myself to be. I looked around, embarrassed.

Paul laughs and takes a bite of his eggs. "I bet he did. I like that you're taking a stand."

"I have a hunch that a new project is coming to me soon, since this one will be wrapped up in a little while. Otherwise, I'll just be home," I sigh. "The kids are the same. And Mark...well, he's being Mark. Always watching TV or working or lazing about, not caring about anyone that's not himself. Charming as usual. And that's my morning moaning done. Your turn now, did all that thinking in your pretty head lead to a plan?" I turn to Paul and give him an encouraging smile.

Paul's gaze turned somber and thoughtful. "I think I have. I just need to really think about the future. Visualize the idea of what would happen if I took it and if I don't take it either. It'll help me decide what to do. So, I've decided that I'm going to meet and talk with Adam today. I think it's time to have a candid conversation with him. I rang him last night and we have a meeting arranged for 10 AM today. Talking to him will hopefully give me some more insight into Ralph and what he was like. I just still can't believe it, you know? An uncle. I will meet him on my own today, I think he will be more open that way."

I agree. It isn't a place for me, after all, it has nothing to do with me really. Though I am very curious to see what Adam would have to say.

"The best thing to do is take your time," I say reassuringly. "This is huge news, life-changing. I think you should talk and think more before you decide. It will be a monumental change in any case."

***

We arrived in London and took a taxi to the office. The Amazon order for the apartment's kitchen had arrived, and Paul asked someone from the store to drop it off at the apartment. The apartment renovation was coming along splendidly. We didn't spend long there because Paul was fidgety, but we did agree it seemed like a home now.

When we got to the office, Nicola informed us that there was a problem in the warehouse. One of the main conveyors was broken, and they were forced to work on the smaller ones, which was straining the operations. I asked what the typical protocol was in such a case, and she explained that they would usually call in a repair company to assess the situation and get the repairs done as soon as possible.

"Alright, so why hasn't this been addressed already?" Paul asks, confused.

Nicola raises her brows like it was something obvious, "I didn't want to make the call to the repair company in case the new owners didn't agree to the repairs. What's the use in getting them to come all the way over if we don't need to get it repaired?"

"Well, for now, you're stuck with us making the decisions," Paul says, swift and reassuring. "Can you just do what needs to be done? We've already reiterated that it's business as usual and we fully trust you to make these day-to-day decisions as you have always done. Just keep us informed about the repair schedule, and let us know if the operations are still hindered, will you?"

I could see an edge to Paul's demeanor when he finishes speaking to Nicola. His voice holds the weight of authority; I wonder if he noticed. He has always been assertive, but I sense a tinge of impatience coloring his voice now. I could see that Nicola senses it too, but she takes it gracefully, "Well, I'm happy to do whatever I can to help. I'll keep you updated." She leaves, and Paul collapses in his chair, exhaling loudly.

Throughout the day, Paul's distraction is palpable. At five minutes to ten AM, he heads off to meet Adam for coffee. I spend the day providing solutions for other unsteady operations and dealing with some stock complaints that had arisen. An hour later Paul calls me to ask if I'm free and would like to meet him at the coffee place. I decide to take an early lunch break, and excuse myself from the office. Paul quickly fills me in on his meeting with Adam.

"Adam told me that he received a letter from Ralph, and he knew I was his nephew when we went to see him together, remember? Adam has known for some time, but Ralph had sworn him to secrecy. He said that he was instructed to fill me in as much as I asked within reason.

"Adam started by telling me that 'they' had met Ralph in 1994. They shared a hobby, which I guess, obviously, is Ralph and Lilly's 'lifestyle'. I asked who 'they' was, and Adam said that he meant himself and his wife, Nicole. Apparently, the couple used to be very close with Ralph and Lilly. They had gotten to know them over time and gone to events together. He said they were a gorgeous couple, happy, and in love. Eventually, they confided in Adam and Nicole that unfortunately, Lilly was married, and they had to make it work as best as they could. Adam said that he wasn't going to get into the details of what Ralph and Lilly enjoyed but if I had any questions, I was welcome to seek his guidance." Paul shook his head, still obviously processing all the information.

"Back in the early 1990s, their lifestyle existed on the fringe, an unconventional realm that was hard to navigate, especially when it came to sourcing high-quality toys and equipment. Eventually, as their friendship and trust deepened, Ralph approached Adam with a proposal. He asked whether Adam would be willing to oversee a potential endeavor: running a shop catering to their niche interests. Adam was overjoyed at the idea, and together, they brought this unique, once unheard-of establishment to life. Ralph's enthusiasm for the project was infectious, and it soon became evident that Ralph and Lilly shared more than just their private moments; they also took pleasure in visiting the shop during off-hours, exploring its offerings, and playing while the shop was closed.

"However, when Lilly tragically passed away, Ralph's world shattered. He seemed to lose his spark, and his interests faded into the background. The hobby that once brought them both joy took a back seat, and even the shop that had thrived under their partnership felt the impact of his loss. About five years ago, Ralph confided in Adam about me. He told him everything, about my mom, me, my career. It seemed like he spoke fondly of me." Paul shrugs but I can tell he would have wanted to know about his uncle if his mother had given them a choice. He extends an envelope towards me, and I look at him questioningly.

"Ralph had this delivered to Adam through his executors once he'd passed away. He said he won't mind if I take it."

"You want me to read it?" I ask, my brows bunched. He nods.

I take the creased, folded pages from him, and look at him before reading the letter.

"Dear Adam

If you are reading this, it is after I have passed away. You and Nicole were one of the few people I could call friends and who I trusted.

I have told you about my nephew Paul and that we have never met, he does not even know I ever exist, and it will remain that way until my death. In my will I have picked Paul's legal firm to sort my affairs, but not to tell Paul until everything is itemised and sorted out. I don't want to ambush him.

Paul will get a letter at the appropriate time telling him he is the sole beneficiary of all my estate. I intend to tell him about our family history. You do not need to know that for the purposes of this letter.

I felt the need to tell him a bit about me and Lilly and some generalities. I would like you to tell him how happy we were, fill in some of the gaps, and help him come to terms with it all. Paul would in all probability have come across some of our toys, though I kept very few, some I kept as memorabilia. He would also have seen my albums, the photos of Lilly and myself from our events and travels. There is nothing explicit in those albums, but I would like him to see us as we were, enjoying life. The revelation is bound to raise a whole load of questions, and I believe he will be curious and wonder about me, which is why I am revealing my life's story to him.

The letter I penned to him gently implies, without imposing any obligation, that if he desires to peek through the curtain and see what profound happiness Lilly and I shared, he might consider dipping his toes into the lifestyle. My intention behind this suggestion is for him to understand me, and not perceive me differently due to the content of the albums and my personal items. I yearn for my legacy to reflect the complete truth to my nephew. Furthermore, I want him to know I am not merely a solitary, embittered old man, but someone who has experienced love and loss. I hoped that granting him candid insight into my life might foster a better understanding.

In the letter, I assured him that he could turn to you for assistance, knowing that you would offer both him and his partner the guidance they needed. I wished for you to clearly establish the fact that Lilly and I found joy in a private world of fetish and exploration. The events we attended like Wasteland and Rubber Ball, if he wants to know more. If he were inclined to inquire, I urged you to provide a genuine depiction of the people within this lifestyle. I couldn't tell my nephew in my life about me, but I entrust this responsibility in your care.

241

All I want is for you to emphasize that our involvement in this lifestyle wasn't about promiscuity or whatever the leading misconceptions are, but rather about reveling in a joyful, playful, and fulfilling experience based on trust. It was about the intimacy that blossomed between us. Our circle of friends, which included you and Nicole, enriched these experiences.

If you don't mind, and you think it may help, give a copy of this letter to Paul.

Now, Adam, my old friend, I have also stipulated that should Paul choose to accept his inheritance all shops will enjoy complete job security for at least a decade. The place is yours as it always has been, and the standard yours to uphold. If Paul decides to dabble, then let him do it at his own discretion. I know you have observed some stock missing after Lilly and my visits and turned a blind eye to it. I hope you extend the same grace to him.

Lastly, I want to express my gratitude for everything. Even though I distanced myself after Lilly's passing, I've always held you and Nicole as dear friends. Seeing the two of you together brought back memories of the happiness I once had. While I had hoped that time might make it easier, I never truly moved on from the loss of Lilly. I hope you understand.

Your friend always,
Ralph"

"I see," I say, deep in thought. I could only imagine how big a deal this was for Paul.

"I am still grappling with this confusion and ...frustration, I think. But in essence there are just two major decisions: what to do about the inheritance and whether I should really delve into Ralph's private life."

"Hey, I'm here. I'll help in any way I can."

Paul's expression shifts with determination. "Come on, grab your coat," he urges, marching on with a purposeful stride. I hurry to keep pace, jokingly reminding him that my high heels are more for show than speed. "Slow down, Paul! Where are we headed?"

"Just follow me," he replies, leading me towards the office. As we arrive, he veers right towards a side door. "You've been curious about those albums, haven't you?"

242

"Paul, seriously? Why now? Not that I'm complaining – the curiosity has been killing me." he just smirks in response.

We enter the office, and Paul explains, "I think I've made a decision on one of those things. If I'm going to peer behind that metaphorical curtain, as Ralph put it, I can't do it alone. I need you by my side for this journey. Ralph said so, too."

I nod, and he brings the safe content to Ralph's desk.

"Whether we like it or not," Paul begins, his tone resolute, "and you may want to run for the hills when you hear this, but you are the woman I love. Complications and all. If I'm going to venture into this, it's going to be with you. I can't do this alone. I won't."

His words hit me like a sudden gust of wind – unexpected, intense.

I stand there, taken aback, my mind a whirlwind of emotions. He loves me. His gaze rests on me, waiting for my response, my reaction. I don't say a word.

Instinctively, I lean closer, press a kiss to his cheek, and whisper, "Well, if you're about to drag me into something, you better show me a peek of what it is first. Let's take a look at those albums." He doesn't look bummed that I didn't say it back; he's had time to get there, and he will afford me the same grace.

He looks at me, somewhat surprised, and I grin. "You heard me. We better check out those albums. I'd do it myself, but that safe looks hostile. So, move it, mister."

Paul retrieves the albums, and I watch him, impatient and eager. He looks at me with a playful glint in his eye, and I wonder for the umpteenth time what the albums are about. Paul pulls out two huge volumes from inside, and tucks them under his arm, "Come, there's no comfortable seating here. Let's go to the apartment."

I can't believe he's teasing me, and I look at him with daggers in my eyes, and he laughs, pulling me into a sideways embrace. "Come, come," he pacifies me. I get his desire to create this suspense for a little while longer. Just a bit.

243

Not soon enough, we arrive at the fully furnished apartment – and I just know we will be spending the night here tonight. We settle onto the couch, side by side, and open the first album. My heart races, excitement and anticipation building within me. The first page unveils a radiant image of Ralph and Lilly, happiness emanating from their smiles, Ralph in his early forties and Lilly much younger than him. They appeared to be on a mountain hike, and the rosy cheeked hue was a tell-tale sign of their enjoyment.

Paul's voice breaks the silence that has enveloped me. "There are two albums. One chronicles Ralph and Lilly's adventures in the great outdoors, just like any other couple might have. The second album, however, captures their more *playful* side."

We settle in, and almost an hour passes by while we go through the first album. It's sweet memories, and I feel a pang of sadness that all this will be destroyed in less than a month now. Each page seemed to be a portal to the past, revealing a life lived, a life enjoyed.

And then, Paul smirks and brings out the second album. As we turn the page, an image of Ralph and Lilly emerges. It takes me a second to make sense of the image I'm seeing. Clad in what appeared to be a rubber one-piece, Lilly's dress was striking, accentuating her soft beauty. She stands amongst a crowd, and everyone's dressed in an array of costumes – rubber, leather, chains and harnesses. I'm surprised to see a much younger Ralph also dressed in a taut rubber outfit.

"Wow," I can't help but exclaim. "She looks absolutely stunning, and so happy. Where do you think they were in these photos?"

We turn a few pages and my question. The next photograph is also from the same night, with the same crowd of people, popping champagne in front of a large sign that read 'Wasteland'.

"What's Wasteland?" I inquire, still flitting through the pages. It's all so alien to me, and my gaze is glued to it. Paul shrugs, equally lost.

We encounter Ralph and Lilly at various events, their outfits and activities changing from one image to the next. Some photos depict scenes of bondage play in the background, though Ralph and Lilly themselves aren't involved. I notice rope artists intricately weaving patterns around willing partners, their postures bent from ecstasy in a dance. All around them people are submerged in different experiences, and the album is like a collage of different worlds merging.

Reaching the final pages, I turn to Paul, and see anticipation and curiosity gleaming in his eyes. "So, what's your take on all this?" I keep my face cautiously blank.

He takes a moment, still absorbing the visual journey. "It looks amazing, to be honest. A bit wild and out there. But what strikes me the most is how genuinely happy Ralph and Lilly seem. I did not imagine Ralph had lived a life of happy companionship from his accounts of most people. Amidst all the- the leather and the collars, the essence of their joy shines through."

His question returns to me like a boomerang. "And now, your thoughts?" he inquires. He also has his poker face on.

I meet his gaze, his words from earlier resonating within me. "Honestly, I've been mulling it over, even before I saw these albums. What I see, more than anything, is their happiness. They lived their truth."

He listens intently as I continue. "You know, Paul, if you think about it, their story isn't too different from ours. Lilly and Ralph had their own double life, a secret world they shared. And we, well, we already have a parallel between here and home. The only question is, I guess, do we take that leap and explore further?"

I feel a shift in the atmosphere, the weight of the decision ahead settling upon us. "Although," I admit, "I think we should recognize that our path forward will be more challenging. My time in London is nearing its end, even if it hasn't already, and though it's just a few more weeks, it will signify a change."

Flipping through the albums and witnessing the freeing, genuine happiness shared between Lilly and Ralph has

245

unexpectedly ignited a spark of hope within me. It's oddly comforting to see that despite any challenges they faced, they managed to make their complicated relationship work.

"By the way, in case I wasn't clear, I've also developed feelings for you – complicated as they might be." That's all I can commit to him, for now. And he accepts it heartily, pulling me snugly beside him and kissing my forehead. "So, what's next... Do we go to Adam and see what stories he's got in store for us? I will certainly not mind learning more about Ralph and Lilly's lifestyle." My mind goes back to that lunch when Paul had first flitted through the albums, and how different he'd been afterwards.

"Okay, so, question. If we explore this and indeed if we meet Adam to talk about this, you are my significant other. You're my partner here. You're also the accountant overseeing the succession so... Are you ok with him knowing our positions? Adam kept Ralph's secret for decades, and he might do the same for us." The gravity of his words lingered in the air, and I felt the weight of the decision ahead.

My mind whirled as I considered the implications. "If we want to go into this, I suppose it's not much of a choice to trust him, unless we want to go into it blindly. Or you talk to him, and we try to cover up our relationship. I think I want to be there when you discover this world beyond the curtain- I want us to be together. Let's only reveal the fact that I'm married if it comes up. Everything we talk to him about stays privileged." I reply, all business-like.

"Alright, yes," Paul acknowledges the fact that we're not like regular couples, "We will always be on limited time. I have an idea. How about I call and invite Adam and his wife to have dinner with us tonight and see what they have to say? Apart from the obvious, maybe hearing him talk will help me- us- decide what to do about the inheritance elephant in the room." It's charming how he thinks his succession was both of our decisions- like we were partners in the true sense of the word. It brings me an odd relief.

As I glance at my watch, reality nudges me back into the present. "I better show my face at work, the others will wonder what happened." A mischievous smile alights my face, "Also, I hear there is a new boss coming in soon, he could be very demanding," I croon, giving him my best 'come get me' eyes. His mouth opens in surprise, and he tugs on my arm and pulls me in, kissing me deeply. I break us apart and whisper in his ear.

"Just think of it, tonight I am shagging the boss. That's a sexual harassment suit waiting to happen, your first day on the job," I quip, and turn to leave.

As I walk away, his laughter echoes in the empty apartment.

***

I get his text at three in the afternoon.

Paul: *Dinner with Nicole and Adam at 7. Brace yourself, he sounded pretty willing to show us the ropes.*

I snort at his naughty gall, then text back.

Maria: *Yes, boss. I'm sure we'll work out the kinks together. (Excited and a nervous wreck!)*

Paul: *Oh, you're good at this. See you back at the love nest at 6.*

***

As the clock ticks toward 5:30, I step into the apartment, the anticipation tingling in every fiber of my being. Paul hasn't arrived yet, so I take the opportunity to explore the newly set up apartment. The furniture, the kitchen, the bathroom – all of it seems to be taking shape as the apartment, a shared space with Paul. Reality strikes me in waves then – was this really happening? Was I really setting up an apartment with Paul? A mixture of fear and excitement stirs within me, a whirlwind of emotions that I can't quite put into words.

I meander into the living room and settle onto the couch, the album resting in my lap. As I flip through the pages, the images of Ralph and Lilly in their shiny, black costumes catches my attention again. My gaze shifts to the wall, back at the hook, a lingering question mark in my mind. Who had been tied to that hook? What sorts of experiences had unfolded within these walls? And what would Adam and Nicole reveal tonight?

Suddenly, the sound of the door opening pulls me from my reverie. Paul enters, his presence grounding me in the here and now. He looks at me sitting somberly onto the couch, with the album in hand. "Hey, Maria, are you okay? What is it? Are you overwhelmed?" he comes over to kneel before me, concerned etched deep in his face.

"Just getting my head around all this, Paul," I admit, still unsure what I was feeling. "Just absorbing that we are here, in our apartment, I guess."

He sits on his haunches, his gaze gentle. "You feeling okay? We can cancel dinner if you want. I know there's a lot of change to get used to, and there's still time to back out. We're in no hurry to sort this out."

"No, Paul," I reassure him, "Just absorbing it all. Let's do this. Now, let's see what I've got to wear to this thing."

As we busy ourselves with preparations, my mind quickly comes up with an apt outfit combination. I settled on high heels, black pants, a grey blouse that struck a balance between casual and elegant. Black lingerie underneath, to keep the vibe alive. Paul looks at me appreciatively, but I don't acknowledge his gaze; we'll get late if I humor either of us right now. Hanging clothes in the wardrobe, I get a funny feeling– a flutter of anticipation and a touch of nerves. This was like a second home- the thought made me feel something so overwhelming I couldn't name it even if I tried. We walk outside the apartment together, into the night ahead that promised us answers, revelations, and a world unknown.

Chapter 17

Paul and I make our way to the table we have reserved, my curiosity building like a crescendo. The evening sun casts a warm glow, and as we settle in, I waste no time in ordering a sizable glass of wine- something to steady my nerves and begin the evening on an apt note. I motion for a bottle as soon as I drain my first glass.

Our conversation flows naturally, but a question burns in my mind, demanding my attention. Leaning in toward Paul, I can't help but ask him, "So, are you just here for stories, or you're looking forward to learning the *ropes*?"

Paul begins to answer but we spot our guests, and instead he says, "Saved by the bell. Our storytellers are here." I'm left hanging, and it accentuates the nerves already wreaking havoc on me. To take my mind off the topic of this evening's dinner, I turn to Nicole, who's a sight to behold. At around fifty years old, her tall, willowy figure stands at 5'10", her dark hair cascading like a waterfall down her back. An aura of elegance and control wraps like a second skin around her. The couple approaches us with an enchanting smile, and I spot a twinkle in Nicole's eyes that hints at secrets untold.

As Nicole draws close, she greets me with a sweet peck on my cheek. Adam and Paul shake hands, and Adam claps Paul on his back; the familiarity makes Paul start, but he doesn't let on. We all take our seats. *This is not weird for me*, I tell myself. After the whirlwind of the past few weeks, nothing feels entirely out of place anymore. *A pleasant evening to discuss some bondage and S&M!* My breath hitches.

Paul clears his throat; I feel he's sorely feeling the lack of a handbook aptly titled 'Guide For Discussing BDSM With Your Dead Uncle's Friend & His Wife'. "Well, Adam, I trust you've shared everything with Nicole. We're immensely grateful for your... help, to guide us through this. This is Maria, my partner, and we're equally invested in exploring whatever this becomes."

I almost whistle; Paul is very adept at discussing difficult and awkward topics.

Adam's lips curl into a warm smile as his eyes meet mine, his gaze inviting, "Oh, Nicole knows everything," he chuckles lightly. "She's been with me before we met Ralph and Lilly. But before anything, how about we order a round of drinks? It looks like all of us could use a bit of refreshment." He looks pointedly at the half-finished bottle of wine in front of me.

We summon the waitress and order our drinks, as well as dinner. The soft ambiance of the restaurant envelops us, lending an intimate air to our impending conversation. The low murmur of other diners' ebbs and flows around us, creating a cocoon of privacy.

As we wait for the drinks to arrive, I feel excitement and curiosity tugging at my frayed nerves. The evening holds the promise of unveiling a hidden world to me that might change Paul and my dynamic, forever.

I can't hold it in anymore, taking the lead, I turn to Nicole, "Nicole, if you don't mind, I'd love to hear a bit more about your journey together. How long have you and Adam been a couple? And, of course, how did your paths cross with Lilly and Ralph?"

Nicole's eyes are warm with memories. "Well, Adam and I have been together since the early 1990s," she begins, her voice carrying the weight of years spent together. "It's been quite a journey, and I can honestly say we've been very happy. Back then, Adam was working a few odd jobs while I was finishing up med school and eventually became a GP."

I can imagine these two as she weaves a perfect tapestry of past time. Youthful adventures perfectly molded around career hustles.

"We've always been a bit adventurous, you see," Nicole continues with a snicker. "And that's what ultimately led us to explore the fetish scene, even though it was relatively limited at the time. Around 1994, we crossed paths with Ralph and Lilly at an event. They were older than us, as a couple, but we were much more experienced. It's funny, really, how connections are made." She pauses for a moment, perhaps sifting through the treasure trove of memories.

"We struck up a conversation and immediately hit it off," she says, her gaze firmly holding the distant memory. "Despite the age difference, we connected on so many levels. A few months later, we bumped into each other again at another event. The evening was just as enjoyable, drinks flowing and a wonderful atmosphere. That's when we decided to exchange numbers."

As Nicole speaks, I can almost hear the tinkling banter that blossomed between them. Whispered secrets and shared experiences of only a world they were a part of.

"We began meeting for dinners and drinks," Nicole brings me back to the story. "We soon discovered that while there's plenty of enjoyment to be had in the fetish scene, there's also a wonderful social aspect. It's something special to share this secret world with friends who understand it so intimately.

"And then, there was the business side of things," Nicole adds with a hint of playfulness. "Adam and Ralph set up the shop together. While I let them handle the nitty-gritty, I must admit I loved the after-hours visits. It's like peering behind the curtain, exploring the stock, doing quality control, and giving feedback, if you catch my meaning."

I certainly did. A world of glossy, enticing merchandise at their fingertips to do with as they pleased. Who could abstain?

"Our friendship with Ralph and Lilly blossomed, although Lilly and I connected on a deeper level, that exists only between women. Whenever Lilly found herself with some free time, we would often meet for coffee, just to catch up and share the new gossip. Adam and I were aware of the complexities of their personal lives, but we respected their privacy. To us, their relationship was their own, something we admired from afar without intruding. Their connection was... incredible; their love for each other was undeniable. Ralph's devastation at Lilly's passing was heart-wrenching. He mourned her deeply, and the void she left behind seemed insurmountable. He never got over her, nor did I ever expect him, too, to be frank. The man was made for her, and when Lilly was no more, some part of him died, too. Despite Ralph's posturing, he withdrew into his own world and his work, seeking solace in his memories of Lilly.

Even then, Ralph remained our friend, a constant, although silent, presence in our lives. But as time passed, it was clear that Lilly's absence had left an indelible mark on him. Our occasional dinner meet-ups felt different; his heart was no longer in scenes, or camaraderie. They had enjoyed life's pleasures together for years, but after Lilly was gone, the spark was extinguished from his eyes. We held out hope that he might find companionship again, knowing how wonderful a person he was. However, fate had a different plan, and Ralph chose their memories over living the rest of his life."

A cloud of gloom settles over the people at the table, and I find myself feeling actual emotions for a man I'd never met in his life and the woman who'd stolen his heart.

Paul clears his throat, "You mention 'scene' several times... I confess I don't know much about what you refer to, but it's obviously what brought Ralph so much happiness. He said in his letter that I could peek through the curtain, as he put it. What exactly lies behind this curtain? Ralph. And what?"

Adam leans back slightly, taking a sip of his drink before continuing. "It's important to respect the boundaries that Ralph and Lilly upheld," he began, his tone heavy with something deeper than loyalty. "They had their personal lives, and that remains theirs alone. What Ralph aims to convey is a broader understanding of the lifestyle they embraced, the scene they were a part of."

Nicole smiles, taking over. "It's a journey of exploration, understanding, and perhaps a glimpse into the broader spectrum of life that they cherished," she added, her voice carrying a sense of gentle reassurance.

"The fetish scene is vast, layered as the painter's palette," she continues, and it begins to unfold. "It's a realm of domination and submission, to the more playful aspects of dressing up, role-playing, bondage, sadism and masochism, and even the allure of humiliation; everyone navigates their unique path. Something yum for one couple is another's yuck. The canvas is large, and each brushstroke represents personal preferences.

"Some among us find joy in dressing up, donning leather, latex, or the iridescent PVC, some may even be into corsets and specific costumes. They attend events and clubs, soaking in the atmosphere without immersing themselves in the physical play – at least not in the public eye.

For them, the preference leans towards the intimacy of privacy. Through fantasies acted out behind the privacy of closed doors, the worship and the punishments. It's a safe haven, away from prying eyes.

"For others, there is a thrill in being observed, remarked upon. The voyeurs. In essence, it's a haven for where reality and judgement are momentarily set aside," Nicole continues, her words painting a vivid picture of this escape into a world of shared fantasies.

"It's essential to grasp some terms. Dominant and submissive roles need no introduction, I'm sure. Often, there's a dominant partner steering the ship while a submissive partner embraces the journey, following their lead. And then, there's the concept of a 'switch,' someone who smoothly transitions between the laid-out roles of dominance and submission."

"But what really, actually matters is personal preference. Doesn't matter if the semantics works, you make it fit accordingly. It's about plunging into the unknown, placing trust in one another, and respecting each other's boundaries. Sharing fantasies openly and candidly with your partner, exploring what might be enjoyed or not- that's the big deal. Balancing the art of pushing boundaries while honouring limits is key, all the while relishing the excitement of each moment."

Her words harden, her tone becomes firm, "Mutual respect isn't just confined to partners, though that's vital. It extends to everyone within the community. Each individual you come across on your journey- their privacy is safeguarded. Whatever you witness at events, parties or in scenes, nothing is to be shared with anyone outside of that event."

Her voice echoes like a mantra, "Nobody is anybody, but everybody is somebody they want to imagine being. So, there's the dichotomy between our two worlds. The world that you live in and the world that you escape to. And so, if you wish to make connections within the scene and extend them beyond, a deep level of respect is needed. Recognize that these people likely never shared these parts of their lives even with their closest friends, let alone family," Nicole articulates, her words dispensing the weight of responsibility.

"Discussing it, again and again until everyone is on the same page is the key, the seed from which this dynamic will bloom. Plus, you guys have the one advantage we never imagined having: the internet! Look everything up, you'll probably find much more information there than we could tell you. But the shop will still be a good place to start; there's toys, costumes, paddles, cuffs, ropes, you name it. Maybe a hands-on exploration would be more apt?" She looks at Adam, and he nods with a small smile.

Paul is fidgeting with the crisp white napkin and I'm swallowing down my wine noisily. Our guests read the room.

Nicole suggests steering the evening's discourse away from the colourful topic. "This must be getting too much all at once. Perhaps, let's just enjoy our meal and talk about this sometime later. You both need to discuss this too, understand what your personal inclinations and proclivities are. Well, you must have the keys to the shop from Ralph's office. A rendezvous in the shop could offer more clarity. See what intrigues you, experiment; it all now belongs to you, Paul," she gently finishes. "It's all about fun and escapism in the end."

A deep red blush climbs from Paul's neck and toward his face, and his ears have already turned a pretty shade of beetroot. He smiles tightly, and nods.

The conversation dwindles, and it becomes even more awkward finding topics to talk about than the conversation we just had.

Nicole chimes in, her attention shifting to Maria's blouse, and soon they're chatting about fashion. The boys playfully exchange comments, teasing about clothing choices. Adam quips, "Lovely shirt, Paul. Where did you get it?" Nicole, with a sly grin, adds, "Somewhere nicer than yours, anyway. Now stop eavesdropping on us and talk about sports or something." She rolls her eyes, and I giggle. I'm really feeling all the wine now.

Adam redirects to a safer topic. "If we must. So, Paul. Manchester United or City fan?" he inquires with a grin. Paul grins back, "Liverpool, when I'm following any bit. Makes me quite popular, as you can imagine."

As the meal progresses, we surrender to the easy rhythm of casual conversation, exchanging anecdotes and relishing the newly formed friendship. Time seems to flow slowly, sweet as honey, or maybe it's the wine, but I feel like we're existing in a bubble. I don't remember my other life, my responsibilities, my worries. Tonight, it's me discovering things about myself with Paul by my side.

With the dinner winding down, Paul asks courteously, "Would you both care for a drink at the bar?"

Nicole's response is coy, "Adam and I think it's time we make our exit. You two have some late-night shopping and thinking ahead." She winks at me and gives me a peck on the cheek. "Have fun," she whispers, her voice carrying an undertone of encouragement. To Paul, she adds firmly, "Take care of her."

Leaving the restaurant, I take the lead with a playful assertiveness. I don't know if I'd usually be so bold, but wine is running like blood in my veins tonight. "So, what's the plan? Are we going to peek behind the curtain?"

Paul chuckles, a glint of mischief in his eyes. "And what do you want?"

I laugh, "I asked you first— besides, you got the letter giving you free reins to *explore*." The word curls in my mouth, and Paul smiles.

He cleverly nudges the decision back to me. "Well, I'm up for it if you are. But only if you're by my side. Over to you, babe."

I grin, embracing the whimsy of the moment, "Well then, let's go shopping."

We make our way to Ralph's old office, slipping in through the familiar door. Once inside the shop, Paul heads directly toward Adam's office, at the opposite end of the merchandise at display.

I ask him faintly, "Where are you going?"

Paul has a mischievous, purposeful twinkle in his eyes, "Adam mentioned some CCTVs. Now that we're exploring, might as well disable the recorder's power. Gives us a bit more freedom."

I nod. *Exploring.*

***

Exploring the shop is like stepping into a world of some alternate world, albeit a decidedly adult one. The array of sex toys and bondage equipment is sprawled across the shelves. The faint scent of rubber lingers, reminiscent of the day we first ventured here. My fingers graze the soft fabrics of the clothing, and excitement flits across my eyes. "Wow, look at these, they're gorgeous," I marvel at the soft, scarce leather harness, fingers tracing the intricate design. "Could you imagine wearing this?" I whisper, not seeking a real answer.

Paul nuzzles my earlobe, and I rehang the garment, still walking through the aisles surrounded by a sensory symphony of textures and sensations that's utterly overpowering. My head

256

is spinning from this heady situation, and my breath is coming in short gasps.

We finally get to the walls that are adorned with an assortment of intriguing paraphernalia—handcuffs, leather, metal bars, ropes, clips, and a host of items that defy easy description. I was sure I could name not even a stick here. *Cane*. Well, that was the easiest one. A shiver runs through my spine, raiding every hair on my body at attention.

"Where do we even begin? What do you think?" His eyes were wide with excitement, and also confusion. "I can totally see why Adam and Nicole said this scene is vast, I mean, so many options!"

I feel overwhelmed. We're not shopping tonight, but I have a suspicion that we will soon be.

As we make our way back to the apartment, conversation flows easily between us.

I confess, "I'm still not over what I've seen, heard tonight. Honestly, I'm still wondering, quizzing myself what this or that toy is used for... used on."

We're back at the apartment by then.

We drop our stuff by the door, and Paul takes me in his arms, "Are you alright with this, Maria? Do you want to close the curtain?"

I giggle and give him a sloppy kiss, "I am so horny right now, and it's from imagining more than just opening the curtain," I clearly enunciate my words, and he gasps. "Although, what I'm thinking about right now is you saying you have some previous experience in this department. So, you likely know more than me. Tell me what it was like for you."

He pauses, then nods. Then takes me to the edge of the bed and sits me down. He pours me some water and watches me swallow.

My heart flutters at his careful attention. He takes the glass from my hand, places it on the glass table beside the bed with a clink. My breath hitches: his comes in gasps, and as natural as breathing, he captures my mouth in a tender, slow kiss. It draws out the last of my breath, leaving me panting. His tongue explores my mouth, and then, as if staking claim, ravages havoc pillaging and devouring while I squirm and moan around his taking mouth. His bottom lip catches on my teeth, and I bite hard, and feel the warm evidence of his life in my mouth, and I relish his passion, his need to give as thoroughly as he takes.

My fingers weave through his hair, pulling each other closer as we're consumed by the intensity of the moment. I realise with a start that I'm off the bed for a while now, standing, although everything feels hazy. In a rush, Paul walks me back, and I'm pinned against the wall, and a memory echoes from the past—another wall, another kiss but equally as all-consuming. I gasp as the coolness of the wall penetrates through my clothes, and he takes my mouth again, diving, searching.

I feel him pressing hard against me, and it spurs a lightning reaction within me. I grate against him and moan, while his fingers fumble at my blouse, and I feel the air when he tugs it halfway down my arms. I move, trying to get it off, but he pushes me back against the wall, my hands back, my arms snared in my blouse sleeves. My eyes search his face, and he whispers softly, "Trust me."

Something silky grazes my skin: a blindfold that Paul places over my eyes, obscuring my vision. Darkness envelops me, heightening every other sense to a state of exquisite awareness. Something in my lower body drops, and I feel an ache… ache building steadily. The anticipation pulses in rhythm with my heart, loud. The tension is almost palpable, each sound, each breath amplified in the absence of my sight.

My blouse is peeled away, discarded with a careless grace. Something about a gesture spurs a moan from me, before I can clamp it down. There's a rustle of fabric, movements: I strain to hear, to decipher the language of his actions. "Don't move," his command caresses my ears, sending shivers down my spine. It's intoxicating, and I surrender willingly. My imagination is wild; *What's he doing? When will he take me? What's coming?*

A gentle pressure on my wrists informs me that he's placed something over them, I feel myself bound, but not uncomfortably so. A tactile dance of submission. "Rope cuffs," he breathes, and the idea alone sends a thrill coursing through me. My wrists are drawn upwards, pulled towards a point above me. *The hook!* I hadn't realised that was the spot on the wall that I'm pressed against.

Hands stretched above my head; my world narrows to the sensations enveloping me. Paul's fingers trace a tantalising path along my stomach, and my neurons misfire from the heady pleasure. His touch is teasing, aching, tempting. His lips find my neck, the tickling warmth of his breath mingling with the softness of his touch. A whisper, a promise woven into the air, "Now, darling, we're back to where it all began. You, against this wall, hands over your head. Only this time, you are mine, and not getting away." He punctuates it with a feather-light kiss on my bikini line. I gasp sharply, squirming where I'm pinned.

He withdraws slightly, and I feel his loss sorely, the warmth, but the anticipation builds. My ears strain to detect his movements, my heart's rhythm echoing through the darkness. Some shuffling and he returns, skin against my skin, his bare chest pressing into mine. His arms enfold me, and I feel possessed, trapped, even though it hasn't begun yet. My senses are heightened, alive with every nuance of his touch, without feeling him, or even looking at him I feel I'm starved.

His lips plant a trail of scorching kisses down the front of my body, from my ears to the crook of my neck, to the valley between my breasts, dawdling there, letting my skin meet his teeth. I know I'd bruise there later, but I cannot bring myself to care. His hands slide over the front of my panties, as his tongue finds the smooth skin there, his fingers teasingly grazing the fabric as he begins to put his fingers around the elastic, then pulling them down. The pace is deliberate, each movement laden with desire, perfected to be teasing, driving my anticipation to fever pitch. The panties cascade down my legs in a tantalising dance, pooling at my ankles.

With a slow, teasing grace, Paul breathes deeply between my thighs, and I pull his face between my legs, and finally his tongue meets the contours of my folds. An electric pulse of pleasure shudders through my body as his lips encase my entrance, and I gasp, my moans dancing in the air. He dives into me with a voracious hunger, his tongue playing me like an instrument. I moan and writhe while his tongue coaxes vibrations of pleasure from inside me.

His fingers sweep down my thigh, to my foot, and he releases the panties from my legs, making sure my heels are on properly. The caress of his fingers gliding back up along my inner thigh sends waves of electricity through me, his lips resuming their journey back up my body, igniting every inch they touch.

His face kisses up the path through my body again, and when I finally meet his lips I taste of my own desire, and it sends a sharp spike of pleasure through my body. He withdraws, touching my lips with his fingers, and I instinctively take them in my mouth. I lick them up and down, teasing him, and his breath quickens. *Fine, let him taste some of his medicine.* I'm breathless, barely able to form words, my body responding with an intensity that eclipses rational thought. "Fuck me, fuck me, please," I manage to grit, my need overwhelming.

"Soon," I feel him smiling against my lush breast, and his long, wet fingers slip into the silky folds between my thighs, the sensation exquisite as he plunges deep into me. The pleasure is almost unbearable, and I tighten around his two fingers, the sensation of him inside me igniting an inferno that consumes my every thought. He moves within me, the rhythm mirroring the crescendo building deep within. I feel mad with pleasure, with desire. His thumb finds my clit, a burst of pleasure radiating from the point of contact. The sensation builds, a whirlwind of desire spinning through me, his pace growing more fervent. And he stops.

I'm left hanging, quite literally, mad and frustrated at the loss. The orgasm that was so, so near recedes from me. I groan loudly.

I hear the soft rustle of fabric as his pants come undone. He steps closer, his nakedness making me smack my lips. His lips explore my neck, a delicate touch that sets my frayed senses ablaze. His breath tickles my ear as he asks softly, "Can you take more?" The answer is almost incoherent, a desperate plea, "More, yes."

The soft hum of a vibration fills the air, and a delightful shiver races up my spine. The device presses against my clit, its sensation oscillating between demanding and spurring. The world around me fades as pleasure takes centre stage again, while Paul kisses me all over, biting and licking. He pushes the vibration device inside me, and I welcome it as it lights every nerve ending on fire. Paul's body melds with mine, his arousal a delicious pressure against my thigh.

The sensation of the device deepens, its rhythm coaxing me towards the edge of ecstasy. My body is on fire, every touch magnified, every sensation electrified, and I'm moving against Paul like I've never moved.

"I'm close," the words escape my lips, part scream and part moan, as the knot in my stomach builds to a crescendo. The sensations coursing through me are overwhelming, a maelstrom that I can't control. The vibrator is removed from my wet entrance, and in the next breath, Paul thrusts deep inside me, his movements unrelenting. The world narrows down to the heat of his body pressed against mine, the ecstatic friction of our bodies meeting in need. My back is pressed into the wall, arms straining above my head, the feeling of vulnerability only heightening the eroticism of the moment.

Paul's thrusts continue, each more brutal than the last, and as the pleasure surges within me, I feel my body respond with abandon. I release with a cry and a moan. The spasms of pleasure are overwhelming, my release washing over me like a tidal wave of ecstasy. My body shudders, convulses, as I surrender to the intensity of the experience, unable to do anything but give in to the pleasure that consumes me. My muscles tighten around him like a vice, and with a cry he releases too, filling me up with warm liquid that drips down my thighs even as he emptied himself.

Breathless and panting, I come back to reality, wobbly. Paul's breathing matches mine, both of us trying to regain our equilibrium. With a deft touch, he removes the blindfold, and my eyes meet his, and I might have orgasmed again at the raw pleasure and care in his eyes were I not made of jelly at that moment. He kisses me tenderly and hungrily, a silent exchange of emotions and understanding. He undoes the cuffs, lifts me and takes me to bed, sliding me within the soft pile of sheets.

He grabs a wet towel from the bathroom and joins me in bed.

His soft voice brushes against my ear, "Hey baby, how did that feel?" All I can do is moan contentedly. "That was the sum of my knowledge, rest we will figure out together if you want." The words are a promise, and I will hold him to it.

I glance at my wrists, noticing a slight redness where the restraints had held me. It's a reminder of the intensity we've shared, evidence of our changing dynamic.

"That was amazing," I manage to say as soon as I gain some awareness. "I don't think I ever felt an orgasm that intense or been so wet before. Do you think that is what this may be like, if we tried?"

Paul turns me to face him and a smile tugs at his lips, his gaze holding mine with unwavering intensity. "You just found out what we can feel like together. We used one toy, our cuffs, and a hook. We could graduate to more stuff in the shop, eventually."

"Oh Paul, you tease, try and stop me. You do know what you are doing. A little experience, you said." I mock-punch his chest, "I was trying so hard to keep my legs apart. But could not help but squirm against you."

A chuckle escapes his lips, and his fingers brushed a strand of hair behind my ear. "Now imagine that on the day you held your hands up first. Forget the blindfold and the bullet. Just imagine being tied and taken like that." He buries his face in

262

the crook of my neck and groans. "I had to hold myself back with a leash."

The intensity of his words sends a surge of heat pooling low in my belly. "Oh, man, I have been imagining," I confess, a blush creeping onto my cheeks. "A bullet, is that what that was? Did you shoplift without letting me know?"

I hear his mischievous smile more than I see it, "When we were in the shop tonight, I saw the rope cuffs, so I put them in my pocket, to surprise you later with. You mentioned them a few times, and I thought they might add some fun. As for the bullet, I saw it on the counter and figured, why not? Now, the bullet I want you to take with you and use it when you want as you imagine tonight."

Afterward, he wipes me clean, and I don't know when he finishes, but I fall asleep, thinking about work tomorrow, but most of all, how sexy the man cleaning me up is.

***

The following morning unfolds with a sweet domestic routine, as we get ready side by side to travel to the office. A quick pit stop for breakfast at the cafe for a sandwich and coffee, and we're on our way. It's there, amidst sips of coffee and bites of croissant sandwich, that a sense of melancholy sweeps over me. Paul picks up on my contemplative mood and asks with a concerned gaze, "Hey, something on your mind?"

I take a moment to gather my thoughts before replying, "I'm just thinking about the London job and what comes next for us. Now that we've started- although I didn't know it would be this difficult- I don't want to stop. I can't." I shake my head, completely at loss.

Paul reaches for my hand across the table. His fingers gently turn my hand around, his gaze fixed on the inside of my wrist. Confusion dances in my eyes as I watch his scrutiny, until his words break the silence, "Not a mark on them. Thankfully."

My brows knit together in momentary confusion until I remember the rope cuffs from last night. I hadn't even thought to check for any lingering marks. I would have noticed them in the shower, surely, if some angry evidence of last night survived. His concern is both touching and endearing.

"And, hey, we will figure something out before then, alright? No need to worry."

But I can't stop myself from worrying.

***

Each of us is summoned to a different part of the office when we reach there. Helen takes Paul to the conference rooms while fussing at his jacket cuff, while Nicola drags me to the Accounts' department. With the team, I meticulously finalise the financial records of the company and all Ralph's holdings for the past quarter. The stores under our care have been holding their own their combined earnings a well on par with expectations. I can't help but wonder what Paul's thinking to do with his life, because this is a ton of money.

The Accounts are done. From a legal standpoint, our affairs are in order. Even Paul knows by now that we are precariously close to the end of this job. At least I am. For Paul, this may just be the beginning.

On the journey back home aboard the train, I'm still thinking if I would be coming back to London again on this job. Leaning against the window, I look at Paul who is observing me keenly, "What's your plan, then? Are you taking it?"

There's still uncertainty in his eyes. "Honestly, Maria, I don't quite know yet. It's a complex decision. On one hand, there's the inheritance - it would provide a security net for the kids. But then, I can't shake the feeling that my mother might not approve. It's a legacy from Ralph, after all, and she's had her differences with him. Plus, there's the kids, again, it's their birthright I guess but. How would sudden wealth affect them? They're grounded right now, and I worry about how their lives would change if I went through with this."

I nod, not saying much. It's his decision through and through. After a while, Paul shifts the conversation, steering it towards the upcoming weekend. "You know where my mind will be, though. It's hard to get over the mind-blowing events of last night."

***

Even after I've said goodbye to Paul at the station, and we've parted ways, I keep thinking about him, about last night, wishing it would stay like that forever. I need to rethink what I'm doing here, where are we going with this relationship, but all I can do is remember his lips between my thighs, devouring like his life depended on it.

I'm met with an unusual sense of calm when I get home. They're all fed and doing their own thing. Liam is off to the cinema with his friends, and he claps me on the back as he leaves. *Huh, have I been gone too long from my house?* Rebecca is somewhere in the house, and while I shuck off my coat and bag, Natalie joins me, excitedly telling me all the gossip at school. I'm invested and we're getting into the thick of it when, as if on cue, Mark comes strolling in, with a wide smile on his face.

"I've got a surprise for you both." he opens, and both our attention narrows on him. I'm genuinely curious, he's not one to prepare surprises.

With a flourish, Mark produces an envelope and reveals tickets, "I've booked a family holiday! We're headed to the Algarve, Portugal. Two entire weeks in August." Natalie shrieks in delight and jumps up and down on the sofa, and she dashes off to share the news with Rebecca.

I don't want to rain on his parade, but what even is this? "It would have been nice if we discussed this before making any plans. I'll need to check with work." My mind races through my schedule, weighing the implications of this decision.

"Hey, I already checked with Joan. Your calendar appeared free except for the potential Thursday and Friday trips to London. "And you did mention that this London job is nearly wrapped up, so." He's expecting me to clap him on his back.

I'm still not clear on what's happening here, "When did you even talk to Joan? She didn't mention anything."

Mark's expression turns slightly sheepish. "I reached out to her a while ago about this surprise. You introduced us last December at the Christmas party. You remember, right? You left me hanging to take a work call, and she and I ended up chatting. I asked her not to say anything because it's meant to be a surprise." I nod in acceptance.

"There could be a new project, or some twist in the current London case. Anyhow I'll handle all the loose ends. It will be good to get out of here and take a break for a little while." I resign myself to this unexpected surprise. Guess it was happening, and I surely didn't mind the off-time I was gonna get.

And then Mark throws another surprise at me. "Also, I have a long weekend planned with the lads in three weeks." He gives me the exact dates. I can't help but grumble a bit about the timing since it clashes with another Thursday and Friday that I've already committed to. This would mean I'll be taking almost half of the next 8 weeks off from the company. My day is on a downward spiral.

Despite the issues, I agree, "Alright, go ahead and enjoy your weekend away. Just be prepared for me to possibly work a weekend or two to ensure everything is covered."

A thought nags at me: How am I going to break the news to Paul about the two-week family holiday? It's a normal occurrence, just a few weeks' worth of uninterrupted time with family, I understand that, but we've deliberately steered clear of involving our families, or more precisely, discussing my own family in detail.

Saturday morning arrives, the anticipation for the upcoming holiday palpable in the kids' excitement. It's hard not to be swept up in their enthusiasm. I suggest we all go out for breakfast and maybe do some holiday shopping. "How does The Trafford Centre sound?" I ask, and smile when I hear loud cheers from everyone's corners. Mark, however, claims he's got some work-related matters to sort out, so it'll just be the kids and me.

Off we go, the four of us, for a breakfast treat in the food court – the mighty McDonald's serving up the best morning meal. We have coffee, and eggs, and the kids bicker amongst themselves. After that, it's a spree in the stores for new swimsuits and summer clothes. We spend the entire morning immersed in shopping and talking, and it's so much fun. It's a lovely day, and seeing the kids so elated improves my mood too. On the way home, I get a whiplash; Paul is in the traffic, holding his shopping. We are shocked to see each other, but exchange an inconspicuous salute. Inwardly, I'm grateful Mark isn't present to witness this.

As I return home, I decide to send Paul a message:

Maria: *Hey, darling. Nice surprise bumping into you today, even if it was just a quick pass in traffic. How do you like seeing me in full mommy mode? And I'm guessing I saw you in full daddy duty mode too. How's your weekend going? I hope you're managing to squeeze in some time for yourself amidst the hustle and bustle.*

Paul: *Oh, I like seeing you anywhere. But, yeah, running around trying to get some shopping done for Rachel. Weekend's okay, no rest for the wicked.*

Maria: *Oooh, got anything nice?*

Paul: *Rachel was happy with it, so I presume so LOL. But I was talking to Sarah, and we have one of our Saturday shopping days next weekend. Will be nice to get time with her. Always a nice day out with her.*

I smile. I love how he dotes on his daughters, they sure are lucky girls.

Maria: *That will be lovely. Credit card will take a nice battering, I suppose. Good for her.*

And then my phone vibrates twice at once.

Paul: *A nice day out. We only do this about twice a year, so it's all worth it.*

Paul: *I miss you, darling. Everything about you. Last week was such a whirlwind for me, and without you I would not have had anyone to talk to. I don't know what I'd have done, I still don't, but I'm trying to figure it out.*

Paul: *All or nothing makes it hard.*

Oh, boy, Ralph really knew what he was doing. Dilemma of a lifetime as a present to his nephew.

Maria: *Whatever you do I will be here. This is a personal decision for you. Only you can make it. But also, I'm afraid I've some news.*

Paul: *Oh, that does not sound good. Sounds like I am not going to like it.*

Maria: *Most probably not. But here goes. Mark has booked a 2-week holiday for everyone for August. In Portugal. He just landed it on me. I am sorry. I know it's going to be hectic with the office, but he got to Joan, and they set it all up.*

Maria: *And there is more, as if my day wasn't ruined enough. He's having a lads' weekend away, going to watch some match or the other. It is in a few weeks. Covers a Thursday and Friday so that is 3 weeks I won't be in London.*

Maria: *Although, I'm not sure if I even should be there since the job is effectively over now.*

Paul: *Oh, wow.*

Paul: *Wait, give me a moment to process all this.*

Paul: *So, Portugal, huh? Well, it is a well-deserved break. Go and enjoy, get a good tan. You really do deserve the break. The kids will love it. I knew when we started you were married, and you never made any secret of the fact you are not going to break up your family. So, I knew I had two choices: walk away, or accept that and live with it. I chose to live with it. I'm still sticking with it.*

Paul: *I know you will have family holidays, as will I. I know you will be out for dinner with friends as a couple, go to parties and do everything else couples do. That is something I must accept if I want to be with you. And I do.*

Paul: *As much as I would like more time with you. I love what we have, and I don't want you worrying about me when you are on family time. You can tell me everything, without worrying if I'd like it or not. I know you have your own demons to fight, and I do not plan to add on to them. So, let's just enjoy what we both have. And if nothing else, Ralph's story has shown me it can work. I can love you and just be thankful for what time we have, whenever we have it.*

Paul: *As for the boys' weekend away and you not being in London, I think we shall have you make it up for it while you stay for a long weekend in London. Making up lost time, of course.*

I breathe a sigh of relief. It really is so easy to talk to him, to empty my day's frustrations into his lap and have him hold them close and make them not scary or as frustrating anymore.

Paul: *As far as London is concerned, we will work it out somehow. It is the same for both of us. My work there is also done. Although, depending on what I decide to do, you may have a difficult boss in the future. Just relax. Let's make the best of the situation we have and see how it works out.*

Maria: *Don't get me started on difficult bosses.*

I grit my teeth, hearing them grind audibly.

Paul: *Well, if you need a pick-me-up, put that bullet to use. Did you bring it home with you? I distinctly remember it doesn't take you much time to... relax when it comes on.*

I laugh, and we say goodnight.

***

Over the course of the weekend, a sense of quiet envelops Paul. Communication from him is scarce and conversation is dry. He seems too busy. I don't even know what he's busy with, maybe it's just one of his blue moods. As Sunday evening arrives, I decide to reach out to him.

Maria: *Are you alright? You've been very quiet. Did something I say bother you?*

Paul: *Hey, no, it's nothing like that. I meant every word I said yesterday. I am just contemplating, I guess. On the big decision. Hemmed in by the four walls around me, listing down pros and cons, considering how either decision could upend my entire life.*

Paul: *This might involve relocating to London or even parting ways with my current job. I don't know. Inevitably. It would impact the kids too. But then, of course, there's the matter of financial security—for both me and the kids. Considerable funds, a number I've never seen before in my life sitting in my bank account... and then the business itself. I cannot even begin to comprehend how it will affect me and the kids, is all.*

Maria: *Of course, I understand. It's a big decision.*

269

Paul: *I apologise I haven't been attentive the past few days... How have you been?*

Maria: *Oh, it's been the usual weekend chaos with the kids. I've been trying to catch up on some work before the start of the new week.*

Maria: By *the way... the bullet solution does indeed hold water, though I must admit, it works better in your hands than mine.*

Maria: *Talk to you later!*

Paul: *Wait, tell me more about the bullet!*

Maria: *x*

Chapter 18

The holidays are soon, I'm on point and the day started on a happy note: Paul's good morning message and my coffee brewed to perfection. The weekend was not bad either; Mark seems to be making an effort with the holiday plans but I'm just looking forward to the welcome break.

When I walk into the office Joan has my work from the previous week all set up for me. The bulk of the work on the Ralph Michaels case has been tackled already, so there's not much of a load. Joan, although is curious and asks if I have any insight into the beneficiaries. She thinks maybe I have some inside information. Oh, boy, do I. I offer the best I can do, "Not at the moment." It's not false since Paul hasn't made up his mind yet.

"By the way, Mark broke to me the holiday news," I add, sighing loudly, "I wish you'd given me a heads-up. It's going to be quite the juggling act to get everything sorted now. If he contacts you again, please let me know."

"Oh, Maria, I apologise. I thought it would be a nice surprise. You know, you're lucky to have him. Not every man would arrange such a thing, especially now seeing you so overworked. You've got one of the good ones," she smiles. I smile and nod. There's something else or we would not be having this conversation.

Joan continues, "I was thinking of taking some time off as well. I presumed it might be easier if I was around during your vacation, given that I'm familiar with your work. I hope you won't have to answer many calls that way. So, I booked off a Thursday, Friday, and the following Monday in mid-July. I figured you would be in London and wouldn't miss me. I only finalised the decision last week, so here it goes. HR said it's fine, as long as you're okay with it."

I consider my options before replying, "That sounds fine, Joan. You deserve your time off too, and I hope you have a relaxing time. Just send me the dates and I'll make sure to put them in my calendar."

She shares the dates with me, and as I enter them into my schedule, I find myself sighing. Those happen to be the very Thursday and Friday when I'll be working here in Manchester, while looking after the kids because Mark was planning to go watch a match with his friends.

Ugh.

My mind seems heavy with weight; there's an upcoming meeting with Jack today, and if he asks about beneficiaries, I cannot pretend to sit there blank. He will sense something is up. He knows I'm too experienced to heed red tape as a warning; I've found out worse things in the past. I need to sit down with Paul and have a candid conversation about what he wants to reveal regarding the inheritance. It has to be sooner rather than later.

The customary Monday planning meeting comes too soon, and Jack, as usual, takes the lead. We dive into the ongoing projects, and inevitably, I'm up for a report on the Ralph Michael case. "It's essentially wrapped up. I'm just overseeing the London team and handling the financial aspects until the new owners officially take over. Babysitting and new records until succession is complete, basically. All the back-end work is done."

We transition to new assignments. There's talk of a local pharmacy chain due diligence- boring! - and a much more intricate forensic analysis of a London-based company, which is being acquired by one of our major clients. I've worked with the London client before, and it seems heavy work, just something up my alley. Plus, the London visits on the table again? Sign me up!

However, Jack's decisions veer in an unexpected direction.

He hands off the coveted London assignment to another associate, with Justin overseeing the task. And on top of it he has the nerve to allocate me to the pharmacy project. It's hard not to feel a pang of frustration, defiance. I look at Jack, a challenge cold in my eyes, "I have a solid background with the London client, and this job aligns perfectly with my expertise. You're serious, handing it off to the kids?"

He's surprised that I called him out. "The decision has already been made," Jack states matter-of-factly. His response stings and I can feel my patience slipping away.

The meeting concludes shortly. Afterward, I linger.

"Jack, what's going on? First, I'm passed over for Partner, and now I'm being handed this boring, grunt work? What the hell is going on?"

He doesn't mince words, "The Managing Director made that call. Something from last week rubbed him the wrong way. I don't have all the details, but it seems you've somehow managed to ruffle his feathers."

"Wow," I exhale angrily. "Way to know my worth here. I push back after being passed over and now I am being punished. Glad to be appreciated."

Jack attempts to calm me down, mumbling comforting words about how he will make sure the next big job comes to me. I'm not in the mood to listen to his consolation so I leave his office and head back to my desk.

I pass by Joan looking at me. "You all right?" she asks.

"No," I say curtly. "Pissed off with all the politics here."

Joan just says, "You are the most senior woman in the business. We are all used to it by now, but I hope you get what's yours."

I sighed as I closed the door to my office. I couldn't wait to get back to London on Thursday. The work here was tedious and boring, and my interest was far off. I could hear the others talking and making plans for the London job, they were getting ready to send a forensic team down to a data room there. I could have been doing that.

My phone pinged with a message from Paul.

Paul: *Hey, hope you're having a good morning.*

Paul: *Are you free for lunch? I have decided and want to run it by you before I report it in.*

Maria. *Of course, even if not, I would make myself free just to hear what your plan is. Any hints?*

Paul: *Great! See you at one 'o'clock. Let's meet where we went for lunch last?*

Maria: *Great x.*

At one, I head out and over to our usual hotel. The quiet corner table in the back we always sit at. Paul was already there, waiting for me. He was dressed in his usual suit and tie, and he had already ordered lunch for us both. He knew my favourite dishes already, and always ordered for me perfectly.

As we sat down, Paul leaned over and gave me a peck on the cheek. It was a surprise, but a welcome one. I smiled at him, blushing slightly.

We started to eat, and Paul began to tell me about his work the past week. I stop him, "Cut the small talk, Bridge. You love torturing me."

He laughs, "Yes Boss."

"I've decided to take the inheritance," he said. "But I have a plan of my own. Ralph wanted me to have it, and I can see his logic. My mother never knew about the money, and I want to secure my family's future for her sake. She would have wanted that."

"I'll honour all of Ralph's requests. I'll protect the jobs he wanted to protect, and I'll take care of Caroline and his secret. But I'll only tell Helen and Nicola that I'm the new owner. I'm going to keep it a secret from the rest of my family. I don't want them to know. I want to give it a year to work out. See where I'm going. Then, I'll see what I can do about my job."

I took a moment to absorb this. "Well, I think you're right," I said. "This is a huge security for you and your family. It sounds like you'll be spending a lot more time in London. It's good that Caroline, Helen, and Nicola are in on the decision. And it's great that you're honouring Ralph's wishes. I really hope this works out for you."

274

I was disappointed. Not that he was taking the businesses, but I didn't see how we would fit together in real time.

"So do I," he said. "But my plan isn't finished. From what I can see, the systems are all outdated. We do need to reorganise to stay competitive.

"I have an idea that fits into my one-year plan. I'm thinking of asking Helen and Nicola to take over running the London operation and report in, but make day-to-day decisions. That means I don't have to live in London and can kind of work as I am. Handling the overseeing from home.

"But then I want to see if I can reorganize by organizing stock management. Possibly set up a chain-wide system and stock control running, so each shop isn't alone and functioning individually. Doing all of that will require manpower. I was thinking that I'll need to have a management team for everything."

Wow, he had been thinking about this.

"I'm going to ask Nicola and Helen to meet us Thursday morning first thing and see how they react. I'm contacting them today to say we'll be having another manager's meeting. This time, I want to have it here in Manchester for Monday afternoon. We will introduce the new owners to everyone and outline a plan going forward.

"I want a meeting called with you and Melanie Wednesday morning. I want Melanie because she knows the business best because she did the analysis on the businesses."

Paul was in business mode. He was very focused, more so than I had ever seen him before. I liked seeing him that way.

He went on, "I'm going to ask that you continue your Thursday and Friday visits for the next ten weeks to allow for a transition. That brings us up to September. I have more plans in mind, but some of that depends on what Melanie tells me about the finances of the businesses. I'll fill you in after the Wednesday meeting. Now, baby, sorry about all the shop talk. How was your day?

Really? Is he asking me that? I thought. "Well, you just filled it with a load of information that I need to process. But about the ten more weeks in London, that's great. I can do that. I have had a crap morning, by the way. An old client I know came in and they have a job for us, and that too is in London. It was given to a more junior team, and I was given a local mind-numbingly boring job. I challenged Jack for answers and was told because I pissed the MD off last week when I wasn't too helpful and told him to ask the new partner for answers," I sighed.

"Now I need something to make me smile. That is your job," I look at him.

"Well, Maria, we have a drink with Adam and Nicole on Thursday at 8. I can cancel that if you wish," he said.

No, no, don't cancel. But did you speak to Adam?" I ask.

"I called him this morning and thanked him for last week. It was really helpful to me, and we enjoyed it. I asked if they could give us some help about the social side the fetish scene, as that is where they met Ralph and it sounded interesting. So, we know what it is like and can decide if we are interested. We both know we are finding new fun things to try," he said grinning, with a glint in his eye. "He agreed and said maybe over a drink on Thursday evening. Nicole will be there too."

"Oh Paul, thank you, that will be fun and a lovely distraction. Fun to hear options. Now for you. What would you like for fun after? I have been thinking of something. But you have to agree to it blindly."

He laughs and says, "Sounds like something I did to you, and I should be scared. But all right, what do you have in mind?"

"Oh, you are going to have to wait until Thursday night," I tease.

Email to: Maria, Jack and Leonard
Subject: Michael's Estate – Next Steps
Dear Maria, Jack, and Leonard,
I hope this email finds you well.
I'm writing to follow up on our recent meetings and to outline the next steps needed to keep the estate progressing and keep the businesses going. I have a list of requests for tasks that we need to carry out soon.

Schedule a meeting on Wednesday morning next between the beneficiaries, myself, Maria Holmes, Melanie (the analyst who worked on the financial status of the businesses), and Leonard from this office. Please let me know what time you all are available on Wednesday.

In advance of the meeting, please arrange a list of each of the shops and businesses, along with their current cash position and cash net of liabilities.

Compile the final tax numbers based on one beneficiary, outlining net of tax and costs what cash will be available to the beneficiary.

It looks like Maria Holmes will need to continue as she has been, the effective financial controller in London for the next 10 weeks, until a transition is arranged, and the new owners can assess their options. The accountancy input can be reviewed at that stage to determine whether the company's auditors can take over. Accommodations will need to be extended for her so this needs to be completed soon.

Thank you for your assistance in advance.

Best regards,

Paul Bridges

Email to: Nicola and Helen:

CC: Maria Holmes

Dear Nicola and Helen,

I hope this email finds you well.

I'm writing to you today to request a meeting to discuss the upcoming changes at the company. I'd like to meet with you both at 11am on Thursday morning to go over the details of the new ownership and outline some of their plans for the future.

The new owners have asked that you share your thoughts on how we can improve the company and our shops in order to secure our future and maintain our market position. This is to be viewed as a constructive request for sharing of ideas and recognising a letter that was left by Mr. Michaels outlining the invaluable position and experience you both hold in the business. They recognize the invaluable position and experience that you both hold in the business, and they value your input.

Please contact all managers and request that they attend a meeting next Monday afternoon at 2:30pm in the Hilton Manchester. Please let them know that the agenda for this meeting will be:

1.   *Meet the new owners.*
2.   *Outline their general plans for the future of the businesses.*

3. Share ideas for streamlining the shops and making improvements.

4. Question and answer session

5. General mingling with the owners

I want to reassure all staff that their positions are safe and that there is nothing to be concerned about. This meeting is for their benefit.

You will both be required to attend the meeting on Monday, and we can discuss the details further on Thursday. Please book rooms for yourselves if you would like to stay overnight. I would not expect you to travel up and down from London in a day.

If you have any questions, please don't hesitate to contact me.

Regards,

Paul Bridges

Paul calls me as soon as I've finished reading the email. His cheerful voice chimes through the phone, "Hey there, how are you doing?"

I chuckle, "Well, I've been diving into your emails. You've got this air of mystery about you – sexy, by the way! Got a master plan up your sleeve for the company?"

Paul responds with a mischievous tone, "Oh, come on now, where's the thrill in spilling the beans? But I am orchestrating a mini-London adventure for you in the upcoming months. Unless, of course, our friend Jack decides to have an issue. By the way, I conveniently 'forgot' to include him in the Wednesday meeting, just a tiny nudge to keep him on his toes. I'm guessing he wasn't too thrilled about missing out on the grand beneficiary unveiling."

I press on, "Alright, alright, quit teasing! Dish the details, I'm dying of curiosity. It's still sinking in that you're seizing the reins of it all. Now, don't leave me hanging, spill the secrets!"

With a laugh, Paul replies, "won't that be telling! But here's the deal: you reveal your Thursday night plans, and I might just drop a hint about mine."

I play along, "Hey now, that's hardly fair. Remember, I'm the accountant here – my mission is to keep your riches shipshape. Consider this a nudge from your employee."

278

Paul adopts a Sherlock-esque tone, "Well, my dear Watson, if you open up, I shall too."

I quip back, "Seems like we're at a standstill then. At least I get a sneak peek before you do," followed by a hearty laugh.

Shifting gears, Paul inquires, "So, how was the world of work post your return? Did Jack's mood cool off?"

Sighing, I reply, "Oh, you know how it goes. I was pretty riled up, I must admit. It's just gnawing at me – I'm so great at what I do, pull in some of the highest numbers in the office, and yet I'm sidelined, always. And when I finally voice it, what do I get? A bottom-of-the-barrel task, grunt work. It's not that I don't like the work, but the spark and excitement is vanishing. It's like a one-way street with no gratitude in sight." I huff.

"It's a tough situation, and I can definitely relate. While I'm not a partner yet, I had to make a choice between family and career myself. In a way, the decision was made for me. But I don't have any regrets, and the support I received here was tremendous when I needed it." Paul says, and I just have to groan. "What about Mark? How's he reacting to all of this?"

"Mark's pretty laid back about it. He sees it as a positive, with less work and more time for the kids. He's content with his bigger projects. Doesn't see that my patience is running thin."

He presses on, "And what about you? What's your own thoughts about all of this? Have you considered other Manchester-based companies?"

"Well, I'm caught in a bind with a one-year non-compete clause in the DAF contract. They're well aware I won't leave Manchester, so venturing to another major firm seems like a challenging move."

"It sounds like you're between a rock and a hard place."

"Alright, hey, darling, I've got Joan on the line here, she's calling about paperwork for the new job. I've got to run. See you on Wednesday. Oh, and don't worry, I'll act clueless about you being the new owner until then."

***

A ping, and I see an email notification on my desktop.

279

From: Nicola
To: Paul Bridges and Maria Holmes
Subject: <u>Thursday Meeting and Abbots Refit</u>

Dear Mr. Bridges and Ms. Holmes,

In response to your previous email, both of us will be available for the meeting on Thursday. We're looking forward to receiving more information; I must say, the team is nervous. However, your reassurance is greatly appreciated.

Regarding Abbots, we received a call today that they're ready to carry out the work in the apartment. They apologised for the delays since last October. They're looking to gain access on Friday at 10 AM. I'm not entirely sure what installations they are referring to. What should I do in this situation?

Best regards, Nicola

Uh, what? I think, wracking my brain about anything regarding Abbots.

I quickly call Paul, my brows furrowed. "Who are these Abbots, and what's the deal with their installations?"

Paul is just as bewildered as I am, "Never even heard of them. Seems like something Ralph worked on last year. He really knows how to keep surprising us. Looks like we're both in the dark until we figure this out."

"Alright then, I'll let Nicola know that Friday works, and we'll find out what exactly they're up to."

"Sounds like a plan. Let's see what happens."

280

Chapter 19

On Wednesday morning, the atmosphere in the office is thick with anticipation, maybe it's just me because I know what's going to happen in a few seconds. Melanie and I are about to leave for the beneficiaries meeting when Jack calls my name. I smile, erasing it from my face as I turn around. "Yes, Jack?"

"You're heading to the beneficiaries meeting, right? I'll tag along." It's a big meeting; the final reveal. In normal circumstances he would be expected to be there. I can see he wants to be there; he can't possibly be left off the invite, right? *Uh, no.*

"Sure, Joan will get your invite," I say, opening up the email from the solicitors' office confirming the meeting on my phone. "Oh, well, uh, your name doesn't seem to be on the invite list. But I'm sure if you crash it, they won't exactly throw you out. Your attendance might not be billable, though," I suck my teeth sharply. I hope it's not obvious how much fun I'm having. He has humiliated me several times in the office. *Payback time is a bitch. I think to myself.*

I sense a touch of annoyance in Jack's controlled voice as he replies, "Right, well, just make sure you report back after."

I turn around and can't help but chuckle to myself. This could have been a fun excuse to get out of the office today for Jack. But now he will be stuck in the office, desperate to hear the minutes of the meeting while doing nothing but delegating tasks from his highchair all day long.

Soon, we're seated in the boardroom at Paul's office, ready for the meeting. Paul and Leonard take their seats across from

281

us. I look at my watch, playing the character of the oblivious outsider. After a few moments, I decide to break the silence, "Here we are again. When are the beneficiaries going to join us?"

There's a long pause, some side-eyes from Lenoard, and then Paul's voice fills the room, "Well, this might come as a surprise to both of you. I *am* the beneficiary. Ralph Michaels was my uncle." He mutters sheepishly.

I let my jaw go slack; beside me Melanie gasps, her eyes wide as saucers.

"Just to clarify, I didn't find out until after our last meeting. So, please don't assume that this was hidden from you intentionally. I was as clueless as anyone else. Mr. Michaels wanted me to explore the companies and understand the staff from an unbiased perspective before making a decision to accept the inheritance." Paul is well-prepared. I give him a meaningful look that Leonard and Melanie both miss. One is suddenly very interested in his shoes, and the latter is still wide-eyed and stuttering.

Leonard sighs loudly, then clears his throat, "Now that we've got that revelation out of the way, let's move on to business. Paul has had a lot to process, and he needs a clear understanding. Melanie, could you please give us your outlines?"

Melanie nods and takes the floor, "Our analysis indicates that Mr. Michaels has refrained from withdrawing any profits for the past decade. All of the shops are free of debt, boasting a debt-free status for a span of 7 to 10 years. This has, of course, led to a substantial accumulation of cash reserves. The individual shop holdings range from £1 million to £2.5 million, contingent upon the size of the shop. The main distribution company holds about £3 million in cash reserves and holds controlling shares in each of the individual shops."

Melanie continues, her words carrying the weight of careful financial assessment, "Considering Mr. Michaels' holdings, the liquid assets at his- and now the beneficiary's- disposal amount to £2.82 million after factoring in all taxes and additional costs.

However, withdrawing funds from the companies would trigger income tax, but there's a potential for intercompany investment without triggering additional tax burdens."

Paul nods, then asks in a measured tone, "Thank you, Melanie. I appreciate your detailed breakdown. Now, I'd like to ask how familiar you are with the individual companies and their financial accounts."

Melanie is excited, a true accounts nerd. We only have a few of those, and I can't help but feel proud that she's come out so well after all the training I've invested in her. Melanie leans forward slightly, her eyes reflective, "Very familiar. I've meticulously studied each company and conducted analyses in case of a potential sale. What's messy is that each company operates quite independently. They each have their own set of accountants and auditors. So, only the head office knows the precise financial position of everything."

Paul nods thoughtfully, absorbing the information, "That's great, thank you. Can you share any overarching observations you've made about the businesses, whether considered independently or collectively?"

That's my cue. "Of course. The companies, while being financially stable, might be missing out on opportunities due to their lack of cohesion. A chain strategy seems to be lacking. They've been operating in isolation which then leads to delays, and functional issues that can only be sorted when the Headquarters comes into the loop. Also, I've noticed an absence of online presence for the entire brand, particularly in terms of online sales. Aside from that, well, they are dated but profitable anyhow. The possibilities arising from a group synergy are significant and have so far been lost "

"Thank you, Maria," Paul says while scribbling in his diary. "Are you able to continue working on Thursdays and Fridays in London for the next ten weeks, as you have been until now?"

"Yes, I can manage that," I respond, my mind already calculating the logistical aspects. "Except for three weeks— one is due to a personal clash, and the other two are already marked as my annual leave. If necessary, I can arrange for someone else to cover those days."

Paul nods, his focus unwavering. "No need for replacements, I think that schedule will work. However, there might be instances where we'll require extra days leading up to your off weeks. Would you be open to working a weekend after one of your Fridays or perhaps a day earlier in the week?"

I consider the possibilities- all of them. "I'll consult with my family and get back to you. It must also be authorised from Jack to see what can be arranged. I'll do my best to accommodate." I paste on my corporate smile.

"Thank you," Paul acknowledges, his tone not betraying any excitement I see in his eyes. "Is there anything else we need to go over at the moment?"

I take a moment to gather my thoughts. "Actually, I was wondering about the larger plans. Should we prepare the books for a potential business sale, or are there other aspects we need to consider?"

Paul consults his diary, "One of the conditions tied to the inheritance is that I have to hold onto the business and retain key staff for at least a period of ten years. So, no immediate plans for a sale." He reveals, "However, we could explore reinvestments using local funding. This will involve assessing the tax implications of transferring cash between the various shops or to the main business."

Deep inside, I appreciate Paul's determination to respect his uncle's wishes, rather than making this about an exit strategy. He's already looking towards growth and optimization of the business while juggling all the difficult feelings that come with it.

Paul continues, "Tomorrow, I'll have conversations with Nicola and Helen. Then, next Monday, I plan to address all the managers here in Manchester during a meeting. I have a broad outline of plans in mind, but much of it hinges on maintaining current operations with existing staff." He looks at Leonard for what he's about to say next, and Leonard nods. "Confidentiality is paramount, though. We don't want the word spreading that I've inherited the business, not before the meeting. From your office's standpoint, your boss doesn't need to know, and I would appreciate it if you don't record this in official record files, you can note that it was a direct request not to. From here on, all taxes will be processed as inheritance taxes and reported directly to either of us."

Leonard nods slowly, "We understand if this creates some awkwardness, but these conditions are critical for the project's continuation."

With the meeting concluded, Melanie and I say our formalities and start gathering our things to leave. Paul offers a cordial goodbye and a gentle reminder about an 11 am meeting scheduled in London for tomorrow. I confirm and we leave.

As we step out of the boardroom, Melanie whispers her astonishment, "I'm still in shock. Did you have any idea about this, Maria?"

I shake my head, surprise evident on my face. "No idea at all. And to be honest, I'm not entirely sure about Paul Bridge's plans moving forward. For us, the clients are the estate, not Paul Bridges. Still, we must be careful to not record his inheritance in the minutes of the meeting."

Melanie nods, but her next concern surfaces quickly, "And what about Jack? You know he'll ask as soon as we're back."

A wry smile tugs at my lips. "Tell Jack that we're unable to disclose the names due to instructions. The solicitors will handle the tax returns. As far as we're concerned, we're working solely for the estate and the solicitors. If Jack has any issues, he can take it up with Paul Bridges, after all he does represent the beneficiaries."

There's a sense of liberation in brushing aside Jack's certain displeasure. This will hurt his ego, and potentially also kill him but I no longer care for his political games and power plays. It's surprisingly exciting.

Just then, my phone pings and I check my phone screen. It's a message from Paul.

Paul: *Hope today went well. If you think it would help, you can let Mark know that I was revealed as the beneficiary today. Since our work doesn't overlap, it might make things smoother for you? Just omit the details about the cash position. Let him know about the shops and business and mention the significant tax liability. No lies there.*

Paul: *Also, you could say that you've been requested to extend your stay for another 10 weeks. If taking weeks off for a holiday becomes tricky, suggest the idea of a weekend continuation in the middle to make up the time. And, yes, I know it's technically work, but that weekend is just for us. Just call it work.*

His message brings a soft smile to my face. The prospect of a whole weekend, under the guise of work, brings a flush to my face. There's something so exciting about our hidden rendezvous. And the trouble we'll get up to in that time...

Maria: *I'm definitely not complaining about a weekend together. Where's this going, though? Care to share?*

Paul: *I do have plans. But it will become clearer when I get to know more, perhaps tomorrow. Once I know more, I promise I'll talk to you about it.*

Paul: *And more plans for you as well… quite a few of them, and not all confined to the bedroom, either.*

I suck in a gasp, then chuckle at his winking emoji. Oh, this is going to be fun.

***

After arriving home that evening, I take charge of dinner for the family. As the evening settles, Mark joins me on the sofa, his steaming cup of coffee cradled in his hands. The kids have dispersed, to their rooms or out with friends. I start the conversation casually, nonchalantly.

"So, big surprise today," I say, blowing over my coffee, "You remember that solicitor we met at the company meeting in London? Turns out he's the beneficiary of the estate I'm currently working on over there. What's surprising is that he only found out last week, right after the meeting we attended."

Mark raises his eyebrows, then whistles, "Whoa, sounds like he hit the jackpot."

I nod with a musing gaze, "It does come with a hefty tax bill for his inheritance. He's just a mid-level solicitor, so he isn't exactly the most well-off, so I wonder what he's planning. He's not exactly the most sociable person."

Mark chuckles. "Yeah, I remember it from meeting him once. About as sociable and interesting as a brick. So, does that mean you're wrapping up your work there?"

I shake my head, "Not even remotely. They've requested that I extend my stay for another 10 weeks. I did mention I have two weeks of vacation planned and a scheduling conflict on one weekend due to your football match. I might need to adjust my working days here and there, maybe even take a weekend if needed. That would work, I think?"

Mark clicks his tongue. "Yeah, I guess. You know my schedule, right? Just make sure Ursula is available to cover the house whenever you're out."

"Will do," I mutter, my mind already planning the weekend off with Paul. He'd texted me if I'd like to have another dinner with Adam and Nicole, and I'd said yes, if only because of the events that had followed after the dinner last time.

The night goes on, I listen to the kids' talk about their week, give them snacks then have them prepare for school tomorrow. They moan and huff but at last the homework is done and they go to bed. Knowing I have an early train to catch in the morning for London, I go to bed early too.

Morning arrives, and I'm at the train station ahead of schedule, taking my familiar spot. Unsurprisingly, Mr. 24A is there as well. I nod at him, and he does the same but doesn't engage more. It makes me cringe to think what he must think of me, now that he's seen me chummy with Mark, and Paul. Just as I'm settling into my thoughts, Paul joins me with his usual charm, remarking, "Looks like my seat is lucky again today." I chuckle and shake my head, and he gets seated.

After we ordered the breakfast onboard, I can't help but let curiosity leak into my question, "Are you going to reveal this mysterious plan to me, or do you want to keep me suffering?" I ask with a glint in my eyes.

His response is a mischievous grin, and he quips, "Suffering sounds rather intriguing, doesn't it?" I pout and mock punch his shoulder.

Oh well, he'd tell me when he's ready. There is some pleasure in waiting when it comes to Paul. I don't really mind it.

"Oh, by the way, I managed to tell Mark about our change in plans." I tell him about the short conversation with Mark about adjusting my schedule for the additional weeks and his reaction to the news. He's relieved it all went over smoothly, and we get talking about other things.

Upon our arrival at the office, I notice a different side of Paul, like a glass wall has gone up– he is being exceptionally guarded and cautious. He holds his cards close to his chest, disappearing into the office on mysterious tasks. It's clear that he's feeling the pressure of the situation, but he's handling it with remarkable discretion.

At 11 am, Paul emerges from wherever he's been and walks into the conference room right before Nicola and Helen. There's coffee and bagels, and from the surprise on Helen's face, I gather that Paul has arranged the refreshments. Sweet as ever. Seated around the table, Nicola and Helen's tension is palpable, and I can see their mind working. *How bad is the coming news? What's happened now?* I can almost hear them thinking.

Paul reads the room and starts talking quickly, "I'm sorry that you're all on edge about this, but it's time I shared the truth. It turns out that I am Ralph's beneficiary, to his estate. He was a close relative, a fact I only learned a week ago. I was completely in the dark about this."

He pauses, allowing the weight of his revelation to settle in. Helen and Nicola exchange incredulous glances, their shock evident. Nicola blinks rapidly, and Helen looks at the wall, a blank expression on her face. They can barely stutter their surprise. Paul grants them a few minutes to process the news.

"You guys okay? I understand how out of the blue this is. It's the same way for me, too." For the first time today, Paul's facade falters, and there's vulnerability apparent in his voice.

Helen clears her throat, then asks the question that's on everyone's minds, "Can I be honest? I'm a bit stunned. More than a bit. But first, could you please explain what this means for us?"

"Thank you, Helen, and of course. Let me preface this discussion by explaining that Ralph's instructions are quite clear: none of the shops or businesses here can be sold for the next 10 years, assuming that they remain profitable. He was adamant about this condition, and I will be respecting his wishes. Also, he wanted to ensure that both of you knew just how grateful he was for your support all these past years. You might not have been aware, but some major decisions in recent years were essentially rubber-stamped based on your recommendations. Ralph described you both as invaluable. In his eyes, you were effectively running things here. And, from what we've seen in the last six months we've been here, that's exactly how it is. You have our utmost respect, and today I just want to acknowledge that we would have been truly lost without your contributions this year."

Helen swallows thickly, and Nicola inconspicuously wipes a tear from her eyes. I can feel these women. It must be wonderful to be acknowledged for your hard work, something that was lost on my bosses. But they deserve it fully, and I'm glad Paul is giving them the appreciation they're owed.

The room falls into a thoughtful silence. Paul takes a sip of his coffee, then proceeds to pour some for both Helen and Nicola. After a moment, Paul resumed with a renewed fervor.

"I mentioned the other day that I wanted to hear your thoughts about potential improvements. Have you had any ideas?" He redirects the conversation.

Nicola produces a sheet of paper, and as she speaks, it's clear that this topic has been thoughtfully discussed between them.

"We've discussed this and from our perspective, a few areas need dire attention. First, stock control is frankly a mess as Miss Holmes must have also noticed since each shop operates independently. Then, there's the matter of the warehouse, which is a bit dated, as is the distribution process. With just a few upgrades and safety installations we could make it more seamless."

Paul nods appreciatively, taking in their suggestions. "Thank you for your insights. As soon as the succession is wrapped up, we will start improving the operations based on your suggestions."

Paul's gaze shifts between Helen and Nicola as he continues, "Now, moving on to Monday's meeting." He exhales in anticipation, and Nicola gives him an encouraging smile, "I expect that my revelation as the new owner will come as a surprise. However, I believe that highlighting the 10-year security aspect might help mitigate any concerns. What do you think?"

Helen sucks in her teeth, "Most of the managers don't have a deep personal connection with Ralph, so their primary focus will be on job security and the well-being of the shops. As long as that's covered, and they're reassured, I don't think there will be any concerns."

Nicola nods her agreement, adding, "I believe the improvement ideas we've outlined today will be some of the main talking points during the meeting. It's not lost on the managers how they have to deal with so many complications due to the outdated system."

Paul nods thoughtfully, taking in the potential concerns that might arise at the managers' meeting. I also can't help but notice that the atmosphere in the room has shifted from horrified shock to a collaborative spirit as Paul, Helen, and Nicola join to work through challenges.

My phone pings and the screen lights up. It's a message notification from Paul. My gaze skips to him as I pick up my phone and click on the message. *Here goes the plan*, it reads. My brows knot and I look at him, his face split in a smile.

"Well, lastly, I have a question for the two of you. Don't look so scared, come on, you two! So, If I were to propose that the two of you take on primary responsibility here, or more precisely, continue in your current roles, while I take over

Ralph's portion of work, would you manage this side of the operation as you've been doing?"

Nicola gasps silently. Helen nods as if she had been expecting this all along. Maybe she was.

"Don't feel pressured to answer immediately. Take all the time you need to think about it. Perhaps a long lunch away from here might provide the perfect setting for a discussion. Feel free to use the company card for a nice meal." Paul slides the card towards them.

Helen and Nicola exchange surprised glances, clearly taken aback by Paul's proposition. They nod in acknowledgment and exit the room to deliberate. I turn my attention to Paul.

"Come on, spill. What exactly are you planning?" I ask sincerely.

Paul leans back, folding his arms. Although I'm curious, the sight of his strong forearms do unspeakable things to my insides. I shake my head to refocus. "Well, I was genuinely curious about the improvements they'd suggest. But beyond that, I need to know if they're willing to remain in their managerial capacities. If even one of them is committed to staying, it would mean a lot for the stability of operations. I have come at a good time for the company, finances-wise but still I must anticipate what hurdles could arise down the line. It's a good time to troubleshoot any weaknesses in the foundation to ensure good future progress."

Something about Paul taking charge and stating his intentions so eloquently makes me breathless. I barely manage to absorb his strategy through the absolute chaos of thoughts.

"Hopefully they will come back with a yes. And if they know their worth, some big benefit negotiations." I wink at him, and he chuckles, "It won't take too long. And lunch sounds like a great way to pass the time while we wait for their decision."

Today, we walked together to get lunch. He's getting a salad bowl, and I wrinkle my nose at his order before requesting club sandwiches with a side of chips for myself. There's a border of chains on the menu, and I watch Paul absently run his fingers over the print.

"Interesting." I mutter, and he laughs, catching himself at it. "Speaking of interesting things, are you looking forward to tonight? I wonder what else Adam and Nicole have in store for us."

"Mmm." I hum and shove a chip in my mouth.

"Also, I remember you saying you have your own plan for tonight. I told you mine. Care to share yours?" Paul asks between bites of his salad.

I snort, "You've only told me the most obvious, littlest fragment of your plan, so here's an equally small piece from me: You're getting very, very lucky tonight." I whisper with an intentional rasp in my voice.

Paul sputters and coughs, then joins in my laughter at his reaction. "Alright, I can live with that. If you're a sure thing tonight—what more could I ask for?"

It's my turn to flush red from neck to ears.

***

After our laid-back lunch we talked more until we finally return to the office at around 2 o'clock. Just as we get settled into the conference room, a call beeps. It's Helen, requesting our time to tell us of their position. I can tell Paul is nervous now that their deliberation has ended, but he doesn't let it color his voice.

Helen and Nicola enter the room and sit opposite us.

Nicola starts, clear and composed. "Alright, Mr. Bridges, we've had our discussion. If we're being asked to continue our current roles and maintain the operations as they are, we're on board with that. Currently, our main priority is to ensure the stability of the business, job security for the employees, and the seamless functioning of this office, which is integral to all the shops."

Paul breathes a sigh of relief and expresses his gratitude for their commitment, assuring them of his plans moving forward. "Thank you, both of you. I promise to share a comprehensive plan with you once I've worked it out in detail. I'm still waiting

292

on some external sources for their opinion. But before that, I want to ask for something from both of you. Be direct with me. While I may have a good grasp of business in general, this specific industry is still quite new to me. If you have any suggestions or insights, please don't hesitate to approach me. Your expertise is invaluable to me."

Helen nods seriously and Nicola smiles. I'm certain they will be direct with Paul when the time comes.

Paul's tone shifts, "And just to clear the air, I can imagine the shock you must be feeling right now. I was only informed about this inheritance last week. My own surprise when I received a letter from Leonard, my boss, saying Ralph was my uncle was unbelievable. To be fair, Ralph's rationale was that after spending months working alongside you and understanding the business firsthand, I could fully appreciate the skills and capabilities he saw in all the employees. All this to say, this arrangement is as new to me as it is to you."

"Of course, we can understand. It's all good, Paul, better the devil we know that the one we don't "Helen murmurs with half a smile.

"Alright, let's reconvene tomorrow to further iron out our strategy for Monday's meeting with the managers. Rest assured; I'll share the details with you. Thank you again."

The two women mutter formalities and leave the room. The meeting concludes, and Paul turns to me with a huge exhale. His eyes have finally lost their nervous edge, and fatigue has replaced it. "It's already 3:30. You've got that 4 o'clock on your schedule. You should head there."

"A 4 o'clock? I don't think—"

"I booked you at your hairdresser's, the one you went to last time, next to the hotel at four. I thought you needed some time to relax."

My eyes convey all the answers.

***

I savour the luxurious sensation of getting my hair done at the salon, letting myself truly relax. He's also booked me for a scalp massage, and I moan as the hairdresser's fingers rub the stress out of my head. When I finally return to the apartment, the aroma of Italian takeout welcomes me, and I smile. Paul has picked up dinner, so we can enjoy a meal together before heading out for the evening.

After dinner, we change into casual clothes and head to the bar to meet Adam and Nicole. The atmosphere is electric as we enter, and there's anticipation swirling in the air.

As we approach, I spot Adam and Nicole seated in a secluded corner. Nicole notices us and stands up, offering us a warm smile and a friendly peck on my cheek. Her voice is silky with charm as she teases us, "Well, look who's back for round two. I hope you've recovered from last week's conversation. It can get a bit intense here and there."

I respond with a touch of humour. "We survived, thank you. And just to own up, we did end up doing some window shopping – that's why we're back, but only window shopping."

Nicole couldn't help but smirk at my choice of words. "Only window shopping, huh?" She winks at me mischievously.

Adam and Paul lean back, their eyes fixed on Nicole and me. I can tell Adam is not a big talking man, and he lets Nicole take the lead in most conversations. It works well because Nicole obviously loves to talk. Paul seems surprised as I get right into the deep end of the conversation, and playfully reach for his drink.

Taking the conversation forward, I turn my attention to Nicole. "So, Nicole, we looked at the shop, we tried out some stuff—" Paul coughs, hiding his embarrassment— "and we did feel out of our depth, it was pretty overwhelming."

Nicole laughs, "Oh, yes, that's one way to describe it."

"You also mentioned a social scene last time – where you met Ralph and Lilly. I think we would like to know more about that. Maybe being at the event would help us explore this more thoroughly." I look at Paul, and he nods his agreement.

Nicole nods thoughtfully. "I think that's a good next step for you guys. However, there's a bit of a prerequisite. You can't just stroll into one of these events and observe. To give you an idea, picture an eccentric nightclub, but on a whole new level. We're talking elaborate costumes, latex outfits to naughty uniforms, leather ensembles, and everything in between."

She pauses, letting the image sink in. I have to acknowledge that I'm intrigued. "It's a blend of fantasy and reality, a place where people can express their desires and experiment with their fantasies in a safe and respectful environment. The events often involve themes and activities that encourage newbies to participate."

Paul raises an eyebrow, his curiosity evident. "So, it's a place where people go to live out their fantasies?"

Nicole nods, her tone matter-of-fact. "Exactly. It's about embracing desires and experiencing something different, something that's often kept hidden from the outside world. But remember, it's all consensual and respectful – that's the key."

"Of course. So, these costumes…?"

"For now, just pick whatever you're comfortable wearing. You will have to go a bit out of your usual style, though. Whatever you dare, make sure it's comfortable and you can tolerate it for a few hours."

"Any tips on what we should pick?" Paul asks. I chuckle, realising that Paul was probably just trying to remind us that he was present in the conversation. Our exchange seemed to be creating a camaraderie between us all.

Adam chimes in. "Well, you guys are newbies, so I doubt you'll be comfortable strutting with everything hanging out. Better look at something conservative." After an initial round of shocked gasps, we all laughed.

"I think what Adam is saying is whatever you pick, latex, PVC, leather… just make sure you can stick with it.

Paul turns to me, places his hand on my inner thigh, and softly says, "I'm game if you are?"

From the shine in my eyes, anyone can tell I'm more than just game.

"Any preference or suggestions for materials which won't suffocate us?" Although exciting, I had to confess that latex, leather and PVC all sounded too... constricting.

Nicole answers, her voice friendly and informative. "Comfort is key. You have options like leather, which is quite comfortable and offers a range of choices. It works the best for us girls. But personally, I'm a fan of latex. It feels like a second skin, and the variety of outfits available is stunning – much more than you'd find with leather. Just a heads-up, though: quality latex can be a bit pricey. But really, it's about what you feel confident in, and of course, the vibe of the event. Different events can call for different moods and outfits."

"Sounds intriguing, and definitely worth giving a shot," I admit, feeling the excitement building within me.

Paul leans in, addressing us with an apologetic smile. "Sorry for interrupting, ladies. It seems we got so caught up in the conversation that I forgot to get you drinks. This discussion definitely calls for a drink. What would you both like?" His thumb is now making lazy circles on my inner thigh, and I catch my breath. I don't know if he's aware of what his touch is doing to me.

Adam adds with a wink. "How about a bottle of wine? Seems fitting for the occasion." The shared laughter and light-hearted exchange continue as Paul gestures at me to accompany him.

"Maria, come, help me pick." With a quick smile, I join him at the bar, realising he wants a brief moment alone. As we stand there, I signal to the bartender and order two bottles of white wine. I figure that sharing a single bottle four ways wouldn't go very far in our animated conversation.

While we wait, he asks, "You seem quite intrigued. You're sure you want to actually attend one of these events?" There's genuine curiosity in his voice, without a hint of pressure.

I confess, "Oh, it does sound exciting. I'm already thinking about what to wear and how it will all work. We'll figure it out somehow."

He holds my hand in his, "As long as you're certain." I nod, reassuring him. I appreciate how he checked in on me to make sure I wasn't agreeing to anything out of obligation or in a flow.

With the wine bottles in hand, we return to the table, our glasses ready to be filled. Adam jumps right in with his question, "So, what's next for you guys? Are you finding this whole experience overwhelming, exciting? What's the vibe here?"

My response tumbles out a bit too eagerly, "It's definitely exciting, but nerve-wracking at the same time." I can't help but blush at my own enthusiasm.

Paul has a wonderful idea, "Nicole, would you be interested in joining us at the shop sometime? Maria and you could explore the options together, and you could offer some guidance. If you're comfortable with that, of course. Having someone who's familiar with it could be really helpful. And hey, like any good partner, I'll just go with whatever she picks."

Laughter ripples around the table, and Adam chimes in, "Paul, you're catching on fast. Happy partner, happy life, right?"

I nod, considering the idea. Nicole's smile is warm and inviting. "That does sound like fun, Maria. It's like a little adventure, you and me poking around the shop. Maybe start with something simple to get a feel for it. Once you're comfortable, you can go on your own."

Adam interjects, a thoughtful smile on his face, "Sounds like the bar chat you had was quite interesting. And we had our own chat too. So, if you're up for it, we're planning to attend an event in a few weeks. You're more than welcome to join us – consider it your first outing with experienced guides."

I'm eager to hear the event dates, so I ask them right away, pulling out my phone to check my schedule. As I scan the dates, I realise that the event falls right before Mark's first boys' weekend away. "Hmm, these dates just might actually work for me. Let me double-check and confirm. But Nicole, when can we swing by the shop to take a look? I want to get some idea of what I'm getting into."

Nicole lets out a laugh and looks at the guys. "Well, it seems like someone's quite enthusiastic. Alright, boys, you keep that wine company for a bit. Maria and I are going to step out for a quick minute."

Once we're out of the bar, she turns to me, mischief in her eyes. "The shop's just a stone's throw away, and I'm assuming you have the keys?" I nod, jingling them around my fingers. Paul had palmed them to me just as I'd taken the last mouthful of my wine. "Let's take a sneak peek now and grab something to get you started."

I wasn't anticipating this sudden turn of events. The wine's hitting my system. "Well, Dutch courage it is. Here goes nothing."

The boys watch us with amused expressions as we disappear.

In a few minutes' walk, we enter the shop through the back entrance, and immediately explore. My eye catches the beautiful corsets on display. I pick one up, holding it against myself to admire the intricate details. Nicole grins and comments, "Absolutely stunning. But remember, whatever you choose, you've got to be able to get into it and, hopefully, out of it." She winks.

We shared a laugh and continue our browsing. The leather and latex section is next. Nicole pulls out a simple latex dress and hands it to me. "Try this one on. It's beginner-friendly and reasonably priced. Zips all the way up the front, so it's easy to slip into and out of. This should give you a sense of how latex feels."

I eye the dress, considering it. "Right now?"

Nicole shrugs playfully, and in a spur-of-the-moment decision, I head to the fitting rooms. I shed my underwear, and the dress clings to me like second skin. I feel like a Christmas present, all wrapped up. It's also incredibly comfortable once it's on. It smooths out all the little imperfections and accentuates my curves. It feels oddly empowering.

Emerging from the fitting room, I grin at Nicole. "You were right, this feels amazing! I might be starting to get the hang of this."

Nicole whistles as she takes a turn around me, appreciating how well it fits me. "Pretty nice, Holmes."

Grinning, I tell Nicole that I'm definitely taking this dress home to try. She chuckles and says, "Hang on a minute." She heads to a nearby shelf and retrieves a bottle. "If you're keeping it, you should shine it. They all come unpolished." She applies a bit of liquid to a cloth and starts rubbing it onto the dress.

As the fabric responds, a lovely shine emerges. "Much nicer when applied by hand if you're wearing it. I love the feeling. I'd do it for you, but you might not be comfortable feeling a stranger's hands over yourself yet. Here, use this cloth to do the rest later." She hands me the scrap of fabric.

With a smile, she rubs the last few drops into the back of the dress with her hand. "Perfect," she concludes. "Now, I must say, I love it when Adam does this by hand. The feeling is just wonderful. His hand glides right over me." She playfully moans and I chuckle.

I glance in the mirror, turning around to look at my back, and I'm taken aback. The dress is now a jet-black, shining masterpiece that clings to my curves in the most flattering way. I hardly recognize myself. The woman staring back at me exudes confidence and adventure. It's like I've stepped into a whole new version of myself, and it's exhilarating, unbelievable. If I saw someone else wearing this dress out, I'd assume she's off on an exciting adventure and envy her for her exciting life. And yet, here I am, in my daring dress on the brink of adventure.

"Thanks, Nicole. You're making this so easy for me. Starting with something simple was definitely the right call. I never would have pictured myself in something like this, but I absolutely love it," I express with genuine excitement.

After carefully taking off the dress and wrapping it up with the shine bottle, we start making our way back to the bar. I can't stop smiling the entire way. Who would've thought that tonight's outing with Nicole would lead me to this unexpected adventure? I slip the dress into my handbag, feeling grateful for its small size. It folds up neatly, almost as if it's eager to be a part of my secret.

As we return to the bar, thoughts of the dress and the evening ahead are swirling in my mind. This little addition to my plans for Paul later on will undoubtedly make him salivate. I can barely control my nerves as I imagine him peeling it off me...

***

We stepped back into the bar, and Paul's playful eyes immediately scan me from head to toe. "No bags. Let me guess. Shop full of clothes and nothing to wear," he teases.

I chuckle and take a seat beside him, feeling the buzz of the wine adding a lightness to my step. I coyly omit that I did end up getting something. It will be a surprise for Paul. As we settle in, the wine flows, and the evening carries on with easy conversation, shared jokes, and a sense of newly formed friendship. Time passes swiftly, and when the second bottle of wine empties, I'm almost disappointed that the evening is coming to an end.

When the final drop has been poured, I offer my thanks to Nicole and Adam with a big hug and a kiss on Nicole's cheek. I know she'll have tales to tell Adam once we've left. Chiming goodbyes, we leave the bar.

We leave the bar and head back to the apartment, and as we walk, I can't help but link my arm through his. I ask about their conversation while we were away. He cryptically mutters, "Tell you later." I can scarcely care what they talked about through the flurry of thoughts in my head. The excitement of the night ahead pulses within me—time alone with Paul, my own little plan, and the new dress tucked away in my bag.

Upon arriving at the apartment, I toss my coat and bag aside, my eagerness mounting. With a playful glint in my eye, I address Paul in a raspy voice, sucking his earlobe. "Tonight, it's my turn." He meets my gaze, and I begin my own version of the surprise I have in store.

Just like he did a week ago, I push him against the wall, and pull his head down to my mouth by tugging on his tie. While his tongue laps at me like he's finally received sustenance after starving, I unbutton his shirt, slowly unveiling the expanse of his chest. With a quick movement, I secure the cuffs around his wrists. He's shocked, but I see his eyes dilating, and his desire growing. With a flourish, I place the silky blindfold over his eyes. His lips open on a sigh, and I plunge my tongue inside. Except his pants and my occasional moans, everything is silent. It enhances the sexy anticipation.

I stay dressed, while he's half-naked, tied to the hook on the wall and blindfolded. *What a sight.* I can't help but observe him, backing away. I appreciate the contours of his chest with my fingertips, savouring every moment. My lips follow the path my fingers have traced, descending down his chest. My hand ventures over his pants, and I gently squeeze the undeniable hardness beneath the fabric. His reaction doesn't escape me— a combination of surprise and arousal.

With practiced ease, I undo his belt and pants, my lips now grazing his neck as I whisper, "You are mine now, to do as I will." He gasps, and I nip along his neck, marking him, following through on my claim. My hands guide the zipper down, and his pants pool at his feet. My fingers slip inside his shorts, and a deep, rumbling moan escapes him as I take him in hand.

He's engorged, solid and eager in my grasp. I work his length, each stroke long and languid. Every twitch and shiver that runs through him fuels my excitement, spurring me on.

I keep my strokes measured, and he makes a pained, frustrated groan at my pace. Smiling evilly, I step back and take a moment to appreciate him undressed, his body now adorned with nothing but his shorts, stretched taut by the arousal tenting them. His breaths come in ragged bursts, and the anticipation in the room is almost tangible.

I retrieve the dress from my bag lying abandoned on the floor, strip, and slip into it. I watch him; he's aware I'm nearby but puzzled at my distance. Ah, the unmistakable scent of latex—a sensory detail that now seems to be following me around like a daring memory. I assumed it was strong at the shop because of all the stock, but even now its undiluted musk evokes something feral inside me.

I close in on Paul, the latex-clad sensation against my skin electrifying. I feel a steady stream of wetness leaking from the pool between my legs. There's something so heady about this. I press myself against him, making sure that he feels every inch of my short dress. I can sense his surprise, eagerness as he yearns to put his hands over me.

Kissing my way down his chest, I move lower, tracing the outline of his shorts with my lips. I nip at his bulging muscles that make a pronounced V, and he sucks in a sharp breath. I can feel the heat radiating from him, and I revel in the power I have over him. Gently massaging his growing hardness through the fabric, I savour his reactions—the hitch in his breath, the twitch in his muscles.

After a few moments, I carefully peel his shorts down, freeing his arousal from its confines, and it springs up at attention. Now on my knees before him, I take him slowly into my mouth, my tongue flat against the underside of his sensitive head. I taste the saltiness of his skin, the thrill of control fueling my movements. I work him slowly, leisurely.

Teasing becomes an art form, a playful dance of pleasure and restraint. I revel in the way his body responds to my touch, his breath quickening, his moans growing more urgent. I work him harder, until he's bucking under my touch, close to releasing. Rising up to meet his gaze, I whisper with a hint of command, "You can finish me soon, but I'm not letting you off that easily." A feral growl escapes him, making me smile.

In those moments, whether it's the dress or the control I exert over Paul—or perhaps a combination of both—I feel an incredible surge of power. I'm in charge, I'm the orchestrator of pleasure, and the newfound confidence courses through me like a vibrant current.

My thighs are wet, and there's an urgency inside me; I need to be filled, satiated, anything…

I unhook him, and lead him by his cuffs to the bed, where I push him until he's laying down beneath me. Before I jump on him, and this finishes, I climb over the bed, the apex of my thighs between his lips. He gets the hint and starts sucking, long flat strokes that have me riding his mouth. His tongue dips inside me, and he drinks from me like a starved man at a banquet.

In just a few moments, he has me teetering on the edge of an orgasm so steep I'm not sure I'd ever come back from it. And as I'm wondering the hazards of a climax this strong, I'm falling, falling or flying. I can no longer tell. He doesn't stop eating me, not even when I shut my thighs so he's barely inhaling a breath.

Finally, I come down from the high, and collapse sideways. The orgasm I just had took only the edge off my hunger; I need his cock to fill me until I cannot breathe from the fullness. I release his hands from the cuffs, and he has immediately got me in his arms. With Paul's embrace, the dynamics shift. His lips find mine, and his hands explore every inch of my body, his hands eager, as if he's rediscovering me. I slide off the blindfold, and his eyes quickly adjust to the scene.

His gaze locks onto me, his astonishment evident. "Wow, you look amazing." He moves closer, his fingers trailing along the fabric, and I'm astounded by the sensation. It's like his touch is imprinted on my skin through the latex, igniting a sensation that sends shivers down my spine. His touch feels ingrained, like it's coming from inside me.

In a swift move, he pulls my zipper down, revealing my breasts. The material still clings to my body, my nipples responding to the surge of arousal, their peaks hard. The dress begins to slip away, unveiling my form inch by inch, and I'm overwhelmed by the fervour in his touch, the fire in his kiss. He takes my breast in his mouth, and rolls it around, making me mad with sensation. He tugs on my nipple with his teeth, and I moan sharply.

The dress falls away, and now we're both naked, him beneath me as I straddle him. In a beat he sits me onto his length, and I slide right on, and we both moan harshly at the sudden contact. I ride him like my life depends on it, and he plunges inside me, then retreats until only the tip touches my folds, and then dips inside me again. On and on until we're both panting, desperate for release. And then he swerves his hips so his head touches that sensitive spot inside me and I burst all around him, tight like a vice. We let go at the same time, flying and falling, but together in a climax so strong it's the best kind of pain.

We're breathing hard, and he lets me collapse on him, then tucks me beside himself. When his breath calms, he whispers, "You look... incredible." He shuts his eyes like an image of me in that glove of a dress imprinted on the back of his eyelashes. "Tell me about it."

"Nicole suggested it— and it was one of the cheaper options, at 50% off! I tried it on and loved the feel. She shined it up for me, too." I tell him about the rest— the corsets and the paddles, how my breath caught in my throat at the sight of other toys.

After some minutes, my gaze catches onto the infamous hook on the wall. "You know, I wonder how often Ralph or Lilly were tied to that hook, and what they did. How much this hook has probably endured. If only it could talk." He snorts and mutters something that sounds like "Ugh, I hope not." Considering I'm talking about his uncle, I understand his sentiments.

"That event Adam and Nicole were talking about?" I spur Paul, who's already half-asleep. He hums his attention. "I'd love to attend it with you. I can probably work it out at home, say it's the weekend I need to work away to make up for lost time. Plus," I nip at his lip, demanding his attention, "We need to dress you too."

He chuckles, and in just a few seconds is snoring like a bull.

***

Morning breaks on Friday, and Paul surprises me with a takeaway breakfast. We dig in, hungry after last night's

304

exertions. Once our meal is finished and the remnants tidied away, the doorbell rings, signaling the mysterious Abbot delivery. Paul opens the door, and two men enter, carrying a long, wrapped item that looks suspiciously like a rolled-up carpet.

They offer their apologies for the delay, explaining that the delivery took a whopping eight months due to some oversight on their part. Since Ralph did not ask for an update, the delivery kept getting missed. We brush off the delay, much more interested in uncovering the mystery of the package. "No worries," Paul reassures them, equally eager.

"Give us 5 minutes and we'll be out of your way." One of the men spoke, and they got to work. With confident ease, they unravel what initially looked like an exquisite floral rug, adorned with a picture of Lillies. We exchange puzzled glances, unsure if this was indeed just a rug.

Witnessing our astonishment, one of the men clarified, "This is a custom tapestry of Lillies that had been here for quite a few years. Mr. Michaels had it sent for cleaning, before hanging it up. We already installed a new hook for its display." He points to the innocuous hook Paul was tied to last night. We look at each other in barely controlled laughter. "Just last October, I put up that hook when we collected the tapestry. It used to be fitted differently, but the hook makes it much more convenient to hang." The man finished.

With precision and skill, they position the tapestry on the wall, ensuring it was perfectly levelled before leaving.

The door had barely shut behind the men when a burst of shared laughter erupts between us as we catch each other's eyes. The situation was so unexpectedly amusing, and it was almost absurd how we had assigned so much undue history to the innocent hook. It had never witnessed any kink other than what we'd done to it.

A bashful grin creeps onto my face. "I'll take the blame for starting this whole thing." Paul's laughter bounces off the walls. "Ah, the curse of having a vivid imagination. At least you're being accountable. Not me, though, I won't take the blame. I'm just here to follow your lead."

Throughout the day, the laughter continued, echoing our thoughts about the silly hook. The light-heartedness of it all was infectious, casting a warm glow over our interactions.

Later at the office, Paul and I meet with Helen and Nicola, who are presenting the pitch he had outlined the day before. Their enthusiasm is palpable, the tension from the previous day seemingly lifted. Paul extends his gratitude for their unwavering support, and their essential role in day-to-day operations.

Then, he unveils another plan, something he picked up from their suggestions – an upgrade to the IT infrastructure, connecting all the shops and streamlining the ordering process. It was a proposal that sparked their interest. He then broaches the topic of potentially launching an online store, reassuring Helen and Nicola that he wouldn't burden them with the intricacies of managing an online platform. "Should online sales become a reality, salespeople would be designated to handle that aspect, while you guys would continue to focus on holding down the fort: stock control and the management of Shop Central."

His tone is earnest as he stresses that these are just preliminary ideas taking shape in his mind. For all this brainstorming to be fruitful, they'd need a robust management team and of course their support. "For now, I do realise the pressing need to upgrade the physical shops, if we are to remain competitive, a robust online presence is crucial." All of us around the table nod in agreement.

Helen shares candidly, "To be honest, the shops are holding their ground, but we've been sort of stagnant for the past decade. We've failed to adapt to the changing times, and while online sales of other brands have made a dent in our profits, we can anticipate a further decline if things stay the same."

Paul agrees wholeheartedly, "I know you care deeply for this business, and from now on our aspiration is to not only see the business endure but thrive. I'm eager to be a part of something progressive."

In a few minutes, the meeting concludes, and Paul mutters his thanks. "Oh, also, for the Manchester meeting on Monday. If you want, you can travel on Sunday. Book your hotel rooms, and just charge it up to the company card." His way of caring for people is so sincere, it makes me glad that I chose this person.

Observing Paul throughout the week has been enlightening. I witnessed a transformation in him, a shift from the usual solicitor engrossed in legal matters to a man absorbing the profound implications of inheriting a legacy. This was not just a financial decision for him. He meticulously weighed the possibilities before finally accepting the inheritance, but to his credit he didn't stop there.

His actions and decisions this week have shown commitment and integrity to the legacy Ralph has left behind. It's clear that he has evaluated the knowledge he has acquired over the past six months and applied it to the running of the businesses. Today's presentation was no spontaneous revelation; he must have formulated this strategy well in advance. This explains the meticulous financial analysis he had requested earlier in the week, likely to ensure that any plans that are finalised can go through without external borrowing.

I can see he has a vision, maybe cloudy, but he is a few steps ahead of what he is sharing. It is attractive to see such strength, but a little annoying that he is not sharing it all with me. I can't help but wonder about the bigger picture – is he planning a move to London, potentially distancing himself from me? Could he be considering leaving his job, now that financial constraints are no longer an issue? It's not like he'll stay in Manchester now for either his job or me.

We're on our way to the train station, and Paul breaks the silence with a joke, "So, which exclusive club are you gracing with your presence tomorrow night in that new dress?" I play along, "And what other surprises have you got up your sleeve? Seems like you're full of them these days."

"Alright, I'll give you a little run-down, but after that let's talk about something else. Office talk has got me exhausted." I nod and he begins. "For now, I've decided to accept the inheritance, but plan to keep it under wraps for at least a year. From a family perspective and even for those who know me well, I don't want to let it impact our lives until I have a solid plan in place. I don't want the kids to be affected by all the trappings of wealth, but they will have a cushion to fall back on if they someday need it. No displays of wealth, but I'll know it's there. I'll continue commuting to London as I've done; they're accustomed to that routine anyhow. But there is more brewing, and I need to join the dots in my head before I can divulge more." he takes my hands in his, kisses my knuckles, "But when time comes to make a decision, I will be depending upon your opinion."

With a playful tone, I tease, "Move over, Richard Branson, there's a new tycoon in town." We chuckle, easing into another subject. He redirects the conversation to the events of last night, and I ask him about his conversation with Adam now that I have my wits about me.

He leans in to share their conversation, "Adam wanted to approach a different topic. I guess he didn't want it to get awkward and waited until you left with Nicole. So, he was telling me about the fetish scene, which often involves swinging. Usually at these events, long term couples are attending but there are also the swingers who couple swap. He was just saying how one must not assume anyone in the fetish scene is automatically a swinger. So, just a note to be mindful of when we're at the event."

"Whoa."

"Yeah, I was pretty out of my depth, too. I told him we're obviously very green and will be sure to not inadvertently get ourselves into a swinging situation. Just there to have some harmless fun, and definitely not into sharing."

"*Definitely* not into sharing, huh? But yeah, glad he gave us a heads-up." I didn't even imagine that could be a thing there. "I appreciate Adam being candid with us."

As the train glides into Manchester, we reach the end of our Friday night journey. "Have a fun day tomorrow with your daughter," I bid Paul farewell with a warm smile.

Chapter 20

Late Saturday as usual, Paul reaches out to me with his customary message, asking about my day and how I was doing. I take a fresh cup of coffee and fold onto the sofa, and our conversation flows naturally, as we catch up on the usual topics: the kids, errands, the week's events, and the routine rhythm of life. I share the details of my day, recounting the little fun tidbits that one gathers living with children.

During our exchange, I casually mention that I saw him in town earlier that day, spending time with his daughter Sarah. It was genuinely pleasant to witness him enjoying a day out with her. I ask about how their day unfolded, and Paul's response holds a sense of intrigue. "Any chance we could have a chat on the phone at some point? It might be easier to fill you in that way," he suggests. My curiosity is piqued, and I agree, "Give me a few minutes." Mark was out for a lads' night, but the kids hadn't settled down yet.

Around half an hour later, I made the call. "Can you talk right now?" I ask.

Paul's voice comes through, his tone bubbly. "Yes, absolutely. Let me give you a rundown of how the morning went. It was quite interesting, to say the least." There's some shuffling and I guess he's getting cosy, too.

"We decided to head out for breakfast, and I was so looking forward to having some quality time with Sarah. So, we headed into town and found a nice restaurant. We discussed the usual topics—how college was going for her and the latest updates in her life. She said she was exhausted, but she'll manage. You know, just the usual. But I sensed that she was building up to something, and I assumed she wanted something for herself, so I started teasing her. God, imagine my surprise when she point blank asks me, out of nowhere, 'So, do tell, Dad. Who is she?' I was baffled and panicked. You know, what did she know? How did she know? She had a playful smile, so I relaxed a bit. But I found myself in such a peculiar position, almost feeling like a child, being quizzed by my own daughter. I played it cool, feigning ignorance and asked her what she was talking about."

"Oh, my God." I intone.

"Precisely. The way Sarah had prodded into my personal life caught me off guard. She rolled her eyes and pointed out how I seemed happier in the past few months, more eager to travel to London than ever before. My heart has been lighter than it has been in a while. Her words touched me deeply. "I've never seen you this happy. So, who is she?" she asked once more."

"God, kids these days are too smart." I exhale.

"And so sweet, too. Get this: She tried to reassure me saying that whoever she is, we can see that you're happy. So, please don't worry about them. And even Matthew was in on the jig, and they've compared notes, so to speak. She said they're both genuinely happy for me. 'Now, do you want to spill the gossip?' she said. God," Paul chuckles.

"So, what did you say?"

"I tried to downplay it. 'Just someone I get on well with.' I said."

I interject playfully, my tone full of mock melodrama, "So I'm just someone you get on with? Oh, the heartbreak." His laughter fills the air, and I couldn't help but smile at the pleasant sound.

"Well, she's convinced that it's someone in London. She associates my happiness with my trips to London and the absence of it when I'm back here. I suppose it just highlighted to her that I never really had a life before you." My heart warms for his solitude and all the love he has to give. *Was I that obvious?* I wonder. *What did my kids see?*

"I miss you," He confesses suddenly, surprising me with the raw honesty of his words. "Sorry if I've been a bit serious at work this week. But I miss you when you're not around and we can't talk."

"I know, it's not easy with just one night and limited contact during the week, aside from Snapchat." I wanted to confess how miserable I was all weekend without him. Now that I'd tasted it once, I was addicted to him.

"I used shopping as a distraction," he tells me. "But she didn't let me off the hook that easily," he adds with a laugh. "She reminded me that they were well aware of my 'activities' and even offered to watch Rachel, so I could enjoy some privacy."

I giggle loudly. It was odd, having your older watch the youngest while you're away enjoying a new life.

"Yeah, I felt like a teenager sneaking away from responsibilities, a bit embarrassed but overall, it was a good day. It was amusing. We strolled along the high street, soaking in the ambiance, and I was in a particularly good mood, so I told her to knock herself out shopping. She certainly took me at my word. She darted in and out of clothing and shoe stores all morning. Something else: I led her into Ralph's sports shop on the main street, to get her unbiased perspective. It was an interesting experiment. I asked her about her impressions before leaving. She was not particularly impressed. Said it was a tad dated and lacking the modern flair of the other shops."

He exhales, the story finally winding down. I have a huge smile on my face just listening to his day.

"As the morning lazed into lunchtime, I surrendered and begged her to take a break from running around in and out of shops. We settled for a lunch, and to my surprise, she ordered wine with her meal. It was a moment that struck me, you know, a realisation that my daughter was all grown up. Her handling of our situation and the conversations we had held throughout the morning were evidence of it." I nod, even though he can't see me. It's bittersweet to see children growing up, becoming their own people. One side of the parents is proud, but the other side wants to keep their precious loves hidden, safe from the world. "All in all, I was surprisingly quite happy that Sarah knows a bit about you," he muses quietly, "Now, you. What have you been up to?"

"I am sitting on the sofa, glass of wine in hand, smiling at you. Mark is out for the night with the lads, so I'm all alone, and the kids are asleep."

Paul must have sensed there was something deeper beneath her words, a hint of emotion that required attention. "So, tell me, how are you really?" he asked, giving me the space to open up.

I paused for a moment, and he waited patiently for my thoughts to form.

After a brief silence, words come to me with frustration and contemplation. "I'm okay, very pissed off with work, except for our job, of course. And annoyed with Jack. I'm starting to wonder where I'm heading there, if anywhere. I even read my contract," I continued, aware that my voice was tinged with exasperation. "It explicitly states that I can't work for a competitor or establish my own venture for the next 12 months within a 100-mile radius of Manchester. They've tied me down tight, making sure I won't be going anywhere anytime soon."

"Huh, that's rough. And unfair." Paul remarks.

But I'm far from done, "And Mark and I, well, we're like two ships passing in the night. He's more focused on his work then the house and kids, right beside his friends. There's not anything between us, —our conversations usually revolve around the household and kids. But that's not really something you need to concern yourself with, it's not your responsibility to listen to me ramble about Mark and our relationship dynamics."

Taking a deep breath, I shift my focus to the topic that's been buzzing in my mind. "I'm still riding the high from Thursday night. When I think about it, which is all the time, by the way, I can't help but feel this surge of pleasure. The entire experience was exhilarating. Going to the shop with Nicole

313

was surprisingly enjoyable. She has this way of putting you at ease, making the whole process feel so normal. And that dress... When I had it on, it was like looking at a different version of myself. I liked that version."

As I continue, my words carry the breathlessness I feel, "When I had you tied up and was wearing that dress, it was such a powerful sensation. I absolutely loved it. But at the same time, when I think back to the week before, that was an entirely different level—knee-buckling, orgasmic, and simply amazing. It's made me wonder if I've missed out on experiences like this my whole life. It's got me contemplating what else I am going to discover about myself."

After a moment, he shares his thoughts. "I don't know which night I liked more, to be honest. Last week was mind-blowing. Seeing your reactions to me, having the freedom to just do as I pleased... It was liberating in the best way possible. But then there was Thursday. I had never been tied up before, and I admit, I was a bit nervous initially. But you taking control, undressing me—those moments were incredible. I don't know if I've ever been more aroused. After about a minute, I think I completely relaxed into the experience. I was fully aware that I had no idea what was coming next, but absolutely sure that it would be something I'd enjoy. I won't mind being tied up by you again." He whispers. "And, oh, that dress. I was expecting the warmth of your skin on skin, but when I saw it on you, once the blindfold came off and my eyes settled, you were a vision. It was something else entirely. You looked absolutely ravishing. It seems like it was made with you in mind. There was this aura of authority, a sense of command and control that you exuded. You really pulled off that look. I could tell you were feeling it all."

Listening to him recount the memory, I find myself smiling, mentally reliving that moment when he saw me in the latex dress for the first time. It was a play of contrasts—me all covered up and him standing there naked, his eyes filled with a mixture of astonishment and desire. "You know," I remark playfully, "I might just start wearing latex dresses on a regular basis if it has that effect on you."

He chuckles, and our conversation shifts to the upcoming event with Adam and Nicole. "What do you think about the event they mentioned? Are we really doing it?" I ask, intrigued to know his thoughts. "I can arrange to get away that Saturday night. It seems like Sarah might be offering her babysitting services for a dirty weekend," I add with a hint of mischief in my voice.

Paul's laughter fills the air as he replies, "Yeah, we're doing it! And there's always a childminder available, but I can just imagine the look on Sarah's face when I tell her I'll be in London for a whole weekend." He shifts the topic back to our wardrobe choices, his voice husky as he asks, "So, would you prefer to stick with latex or try something else for the event?"

I grin at his question. "I loved the latex experience, the way it felt against my skin. But for this event, maybe we could opt for something a bit dressier. We might end up going shopping again, and this time, perhaps we can both pick out some outfits. They had quite a selection of interesting men's options there," I tease. "Don't worry, you'll look fantastic in a leather harness" Laughing.

A glance at the clock surprises me—it has been two hours since we started talking. I realised it was getting late. "I hate to cut this short, but I really need to catch some beauty sleep," I admit with a chuckle and a yawn.

"Of course, sleep well," Paul replies. We say goodnight to each other, and as I hang up, my phone immediately pings. It is a Snapchat from Paul—just a simple "Nite x" along with a selfie from our day in Scotland. I can't help but smile at the memory, curling up comfortably in bed as I drift off to sleep.

***

I stir when Mark stumbles into the room drunk, clumsily tripping over the footstool and kicking the edge of the bed. His pained moans mixed with slurred words fill the air. He propels himself up and climbs into bed and, with a certain audacity,

315

starts nudging me. He taps my shoulder and fusses at my strap, but I meet his advances with an unwavering resolve—I wouldn't entertain him, not after he has to resort to alcohol to conjure any semblance of desire for me. If he needs to be intoxicated to want me, then he can keep wanting. I'll see how much he desires me when sobriety comes calling.

Feigning sleep, I remain motionless, my breathing even as I ignore his pitiful attempts. Eventually, he gives up, and as he collapses in bed, the room descends into silence once again. As I lay there awake, thoughts swirl through my mind. I can't help but compare Mark's behavior with what I know of Paul. In all the time I'd spent with Paul, I'd never seen him inebriated; a few glasses of wine make him relaxed and jovial, but I had yet to witness him drunk. And his desire for me was sober and spontaneous. These thoughts lull me back to sleep.

The following morning, I woke up with the kids, and we watched morning TV for an hour. The children lounge about, cozy in their pajamas, and it isn't until nearly noon that they think of breakfast. Mark was also moving, finally sleeping off however many beers he'd thrown back. Before he fully woke, I call the kids, "Come on, loves. How about a lazy Sunday trip to the Trafford Centre for lunch?"

We leave just as Mark is descending the stairs, still in his pants from last night, now completely ruined. Strangely, I feel an uncharacteristic intolerance for him today, I don't really know why. These drunken episodes of his were nothing new— four or five times a year, he'd return home in this state. That's pretty normal, I used to think. Yet, today, it irks me more than usual. It's as if I was losing my patience with him, my dissatisfaction spilling over the brim.

We settle into the bustling food court, each of us choosing quickly. We are really hungry. Once we're full, Liam and Natalie want to go exploring the shops. I give them some money and clear instructions: stay together and return in one hour to the same table. With Rebecca in tow, I go on my own stroll through the Center.

As we walk past the shop windows, a fleeting smile crosses my face. Victoria's Secret and Ann Summers is lined with lace, scarce pieces of clothing that I was coveting just a few weeks back— and now, latex. I chuckle softly, 'Here to the toy shop" aloud, a comment Rebecca caught. She cheered in response, saying 'Yes, Mommy" over and over. I snort and say, "Come on, let's find you something fun." And with that, we ducked into the children's toy shop.

Rebecca darted straight into the Disney Store, clutching several dolls in her arms. She meticulously assesses about five of them before finally settling on one that ticks all the boxes for her. Smart girl. The smile on her face radiates pure joy as we exit the store. As we leave the shop and walk towards the spot, I'd asked the children to return to, I find my mind wandering, contemplating the double lives I was living. On one side stood Mark, unsatisfying work, being a mother and a homemaker, and the stagnant predictability of suburban life. And then, on the other, there was Paul—a world of excitement, working at the London headquarters, latex, toy shops and the uncharted territories of pleasure. These two lives were as different as night and day, and yet I wanted both in their capacities. Could they coexist, I wonder, or were they destined to never meet, two paths I treaded one in darkness and the other in light?

My reverie is interrupted as Liam and Natalie approach me, shirts clutched in their hands as trophies from their shopping alone. Natalie chose a beautiful baby-blue button down top, while Liam- as always- got another football jersey. With the lunch eaten, and purchases made, it was time to head home. The kids piled into the back of the people carrier, their laughter and chatter filling the air as we set off home.

As we arrive home, a surge of energy propels the kids upstairs, chittering and ready to do whatever they did on the weekends. Mark emerges from the house, "Where did you go, Maria? I woke up, and the house was empty," he asked, mildly perturbed.

I wasn't any less irritated than this morning, but I decided to play nice, "Well, considering your impressive hangover from last night, I thought it best to let you rest and recover. I took the kids out to give you some peace while you slept it off. How do you feel now?"

He nods sullenly, but doesn't say anything. "Alright, I'll warm up something for you if you haven't eaten yet. And, oh, you owe me, you know. Next time I have a late night." I smile and go into the kitchen.

In the evening, I call the kids out, and Mark makes them barbecue. Afterwards, we laze in the sun with a bottle of wine and gentle breeze on my bare feet.

Later that night, I retire to bed early, my mind already occupied with the tasks that will plague me tomorrow. I had to get up early to manage the pharmacies and straighten up other work before the manager's meeting with Paul in the afternoon.

***

My alarm clock rings unforgivingly at five AM, and by six, I'm already seated at my desk in the office at DAF. The room is dimly lit, and there's a tranquil solitude in these early hours that allows me to focus without interruption. With a steaming cup of coffee by my side, I dive into my work, making the most of these two precious hours before the rest of the world pours in.

Joan arrives sooner than I was expecting her, probably having had the same thought as me. She glances at the array of documents and notes strewn across my desk, "You were in early today." I pause for a moment, looking up at her, nodding.

"I've spent the morning dictating a list of tasks for the team and running the analysis for the Pharma chain." I hand her the list, and her eyes quickly rove over it, her jaw setting in determination.

"Alright, I'll see to it. Oh, also, management was looking for you on Friday. I told them you were in London, and only got back in the morning. They said they'd like to see you in the conference room for a meeting at ten." I grimace; I don't have

318

time for this useless meeting. I do, however, wonder what this unexpected meeting entailed. The memory of the MD's lingering annoyance from last week briefly crosses my mind, but I can scarcely bring myself to care about it.

Lost in work, I manage to down my fourth cup of coffee just before the clock struck ten. With a sigh, I rise from my desk and walk to the conference room. Joan offers a simple, heartfelt "Good luck!" as I leave, and I can't help but wonder if she knows more than she's letting on. Joan does have a way of being on top of office gossip, after all. Despite it all, I still cannot care about it. Whatever happens will happen. I'm overspending every minute of my waking hour worrying about the firm that couldn't care less about me.

Upon entering the conference room, I notice the MD and Jack seated at the head of the table. My eyes briefly meet theirs before I take a seat further down. As I settle in, I take a deep, calming breath, reminding myself that whichever way the meeting goes, I'm fine.

The MD's voice breaks the silence, 'So, Maria, what's the progress on your current assignments?"

I respond with measured confidence, The Michael's estate is done, I was requested to work for ten more weeks, putting in the two days per week to help with the transition. I have some holiday plans and a personal commitment that might affect my availability, but I'll make it up with weekends or rearranging my schedule. It's all cleared up with the HR, and I assume, Jack. I've started working on the pharmacy chain and delegated the tasks. I'm sure we'll be done well before the deadline." I finish and realise neither Jack nor the MD really needed an update. It was just a conversation starter. I can barely stop myself from rolling my eyes. "Everything alright?"

"Well, you were annoyed that you did not get the London job that day."

"I am not questioning the directives, Jack. It's alright. It's above my pay grade anyway, that's been made clear to me. I'll let the new Partner handle it," there is a cutting edge to my voice which makes them uncomfortable, "I've not been following it since it's not my problem, and the pharma job is working out well with my London estate work, so what's this now?" Now that I thought about it, I did hear a rumour going that Justin was not doing well, that there were too many personality clashes, and the project was struggling.

"We were just thinking of changing things around. Do you want the London forensic job, anyway?" He asks me with a tone that says I'll jump at the chance.

This would work so well; I would spend much more time away in London this way...

To hell with him.

"No, but thank you for reconsidering. I have a lot on my plate, and as I said, the pharma job has worked out well with my schedule."

The two exchange a surprised look, "Well, the management thinks we need someone more senior for the job. Which is why we reconsidered."

"Well, now you know my position. Plus, Justin's all over it. How senior can you get than a Partner, right?" More time in London would be good, but that job won't last more than ten weeks that I was already going to spend there. On second thoughts, I loved seeing them sweat for it.

They look at me in surprise, then look at each other. I've always been more cooperative than anyone, always making it work for them at my expense. But this time, things are different. I've been a doormat for more years than I can count. They don't know how to handle this side of me.

"Anyway, I'm already all planned for a two-week vacation in the middle of this month, so I think that would be interruption enough with the London work."

The Director clears his throat, squinting at me, "Maria, are you being like this, refusing this job because you were not made Partner?"

"Refusing? No, I was asked what I think about taking Justin's job, and this is what I think. There's nothing to refuse. As long as the Partner thing goes, the management made their decision, and maybe, as Jack said, it's not my time yet. That's my place. And frankly, I genuinely don't have the time to do the Partners' jobs too with everything on my plate."

"Alright, then you don't want the London job?" He fixes me with a withering stare, his nostrils flaring. I've thoroughly annoyed this man, and I've never been more satisfied at the workplace before.

"No, sir," I murmur nonchalantly. "Is that all, then? I have an afternoon meeting to prepare for."

Jack mumbles a 'yes' and the Director huffs and puffs as I promptly leave the room. Once outside, I can't imagine I did that. I never would have thought I could say no to the managers or leave like that. As I walk past the coffee station, I spot Joan. "My office now, please." I say brusquely.

"Joan, what's the buzz on Justin's London gig? Give me the latest." I ask, exasperated but curious.

Joan, finally glad that I'm interested in the office grapevine, leans in a bit, lowering her voice. "Well, I've heard it's been a bit of a disaster. Justin butted heads with the clients, got a little too cocky with the wrong person. Rumour has it that the clients might be jumping ship because of it, though I don't have all the details. Someone in the client's company told me that we might lose the account."

Whoa, that's big. "Thanks for the scoop," I reply, making a mental note to never get on Joan's bad side. The woman had eyes everywhere.

Joan clears her throat, "So, what about you? What went down at the meeting?"

I take a moment to gather my thoughts, then divulge, "They asked me to step in and salvage the project, I guess, although they didn't say it was that bad. I turned it down."

Joan's eyebrows shoot up, clearly surprised by my decision. "But you've always enjoyed working in London," she says, confused.

I nod, "It's all work, but it's true, I do. But between overseeing the pharmacies and sports shops and the fact that they have a Partner handling the London client, they can sort out their mess on their own. I don't see why I should step in after they chose to sideline me." She sees the look of determination cross my face as I add, "Playing the doormat hasn't worked for me so far, so maybe it's time I assert myself. If they want to let me go, let them."

Joan eyes me with a strange expression, "That's a bold move, and it might ruffle some feathers in management. Are you sure about this?"

I flash her a resolute smile. "Absolutely. It's high time I stood my ground. Now, can you fetch me the folder for the afternoon meeting? I won't be back here afterward."

***

By 12.15, I've wrapped up my work for today at the office and head to the hotel for lunch, where I'm meeting Paul. As I walk in, I greet him, smiling teasingly, "Hey boss, ready to rally the troops?"

Paul returns a half-smile, laced with a touch of nervousness. "Just feeling a bit jittery about addressing all the managers. I've never been the one in charge before. Not of a company, of this scale. Not sure how long getting used to this will take," His gaze zeroes in on me, "You need to rush home right after?"

I shake my head. "No rush."

Leaning closer, Paul slides a hotel room key into my hand. "Maybe we can indulge in some room service for dinner. I've missed you." He whispers, "No toys, just us."

The change in his voice and the heat in his eyes takes me by surprise. My heart skips, mmm, this was going to be fun.

"Actually, I'd love some alone time with you," I respond with a warm smile. "That's what'll keep me going. But first, let's focus on work."

Paul proceeds to outline his strategy for the pitch, much like how he'd briefed Helen and Nicola the previous week. Just as Helen and Nicola join us, Paul greets them with an amiably. "Well, how are the London managers today? Still eager for the job, I hope?" He delivers it with such affability and ease. It's clear that Paul possesses a remarkable knack for putting people at ease, making them feel valued and heard.

Nicola helps herself to a cup of coffee from the table, thoughtfully arranged for the arriving managers. "You gave us quite a shock last week. We came here to discuss it over dinner, in fact. Yes, we definitely want the jobs, and to see the company move forward once again, like it did in the first ten years we were here. It's in everyone's interest, yours, ours, and the staff. This could be exciting, although we're a bit nervous. We've always had a boss who made the final decisions."

Paul offers them reassurance, his voice soothing. "Don't worry. I'm always here if you need a sign-off. Ralph was clear that he trusted you, and he'd simply been rubber-stamping your decisions for the past few years. So, in reality, you've been running the company all along. I'm extending the same trust to you, but I'm looking for decisions that will not just keep the company afloat but propel it forward." He sipped from his coffee, and the women followed suit.

He continued, "Not all decisions will be right, some may not work out. That is ok, too, expected even. Remember the person who never made a mistake, never accomplished anything. Anyhow, you have heaps more experience than I do, so, let's do this together."

Both Helen and Nicola nod, appearing reassured and encouraged by Paul's pep talk.

The managers start to arrive for the meeting, there's some mingling, and a few curious ones ask about the whereabouts of the new boss and joke if they should be concerned. I answer glibly, "All will be revealed. What's life without a little suspense?"

Once everyone is settled in the meeting room, Paul began his address.

"Thank you all for coming. We've had the pleasure of meeting most of you recently, so no need for lengthy introductions. You're already acquainted with Helen and Nicola, and Maria here is our main accountant, currently handling estate matters and assessing our financial positions."

Paul pauses for a moment, letting out a chuckle. "I know, solicitors and accountants, quite the thrilling bunch, aren't we?

Half of you must be on the verge of sleep at the prospect of dealing with us."

There is scattered laughter.

"Mr. Michaels, or Ralph, depending on how you knew him," Paul continues, "left a letter to accompany his will. In it, he spoke highly of the quality of our managers and long-term employees. He emphasized your competence and loyalty to the company. He wanted the new owners to understand, appreciate, and recognize this fact."

Paul leans in a bit, engaging his audience. "Which is why he made it a condition that, as long as the shops remained profitable and everyone continued doing their job, your positions would remain secure. Subject to these conditions, none of the shops or the distribution business could be sold for at least a decade. In his own unique way, he remembered each and every one of you in his will, not by name, but by your roles as loyal, long-term employees and managers. Now, does anyone have any questions about this?"

From the back of the room, a manager offers a simplified summary, "So, in simple terms, the new owners' hands are tied for the next 10 years as far as we and the shops are concerned."

Paul pauses briefly and then continues, correcting the statement, "No, that's not entirely accurate. The shops and managers are indeed safe, as long as your shops continue to perform as they have. This doesn't mean that nothing can change. It doesn't prevent the new owners from trying to grow or improve what's already here."

That seemed to take care of anyone who was thinking they could take advantage of Ralph's- and Paul's- goodwill.

"Alright, now let's talk about the new owner," Paul continues. "The new owner only found out about this inheritance 10 days ago. So, I ask you all to cut them some slack. They understand Ralph's conditions, and your jobs are secure. Is that understood?"

A collective nod and murmurs of agreement ripple through the room.

"Now, for the big reveal," Paul announces with a hint of amusement. "The new owner is a solicitor, so, as you rightly guessed, he's not the most thrilling person. He's also me. It turns out that I'm related to Ralph. I was appointed as the legal advisor for the estate to get to know all of you and the shops and businesses with an objective perspective. Ralph was rather clever in his planning. I see what he saw in each of you, and I know he wanted to ensure the business and your jobs remained secure."

Paul pauses, scanning the room for any questions. Silence hangs in the air.

"Alright, so now that we've clarified that, I'll let you know how we plan to move forward. Helen and Nicola, who've been here longer than most, will run the London office, as Managers . Since that's what they've been doing anyway, it's not a big change." His gaze sweeps the room, "So, any other questions? As managers, there are no wrong suggestions here. I'm opening the floor for any suggestions you have, either in your shop or across the group."

After a few moments of quiet, a voice gingerly breaks the silence, "Well, it would be helpful to know what stock is in other shops, especially specialized items that most shops might not carry."

The next suggestion comes swiftly, "We should have the ability to post or send orders in an organized manner. We're often asked for delivery, and we can only manage it occasionally. The shops also need a bit of modernising, particularly in terms of lighting."

Paul nods appreciatively at these suggestions, then continues, "I've had similar discussions with Nicola, Helen, and the accountants, especially the stock section. So, here's what I'd like to propose, but it will only be done on trial basis for a period of three months. At the end of this period, we will review reports and then decide which way to go."

It's a clever thing he did; make them think it's their suggestions he's taking forward when in reality it's always been his priority number one.

He takes a moment to gather their attention before outlining his plan, "I want to upgrade the stock and sales IT systems, transitioning to a central system. This way, each shop can see what's in stock across all locations, including our warehouses. If an item isn't in stock at one shop, we can arrange for orders to be filled from another. Of course, this will require some time and coordination, especially since we need to ensure our head office system is up to speed on this."

Paul pauses, allowing his proposal to sink in, then continues, "Apart from that, the spruce. Each shop should also evaluate what needs to be modernised to freshen its image. We have two options for this. We can either take individual shop requests or hire a company to handle the job, modernizing lighting, displays, signage, and ensuring a uniform image across all shops. What do you all think?"

The consensus among the managers leans towards hiring a company to manage the image.

"Excellent," Paul responds. "Now, each shop will be responsible for financing its own upgrades from its available cash reserves. Luckily, each shop has ample reserves, so this shouldn't make a significant dent in them."

The room seems to collectively agree with this approach.

"As for mail delivery, this is an area we really need to address. Currently, we're falling behind our main competitors who offer online sales. This will be the next phase of advancement for us, allowing you to sell stock from central stores even if it's not available in your shop. Eventually, we may even move towards having an online store that offers delivery or local pickup.

I understand that this is a significant leap forward, but to ensure that everyone stays competitive, and our business keeps growing, we must make these investments. I'm committed to improving our operations, and online sales shouldn't pose an issue for our existing shops. You'll even have the option to order items for delivery for customers if they aren't in stock in your store.

Naturally, these changes will bring about challenges and problems. To address this, we will have a team to help successfully implement these advances and dedicated to address these issues plus bonuses for each manager. These bonuses will be based on your cooperation with the changes, your input, and the advancements you help bring to our business. In essence, those who work to make these changes succeed will see that reflected in their bonuses. Those who don't, well, that will also be reflected.

Remember, these are your shops, your statements. It's up to all of us to make them work. Now, unless anyone else has any questions or additional points to add, how about we call it a day? If you're staying, feel free to charge dinner to your room. If not, please go ahead and grab something to eat or drink, and you can charge it to this meeting room." Paul waits a beat and then hurries out of the room.

As the day concludes, I signal to Paul that I'm ready to leave. About five minutes later, he joins me.

In our hotel room, he appears fatigued. "Hey, darling, you had them eating out of your hand. Are you okay?"

He offers a tired but content smile, "I'm just glad it's over. There's a lot for me to sort out. But now, let's not talk about work."

With those words, he wraps his arms around me, and we share a warm kiss. It feels wonderful, and as the intensity of the kiss grows, I know the next few hours will be wonderful.

**

The following two hours are spent in each other's company, enjoying this precious time together. Afterward, we take a relaxing and mischievous shower together. I can't help but wonder if this is what our future will be like – hotel rooms in the afternoon or evening and when we have some free time during our time in London.

Chapter 21

I arrive home to a quiet house. To my surprise, the kids are all fed and taken care of, Mark was watching TV, and all was quiet.

"What's going on?" I ask, looking around the house.

Mark barely looks at me. "Nothing. Everything's fine."

He asks me how my day was, and I tell him about my mini revolt with the boss this morning. In a few sentences I explain how they wanted me to do the job that I was sidelined for in the first place now that it's messed up, and I'd stood my ground and said no.

"Is there any chance they could fire you?" he asked, sounding worried.

"At this point, it might be a push I need," I said, shrugging.

He encouraged me to think about it. "I mean, you're up and down to London anyway. What difference would a few more months make?"

I thought about it for a moment. "No," I said. "I'm spending enough time there as it is. They had their chance to give me the job. Instead, they're trying to punish me for getting upset about not getting the promotion. And what about the extra work? When I didn't get the promotion, you were happy because it meant less work for you. Now you're perfectly fine with me taking on more work and staying in London more."

I didn't want to get into a fight with Mark, so I changed the subject and moved on. "Let's see what they do," I said. "If I bail them out now over their choice of Justin, then they'll think I'm just their good little girl all the time and they'll know they can walk all over me."

We went to bed, both of us tired. It was unusual for Mark to come to bed with me, he usually didn't even try to sleep at the same time, almost seemed like he avoided it. But that is as much as we do, head to bed and go to sleep.

The next day, I headed into the office and Joan was already at her desk before me. "Jack was here five minutes ago," she said. "He's looking for you and he really seems like he woke up on the wrong side of the bed this morning. He said you should call him as soon as you get in."

I called Jack, and he was indeed annoyed. "We just lost a major client because you wouldn't do your job and take over the London work from Justin," he grumbles.

"Well, you didn't tell me," I replied. "You asked me. And to be fair, I didn't have time even if I wanted to. So why is this my fault? Blame your new partner. He's the one who lost them, not me," I say angrily. I knew Jack knew that as well as I did, and he was just looking to rant and blame someone.

I stay busy with work as the week goes by and Mark keeps asking me how work is. He seems more worried about my job than I was, which irritates me.

"Why are you so concerned?" I ask. "So, what even if I was fired? We can manage for a while. Your job is good, you're staying busy, and we have low enough borrowings. Besides, I'm sure I could find another one easily."

I roll my eyes and leave. Why's he being super weird?

***

Finally, it was Thursday, my favourite morning that I'd been looking forward to all week. I headed off as usual, and found Paul was waiting on the train. We headed down and I talked about my week and problems at work. Paul just listened for the most part, reacting and reassuring me.

When we arrive at work, Helen and Nicola are already there, working away. When we settle in, they ask us to join them for a meeting at eleven o'clock. Paul and I share a mystified look, wondering what was coming in the meeting. At eleven, we reach the meeting room, and Helen and Nicola arrived, bringing with them an air of confidence. "So, what's up? What's this meeting about?" Paul asks.

Nicola began to explain that after Monday's meeting, they had heard back from most of the managers. The general consensus was a positive one and everyone was happy with the arrangement, and wanted to know what was next. Helen had already asked each manager to send in photographs of their shop and a wish list of work and ideas for what should be done. They spent the next hour compiling common suggestions and requests.

Paul asked, "Have ye found any shop fitters yet?" Helen said that they had contacted three national companies and were asking for quotes from places all around.

Paul said, "Well, it looks like I'm already being retired here. Well done, keep going and let us see the final plans and prices. Now, by the way, who does your IT?" he asked. "We need to look at connecting the shops to the central servers."

Nicola replied that they had an IT company, but they didn't know if they were used to stock control software and shop chains.

"Do you want Paul and I to look at that while the two of you take care of the shop outfitters?" I asked. "It would be less of a national job, as once the systems are in place they could be implemented everywhere."

Everyone agreed that this seemed the best way to go about it and we discussed everything until lunchtime, and then decided that everyone knew where they were going and let them off.

We decided to go to Starbucks for coffee and a light lunch. Sitting in the busy cafe where we've thankfully found a table I ask Paul, "So what's the plan for tonight?"

"Let's head out around seven after work. I was thinking we could have dinner somewhere, maybe some spicy food?" he suggests.

"I'm definitely in the mood to enjoy this nice night out," I say. "Then on the way back, you and I can take another look at the shop, and you can show me around. After all, it's only two weeks until the event with Adam and Nicole. I don't know what I should wear."

"That sounds like fun," Paul perks up at the thought. "Helping you with clothes is always fun," he grins at me mischievously.

We spent the afternoon working and finished up around five o'clock, before heading back to the apartment. It was always comforting to get back there; it had started feeling like home. We took a bottle of wine from the fridge and poured ourselves a glass each. A while later, we changed and got ready to leave. I had changed into some casual clothes I had brought with us. 'I had better wear something that I can get in and out of easily, in case I try anything on, I thought.' Getting dressed together and going through the motions of a quiet, blissful domestic life felt like we were just a normal couple living life.

We went out for dinner, and walked around till we found a nice Indian restaurant. We ordered dinner and a bottle of wine, and chatted about life, home, and our kids. We had a laugh over Sarah's suggestion of having a dirty weekend.

After we finished dinner around nine, it was time for our plans at the shop. Paul and I entered the shop through the back door, and Paul unplugged the CCTV security cameras. Paul showed me all the different sections of the shop, told me all the terms used in the fetish scene that he had just found out and then left me to take my time looking around.

I walked around in awe. A little while later, I came back to Paul who was looking at some of the toys and restraints the shop had stocked.

"Not a lot we can do their babe," I laugh. "The Lillie's on the wall took our hook. We may have been wrong about the hook, but hey, there were Lillie's on it!"

"Oh, ye of little faith, there must be something here to work with", Paul chastises me laughing along. "After all, I presume most of these don't come with hooks on the wall."

We look over the toys and restraints display, until I find a box. "These are over the door restraints," Paul says.

They looked like a little bar at the end of the cord with a ring at the end. "Well, they do look interesting," I say.

"And portable," Paul adds, laughing. "But they will need cuffs, babe. Over the door, yes, not a hook to add the rope cuffs to."

Paul walks over to another display and picks up a whip, "So, Mistress Maria, is that what you want to do at our next rendezvous? "

I blush at 'Mistress Maria' then recover quickly. "Perhaps, but you better be careful, who knows. But look at the options. There must be twenty different variations of it on the wall. Anyway, we are here to dress you up like a giant condom. Where do they keep the latex?"

Paul laughs, "Mr. Durex, will it be?"

We found the clothing section of the store, and I walked towards the men's section. Paul said, "Let's see what you're wearing first, and go from there," taking me by the hand and guiding me gently to the women's side.

The women's section was dimly lit, with plush velvet curtains and tables and shelves racked with lingerie in an array of colours. Besides the obvious corsets, dresses, shirts, skirts and robes, a section was dedicated to accessories like satin gloves, feather boas and masks.

I gasped at the large collection of options presented to me as I walked around. I glanced at the price tags as a matter of habit. When I saw the price of the dress I picked up, I exclaimed, "Bloody hell, this is nearly £300!"

Paul laughed. "It's just as well you're on stock control duty, so you're not paying. You're just liberating it from stock. Advertising it, even."

The dress is a lovely pencil style dress in a deep shade of burgundy, with some pretty white trim and latex lace details down the front. I try it on and come out to show Paul.

In the large, ornate mirror that stand in the corner of the room, I admire myself, feeling powerful. The dress had a low enough chest line with cups for my breasts, a big step up from what I was wearing last week.

Paul said, "Looks like we have a winner. Now for me."

The men's options were much more limited. Paul found some pants, which were perfect, but the question was a shirt. There were some uniform shirts, which didn't really match the look we wanted. But then, he found a black shirt with the outline of a bow tie on it. It looked like a dress shirt at the end of a night out.

He puts them on, "Great, now we look just like a couple at a dinner, just in latex."

"Would you like to find those cuffs now, so we can take them home along with the over-the-door restraints?" I asked. "Let's see where this leads us."

We continued to explore the store a bit more, and then I stumbled upon the playful lingerie section. There were plenty of lacy, see-through options, and I decided to pick up a box that read, "One size fits all"... what on earth?

"Let's head home," Paul suggested. It was the second time he mentioned going *home*. That sounds nice, I thought. Too bad it isn't.

Once we returned to the apartment, both of us were a bit horny from our visit to the shop. As soon as we entered, we began kissing, touching, and undressing each other. When I was nearly naked, I instructed Paul, "Find a door for those cuffs and put them on."

Paul, dressed only in black shorts, smiled and replied, "Yes, Mistress Maria, whatever you say." I made my way to the bedroom to change, putting on the lingerie from the shop—cheap and cheerful—and decided to add heels to the mix.

Upon returning, I found Paul with the restraints set up over the kitchen door and the cuffs already on. "Against the door," I say. He complied, raising his hands to the restraints. I walked over and attached the clips without saying a word.

Why does this feel so good? Being in control. Here is a grown man, educated and strong, bending to my will. I look at him, standing there. At my mercy and completely aroused by it.

I walk over and just enjoy kissing him, hard on the lips first, touching his face. He pulls against his restraints, trying to reach out and kiss me back. I can pull away and move back in if I want, so I walk to the bedroom, and laugh, "'Night, see you tomorrow."

I go and get a bottle of lotion from my bag. Walking back to Paul, I slowly apply it to his chest and take my time rubbing him down, savoring it. I massage him all over, leaving his shorts on, but massaging him over them. He feels good, really good.

When I am ready, I go in and kiss him again teasingly, then release the cuffs. "That was fun, baby. Your turn to take charge now..."

Paul takes the cuffs off and drops them to the floor. He pulls me in for a kiss, "Now, honey, you are mine." He heads into the bedroom and stretches me out on the bed. The rest of the evening... oh, he took charge.

We ended up curled up and spent, falling asleep in each other's arms. The morning was like a morning in any other household; we get up, I make us breakfast, and he puts away the cuffs and restraints. Alright, maybe not exactly the same as any household, but it felt normal, natural. We just worked around each other.

At least it's casual Friday in the office today. Paul said he will look at the stock control companies. He asks me if I have much to do today and I must admit that I don't have a lot to do. A day a week would be suitable now, but I am not missing taking the overnight.

Paul asks if I can look at the options Helen and Nicola presented to centralise the accounting system in all the shops, so we can have a single set of auditors. Paul wants to make sure the accounts are all centralised, so we don't have to wait around for shops to report to come in. The IT company should be able to support the centralization and whatever we are doing wherever we wish to set up.

We began our workday as usual, splitting our tasks between us. Paul wanted to use the boardroom, even though we could have shared an office. At 11:30, he left for two hours. He texted me at 1:00 to say that he would be at the pub down the road if I wanted to join him for lunch. I asked him where he had been, but he said it was nothing important, just a few errands. I knew he was being evasive and coy, possibly up to something, but I let it go. He will tell me if he wants to. He had other shops to manage in the area, so I figured he was just checking in on them.

I supposed I would need to get used to the changes. Paul was clearly ambitious and had a plan for the business. I wouldn't be a part of it, but that was okay. I was happy to support him from a distance.

After work, we headed back to Manchester on the train. We had dinner on the train and enjoyed each other's company. Paul seemed excited about his new life. He was adamant that his children shouldn't know anything about it, at least not yet. He didn't want to make any major changes or purchases that would draw attention, no new cars, or big presents. They should live within the means they'd always had. He said he might need to talk to his boss about reducing his workload. He was currently billing the estate for his time, but that wouldn't last forever. He would need to free up more time to focus on his new business ventures, because if he quit his job, his kids would get curious. Also, he was effectively paying his employers so he could spend time in his own business. It did not make sense.

I thought about what Paul had said. He had talked about negotiating a three-day week; Monday to Wednesday in the office, Thursday and Friday in the shops and the business. He would be in London two days a week this way and I wouldn't be going with him, so I wouldn't be able to see him as often. I couldn't possibly justify continuing to go down and bill him for my time. That would feel strange and wrong. It would be like he was paying me to spend time with him, which was not a feeling I liked. Anyway, I thought. Let's wait and see.

As the train was pulling into the station, Paul put his hand over mine and said, "Before we go, I remembered you never got a chance to wear that new dress and heels we bought a few weeks ago. How about we book the restaurant we went to on our first real date? I still remember how gorgeous you looked that night. Oh, that was one amazing date."

All the feelings and memories from that night suddenly rushed back to me. "That sounds perfect," I said.

"It does," he smiled. "I'll book the reservation as soon as I get home. If you want to get pampered and primed for the date, tell me what you want, and I'll book you a hair appointment. Get a massage, get your nails done too. I'm sure your boss is quite alright with letting you leave early," he added teasingly.

As we were getting off the train, we bumped into Mr. 24A. Paul smiled at him and then said to me, loud enough for Mr. 24A to hear, "Coming, honey." I smiled at him and out of earshot of Mr. 24A, said, "Don't be mean!"

We parted and went our separate ways. It was a lovely evening, and all I could think of was our date next week.

Chapter 22

The weekend carries on much like any other; there's the routine of dropping off and picking up the kids from playdates. When I get home, I'm surprised to find that Mark has taken care of the kids' meals again. It's unusual, and I can't help but wonder if he's trying to change his ways. *Isn't it too late now?* A voice inside me whispers.

"How's work in London?" He asks, a question so rarely posed that I'm taken by surprise.

I still fill him in on what's happening, the search for new accounting software to connect our shops for centralized accounting. I can see he's trying to feign interest, and it strikes me as odd. He usually doesn't even bother with a percentage of this pretense. He brings finger snacks for me and even pours a glass of wine.

I can't resist teasing him, saying, "Are you feeling alright? You never do this."

He blushes, "You've had a long week."

Perhaps it's a combination of exhaustion and wine, but I playfully add, "Or just guilt," and we both share a laugh. I sense there might be something more beneath the surface about my comment there, but I decide not to push it. After all, I have no right to judge. In some ways, it might even be simpler if he were having an affair.

I change the topic, asking, "Well, how was your week? Are those Thursday evening site meetings going okay, or are they almost done?"

He looks serious when he replies, "They're fine. We're sticking with Thursdays since the week is almost over, and it gives us time to plan for the next week."

There's silence afterwards, and we swiftly move on to another, lighter topic.

On Saturday morning, I drop Liam off at his match and Natalie at her friend's house. With Rebecca in tow, I go grocery shopping. Mark settles in for a day of watching sports, which is his usual weekend routine. The day passes without any significant events. Later in the evening, I decide to cook a nice dinner for everyone – a simple family meal, while watching a movie.

After the movie, Mark seems to be back to his attentive self. It's weird how quickly he can switch this side of him on and off. He brings me a glass of wine and offers to help tidy up and wash the dishes from our dinner. I say yes, mostly because I'm surprised he's asking. While we work together, he asks about my work. "What are you going to do about the new London job and what's left in the existing one?" he asks, in the mood to chat again.

I remind him, "In two weeks, I'll be away in London until Sunday for work, and I know you'll be away the following week, starting on Thursday, so I won't be in London at all that week." Mark seems perfectly fine with this arrangement. In fact, he's quite encouraging about the idea of me considering the second London job.

I shake my head, "I'm not too interested, and it would mean I'd be back in hotels since I can't use the apartment as it belongs to the client's company. At least in my current situation, I can leave a change of clothes and toiletries, making it easier to travel light." I can't help but think about the cuffs and all the kinky paraphernalia that weighs us down these days. "I'm not happy in my current job," I admit, "and unless there's a change in attitude from higher up, I don't know what I'll do. I can't work for an accountancy firm in Manchester or within 100 miles for 12 months as an accountant. Who knows, I might

338

take a year off. I'd be around all the time, then." I smile ruefully and look at him- he's so shocked he can barely speak.

I probably won't stay at home for a year, and if Mark knows anything about me, he'd know that. Shaking my head, I ask him about the children's parent-teacher meeting he'd attended while I was away in London.

As I head to bed, my mind is racing with all the possible options. It would certainly help if I knew what Paul was thinking – is he planning to stay around or make the move to London? He said that he will only come up when he was needed, but that could be all the time now. He was running a company, for God's sake, he couldn't live away from headquarters. I also can't shake the feeling that something is up with Mark; his behavior has been rather strange lately.

Sunday arrives as a quiet day. I decide to go for a walk on my own, popping in my earphones and losing myself in music. It occurs to me that if I'm going to look good in latex, I might want to start working on toning up.

***

Monday arrives, and my morning follows the usual routine: getting up early, getting the kids ready until Ursula arrives to take over, and then heading off to work. I find myself back in the routine of dealing with pharmacy accounts, which, to be honest, is rather mundane. I start regretting my decision to keep this account several times. As I sift through the reports from my team, nothing particularly exciting catches my eye. The turnover is as expected, although there's one shop that's slightly underperforming, but considering its location, it's not entirely unexpected.

Thoughts of taking the forensic job cross my mind. Had I made a mistake by turning it down? While it might have given me more time in London, it would also mean missing out on spending time with Paul on those days, and the job would still wrap up around the same time as my work with the sports shops. It didn't seem all that inspiring once I thought about it.

I decide to send a message to Paul:

Maria: *Hey darling, how was the rest of your weekend?*

Paul: *Very quiet, the kids were out and about, and I was catching up on some work. How about you?*

Maria: *Same as you, nothing interesting.*

Maria: *I have a question; I was about to email it. But I thought I didn't want it on the record. Would you consider my office here for your auditors and accountants?*

Paul: *I considered it, but no. I don't want to use your office. Anyway, even if I did, you're not in that section, so it's not like we'd be working together.*

Paul: *While we're on the topic, what sort of manpower would be required to manage the accounts for all the shops and an online shop?*

Maria: *A good mid-sized practice could easily handle it. One overseeing accountant, and the rest would be mostly assistants. Nothing major. It depends on how much you want them to do. Why do you ask?*

Paul: *Just curious. It's quite messy having seven different sets of accountants, one for each shop, and one for London. It would require much more management and time with seven different offices to coordinate.*

We move on and talk about different things, but I can tell is pre-occupied, so I say goodbye quickly. Around 30 minutes later, I receive an email. It's from Paul's office.

From: Paul Bridges

To: Maria; Jack; Leonard

Good afternoon all,

London is winding down, and the new owners are putting a plan in place. Thanks to Maria for agreeing to the extra time to transition and to DAF management for seconding Maria to this job. We know they were employed by the executors here rather than the client's companies.

We need to complete the estate wrap up and get all the bills in. DAF, I presume, are invoicing us here, and all of their accountancy and estate records might be made available for the client's accountants at the end of the transition. The tax calculation is being finalized here, and hopefully, that can be paid off shortly.

Jack, you might confirm agreement to the above so we can move to closure and handover. If any of you have any further issues that need to be addressed, please let me know.

Regards,
Paul Bridges

I read the email and can't help but wonder what it's all about. We all know we're in the process of winding things down, and the clock is ticking. Why did Paul ask for Jack's sign-off on this matter and not mine? It should have been my job.

I thumb him a message in confusion.

Maria: *I got your email. What's that about? Why didn't you ask me to sign off? I'm expected to do it, by the way.*

Paul: *Don't worry, darling. I'm just doing a little advance planning here.*

Maria: *Secretive and coy, aren't you?*

Paul: *LOL, just trying to keep some mystery going. What shall I do if you tire of me?*

Maria: *Austin Powers, you are not. LOL, international man of mystery. I'll get tired with you, not of you.*

Another email pings. I click on the thread.

From: Jack
To: Paul, Maria, Leonard
Thank you, Paul,

Yes, the above is in order. We will invoice the executor at your office and close matters off here. Thank you for engaging us, and we hope that Maria and her team met all expectations.

Regards,
Jack

There's another email in the thread. I click on it.

From: Paul
To: Jack, Maria, Leonard
Jack,

Thank you, and yes, Maria and her team were invaluable. The staff in London had nothing but good things to say about her, and they are making the transition very smooth. I am sure she's a valuable asset to any organization.

Regards,
Paul

I couldn't help but text Paul, giggling this time.

Maria: *LOL, are you winding Jack up on purpose?*

Paul: *Well, praise where it is due. No lies being told either.*

Maria: *Thank you ... that will help me here plus it annoys Jack, especially now. That's what they call a win-win.*

Paul: *Ok, baby, I better get some work done. I can spend all day- and night- singing your praises, but then who will run the company?*

Paul: *xx*

Maria: *Yes, boss. No slacking on company dime.*

I get back to work, focusing on clearing my tasks. Later, I ask Joan to shortlist three reputable accountancy firms for taking over the Sports shops. "What about us here?" She's defensive and confused. She knows how hard I've worked for Paul- the client- and yet they didn't want to keep us?

I shrug, "The client has not explained. I'm not sure why. But he has asked for three recommendations."

Joan diligently works on the task, and takes her time since the workload isn't too heavy at the moment.

Tuesday night, while Mark is out, I give Paul a call. "Hey darling, how was your day?" I ask.

"Very interesting," he replies, chuckling.

"Really, do tell," I say, intrigued.

"I took a walk after work and went to the Manchester shop. I got there just before they closed up. I met the manager and asked him to show me around. He was quite relaxed and asked me about the refit. I told him Helen and Nicola are controlling that, so be nice to them before handing them the wish list."

"And?" I urge him. He always stalls before revealing something exciting.

"I then asked him to show me the rest of the building. The upper floor was recently vacated when tenants moved out. The top floor was an old apartment, vacated last year and never relet.

The shop also has a few parking spaces in the nearby car park. They only use 2 of the 4. I told them I would take one since it's close to work, anyway. Shame to waste it, and me paying for parking every day," he explains. "Looks like those vacated offices could be rented out easily enough. Already modernised since the last tenants required a face lift before moving in," he adds.

"Surveying your new empire, are you?" I tease.

"Just something that was on my to-do list. I will really have to visit them all at some stage. Only seen London, Manchester, and Fort William," he muses. "So, dinner Thursday, I am looking forward to it. Lovely to be able to get out and about with you."

"I can't wait, and then thinking of the following week, we will have three nights and Saturday to ourselves! Unless the boss is making me work. So nice," I gush with enthusiasm anticipating our upcoming time together.

***

Thursday arrives like clockwork, and we fall into our usual morning routine. As we chat, Paul shares more about his plans and his decision to keep his children in the dark about his inheritance for at least a year.

"I really only want to spend on two fronts," he elaborates, his eyes alight with determination. "The first being the shops, business and properties. Second, us. Ralph wanted us looking through the curtain and see that side of life together, then it's only right we use and enjoy the money from him for that. But I doubt that would even dent it."

His tone is serious when he continues, "Now I know, I have been secretive, a bit anyway, about my plans. But trust me, please." He looks deep in my eyes, "Now I want you to agree to something without questions," he implores, a mischievous glint in his eyes.

Unable to resist, I joke, "That could be dangerous for me, for all I know you want me to agree to you having your wicked way." Our laughter fills the room.

"A bit late for that." Paul murmurs.

"Do I have a choice?" I ask with a playful glimmer in my eyes.

Paul responds with a hint of a smile, "Of course, the answer is yes or no, so you have two choices."

I consider for a moment and reply, "Well, at this stage, saying no is getting us nowhere, so what the hell, yes."

Paul reaches into his pocket and retrieves an envelope. I glance at it and then back at him, asking, "Shall I open it?"

He nods affirmatively but looks a bit apprehensive. I wonder what it could be, and carefully tear open the envelope and find a credit card inside, along with a pin number. The card bears the name of a property company and my own.

"Uh. What is this about?"

Paul explains, "Well, the property company is what Ralph lived off, and in fairness, there's plenty of money in it. So, if we are to explore a new life together in whatever shape or form, that will cost money, and we both know you can't show it on your credit card or bank statements. So here is a card you can use. All the statements will be in the company's name and will be sent to Ralph's- my- private office. I also have a card now from that account. I want you to use this for anything related to us, whether it's for play, travel, clothes- whatever you need or if the apartment needs anything. Whatever."

I examine the card, a sense of unease washing over me. "I can't take this; it feels all wrong. It won't feel right."

Paul's expression softens as he reassures me, "Maria, I want you to have it and use it. You don't need to go overboard; it has a credit limit." He smiles warmly. "But you can't use your card for certain things, and this is just for practicality's sake. Last Monday in the hotel was gorgeous, and if we want to arrange that again and you check in, you will need to swipe a card. Now take it, and please don't argue. If we are together, it will be on my card anyway, so it's all the same. I will get the new accountants, when hired, to register you as an employee of the company, and you can keep records, earn your keep."

I reluctantly agree to accept the card, although I know I will rarely use it. My sense of independence runs deep, but I also understand Paul's practicality and the need for discretion in our situation. Still, it feels off and I can't completely erase the feeling.

***

As we arrive in London and make our way to the office, I notice the atmosphere is notably different. Nicola and Helen, who typically are professional, now seem to be infused with a newfound vitality. The office itself feels more vibrant and bustling than usual.

I can't help but ask about it, "What is going on?"

Both of them exchange glances before Nicola responds, "The mood has lifted. Everyone seems happier. They are thrilled that Paul is the new boss, as everyone here genuinely likes him. But more importantly, the prospect of new investment has given them a sense of security for the future."

Paul flashes a smile and chimes in, "Great, just wait until I drop my next idea." He chuckles playfully before heading off.

I can't help but smile tightly. *"What is he up to now?"*

Paul pauses midstep and glances back at us, adding, "Oh, I almost forgot to mention. While we were making all those plans for the shops last week, I forgot something. Can you either delegate or decide who will handle the next task?"

Helen nods cautiously. Oh, he enjoys keeping them on their toes too much.

He continues, "I want this office revamped as well." He says, looking around the dilapidated building, "We have plenty of unused space. I'd like you to modernize the entire office, including the old canteen kitchen. A separate office for each of you. I want everything painted, new floor coverings, and furniture replaced where needed. And the boardroom needs an overhaul. It should feel like a proper head office here. Have electricians check the wiring and computer connections and designate a small server room that's both secure and fireproof.

If we're going to link all our systems with the shops, we need appropriate infrastructure."

Then, as an afterthought, "Ralph's office space should be retained but modernized as well. I assume I'll be spending some time here, so I'll need a suitable workspace."

Helen asks, "When do you need to sign off on this?"

Paul, wearing a knowing smile, responds, "You're running this office, so you will sign off on it whenever you get the quote. Just be reasonable, we're not made of money here. Make sure we are efficient, ensuring value for money. Ultimately, the accountants will scrutinize the invoice, and Maria here is known to be quite meticulous. So, do it well, and make it last. Also, whoever ends up signing off will need to stay here and look at all the renovations. And consider getting an architect to look at it before anything goes through."

"Now, the next task isn't one you can delegate. Your job titles need a review. Helen, especially, our London Manager. You're managing this place now, and it's about time you had a proper title. Nicola, you can stick with 'In-House Legal' or opt for a more generalized managerial title, as I announced in the managers' meeting. I'll need to approve these, but unless they're way off the mark, I'll be practical about it."

With that, Paul coolly strides off, leaving behind two ecstatic colleagues. They're overjoyed that their promotions are not only being acknowledged but also accompanied by new job titles. Helen, in particular, seems pleased that her hard work is finally being recognized.

As the conversation shifts to the office revamp, I note that it's long overdue but a great opportunity for them to shape the space as they see fit.

Soon, it's time for Helen and Nicola to return with an update on the shop renovations. At eleven sharp they bring booklets filled with images from each shop and explain that, thankfully, all the shops are up to code, so the majority of the work will focus on cosmetic improvements and displays. New computers and sales terminals will also be incorporated. Paul hums, satisfied with their progress, "Great. Thank you."

Curiosity gets the better of them and they can't resist asking, "What's the next big idea?"

Paul responds with a laugh, "Now, now, hold your horses. One step at a time."

After they leave, I tsk-tsk at him, "This all seems so natural for you. You're quite the charmer. You could've told either one of them, and still you keep them in suspense. If they weren't smitten with you, I don't know how they'd avenge all this suspense."

"Well, I am actually enjoying this, the running of a business," Paul says, "but I know my limitations. Also, I know Ralph wanted everyone taken care of and shown the respect they deserve. Lastly, I need them; can you imagine the mess I would have if they weren't here while I was trying to do this? Show people respect, and loyalty should follow. Establishing rapport is all part of the great scheme."

Well, no arguments there.

"Now, I need to head out. It's 12 now, how about we meet at 1 in the restaurant down the street?" he suggests.

I nod, but I can't help but wonder where he's off to now. What exactly is he doing? Could he be going to Ralph's other office, the one where Ralph had those 12-2 lunches?

***

I arrive at the restaurant a little early and place an order for our lunch. Paul shows up a little while later, looking a bit dusty. I gasp, "What have you been up to?"

He brushes some dust off his shoulder with a chuckle and replies, "I'll tell you later. What did you order me for lunch? I'm starving."

I fix him with an unyielding stare, "I got your usual, but I get the message—don't ask. Although, I might make you pay for this later."

He snickers, "Promises, promises."

Over lunch, we enjoy a pleasant chat, and Paul reminds me about my hair appointment at four in the evening. As we're leaving the restaurant, he kisses my hand and tells me he's really looking forward to tonight.

I return to the apartment at around six, eager for our dinner date. Paul has not yet come back from the office, it seems. Having just had my hair done, I feel refreshed, and I start getting ready for the evening, changing into my new dress and a pair of heels I've been looking forward to wearing. Paul arrives at around 6:15, and hurries to get ready.

At 6:50, our taxi arrives, and we make our way to the restaurant. It's a charming place, warm and impressive. We enjoy a delightful dinner accompanied by a bottle of wine. We're so engrossed in each other's company that we hardly notice the world around us, not caring who might see us.

As we drain a second bottle of wine, Paul leans in with a playful glint in his eyes. "Well, Mistress Maria, are you top or bottom tonight, just so I know?"

I raise an eyebrow, "Top or bottom, you say? Let's see where we land on the bed, I guess," I respond with a laugh.

Paul shakes his head slightly. "Tut tut. I see I'm the only one doing homework. Since I had plenty of time on my hands in the evening, I was doing some research. Top is Dominant and Bottom is submissive. There's even topping from the bottom, where the submissive takes control, that's a Switch."

I contemplate for a moment. "Hmm, I see."

"So, babe, what are you in the mood for tonight? Ladies' choice. Should we play as we have for the past few weeks, or do we skip the toys tonight?" Paul is almost slurring his words, but I know from experience he'll sharpen quickly when we enter our room.

I'm not entirely sure about the labels, but I decide to go with the flow. "Can you do what you did to me two weeks ago? Maybe I'm leaning towards a bit more on the Bottom this week."

Paul grins mischievously. "Sure, baby... but I may add a twist if you're up for it."

"Oh, after two bottles of wine, twist away."

We call for the bill, settle it, and then head back to the apartment. As we enter, Paul takes charge.

"What twists and turns do you have for me tonight?" I ask breathily.

Paul smiles and suggests, "Let's start with a little mystery." He places a blindfold over my eyes, and my anticipation builds as the world before me is clouded, then disappears. His lips meet mine, and his hands start to explore, sending shivers down my spine. He moves around me, kissing my neck, and I can feel the slow descent of my dress zipper, each gentle motion of his fingers brushing over my skin, making sparks fly. I step out of my dress, and Paul cuffs my hands, one at a time, teasing me with a delicate touch.

Leading me to the door, Paul turns me around so that I'm facing it this time. Then he breathes over my neck, and his hands glide sensually over my skin, tracing the curves of my back, my ass, and my thighs before sliding my panties off. As his hands journey back up, sliding fingers into me, I can't help but squirm in delight. The sensations are intoxicating, my body responding to his touch with an undeniable heat, and pooling liquid in my core. I fight against the urge to close my legs, and he takes one, and while massaging my clit, cuffs my leg to the side. He does the same with the other. I can't help it; I feel so exposed, and I want to shut my legs but it's impossible now; I'm completely restrained.

His hands resume their journey upwards, slipping inside me once more. Paul leans against me, his warm breath teasing my earlobe as he whispers, "Who's a bad girl trying to close her legs?" He punctuates his words with a firm slap on my bare ass. It's hard so that I still in surprise, but not as hard that it hurts. A shiver of pleasure arcs up my spine. I shift a bit, pushing back against him, the sensations electrifying.

"Do you like that?" he murmurs, his voice husky.

"Yes, yes," I gasp in response, and he rewards me with another tantalizing spank. Then, his hands encircle me, pulling me close to his chest. He leaves me for a moment, and I feel cold without his touch, but he returns quickly, kissing down my spine. I squirm, gasping, which is when I feel it: a light but firm whip on my thigh. It's his tie, I realise. He whips me with it for a few seconds, and I moan and gasp, telling him exactly how it felt.

He steps back, and I hear his clothes shuffling to the ground; he's undressing. This moment feels simultaneously intense and tender, as if I'm both restrained and safe in his hands. He spanks me a few more times, until I'm a gasping mess, and then Paul eventually takes me from behind. By this point, my desire is flowing like a river down my thighs, intensified by everything he's done to me – the cuffs, the ass spanking, and his tie, which I surprisingly find myself enjoying.

He moves inside me, the friction delicious against my clit, and soon we're both coming all over each other. Completely spent, he gently undoes the cuffs on my ankles and then my wrists. He takes me in his arms and leads me to bed; my legs are like jello at this point. Stretching out on the soft sheets, I let out a contented sigh. Paul spent the next ten minutes giving me a soothing massage. He used oil, his skilled hands gliding over my skin and paying special attention to my ass.

Leaning in, he whispers, "Your ass is a little red, darling. Are you okay?" I am barely awake, thoroughly fucked, my body still floating in the aftermath of our sex. "Better than okay," I murmur.

Paul stretches out beside me, and we both succumb to sleep.

***

The following morning, we rise early for work and take a refreshing shower together. As I glance at the restraints still hanging on the door, last night's memories haunt me, making me gasp. I couldn't help but smile as I got ready for the day.

At work, we delve into the plans for the shops, and Paul has arranged a meeting with an IT company that specializes in stock control and interlinking the shops with our main office. We discuss various options with them, to decide if their system could accommodate online sales.

As they're leaving Paul thanks them for their insights and informs them that two other companies will be presenting their proposals next week. He requests an inclusive quote for their services and bids them good luck.

Afterwards, we travel home together, our minds and bodies remembering the events of last night in intimate details. I say a sorrowful goodbye at the station as we do, and then head off home.

Upon returning, I notice that Mark was being attentive once again. It was becoming a noticeable trend, and I couldn't help but wonder what was going on with him. His sudden attentiveness discontinued when we went to bed, as if I were somehow contagious, but here in the living room and in the kitchen, he had eyes just for me. It was becoming exhausting.

Over the next week, I focus on my work, even though I am not yet assigned any new substantial projects. However, it doesn't bother me: I'm eagerly waiting for the upcoming weekend, my nerves and excitement building as I imagined the following Saturday night.

Chapter 23

On Thursday, while the train soundlessly carries us to London, Paul mentions that he has something in mind for the next few evenings. Naturally, my curiosity is piqued.

"Tonight," he says, "I want to go through the chest, and look through all the brochures, tickets, and mementos from events that Ralph and Lilly attended. Who knows, it might give us a glimpse of what to expect on Saturday evening."

I readily agree, excited to look through the brochures, now that I know what the events were about. "How about we order some take-out, make it a cosy evening?" I suggest.

Upon arriving at the office, we discover that the redecoration has already commenced. The space was being cleared to make way for the renovation work. One side of the office is completely barricaded, tarps covering every surface and some furniture. The offices were relocated to the other side, and until the work was completed, all rooms will be taken up, even the conference room that were previously only used for meetings. That left our current office to be used for meetings and discussions.

Around 11 AM, Nicola and Helen join us to provide an update on the renovation progress. The report is succinct, covers all aspects, and even gives us an update on what companies we've hired for work. Paul is pleased, and so am I; we detest reports that drone on and on.

"Thank you, Nicola, Helen. Please keep us updated. What about the furniture, where are we on that?"

While Paul gets the report, my mind wanders, craving for another coffee. Once they leave, Paul chuckles, "It seems that

Thursday 11AM is shaping up to be the designated management meeting time." I shake my head and get to work.

By noon, we have our first presentation from an IT company scheduled. Paul requests that both Helen and Nicola attend to gather their input on what we need. The same routine follows in the afternoon, with the two companies offering software solutions that appear quite similar to what we have already seen the previous week. Paul asks Nicola and Helen to provide their recommendations, taking into account the specifications, services, and quotations. I am tasked with evaluating the proposals from a cost-efficiency perspective. Another meeting is scheduled the following afternoon at 3 p.m. to review all three options and make a final decision to hand over this assignment and begin the changes.

As our workday concludes, Paul mentions that he has a few errands to run and will meet me at the apartment at six PM. I can't help but wonder where he was going; was it to the shop, Ralph's office, or some other undisclosed location? Still, I smile and wave him goodbye.

When Paul returns home, we decide on ordering takeout for dinner. Our collection of menus has grown over time, a consistent sheaf of glossy pages pressed under the paperweight on the living-room table. Tonight, we explore the secrets of the chest tucked away in the corner of our bedroom. While we await the arrival of our food, Paul lugs the wooden box out to the living room, all ready for tonight's adventure.

By seven PM, our dinner has been delivered, and come eight, we find ourselves seated in the living room, satiated and a bottle of wine within arm's reach, and the contents of the chest laid out before us.

We dive into the treasure trove of memories, selecting brochures and mementos at random. The first item to catch our eye is a ticket to an event called the Rubber Ball. I've heard of it from Nicole before, but she didn't give me many details. Judging from the date, it seems to be one of the last events Ralph and Lilly had attended. I halt Paul mid-reading through the brochure and run to my room to fetch my laptop. Although these events were not very mainstream, I am sure we'd find something about it online.

With the help of Google, we are treated to a visual spectacle of the Rubber Ball. The costumes were extravagant, and the attendees appeared unbothered- even ecstatic- to be photographed. Next, Paul holds up a brochure to an event known as Wasteland, hosted in Holland. It appeared to be an annual tradition for Ralph and Lilly to attend. The photographs showcased the diverse attire people wore; chains, leather, latex, hoops of various sizes, and in some cases, absolutely nothing at all. These events seemed to be a spiritual experience, the attendees glowing, sweaty, and overwhelmed with pleasure. I run a finger over their uninhibited faces, imagining what it must be like to participate freely in these festivals.

Among the memorabilia were also movie tickets and hotel bookings, not only in London but also in Holland and even farther-flung destinations. This chest, I realised, was a vivid diary of their shared life, documenting the places they had explored and the events they had reveled in together.

As we sift through the contents, we encounter a few photographs of Ralph and Lilly, similarly dressed in elaborate outfits. Latex and leather seemed to be recurring themes, and Lilly's beauty, especially when adorned in corsets, shone brightly in those images. I could tell from the fearless set of her eyes and the intelligence in them that she was up for anything she enjoyed.

For three captivating hours we flip through this diary of sorts, now looking through the lens of someone who was in on the secret. It was a treasure trove of experiences, and despite the constraints of time, Ralph and Lilly had truly seized every opportunity to live life to the fullest when they were together.

It's past eleven when we call it a night, but our conversation carries on as we head to bed, our minds still abuzz with the exciting discoveries from the chest and the memories of the couple's vibrant life together.

Friday was a typical workday, and once again, Paul does his mysterious disappearing act. I wonder again where he was sneaking off too, but Joan had promptly called me about some discrepancy in the pharmacy accounts and I went in my office to talk about it with her. He was still not back when I was done with the call, and the curiosity was killing me. I was about to ask Nicola what this time slot was scheduled for in Paul's calendar when a message popped up on my phone.

Paul: *The usual pub for lunch, and Adam will join us so we can make arrangements for tomorrow night.*

The event! Tomorrow!

Maria: *It'll be great to make a plan. See you there.*

My message couldn't even begin to relay how excited I was for the day to arrive, and now that it was close, the only thing keeping me sane and not screaming out with anticipation was simply not thinking about it. As soon as a thought about it pooped into my brain, I willed my brain to think about toothpaste, or my creaking chair at DAF. Anything inane over it.

I arrive at one in the afternoon at our usual place, but Paul is nowhere around. Instead, I see Adam at our usual table, gazing at his menu. Well, I know exactly where Paul *isn't,* so I go ahead and take a seat opposite Adam. While we wait for our food, we make a bit of small talk. I ask Adam, "Paul also seems very excited for tomorrow. Have you two been talking much these past days?"

"Oh, I'm sure he is. Although, no, other than a couple of phone calls, I haven't seen him since the last night we were all out together." Adam raises a brow but doesn't pry.

With our food also comes Paul, looking hurried and flushed, and we make our plans for tomorrow. The event is only a ten-minute drive from our place, and Adam suggests Nicole and he pick us up around eight, and we go onwards from there. Paul extends him an invitation to stay overnight at our place since it would be over an hour's worth of drive from their home, and Adam graciously thanks him.

"Nicole likes to be with her knick-knacks, but I'll ask her what she thinks." Adam wipes his mouth with a napkin.

I don't mind having these two over, because we do have a spare room, and I know for a fact that having Nicole accompany me would be a huge help. Before, and after the event. We ask a few more questions, and Adam nonchalantly answers us, even some of the stupid ones, like *Is there a code word to enter the establishment?* To which the answer was of course, *No, you just have to whistle thrice.*

Back at the office just as things are winding down, Helen and Nicola unveil their analysis for the IT companies. They have a preference system in place, and I have meticulously reviewed the costs. Regardless of which of the three options we chose, the cost was pretty much on par. So, it came down to selecting the right system, bundled with a company that could offer nationwide support. By the end of the day, Paul gave his nod to his managers' choice and signed off on the order, suggesting they try to negotiate the price down a bit but ultimately go with the chosen company.

That night after a laid-back dinner, we decide to go out for a stroll through Leicester Square, soaking in the vibrant atmosphere. The streets were teeming with theatregoers, and we couldn't help but revel in the buzz. We made it back to the apartment around eleven, contentedly enjoying each other's company before going off to sleep.

***

Saturday morning arrives, and I am absolutely giddy with excitement. I can't contain myself, so I gently nudge Paul awake. "Tonight is the night!" I exclaim, practically vibrating with enthusiasm. He blinks at me, still half-asleep, with a bemused expression. "You're like a giddy teenager," he teases. "Alright, let's make the most of the day. Breakfast in Covent Garden?"

Thankfully, Covent Garden isn't too crowded, and we snag a table without much trouble. We indulge in a leisurely breakfast- creamy eggs and crispy bacon, with a tall latte-before taking a stroll down Strand Street. The morning is sunny, perfect for some window shopping. We meander past clothing boutiques, furniture stores, and electronics shops, all the while relishing the warmth of the sun on our backs and each other's hands at our waists. There's much time to kill; the air feels electric with anticipation, like we're holding our breath, waiting for something to happen.

I have my hair and makeup appointment booked for three, so we enjoy a leisurely walks and window shop. After a quick nap while Paul read a book, I head off to the salon for a delightful two-and-a-half-hour session of pampering and primping. I luxuriate while my hair gets done, thinking for the hundredth time what the event would be like, what I'd look like there. How would Paul feel?

I come home to find Paul sprawled on the sofa reading his books. As I'm passing by him, he grabs me by my hand and pulls me in his lap, capturing my mouth in a kiss. I gasp in surprise and my mouth opens, and he dives inside, making me moan. I don't care about my lipstick or hair, I try to deepen the kiss, but he lets me go, a mischievous smile playing on his lips.

The clock was inching towards 7pm, and it was time to get ready. Paul lends a hand as I slip into my dress, and then he lovingly applies the finishing touches, rubbing a shine onto the fabric. His touch feels incredibly sensual, like he is caressing my very skin through the black cloth that molds over my body.

I feel incredible, almost like I am living in a dream. I slip on a light coat over my dress, while Paul turns around to get into his outfit. He looks dashing, all chest and broad shoulders, but the design makes him look like he's already had a wild night out. I wonder if his outfit came pre-shined, but he catches me watching him confusedly.

"Did it come like that?"

"Like what?"

"All cool and shiny?"

"You think I look cool?" He smiles his charming smile, and I almost melt right there.

"And shiny."

"I did it while you were at the hairdressers."

Paul's phone rings and he picks it up, mouthing 'Adam'. I nod and turn to fix my lipstick.

"Adam called to say they are only five minutes away."

We wait eagerly as they turn around the corner, and then hop into the taxi with them. Our destination was a mystery to me, and I was convinced Paul had no idea either. The ride was just over ten minutes, as Adam had promised. It gave me barely enough time to process my excitement and nervousness.

When we get out of the taxi, all I can see is the massive entrance to an exclusive nightclub. As we approach the entrance, Adam smoothly produces four tickets, and the concierge greets him like an old friend. It is clear they are well-acquainted with each other.

As we enter the venue and check our coats, our eyes widen in astonishment. Nicole couldn't help but chuckle. "Come on, let's find the bar. You two look like you could use a drink." Wise words, I think, and eagerly followed her lead before she had to scrape my jaw off the floor.

At the bar, we order a round of stiff drinks and take a moment to take in the surroundings. The scene before us was a kaleidoscope of latex, leather, costumes, corsets, and outfits that defied conventional description. It was like stepping into a fashion carnival. People wore heavy chains around their neck —and genitals — being led around by other people.

Adam leans in and whispers. "House rules to get you started: No sex on the premises, and no full frontal, among others," he says with a sly grin. "But, you'll notice that some rules are, well, bent a bit, especially in the playrooms. Out here, we've got the bar, the dance floor, and the main areas. But this place has multiple floors and some dedicated playrooms."

"Playrooms?" I ask, raising an eyebrow. Adam nods, and Nicole adds, "Yes, in those rooms, you'll see just about everything. People tied to crosses, in cages, being whipped, flogged, spanked, restrained, and rope suspension. Really, anything they consent to. You're welcome to watch and use the equipment if you like. Although, maybe that's a bit too much for night one." She looks at my wide mouth and Paul's creeping blush.

I chase my tequila shot with a quick laugh. Paul joins in, clearly as nervous about tonight's adventure as I was. We wander through the crowd, gawking at the astonishing array of outfits and costumes. Nicole advises us to meet back at the same spot in the bar in two hours if we happen to get separated. They guide us for about half an hour, and then Nicole says, "Alright, playtime." With that, they led us into a room that buzzed with a completely different vibe. You could practically feel the anticipation—and something else— in the air.

The first thing that catches my attention is a cross- it's in the center of the room. A woman, her back facing the audience, is cuffed to it, while a man expertly wields a flogger, sweeping it gently over her back. I watch as the man jerks the flogger before it kisses the woman's skin, and a shiver of anticipation courses through the room. The impact is sharp; at first, there is a bite of pain, a fleeting sting that sends ripples of sensation across her body. Her back arches, and she lets out a soft gasp, of surprise and arousal.

The crowd watches the skilled practitioner with the flogger, and it's evident that this wasn't merely about pain; it was a delicate art of sensation and connection. This was about after the strike- when, almost like magic, the pain transforms into something entirely different. It shifts into a delicious pleasure, radiating from the points where the flogger has touched her skin to every nerve ending of her body. Each strike awakened a dormant fire within her, igniting a desire she wanted worshipped. The rhythmic impact of the flogger becomes a dance, a sensuous caress that seems to pull her deeper into a trance of sensation. Her eyes close, and she surrenders to the experience, her body reacting with a symphony of pleasure and desire.

It was a unique and intoxicating blend of pain and pleasure, a delicate balance that leaves her yearning for more when the man pauses to run a hand over her behind. His actions are filled with genuine care for the woman he was flogging, ensuring her well-being. I don't realise how close I'm standing to them until the man addresses me directly, "Do you want to try?" He asks, like that wasn't the most insane thing.

I quickly blubber a no, and look at Paul for confirmation. I can tell by his expression that he's aroused by the exhibition before us- I am, too- but he isn't enjoying it so much. We continue wandering, venturing further down the playrooms, and encounter a variety of scenes – a man dressed up inside a cage, I baulk unbelievingly, and Paul pushes me onward. In the next room, a young woman is bent over a bench, her wrists clasped to the chains buckled in the ground. I notice amusedly that her skirt barely covers her behind- but my smile falters and then disappears as a man, dressed in a crisp suit, brings down a slim cane in an arc over her bottom. The cane leaves an angry red line behind, and I almost scream as tiny pinpricks of blood ooze from the line.

Paul shivers beside me and wraps a protective arm around me, "Oh. Oh, no." he murmurs, his voice trembling, "That is not my cup of tea." I nod my agreement. That looked more painful than what any pleasure could be worth.

"The cross was fun, though," I say, and watch as expressions fly across his face.

As we were going in and out of playrooms, Nicole and Adam wandered off, leaving us to our own devices. We're going towards another playroom, leaving the painful caning and shrieks behind, when my attention is drawn to an amorous couple in the corner, the woman is sitting in the man's lap, his one hand supporting her back, and the other between their legs. She's lost in the movement, languidly moving over him, and his head is thrown back in ecstasy, as her lips suck the nook of his neck. Well, a rule or two was broken but they seemed to be enjoying themselves. A lot.

Observing discreetly, I murmur to Paul, "And here I believed that wasn't allowed."

Paul looks and tries to say something, but his tongue falters when he realises what's actually going on.

360

The woman is still moving slowly over the man, as the knuckles of his hand tighten over her waist urging her to bounce, but she keeps the pace slow, torturing him. Meanwhile, his hand is working steadily between her legs. She's wearing a short skirt and a corset top, which conceals some of what they're doing, but the quiet corner does help them from being escorted out of the premises.

We're still discreetly watching the couple in the corner, when the flogging couple on the cross are exiting the playroom.

The man catches my eye, "Hi, again. New to the scene, huh?"

Maybe it's this heady place, the absolute ridiculous things going on, or maybe it's just us, but we laugh boisterously. "We look that green?"

The woman— her eyes gleaming, and her cheeks flushed with pleasure— smiles, "Just a guess. Love what you guys have on. Sure, you won't try the cross?"

"Maybe next time." I say, at the same time Paul says, "We're complete beginners."

Paul and I exchange a glance. I'd hate to look silly with the thing, and it looked like it could do real damage if used improperly. From the look on his face, I was glad that Paul had the same thoughts going on in his head. The couple looks at me, to Paul, then back at me. The man raises a brow, but nods in understanding, "Ah, you'll get there. You've never used a flogger before?"

Paul clears his throat, "No, not yet."

Not yet. I smile widely.

The man hands Paul his flogger, and gestures at me to feel the tails. I run my fingers over it, surprised at how soft they feel.

"You'll see many varieties in the market, cheaper ones that are harsh, they could draw blood. Feel the tails, if they're soft you're on the right track. A good one like this is like a feather's touch, soft but provoking." He explains, "Would you like to feel it?"

361

Paul and I exchange a glance and then cautiously nod.

"Feel the tails." He says, raising the flogger over our extended arms and bringing it down in an arc; the flogger lightly kisses my skin, and I hear the distinct crack of its tails. Surprisingly, it isn't painful; instead, it feels oddly pleasant. Like fingertips on so many parts of my arm. The tails are soft, almost sensual to the touch. He places the flogger in my hand, and I marvel at its silkiness.

"There are floggers that are beaded at the end. That's some high-end stuff. Don't start there, the pain could easily put you off this whole thing. Explore gently, and you'll find your zone." He smiles and the woman takes his arm. "See you soon. Say hello if you spot us," she says, and they saunter off. Only after they've left that I remember we did not even ask them their names.

We continue our playroom exploration and enter another room. This one was dimly lit, shadows dancing sensuously on the walls. A soft, sultry scent hung in the air, incense and something more primal. In the center of the room, a sensual scene unfolded. Adam was restrained, his muscular form pressed against an inverted cross. Nicole, a vision of commanding sensuality, stood beside him. Her leather-clad figure oozed dominance and control.

She held a whip, its slender black tail glistening in the dim light. With a seductive grace, she raised it above her head and then brought it down upon Adam's back. Paul's hand tightens over mine. The sound is sharp, shocking, a symphony of pleasure and pain that leaves the room heavy with tension.

Adam gasps and shudders, but makes no noise. Nicole strikes again, and again. Every strike of the whip sends shockwaves of sensation through him, ecstasy dancing on the fine line of between pleasure and pain. Nicole whispers something in Adam's ear, and he nods briefly, finally losing the tension in his jaw. From then on, he punctuates every strike with a moan, his sounds making the audience lick their lips and tighten their arms around their partners. I watch as one of the couples breaks apart from the main audience, pressing against

362

the wall to ravenously make out, their hands going everywhere, their noises spurring on the couple in the center of the room.

We watch, captivated by the erotic dance of the whip lashing and curling over Adam. The rise and fall of Adam's chest, Nicole's practiced hand, every strike coming from her shoulders. An intoxicating scent of arousal hangs heavy in the air, and our hearts race in tandem with the intimate, unspoken connection between Adam and Nicole.

Suddenly mindful of their privacy, we eventually tear ourselves away, and retreat to the bar.

The drinks flowed, and Adam and Nicole checked in with us from time to time. The clock's hands steadily approached 2 am, and we decided it was time to call it a night.

Adam and Nicole, accepting our offer to stay the night at our place, had left their bag in the Toy shop. We picked it up on the way back to our apartment. When we return, the atmosphere is still charged with the night's excitement. We all shed our coats, and sit around the living room table, still dressed to the nines, eagerly recounting the events of the playrooms we'd visited. We described the rule-breaking couple in the corner who carried their secrets beneath loose skirts and cleverly selected corners.

Adam and Nicola giggle. "Oh, that does go on. Although very discreetly. Voyeurs are not very happy with that rule, but alas, it *is* the rule."

Nicole, always perceptive and playful, gently teases us about catching our open-mouthed observation of their exhibition earlier in the evening. Blushing, I begin to stammer a response, but she interrupts me, "Don't worry, if we didn't want you to watch, we wouldn't have played there. Plus, half the fun is being watched, in the thrill of the people's eyes." She smiles, "Plus tonight I wasn't naked, so, it's all fine."

"Uh, not naked *tonight?!*" I gasp.

With a knowing smirk and a wink, she bites her lip, "Sometimes I am," she shrugs, "In places more exclusive, not on visitors' nights. Anyway, go off, you two, go to bed. I'm sure both of you have lots to discuss. We can talk more if you like, tomorrow over a late breakfast or early lunch."

Although my mind was buzzing, we agreed, realising we did indeed have a lot to think about, both as couples and individuals. Finally alone, tired, but faintly excited, we shut our bedroom door behind us. Paul helps me out of my dress, and we immediately collapse into bed. Wrapped in his arms, I kissed his bare chest tenderly, my mind still racing with the night's memories.

"Darling," he begins, his voice soft and thoughtful, "what did you think about everything? His fingers trace delicate patterns on my back. His touch is both soothing and electrifying, sending shivers down my spine.

"It was amazing," I admit, a warm smile spreading across my face. "It was a big club, full of consenting adults having a blast. The average age was probably close to ours. The play was … varied, but I enjoyed looking at most of it. And you? What did you think?"

Paul's fingers dance lightly over my skin as he replies, "I had a great time too. It felt safe, and everyone there was just out for a good time. As for the play, it was varied, as you said. The cross looked right up our alley, just a step up from our door restraints and hook. And the tails on that flogger... surprising, right? It's definitely something I'd like to try someday, if you're up for it."

"Oh, I am," I whisper into his chest, giving him small kisses. Even though I'm sleepy, I have an insane urge to feel him, against me, over me, inside me. I look up at his hooded eyes, and realise he's half drifted off to sleep. Smiling, I close my eyes, surrendering to sweet slumber, wrapped in each other's arms.

***

I stretch awake at 10:30, yawning, and squinting at the persistent sunlight streaming through the window. Paul is still asleep beside me, but I catch his glory, warm and stiff beneath the sheets. I roll onto him straddling his length as I wake him,

364

trailing kisses over his neck to his chest. I palm him, massaging him slowly, then fast.

"I never expected to feel like this about anyone again," he murmurs, sealing the sentiment with a tender kiss. He holds me close, his sleepy words slurred but touching my heart. I pause my administrations, taking in his sincerity, and then resume, my hand roving over him slowly. His fingers trail feather-light touches along my spine, coming to rest over my ass, fingers splayed and digging into my skin.

I move to remove the sheet from between us and wrap him inside my warmth when our intimate moment is interrupted by movement in the living area. I realise belatedly that we have company over, and a new day has begun. Paul groans, then laughs, kissing me deeply, and then plunging his fingers inside me. As he moves, I move too, until his thumb comes to play over my clit and I cease all movement, helplessly taking in all the sensations. His thumb makes circles over my clit, while his fingers start a punishing rhythm. He takes my breast into his mouth, and soon I'm coming, releasing all the pent-up energy from last night onto his hand. He coaxes the last of my orgasm from me, and I lay there panting as he kisses me deeply.

Spent, but not satiated, I don a robe, throw Paul's over to him, and go head for my shower. Paul hangs back, a smile on his face, the sheets now crumpled at his foot.

Outside, on the way to the shower, I encounter Nicole, who greets me with a playful smile and a knowing smirk. "Have fun!" she teases, her eyes twinkling mischievously.

After my shower, I return to the bedroom, and Paul heads for his own. I overhear Nicole's cheeky comment to him, "You need an even bigger shower." Her playful spirit is contagious, and I find myself growing fonder of her with each passing moment.

Once we are all dressed and ready, they suggest we go for an early lunch. We leave the apartment and soon find a restaurant where we settle in and place our orders. Amidst the clinking of cutlery and the murmur of conversation around us, Adam broaches the topic of our recent adventures.

"So, guys," he begins with a grin, "how was your journey to the dark side? Ralph wanted you to look through the curtain, and it seems you've had a good look and maybe even sampled some stock from the shop. So, is this the end of the road, or just the beginning?"

I can barely contain my enthusiasm, "Definitely the start! We absolutely loved the event and the club, not to mention watching the play. There's so much for us to think about and explore." Paul takes my hand in his.

Adam chuckles heartily, seemingly unsurprised by our eagerness. "We had a hunch," he quipped, "Well, welcome to the world of possibilities. If there's anything we can do to help or if you ever want to tag along to other events, just give us a shout. Last night was visitors' night- they happen twice a month, so we'll keep a lookout for you two."

Eventually, curiosity got the best of me, and I asked about Wasteland, recalling the numerous old tickets we had found among Ralph's papers. Nicole's laughter fills the air as she responds, "You two are quite the adventurers, aren't you? Wasteland is like last night, but on a grander scale. It happens twice a year in Holland, and Ralph and Lilly attended most of them. They stayed the weekend in Amsterdam while they were there. My advice would be to explore more of what you like in terms of play and go from there."

I nod, "Thanks. One last question, the whip you had last night, could I see it before we head back? And perhaps, where could we get one like it?"

Nicole graciously agreed, "I'll show you, maybe even teach you if you'd like. It takes quite a bit of effort to get used to it- not hurting yourself or your partner." Adam adds with a laugh, "You're welcome to see it, but the funniest part is that they're in the shop—you know, the same shop you were checking out earlier. We have dozens on sale."

The thought evoked all kinds of feelings inside me, but I'd need to talk to Paul before going forward with anything. This was for both of us, always.

After our lunch, we return to the apartment to retrieve our bags and prepare to leave. Adam kindly shows us the whip, its tail as soft as the flogger the couple from last night had demonstrated for us the night before. Adam and Nicole take their leave amidst warm goodbyes, and soon we're ready to catch our train back home.

The train ride home is relatively quiet, filled with a contemplative silence. We knew it would be two weeks before I could return back to London. I wished, in that moment, that my vacation was with Paul, instead of Mark. Resentment and regret built inside me, but Paul caught onto my mood, and kissed away the negative thoughts.

As I disembark from the train, Paul lingers behind. Mark had texted that he was there to pick me up with the kids. When I spotted them, I acted excited, but tired.

"I'm exhausted," I tell Mark with a sigh. "Work has been so demanding lately, especially yesterday and this morning. I had to get everything sorted out until the minute I was leaving."

Chapter 24

For the next two weeks, I find myself entrenched in the bustling projects in Manchester and the daily grind of my pre-Paul office life.

Meanwhile, Paul was on a mission to reclaim his time. Although Leonard was a good friend of his, negotiating for a three-day workweek was proving to be difficult. He was also making appearances at the Manchester store of the sports shop sporadically. The building had been empty for a while now, except for the ground floor occupied by the shop, and he dropped hints about potential tenants for the first and second floors of the building. There would be the necessary cleanup and renovations to prepare the space, and some sprucing up, but it all sounded quite promising, and it was evident that he relished these new challenges.

"Tell me more about these tenants," I prod, missing more than just his voice.

I imagined him shrugging, "They're gonna rent the offices, similar to the previous tenant. Nothing particularly interesting—typical administrative offices and staff."

In the back of my mind, I know that even if his current employer refused to condense his workweek, Paul has the means to walk away. His new-found wealth and his role in the various companies afforded him that luxury. It was clear that his priorities had shifted, aligning more with the future of Ralph's estate than his career as a solicitor.

As for my own work, it remains a monotonous affair, devoid of any excitement. Daily phone calls with Paul are my saving grace, a connection to a world that doesn't make me want to scratch at the walls with my nails. Every Thursday, like clockwork, he messages me from the London train as soon as he's seated, as if travelling there without me in any form is incomprehensible. Arrive in London he calls me, knowing I am on my way to an office without him.

Paul's voice crackles through the line, filled with subtle amusement. "The journey felt different without you. I ended up sitting next to 24A on the train," he chuckles, "The cheeky punk said, 'looks like you aren't as lucky with the seat this week.'"

I snicker, "What did you say?"

"I said 'Well, not every week can't be perfect, can it?'"

I laugh, teasing him, "I suppose payback's a bitch. You deserved that; you know. Making fun of that man every week."

"He had his eyes on mine. Anyway, how's everything going at your end?"

I sigh, contemplating the situation. "It's the same old routine here. Working away, missing London more than a bit this week. But I'm there in spirit. On top of it all, Mark left this morning on an early flight, so I'm on kid duty tonight. Joan's away for the weekend, assuming I was in London, so she booked her holidays. It's like my right hand is missing. I absolutely despise dealing with temps."

I inhale deeply, centering myself, "What's on your agenda for this week?"

I hear the traffic pass by him, even so early in the morning; he hails a taxi, and the world is muted again, "The usual meetings at 11 a.m., overseeing the ongoing work, and attending to renovation work. So many papers to sign, you won't believe. By the way, are you available for an 11 a.m. conference call with Helen and Nicola?"

"Sure, I'll be there." I readily agree, knowing that even amidst the mundane, our conversations provide a much-needed spark in my day. And as soon as our call ends, I'm sucked into the aforementioned mundane again.

The clock strikes eleven, and my phone comes to life with a ringing tone. On the other end are Helen, Nicola, and Paul, ready to dive into our conference call. Without delay, Nicola and Helen launch into a rapid-fire update.

They inform us that the stock control software has been ordered and is on its way. Installers are currently conducting thorough shop audits, assessing the state of our existing IT infrastructure and identifying areas in need of replacement or upgrade.

Paul listens attentively, letting them finish before he speaks. "Alright. Is there anything else on the agenda, ladies?"

Helen and Nicola are quiet, likely wondering what Paul has up his sleeve now. Nicola's voice comes through, "That covers the main points for now, Paul."

Paul leans back, from the audible creaking of his chair, "Alright, now for the final piece of my master plan."

"Go on, then. We're all ears."

Paul began, "We're making great progress with the shop upgrades and centralizing our IT. Soon, our online store will be up and running, and the only decision left is where to manage our distribution. We need to determine if our existing warehouse can handle it or if we should consider a new one. But here's the thing, Brexit is looming on the horizon, whether we like it or not."

He taps his fingers gently on the desk. "If it indeed does happen, we don't know how our exports will be tariffed. To Brexit-proof ourselves to some extent, we should explore the possibility of setting up another physical shop. In an EU country. This way, if orders come in, we can service them from within the EU itself. We'll need to carefully consider where and how we'll manage EU sales, but the concept is fairly straightforward."

There's a pregnant pause, and then he clears his throat. "So, what are your initial thoughts, everyone?"

Nicola's clear voice comes through the speaker, "That is a bold move, I must say. The EU market is not saturated yet, but it will be hard to break through. But going online means more reach. And we should be ready to service it. You think we can sell outside of the UK?"

"Well, I'm optimistic. With the right strategy, partnerships, and a strong brand presence, I believe we can. Starting with selling on platforms like Amazon and expanding from there. But it won't be a walk in the park, that's for sure." Paul says.

I give my two-cents, "I think it's a smart idea, from the tax POV. Many UK companies are doing something similar to safeguard their EU trade, given the uncertainty surrounding Brexit. It's a proactive approach."

I hmph, and then ask, "Why don't we all take a week to think about it? Research potential locations and weigh the pros and cons. Let's not only consider it as a shop but also as a hub for managing EU stock and handling shipping for EU sales. If we can grow that side of the business, it could be a game-changer."

With a plan in place, we wrap up the meeting. Later that evening, Paul calls me again, this time from the apartment, "This place doesn't feel the same without you. Not like a home... very lifeless and empty. I miss you," he confesses, yearning for my presence. "A glass of wine, dinner, and just being together would be perfect."

We spend the evening chatting intermittently. Once the kids are off to bed, I call him again. "Tell me a story. What would we do if we were together right now?" I croon from my bed, drowning myself in the soft sheets and pillows.

He tells me about the things on his mind right now: the EU trade, the renovation, his career. He tells me how gorgeous a night it would be if we were together, and goes into detail about what we'd do together, all the screaming and the moaning that will be involved.

I drift off to his voice caressing my ear.

***

Mark returns home on Sunday, looking utterly exhausted after his long weekend in Holland with the lads. I muster some feigned interest in his football match and weekend escapades, although the world of sports is as interesting to me as a garbage patch.

"Did you have fun there?"

"Mhm." He replied, not in a very chatty mood.

With fatigue hanging over him, he headed straight to bed. I unpack his luggage, sorting out the laundry. I can't help but notice the lack of a gift, even a small souvenir from his trip for me. There used to be perfume bottles or chocolates grabbed at the last second as an afterthought a few years back— now, not that either.

***

Monday brought news from Paul, who shared that his boss had reluctantly approved the three-day workweek arrangement. However, the concession came with a condition: all external legal work from Ralph's shops and the business would be directed to Paul's law firm. Leonard had snagged a big piece of business in this deal. It was a shrewd trade-off, but I couldn't help feeling relieved that this new work schedule was falling into place.

"How's the news of the EU warehouse come outlet going over at the office?" I ask, knowing for some of the staff this project was going to be the most exciting thing they'd ever work on at this company.

"Oh, ho, ho. It's like Christmas. The office is buzzing with discussions about the EU and potential trade challenges. Lots of discussion, plenty of back and forth. Checking with supplier to see will they supply outside the UK to us. I wonder what Helen and Nicola will come up with."

Curiosity got the best of me. "Are there any specific criteria we need to consider for this venture, though? What have you found out yet?" I ask. I know for a fact Paul wouldn't touch anything new with a ten-foot pole if he hadn't looked into it extensively.

Paul responds nonchalantly, "Well, we'll need a robust shipment facility across the EU, efficient courier systems, and the like."

"Hm, I see," He was holding his cards close, but that was just Paul. "So, this Thursday's going to be our last night together for a while, do you have anything special in mind?"

"Whatever the lady says, gets done," Paul says amusedly.

"Cop out," I smile, laying out my plans. "Alright, you're going to book us a nice dinner, and we'll head out early. Then, you're going to take me back to the apartment, and we'll have some fun playtime. Oh, also, pick up something new from the shop to play with."

Paul chuckles, resignedly happy. "Well, I better get busy then, don't I?"

"That's my good boy." I chuckled and hang up.

***

Tuesday brings Joan back into the picture, and I can't help but sigh in relief. Joan gets half my work done, and just the way I like it, too. She looks bright and glowing, and I ask her about her holiday. She recounts a great long weekend spent with friends, filled with fun, drinks and adventure.

Tuesday and Wednesday I throw myself into tying up all the loose ends before my upcoming holiday. All the paperwork is up to date, signatures have been done, reports have been mailed in and I have also briefed the team on all proceedings in case something comes up while I'm away.

Jack asks me for a meeting on Wednesday, late in the day. He asks for an update and looks over the work and skims the reports I have prepared. I give him a scoop on the London job, but since that is also in the last stretch, there's nothing significant to report. "So, what's in the pipeline for when I come back?" I ask conversationally.

"We have a few handy jobs on the horizon that we can slot you into," he finally says.

"Alright. What about substantive due diligences or mop-up jobs? I could really use a challenge after this pharmacy thing."

Jack's response is measured, and he chooses his words carefully. "Maria, I don't foresee you handling large projects in the near future. You've ruffled a few feathers within management, especially when you declined the London assignment. That led to us losing a client."

373

I bristle at the implication. "Jack, let's be clear. I didn't lose that client. Justin did. I had my hands full already, commuting to London two days a week. It's not fair to offer me nothing and then expect me to cancel the first holiday I've taken in years."

He looks shocked, but his response is unwavering. "You'll need to rebuild some bridges, Maria, and show that you're a team player. I'm confident you'll bounce back quickly, don't worry."

Jack catches the frosty, frustrated look on my face and almost stumbles on his way out the door, realizing he might have pushed a bit too far. But that doesn't change anything. It's become evident that my attempt to assert myself has handsomely backfired, leaving things no different than they were before. But I've come this far, and hell if I'd take the fall for Justin's mess anymore. I want to call Paul and vent to him, but I decide to talk this over with Mark beforehand when I get home.

I take a glass of wine to the sofa where Mark is watching the television, and tug at his hand for attention. He takes the hint and switches off the TV. I regale him with my frustrations and worries, pouring over all the anger I've been feeling. Mark, ever the realist, listens to my account of the situation and doesn't mince words. He more or less echoes an "I told you so" sentiment and urges me to work on rectifying the situation-same as Jack had told me in the afternoon. His support feels lukewarm at best, and I can't help but feel disheartened. It quickly devolves into a chilly evening, and as Mark encourages me to make amends, something inside me breaks.

All my anger and Mark's surgical sharp words culminate in a bitter argument, the first in a long while. Frustration reaches its boiling point, and I unleash my pent-up emotions on Mark.

"Yes, why would you care if I'm *happy* or god forbid *content* in my career? All you need is a paycheck and childcare!" I scream, not caring if the children hear us.

"I'm just saying, you need to think about becoming stable again." Mark says, like he's talking to a child.

"Becoming stable? Are you hearing yourself? Becoming stable just means getting numb again, bearing every humiliation, looking the opposite way every time, I'm passed over." I'm breathing harshly, but Mark is as confused as ever.

"Maria, come on, calm down—"

After that, our argument escalates into a shouting match, a less-than-ideal way to prepare for our upcoming vacation.

"-I'm telling you that I'm fed up with it and you don't give a rat's ass about it!"

"Fine!" He screams back, "Do as you want, you will anyway," he spits before storming off.

***

As Thursday morning arrives, I find myself on the train, the weight of the previous week's turmoil heavy on my shoulders. Tears well up in my eyes, thinking of how disappointed I felt when I told Mark about the emotional burdens I am enduring. I fight to keep them at bay as I think of Paul. Unable to contain my distress any longer, I dial his number.

"Paul," I begin, my voice shaky, "I've had an absolutely horrible week. Jack's furious with me, and it's become crystal clear that I've been demoted to do the most menial of tasks, and I'll be stuck there until I 'learn my place.' I told Mark, and we had a colossal fight about it. He just wants me to suck it up and bear it." I say in a rush, sobbing heavily.

Paul is quiet as he takes it all in, then his soothing voice comes through, immediately calming my frayed nerves. "It's going to be alright, darling," he reassures me. "You'll get through this. Wait, I'm close by." He says, and I feel a hand over my shoulder. He smiles at me and both of us disconnect the call "Now, listen to me." He starts, taking my hands in his, and wiping the steady line of tears from my cheeks, "Let's head down to London, take care of what needs to be done there. Tonight, I've got a restaurant reservation for us, just as you wanted. Trust me, I know what will help you. We'll channel that anger and frustration and get you ready to move forward."

He pats my head lovingly, and although the gesture looks out of place, I am calmed by it.

I nod weakly and melt into his arms.

During the train ride to London, I pour out my heart to Paul, my grievances about work, Mark, and every other frustration that has been gnawing at me. He listens patiently, offering comfort and support, his presence a reassuring balm for my troubled soul. Just as the train is entering the station, Paul lifts my chin to face him.

"Now here's what you have to do," Paul begins, his tone firm yet reassuring. "You're not back in the office for over 2 weeks. That was your last day there! Take your holiday and think about what you want. Really think. List it all down, and then consider how you might accomplish those goals. When you come back, you and I are going to meet and have dinner, somewhere quiet, and talk. You'll tell me what you're thinking, what you want, everything. I'm here for you, Maria."

His words resonate with me, and I nod in agreement. It makes sense. I have the luxury of time away to reflect and plan for my future. But one thing I'm sure about: I feel stagnant at this time, in my career, at home. It feels like being stuck in mud, exhausted and dirty and just the intense urge to escape it and leave it all behind.

Paul and I head into the office, where a buzz of activity greets us. Painters work diligently, and a new kitchen and canteen are almost taking shape, complete with water heaters, microwaves, and a grill. A large fridge stands proudly in the corner. Paul observes the scene keenly but makes no comment.

As 11 am approaches, Nicola and Helen enter the room and take their seats. They launch into their report, detailing the ongoing renovations and the schedule for completing the office revamp. Paul listens attentively and then, with a smile, commends their work, adding, "Let's do this right! We only get to do this once."

Then, turning to the matter at hand, he prompts, "Now, what about last week's discussion? Any suggestions for a new shop or an EU hub? Maria, why don't you start?"

I take a moment to collect my thoughts before responding. "Alright, let's rule out Ireland due to the lack of a land bridge. I think we need to be close to a major airport hub. So, naturally, Paris, Berlin, or Amsterdam airports come to mind. I would lean towards Paris or somewhere in Holland for a shop. Simply because it's more accessible from here as well."

Paul nods and turns to Helen and Nicola. "Have you both come up with separate ideas or reached a consensus?"

Nicola speaks up, her tone confident. "We've looked at our individual lists and found that they align quite closely, so it's easier to present as one. We've settled on Holland due to Schiphol's status as a major air hub. We considered Belgium because DHL and other major couriers offer warehousing services there, which could be beneficial in the long term. We might be too small for that now, but who knows what the future holds. Paris is also a viable option."

"Thanks, Nicola. Great job on the DHL hub research, you two," Paul nods, his eyes gleaming with approval.

"I've also been looking, and it seems I've arrived at similar options," he reveals. "What if we aim to secure a shop in the Rotterdam area, maybe somewhere in South Holland? This would give us proximity to both Belgium and Holland, and it's close enough to the DHL hub that Nicola and Helen suggested. Over the next few months, we can go deeper into this."

All three of us nod in agreement.

"Thank you all for your contributions. Let's focus on getting the UK operations sorted and explore our sales options here. We have ample time to establish our EU base." He claps his hands, and exhales loudly.

The meeting concludes around noon, and Nicola, Helen and I shuffle out of Paul's office. I quickly get lost in my work, tossing back coffee after coffee. After half an hour, I notice Paul heading out, and I frown. I didn't think there was anything scheduled at this time in the weekly calendar he'd shared with me. A sense of curiosity about his whereabouts nags at me. Around 12:30, my phone buzzes with a message from him.

Paul: *Can't do lunch today, see you later or back at the Apartment for 6. Dinner booked for 7.*

Maria: *Alright... my man of mystery.*

At sharp six, Paul arrives at the Apartment, exclaiming, "Honey, I'm home," in a playful tone. I shoot back, "Your slippers and cardigan are by the door."

"May we never become that," I tease, as he comes to collapse beside me. "So, are you going to share where you go?"

He chuckles, "Ah, you know. I have to go through all the post that comes into Ralph's office. You'd be surprised what arrives. Also met the other tenants, and then, you know, there are things to do, places to go, and people to see." He trails off vaguely. I shake my head, squinting suspiciously at him.

***

"I'm ready. Hey, can you zip me up here?" I ask, deliberately giving him a glimpse of the lacy lingerie and suspenders, I am wearing. Tonight, I was in the mood for some play.

"Yeah, sure," he comes over innocently, then his eyes catch on the lace and his mouth waters. He clears his throat, his hands pause on the zip, holding his gaze on my back, "There, all done."

A taxi promptly arrives to ferry us to the restaurant for our 7 o'clock reservation.

As we savour our meal, Paul looks deeply into my eyes, his gaze studying every expression on my face, "How are you feeling now, after yesterday?"

I contemplate for a moment. "I'm still annoyed and a bit frustrated. Could really use something to hit," I admit with a laugh. "Maybe I need to take up self-defense classes. Good excuse to beat up things." He laughs, holds my gaze, then looks away.

After the delightful dinner, we decide to cap off the evening with drinks in the bar. Paul takes charge of calling a taxi, which whisks us back to the apartment in no time. Anticipation is bubbling inside me; I haven't forgotten, I asked him to pick up a new toy from the shop, and I have no idea what he's picked yet.

Once inside the apartment, Paul suggests, "Pour some wine; I'll get things sorted." He flashes a mischievous grin, a promise of something new and exciting, our own version of 'fun games'.

I take a swig of wine from my glass, and watch heatedly as Paul places restraints over the door, just the top ones. His actions are deliberate, and I can sense the anticipation building in the room. With a seductive air, he retrieves more cuffs and lays them out, then removes his shirt, revealing his bare chest. My eyes are glued to him as he stands there, shirtless and confident, waiting for me.

It's clear who is going to be the one tied up tonight, and tension bubbles deep, low in my belly. Paul looks at me with a hot gaze, "Darling?" he breathes, imploring me, positioning himself against the door, his back to me. I take off my heels, and softly move to the door, then lean against his burning skin. I kiss his back softly, and he breathes in, all heady sensation.

I secure him firmly to the door, then use the other pair of cuffs to bind his legs. "The chair," he murmurs, his cheeks flushed. I'm puzzled, and then his gaze meets mine, and without further question, I walk to the chair.

A towel is thrown over it, and I pick it up, the object under it stunning me, and my eyes widen in surprise. My head snaps back to him on the door, and a new sensation runs through me like lightning. Power. An overwhelming need to do this. To hear the tails of the flogger against his skin, the anticipation in his muscles for the next strike. I need it like I need my second breath. One flogger has a black leather handle with long, sensuous tails, while the other is slightly shorter with a steel handle, and shorter tails.

I glance back at Paul, feeling the weight of his gaze upon me. Before I lose my mind in desire, I ask him, "Are you sure about this?" There is no hesitation, only careful consideration. I want this; we're ready for it.

Paul reassures me through laboured breaths, "Yes. If it hurts too much or gets uncomfortable, I'll let you know. I know you're frustrated, darling. Channel it."

That was all I needed to hear. With a sultry confidence, I shed my dress, now in just my black heels, lace stockings held up by garters to my panties, and the sexy, lacey bra. The room crackles with tension as we venture into this new realm of sensuality and exploration.

With the whips in hand, I walk closer to Paul, my hands tenderly caressing his back, then I scour it lightly with my fingernails, and he gasps, his head turning back. Leaning in, I whisper softly, "Don't let me hurt you." Then I bite his earlobe, hard. He groans, his body going limp against me. I hold the steel handle against his skin, so he feels the hardness of it. Desire swims unashamed in his eyes as he nods and opens his mouth as if to ask for it.

I draw back, surveying his back like I was an artist and he, my canvas. And then, very deliberately, I draw back the flogger, raising it high, and bring it on his back with a crack. He shudders, but no sound escapes him. I bring it down again, this time a tad harder, and his chin falls against his chest. I flog him again, this time harder, and watch the tails dance through the air, beautiful and threatening.

"You doing okay there?" I ask, rubbing my palm across the faint red stripes across his back. He nods enthusiastically, urging me to continue. I whip him again, and again, and again, in quick succession, barely giving him the time to process the bite of the tail before bringing it down again. He is squirming now, his desire hard against the door. He moans in need, and I get the not-so-subtle hint. This time I strike him the hardest I've ever gone.

I see parts of his back turning a subtle shade of red. I tilt his face up to meet my gaze, "Doing okay?"

He licks his bottom lip and nods, "It sounds way worse than it feels. It's actually quite nice." he smiles, and I can't help but swoon. He looks absolutely ruined; his hair is a mess; his lips are swollen and wet and his face is a beautiful shade of pink. I nod, and swap the leather handle flogger for the metal hilted. I wonder how the different tails feel, are they softer or harder on the skin. Tonight is a night to explore.

Emboldened by his words, I trail the shorter tails teasingly over his back; then comes the swish and thud of the whip. A loud groan escapes his lips, and I feel myself dripping. My desire has been pooling since I realised Paul's intentions for tonight, and now it's spilling over, running down my thighs. I revel in the intoxicating sensation of power and release. This is escapism, the transcendence of sensuality and liberation.

Angry marks are left behind from the flogger's kiss, and I finger them, enjoying the look of him. Paul reacts under my touch. I bring the flogger down on his back again, then again. Repeatedly, until each strike elicits a moan from deep in his chest. Until he's panting, his mouth hanging open, his head bowed against his chest. Until there are tons of red streaks across his back, and it looks like a crazed painter took a brush to his back, haphazard, angry strokes against the canvas.

Leaning against Paul's warm body, I kiss the marks I've created on his back. He's breathing deeply, inhaling in small sharp bursts. My hand ventures lower and I find him rock hard; I'm glad he's enjoying this as much as I am. With each kiss, he groans harshly, squirming away from, and welcoming my touch at the same time.

We carry on for a while longer, the room filled with the echoes of our desires and the soft whistling of the whip. Eventually, it is time to unhook him, and I turn him around, and he joins our lips in a passionate kiss. "Oh, darling, that was-," he murmurs, thoughts evaporating from his mind as I start to pump him.

We kiss for a long time; him half restrained, me still holding the flogger in one hand, our lips like snare and prey at the same time. "Come on, let's go to bed." I murmur. I unhook his legs, then lead him to the bed, pushing him on the bed, his back raw against the soft sheets. He quickly adjusts, his eyes dark with desire. I shed off my bra, and his eyes latch onto my breasts as

I proceed-to straddle him, then slip slowly- torturously slow- over him, enveloping his length in my warmth.

He gasps, his breath strained, as if it's too much pleasure, and I see him reel against it, absorbing it all, but I don't slow now. I ride him like my life depends on it. His head falls back, and he's lost, and so am I, and soon, I'm falling over the edge, taking him with me. He screams when it hits him, holding my thighs in place so hard I'm sure I'll bruise. My orgasm rocks through me like a hurricane, stripping away everything from its place, making all my thoughts swirl widely. Even after I'm done and he's done, I continue sliding over him, until he begs me to stop.

We lay in the bed afterwards, boneless and spent, giggling and smiling. I tease at the now fading red lines on his back, scraping at them with my fingernails, and he reacts but doesn't move away, looking at me deeply. There's massage oil on my bedside table, something that always to hand here, and I apply it gently over the softening streaks on his back, as they fade to nothing. Paul sighs in utter contentment, then turns around and spoons me, enveloping me in the cage of his limbs.

As sleep overtakes me, I whisper, "Where did this idea come from?"

"You said you wanted to try it." It's all he says before both of us fall into deep sleep.

***

Friday morning arrives, and we get right into our little domestic routine. Paul pulls me into the shower with him, which takes way too long to finish, then we brush our teeth beside each other. Next, we untangle pieces of clothing from around the lamp, and retrieve some from under the bed where it had ended up last night. We eat together, then pack our bags.

I glance around the apartment as we're leaving, knowing I wouldn't be here for the next three weeks. I would miss this place terribly and, more importantly, him. Despite the impending gap in our time together, we carry on like usual at the office, focusing on work, deliberately avoiding any discussion about the separation ahead.

But the day wears on, and soon we're on the train back home. We share a leisurely dinner on the train ride, and our conversation flows easily, but as we near Manchester, Paul can sense my mood darkening. He nudges me, smiling and gently reminds me, "Enjoy the time off, alright? Whatever the circumstances are, you deserve this time to yourself." I nod but say nothing. I'm beginning to realise what three weeks without Paul's company would feel like, and I don't like it one bit.

"I won't text you, unless you text me first. This is entirely your holiday, no distractions." He flicks at my chin, and I finally smile. The lines around his eyes ease.

Before parting ways, I squeeze Paul's leg, a silent gesture of goodbye. We disembark and head off in our separate directions. With each step I take, I feel like I'm losing pieces of my heart, that Paul is taking away with him the best of me.

***

Upon arriving home, I find the children brimming with excitement as they finish packing their bags. Although most of the packing is done thanks to Ursula, everyone's running around the house looking to pack the last-minute knick-knacks.

Mark, who has been somewhat sheepish and withdrawn since our argument, inquiries about the children's passports. Irritation flickers inside me. *We're literally leaving, and he's worried about the children's passports now?!* I assure him that I have already taken care of them, annoyance clear in my voice.

"Well, uh, how was work?" He asks, still awkward. So many years of being married, and he is still acting like a teenager.

"London was fine. I won't be there again for around three weeks, so I had much to sort out there. As far as DAF goes, I'll take this time to really think about it. About what I want in the context of what's been happening recently." I reply curtly, then look at him with a challenge in my eyes to see if he's going to say something infuriating again. I conveniently leave out that this was Paul's suggestion.

He stays silent.

I shake my head and pack my Kindle with a selection of new books and prepare for a few weeks of relaxation by the pool in the warm sun. Maybe when I get back here, I will have a tan, and perhaps, some clarity about my future.

Chapter 25

We set off for the airport bright and early, eager to begin our family holiday. The children are playing loud summer songs, teasing each other and trading snacks. They have their straw hats, chiffon scarves, and suntan lotions all ready to go. I laugh loudly for the first time with my family in a long time.

Mark has packed his golf clubs, and I can't help but comment, "Isn't this supposed to be a family vacation?" I raise my brows.

He replies casually, "Well, I might get a round of golf or two in, see how it works out."

I decide not to push the issue any further, not wanting to start a fight in front of the children.

While enroute, I take a moment to check my phone habitually and notice an email from Jack. It was sent on Friday evening, and its contents immediately rubbed me the wrong way.

From: Jack
To: Maria
Dear Maria,

Can you send me a summary report on the Pharmacies, flagging any areas of concern? Can you also send me your end-of-the-month expense report in the next few days?
Regards,
Jack

All I can think is, 'What an asshole'. He is well aware that I am on holiday for the next two weeks. Was he trying to sour my vacation or add stress to it? Exasperation overwhelms me and I quickly fire back a response:

From: Maria
To: Jack
Jack,
I am on holiday for the next two weeks, as you are aware. The pharmacy reports are already available, and you can check with the team for any other questions or concerns. I will address any queries when I return.
Maria

I log out of my work email and throw my phone in my bag.

Upon arriving in Portugal, the children are overjoyed. The heat hits us hard as we step out of the airport, and their excitement is palpable. We pick up a rental car and make our way to the villa Mark has booked, conveniently close to Vilamoura.

The villa is lovely, with ample space and a beautiful pool. I can't help but feel a sense of relaxation wash over me. The children have the freedom to walk into town or to the nearby supermarket, while I plan on lounging around or inside the pool for the rest of the days. There are also a few sights nearby that we could check out for a day trip with the family.

As we enter the villa, we are greeted by glaring sunlight streaming in through the tall windows, white interior and plenty of couches and cushions to go around.

Mark gestures at the kitchen, addressing me, "Check to see if everything works," with an implied expectation of my involvement in cooking.

I shoot him a look and retort, "Unless you plan on being the chef, the state of this kitchen won't matter much. It'd be nice of you to remember that all of us are on holiday."

His jaw works, but he wisely chooses to simply say, "Of course."

For the next two weeks, I relish the warm weather, indulging in long walks to soak in the serene surroundings.

386

Mark ventures off with his golf clubs most days. In the beginning, I remain quiet, silently observing his daily outings. But eventually, I can't contain my frustration and ask, "Are we ever going to see you during the day?"

He sighs, "How about we plan a day trip tomorrow?"

"Anything would be appreciated," I say. "The kids need some activities too, you know. And if you're out every day, and I'm here entertaining them, where's my break? Maybe you should've brought Ursula if you wanted a babysitter while you golfed the day away. I'm entitled to some time to myself." I finish firmly.

He nods absently.

Over the next few days, I ensure I have a few hours to myself, and I go on solitary walks to clear my mind. By the end of the first week, I tell Mark that I have booked a sitter so we can have dinner alone. His forehead creases but he nods, saying nothing. During our meal, he asks, "So, why the dinner alone?"

"I want to tell you what's been on my mind these days. I've thought and thought about it, and I've come to this conclusion: I'm way too dissatisfied with work, there's no challenge, no excitement. I don't know what I'm going to do, but I will be looking for more opportunities as soon as we're back home."

Mark is silent. When I finish, he simply remarks, "We need the money, and you need to work. Can't you just stick it out?"

Frustration bubbles within me as I counter, begging him to understand, "Why should I? You love your job, your grand projects, and your towering buildings. Why can't I have the same? I want to be able to enjoy my work again." I'm completely vexed at this man, drained to the last drop of energy.

"Maria, I want you to enjoy work again. But enjoyment is secondary, and money is primary, isn't it? You're just having a rough patch," Mark says like that is reassuring.

But all I can think is why can't he understand my yearning for job satisfaction too? I can't take this; I ask him point-blank, "Is my paycheck all you're interested in every week?"

Mark's response is reserved, which tells me everything I need to know, "Let's just enjoy the holiday. You need a break."

"Okay," I reply, a tinge of bitterness in my voice, "At least I know that as long as I'm earning, you're not concerned."

We say no more about it. The night is spent in strained silence. Over the next week, Mark plays golf for four days, and we go on a few day trips with the children, visit Lagos, go shopping at the Center, and also cover some tourist spots. I indulge in plenty of beach and pool time, for my part.

Seeing our three children so happy, playing together without the usual bickering, is a delight. I maintain daily contact with Paul, sending him selfies by the pool or while out walking. I wish he was here with me, someone to talk to who would listen and provide support.

Mark refrains from bringing up work during our vacation. As we are packing up the night before our flight home, he casually remarks, "I hope you enjoyed the holiday and are feeling better. Back to work on Monday, and you'll be just fine."

I remain silent, choosing not to respond. To Mark, I am just an emotional woman who does and says things she doesn't mean. But I meant each word I said to him at dinner that night.

As we settle into our seats on the flight home, luck is on my side - my seat is two rows behind Mark and the kids. I close my eyes, pretending to sleep, but my mind is racing.

Over the past two weeks, Mark had hardly shown any affection toward me. He was pleasant most of the time and enjoyed his moments with the kids, but he made the holiday all about himself, making no real effort for me. Even when I lounged by the pool in a bikini, and I didn't think I looked too shabby, he didn't offer a single comment, not even in jest. It takes us two weeks to get into bed together, and even then, alcohol is involved, and I can tell he's doing it half-heartedly. I sigh loudly, thinking, *what am I doing with my life?*

Chapter 26

On Monday morning, I step back into the familiar hustle and bustle of the office. The holiday has been a much-needed break, and I'm adequately recharged for the difficult times I'm sure are right around the corner. Joan welcomes me back with a warm smile and a hug, and I promptly present the customary airport chocolates that everyone expects when a colleague returns from a holiday. She pops one into her mouth, relishing the treat.

"So, what fun did I miss?" I inquire playfully.

She chuckles, but her expression has changed. She's serious when she replies, "Well, you missed a less-than-cheerful Jack. He seemed to be in a sour mood, nitpicking about everything, asking for reports on your projects. And, of course, he's still on about those sports shops, wondering who the beneficiary is, and why we aren't getting their accounting work to compensate for the London client you lost."

I sigh and ask, "What did you tell him?"

With a mischievous glint in her eye, Joan responds, "Oh, I just gave him a dose of 'I don't know' medicine. After all, it's not our department, right? I told him as much. He's been wanting to see you as soon as you're back."

I roll my eyes good-naturedly. "Well, here goes nothing," I mutter to myself as I make my way to Jack's office. Upon entering, I try to keep things light.

"Hey Jack, you were hunting for me?" I greet him casually. I know it drives him insane that I'm not bothered anymore by his shenanigans.

He glances up from his desk, his expression unchanging. "I've been reviewing some of your work. Why haven't you submitted your expense sheets? I asked for them two weeks ago," he grumbles.

I respond with a touch of amusement, "Jack, that's what they call a vacation. It's the first one I've taken in over a year, and I consciously chose not to bring work along." His mouth tightens. I think I'm enjoying this much more than I should.

He doesn't seem impressed. "Senior staff members need to be reachable and stay connected while on holiday. That's just standard procedure, Maria."

I grimace slightly, "Well, Jack, I'm not in a senior role, as you've made that abundantly clear. No promotions, and I was explicitly told that I'd be working on lower-level tasks before I left. So honestly, you can't have it both ways," a hint of playful exasperation colours my tone. "I hardly ever take holidays, and that didn't get me anywhere. Now, when I do take one, you complain. If I were a senior, I'd probably be as 'contactable' as the rest of the partners when they're on vacation."

I know for a fact that me being unreachable has nothing to do with his mood. It started way before I went on vacation.

"Now, in order of priority, just tell me what you need?"

Jack gives me a stern look but answers my question, "Just get your pharmacy report finished. And bring me the expense report, the list I asked for before you left. I want to finalise the sports shop billing since it seems like we won't be getting that work."

"Okay, Jack. No problem," I respond with a diplomatic smile, concealing my internal eye-roll. "Thank you, by the way, I did enjoy my holiday." I turn and leave his office, shaking my head. There is exhilaration, but also sadness at realising what's become of the people I have spent most of my adult life working with.

As I'm returning to my desk, a message pops up on my phone screen.

Paul: *So, how's my bronze beauty? Hoping I get to check for tan lines soon.*

I can't help but smile at his message. Oh, how I wish.

Maria: *Doing good. Will definitely whip you if you don't come through on that promise soon.*

Paul: *Promises, promises. So, am I going to have to wait until Thursday to see you?*

Maria: *I would love to have dinner soon, but I don't think I have an escape. Looks like it will be Thursday after all.*

Paul: *Ugh :(London's not the same without you. But I do hope you had a great holiday. You needed and deserved it. I hope it brought you some clarity.*

Maria: *Some, but only some. All ancient history, though, because Jack has been acting like a pig, and I've only been back a few hours.*

Paul: *If you can get a coffee or lunch before Thursday, let me know. I'm office-bound all week, so I can get out.*

I smile at the screen.

Maria: *Lemme see what I can do.*

Unfortunately, my schedule didn't allow us to meet until Thursday morning, when I finally laid eyes on Paul. After nearly three weeks' worth of separation, I hung back on the train, drinking him in while he sat oblivious to my attention. I wanted to throw my arms around him in excitement, but we had to be careful. After all, we were in public, in Manchester, and against my very instincts I had to maintain some semblance of composure. So, I settled for a cheeky smile and a playful remark, "Fancy seeing you here, on your way to London, in your lucky seat."

He startles at my sudden appearance, then a megawatt smile alights his face, and he lurches forward as if to wrap me in a hug. But then he hesitates and looks around, remembering our surroundings. I give him a wry smile and we settle for hand holding instead.

When he starts talking, it's like I never went away, we never parted, and we'd only met just yesterday. "How was your holiday? You look great, all tanned." He asks, his eyes roving over my body.

I nod, "It was a nice holiday, the kids loved it - sun, sea, and sangria. There was a lot of time to think."

Paul nods in return, then turns to me, looking deeply into my eyes, searching for something. Whatever he was looking for, he found it because he shakes his head and sighs, "And how are you really feeling now, Maria?"

I exhale slowly, finding comfort in finally confiding in him. I know that whatever heights I fall from, if there's Paul waiting beneath me, I'll land alright. "I received some emails from Jack right before I left, I ignored them, naturally, and he made a big deal out of it today. I was expecting it though, not a major shock there. It just feels like he's got a vendetta against me now."

Paul's hand clenches mine— so hard that it almost hurts. I relish it.

I sigh, frustration evident in my voice. "I hate working there." I rub my temples, "I spoke to Mark about it, but all he cares about is the paycheck I bring in, despite what it's costing me. He effectively told me to suck it up and stay. Plus, this non-compete clause in my contract makes it nearly impossible to leave, to work for other accountancy firms. I'd practically need a complete career change to stay local."

Paul rubs circles on my hand with his thumb, "It sounds like you're determined to get out, but there's no way to, and no support from Mark."

I shake my head at his succinct summary of my circumstances, feeling a mix of emotions. "I don't think Mark would care, as long as the money keeps flowing in." I inhale deeply, unlatching my fingertips from my temples, "Anyway, I want to enjoy the next two days and not think about this. So, has anything exciting happened to you in the last few weeks?"

Paul's face lights up with a smile. "Well, as of last week, the office refurb is going very well. Nicola and Helen really threw themselves into it, they're determined to get it all done ASAP. I think everything in disarray is throwing them off. The conference room was finished last week, and most of the painting and carpeting were done. I hope it's nearly completed by now. Your office was halfway done when I left— the ladies halted the work on other rooms to get yours done first. I think they wanted it ready for you when you got back." He pauses, taking me in, "They really like you; you know. They asked about your holiday and how you are doing."

"How precious," I murmur, and the blanket of gloom lifts off of me.

***

We arrive in London, and promptly grab a taxi, and head to the apartment to drop off our bags. The apartment too has gotten a facelift since the time I was here last. Right from the front door, I'm greeted by freshly painted halls and new stairs. I run a hand across the walls, "I love the paint job. It's so bright and cheery. This place always looked drab and old."

Paul chuckles, and wraps me in a side hug, "Yes, I took advantage of having painters around while you were gone. After all, I expect we'll be up and down here for quite a while." His words sting a bit, the realisation hitting me that he'll be the one spending more time here, not me. But I quickly shake off the thought, not wanting to ruin the mood.

We start up the stairs, and I quip, "You'd better fix that elevator next."

He winks at me. "I did. I just didn't mention it. Besides, the view is much better following you up." I smack his shoulder with a file as he snickers like a teen.

As I turn on the second-floor landing to the stairs for the third floor, Paul grabs me from behind. We stand at the door to the apartment on the second floor. "Hey, wrong floor," he says with a mischievous grin.

I'm puzzled until he inserts a key into the door and walks in. I follow him, utterly surprised by the transformation. I haven't seen inside this place so I'm not sure if it really is a transformation, but it looks recently redone. "What happened here?" I gasp in amazement. The place looks absolutely incredible, completely modern in both décor and furniture.

"I figured since we'll be going up and down here a lot, I could renovate this apartment first, make it completely modern and new. Ours if you want. Or we can go upstairs and stay there if you prefer. Take a look around," Paul gestures.

393

My heart clenches at the sadness his words bring me—*you'll be here a lot, Paul, not me,* my heart echoes hollowly— but I eagerly nod, and explore the apartment. Paul is following behind me, drinking in my expressions.

The living room is beautifully furnished, exuding comfort and homeliness. There's a lovely desk in one corner, facing out towards the window, just like Ralph's old setup. A computer, TV, and entertainment system are tucked away in another corner. As I glance around, I see Paul is grinning, almost chuckling. "What?" I ask.

He points to the wall, and a laugh escapes me unbidding. "Well, this all started with a hook, so I figured it wouldn't be right not to bring it a full circle. Plus, the wall was right there, all bare."

I snort and lead the way into the bedroom, where a beautiful traditional-style bed sits. The room is furnished with a cosy but modern bedroom set. I smile mischievously, teasing, "Plenty of places to tie you to that bed." He rolls his eyes, but I see the flush creeping up his cheeks. The wardrobes are the sliding, mirrored double doors type. There's a huge double wardrobe for hanging clothes and drawers, already set up for a his-and-her arrangement. At the end, there's a smaller wardrobe. When I try to open it, it appears jammed. "Is this locked?" I ask Paul.

Paul tugs at the discreet lock, and the doors swing open, the wardrobe empty. "A locked wardrobe might come in handy for a little privacy with the … less conventional clothing," he winks.

Paul leads me through another door. He's managed to fit an en-suite with a large walk-in shower. "How did you make space for this?" I ask, impressed.

"I took a little room from the bedroom and made the main bathroom smaller to fit it in. Figured it was nicer than having to go to a separate bathroom."

The second bedroom mirrors the first, complete with a comfortable bed and slide-robes, missing just an en-suite.

"I can't believe you did all this— and the furniture! When did you find the time?" I ask incredulously.

Paul grins mischievously. "Remember all those mysterious Thursday disappearances? Well, I was meeting the renovation crew and sorting out the furniture. I wanted it to be a surprise for you, something new and truly ours. Plus, Ralph had already set out plans and budget to renovate the entire building, including the top floor which we can lease out if we choose."

"Now, come on, Maria, get moving. Let's get to work-Helen and Nicola will be expecting us. We can move our belongings down tonight, if you want," he whispers the last sentence against my neck, and I shiver in response.

We head into the office, and right from the entrance I'm completely floored by the transformation. It's as if I've been away for months, not just three weeks. The space is thoroughly modernised, with new lighting, and furniture. Helen and Nicola have neighbouring offices, which is a nice change from the previous layout. One office occupies what used to be the old canteen, and a brand-new cafeteria space has been added upstairs. The conference room has been revamped with a modern design, all sleek and grey, and features a video conferencing setup on one wall.

Finally, I step into my new office, which was previously Ralph's. It's beautifully furnished with a new desk, a high-back leather chair, a computer and printer, and a filing unit behind the desk. There are new cabinets for storage and even a cosy couch with a coffee table against one of the side walls. A beautiful painting of a cerulean sea against a yellow coast graces the other wall.

"Paul, this is absolutely gorgeous." I murmur, taking it all in, "This will be a fantastic office for you as the Managing Director," I remark, subtly telling him that this will be his place, not mine- not anymore.

Paul smiles and corrects me, "Actually, this office is for whichever one of us is here. And there's a spare office, too, on this floor in case we need two."

I smile quietly, not correcting him.

At 11 am, Paul peeks inside the office, "Hey, let's gather in the conference room for a meeting with Nicola and Helen." I nod, and we go to the newly minted conference room. A few moments later, the ladies enter, both wearing beaming smiles. Helen greets me warmly, "Welcome back, Maria! How was your holiday? You've got a great tan, by the way."

I've never seen them so friendly. I return their smiles, feeling a sense of camaraderie. "It was wonderful, thanks. And I love what you've done with the place. I bet you had a blast shopping for the furniture."

Nicola chimes in, "Oh, we absolutely did, and it's been a hit with everyone here. Thank you again, for making this happen, Paul."

"You're very welcome, and this is all you guys, by the way. So, ladies, where are we at?" Paul calls the meeting to order as we take our seats.

"Well, the office here is all done, just the last few touches remaining. There's some wiring work that needs to be finished for the server room," Nicola begins, her tone brimming with enthusiasm. "We've also spoken with the IT stock company, and some of the shops will need new computers and modern registers that can log all sales. They'll need a few weeks to get everything in."

"They recommended that every shop does a proper stock inventory, or we hire someone to do it," Helen adds, her fingers tapping on the sleek, new conference table. "This way, we can have accurate records in the system from the get-go. Some of the shops have pretty lousy stock control, just outdated systems, and loads of unsellable stock cluttering up their storage spaces."

Paul nods thoughtfully, absorbing the information. "I see. Let's see if we can hurry up the computer delivery. And what's the plan with the stock issue?"

Nicola leans forward, "I'm suggesting we take one or two days to close for a full stock take. It'll give us a clean slate to start with, especially since we're modernising our systems. It's a bit of a reset button."

Paul gives a decisive nod. "That sounds reasonable. Let's do that."

Helen nods in agreement, "Once we have all the stock centralised, it'll be easier to manage accounting and sales. But there's one more thing, what about the warehouse and dispatch for online shopping?"

Nicola pauses, considering. "I don't think it will work, Paul. The warehouse currently ships full boxes of products to the shops. For online orders, we'd need a separate area for packaging and shipping, and honestly, the warehouses are already quite cramped."

Paul furrows his brow in thought. "Could we explore the possibility of purchasing an adjoining warehouse if available?" he suggests. "Otherwise, we might have to consider relocating. We need space— that's vital, especially if we plan on opening more shops and increasing sales. We have to prepare to run an online shop with physical stores."

Nicola and Helen nod in agreement, and they all make a mental note to investigate the option of expanding into an adjoining warehouse.

"On another note, we're exploring some possibilities for Holland," she begins, and I can't help but feel a twinge of unease. "There are vacant units in the shopping district in Rotterdam that could be promising, and a few empty warehouse units on the outskirts that we could rent or buy until we figure out which direction to take."

As I listen to their plans for the future, I can't shake the feeling of being left out. This was their vision, their exciting adventure, and it was becoming increasingly clear that I wouldn't be a part of it. I had played my role, done my job, and they were still making plans for a future I wouldn't be a part of.

"Where are we going to manage the new central admin from?" Helen's brow furrows with worry as she consults her notes. "To be honest, we're already managing stock, distribution, legal and some admin and HR for the shops and the warehouse. I'm not sure if we can handle much more here."

"Leave it with me for now," he assures Helen. "Don't worry; I won't be increasing your workload. Your job will remain focused on managing stock for the shops, handling buying and ordering, and coordinating the shops. The new layer of admin for the online shop is a different issue."

The managers look relieved, and after sorting out a few more kinks, the meeting concludes. As soon as the ladies walk out, I can't resist asking Paul, "How many steps ahead of us are you?"

He chuckles softly. "A few, I hope."

After the meeting, we head to lunch. Paul has an idea, "Why don't we invite Adam and Nicole to dinner tonight? It would be a nice way to thank them for their help."

I readily agree, loving the thought. A night with Nicola always promised good company and fun. "Alright, will you ring Nicola, then? Tell her it's a thank-you dinner, and they simply must come."

I call Nicola and we decide to meet at our favourite restaurant— the perfect setting for showing our gratitude.

Paul and I return to the apartment around 5:30, and I start to get ready. Paul has thoughtfully arranged everything, equipping the vanity from a hairdryer to the smallest details. I can't help but wonder how he managed to pick out everything so perfectly, down to the linen.

"I had a little help," he confesses with a grin. "Rachel sorted out a lot of this for me. She's been a great help. She'll come in every Tuesday to clean and change all the linen and beds. I asked for Tuesdays, just in case we ever decide to spend a weekend here."

"Aah, Paul," I pout, and he kisses me deeply.

***

At the restaurant, we meet up with Adam and Nicole. It is a delightful evening spent in the company of wonderful people.

398

Naturally, we reminisce about our last night at the club and the event we attended. We share anecdotes and encounters, toy shopping, and ask them about future events. But it isn't just about the club and the lifestyle; we talk about everything under the sun. It feels like four old friends catching up over dinner. We linger until ten before deciding to call it a night. Paul tells them about the new apartment, and our little move. Adam and Nicola are delighted and urge us to hurry back. We exchange our customary goodbyes, giving each other pecks on the cheek.

Back in the apartment, we survey what needs to be moved and pull out our latex outfits from a box under the bed. I'm grateful I'm getting to see this whole different life take shape, even though I will soon be disappearing from the scene, it was a nice thing. We hang them up along with our collection of toys. It takes us a while because we can't resist messing around and playing with each other. Then we enjoy christening the new bed, revelling in its freshness and newness. All the while, there is a tinge of sadness knowing that I would only get to use it for a few weeks.

Despite my complicated feelings, Paul appears genuinely happy and enthusiastic about the shops, the apartment, and the business. Over breakfast on Friday, he mentions a few papers he wants me to take a look at from an accountancy perspective regarding the Manchester shop. "They really aren't making sense to me, could you review them when we get back this evening?"

"Mhm."

He suggests we take an earlier train so that I can get home at the regular time. I agree, knowing that things were running smoothly here in London, and there was no reason to extend my stay. Better get used to it from now.

We spend a good part of the day discussing the shops, and I bring up the topic of the new accountancy firm that would handle the shops in passing. "You know, Jack is pretty upset that we're not even in the running for that contract. It could bring a substantial amount of work to one of our offices. It's very satisfying seeing him deal with losing it."

He nods knowingly, uncharacteristically serious "I can imagine. But centralising our system will create a significant workload for one accounting office. I have something in mind for it, and I want to explore that option before finalising this."

I shrug and get into reviewing other materials he's gathered for me.

As the day passes, we decide to take the 3 PM train back to Manchester instead of our usual 5 PM. During the journey, I can't help but burst, "You know, I've only two weeks left with you, here in London. I ... honestly don't know what's gonna happen between us once I return to Manchester."

Paul smiles faintly and replies, "We'll figure it out. We can try hotels when we can, aim for city centre lunches instead of dinners, and see if we can squeeze in the occasional weekend getaway."

It did little in the way of comforting me.

When we arrive back in Manchester, I follow Paul to the shop's parking spaces, which are conveniently just two minutes away from the shop and the city centre. We decide to grab a couple of takeaway coffees as we head toward the shop.

Paul leads the way to a side door, and I assume he is heading to the office. My mind is still preoccupied with our conversation. He did not seem much perturbed by the distance that will stretch between us. And then- then we enter and make our way upstairs, I am greeted by a completely transformed office. The air is filled with the scent of fresh paint, and the space is adorned with brand-new desks and chairs. The office looks brand new, yet it's still empty, devoid of computers or any other equipment.

With a proud smile, Paul pivots on his heels and gestures to the space around us. "Welcome to the new admin centre for the company," he declares. "I'm thinking of establishing an in-house accountancy department here, rather than outsourcing the work. We can also handle online sales from this location, with orders dispatched from wherever they need to go."

At my puzzled look, he explains further, "This area will serve as our online sales and accounting. Warehousing elsewhere, and I'll have my office right here." "I'll be travelling to London when necessary, and we can set up video conferencing for all our meetings."

We. The word rings loudly in my mind.

"So, I'll need someone to head this operation, essentially a CFO, who can manage all the financial aspects."

"Good planning ahead. It makes sense to run this from where you are. If you're bringing accounting in-house, it will require new staff and management. If you'd let me know I'd have recommended someone. So, have you been advertising for the positions? Did you already decide which company you're hiring? And why all the secrecy?" I confess I am hurt about this. It's been too many secrets, too many surprises in the span of a day. It's like he's already living a separate life than me.

"Maria… It's you. I want you to do the job. As for the secrecy, well, I was waiting for the right moment. I wanted to see if you were content with your current job or if you were really up for a change. I didn't know if you were really unhappy, or it was just a rough patch you wanted to stick through."

I process the information slowly, not wanting to build my hopes up then have them dashed, "So, what you're saying is…?"

He leans in, his gaze unwavering. "I want you to lead this initiative, Maria, if you're interested. You'll be responsible for establishing the admin and accounts department and overseeing its operations. Your current contract doesn't prohibit you from taking on a role like this, as long as it doesn't involve working for another accounting firm or client. And just to clarify, Jack confirmed via email that the estate was his client, not the shops."

I am stunned, lost for words. I haven't seen this coming at all, and it is evident that Paul has put a lot of thought into it. "I... I don't know what to say."

Paul nods in understanding. "Maria, I'm not asking for an answer right now. Take your time, discuss it at home. The compensation package will match your current one, with an added bonus. You'll have a formal employment contract.

There will be some travel involved, likely to London and potentially to help set up operations in Holland. The next move is entirely up to you."

I nodded, still absorbing the weight of this unexpected offer. "Thank you, Paul. I'll need some time to think about it, for sure."

He smiled warmly. "Of course, Maria. It's a significant decision. Take all the time you need, and we'll discuss it further when you're ready."

As we walk away from the office, my head is swirling with questions and uncertainties. *Was this a real job opportunity? What would Mark think about this? Could I really leave my current job? Was this the chance for Paul and me that I'd been waiting for, or the beginning of a disaster? What if things didn't work out between Paul and me?*

Paul senses my inner turmoil, and offers a warm smile. We're walking out, towards the car park. "Have a great weekend, Maria. I'm sorry for springing this on you, but I wanted to be sure you were genuinely considering leaving your current job before discussing it further. This is not personal, business only. Please consider it a job offer. You have the skills for it, and overseeing the setup of new systems and managing finances will be quite challenging to anyone who's not you. Take your time to decide, alright?"

I nod numbly, and we part ways.

When I finally get home, my thoughts are still in a whirlwind. The kids are settled, and I quickly grab a bottle of wine, pouring myself a glass to help me think. Mark notices my distracted state and asks, worry tinging his voice, "Is everything okay? You seem quiet. Did something happen at work or in London?" He probably just thinks I quit in an emotional outburst and now I'm unemployed.

I take a deep breath and look at Mark, pausing for a moment before responding, "I was offered the position of CFO for the sports shop companies. They're establishing an administration base here in Manchester. It would involve occasional travel, some time in London and possibly Holland. They're even considering setting up a European base and a new shop to handle Brexit and sales in mainland Europe and the EU." I say it in a state of pure calm; something I wasn't sure I was really feeling. But Mark needs to know that this is a serious offer.

Mark's expression shifts from curiosity to shock. "When did this happen?" he asks, clearly taken aback. So, he was expecting me to be unemployed, huh.

"Earlier today, about half an hour ago," I reply. "I had to make a quick call and check some paperwork in the Manchester shop, so I took an earlier train back. Paul accompanied me. He showed me the new office space here, a whole furnished floor above the shop. He laid out his plans and offered me the job. I had no idea any of this was in the works. He never even hinted at the possibility of centralising operations here or bringing accounting in-house." This was true enough.

"What will you do?" Mark's voice is tinged with uncertainty, mirroring the whirlwind of emotions raging within me. "It's a significant risk, Maria. What if you end up not liking it, or worse, what if the shops fail? Is Paul investing a lot in this?"

I turned to look at Mark, determined but drowning in trepidation. "From a financial standpoint, it actually makes sense," I answer, my voice firm. "It means they'll be paying staff for in-house accounting rather than maintaining seven different accountants, one for each shop. So, financially, it's a solid move. All the shops are profitable, so I don't see much risk there. And his investment can only improve them. Bringing it in-house offers significant savings and better control."

But in the depths of my mind, a different thought looms large. What if Paul and I have a falling out? Mixing pleasure and business has never worked out well-well, except for Ralph and Lilly. What if this decision ended up affecting us negatively? That was the true risk.

Mark continued to fix me with his gaze, his eyes probing mine. "And your current job... You do realise you're beholden there, right? You can't just work for a competitor or client. They won't be happy about this."

I nod slowly. "I'm aware of that," I admit, the irritation setting inside me. "But Paul has already looked into it. He said that the role of a CFO is different. The shops were never our client; it was always the estate. That takes care of the non-compete clause. So, while they might not be thrilled, there's not much they can do about it."

With that, I excuse myself, saying I'm tired, and head to bed. The day's events have been a rollercoaster, leaving me utterly exhausted, and I really need time to think.

As I lay there in the dim light, I ponder the weight of my decision. Was this the beginning of a new chapter or the end of something that has become so familiar? I can't help but wonder what would happen if I take this opportunity, and perhaps even more hauntingly, what might occur if I didn't. It wasn't the job or the benefits, or the thought of leading a new, exciting team that occupied my thoughts, but rather, it was the uncertain path my relationship with Paul might take.

TO BE CONTINUED

www.ingramcontent.com/pod-product-compliance
Lightning Source LLC
Chambersburg PA
CBHW070900120626
46546CB00001B/70